5/3

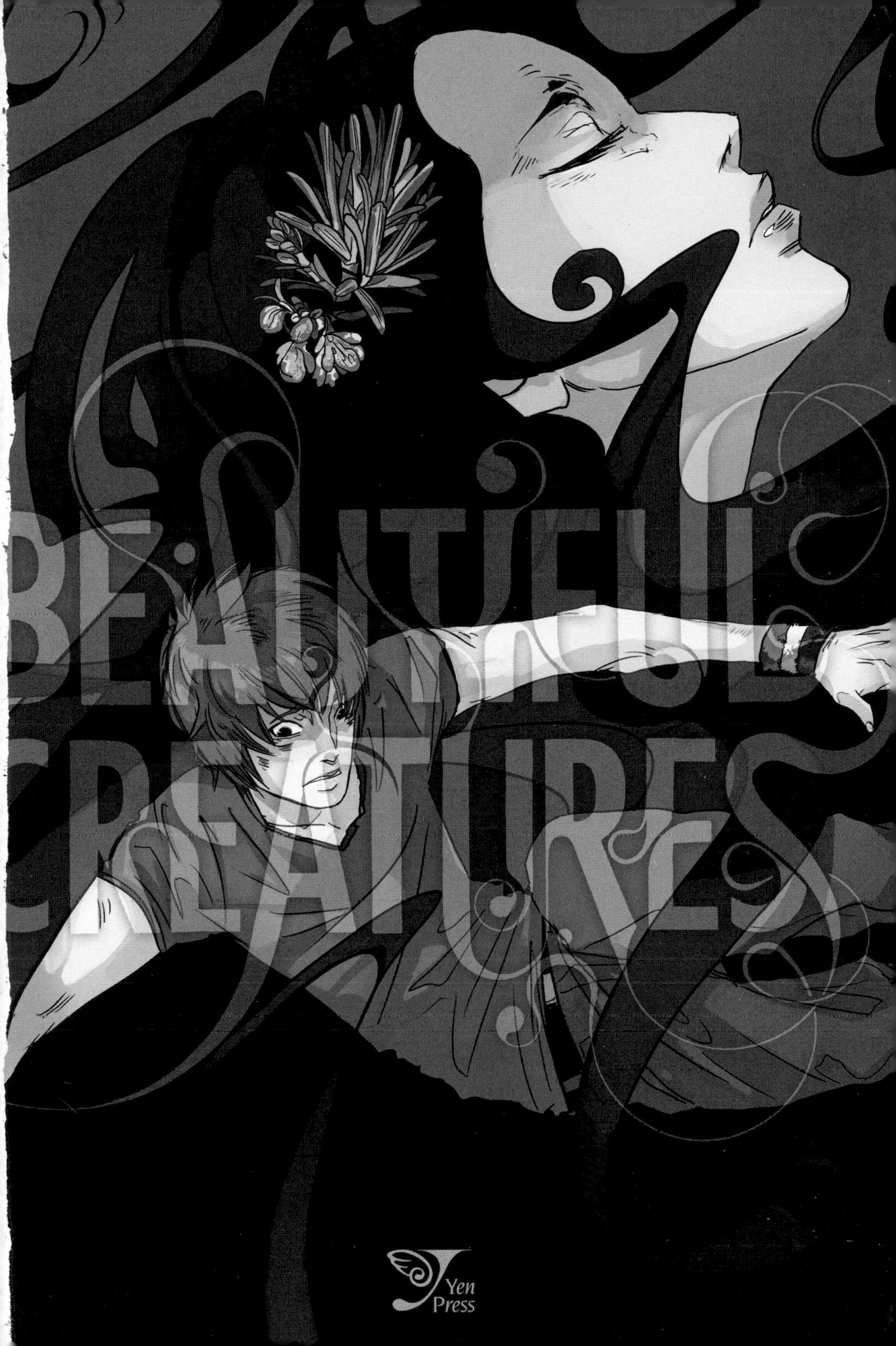
Yen
Press

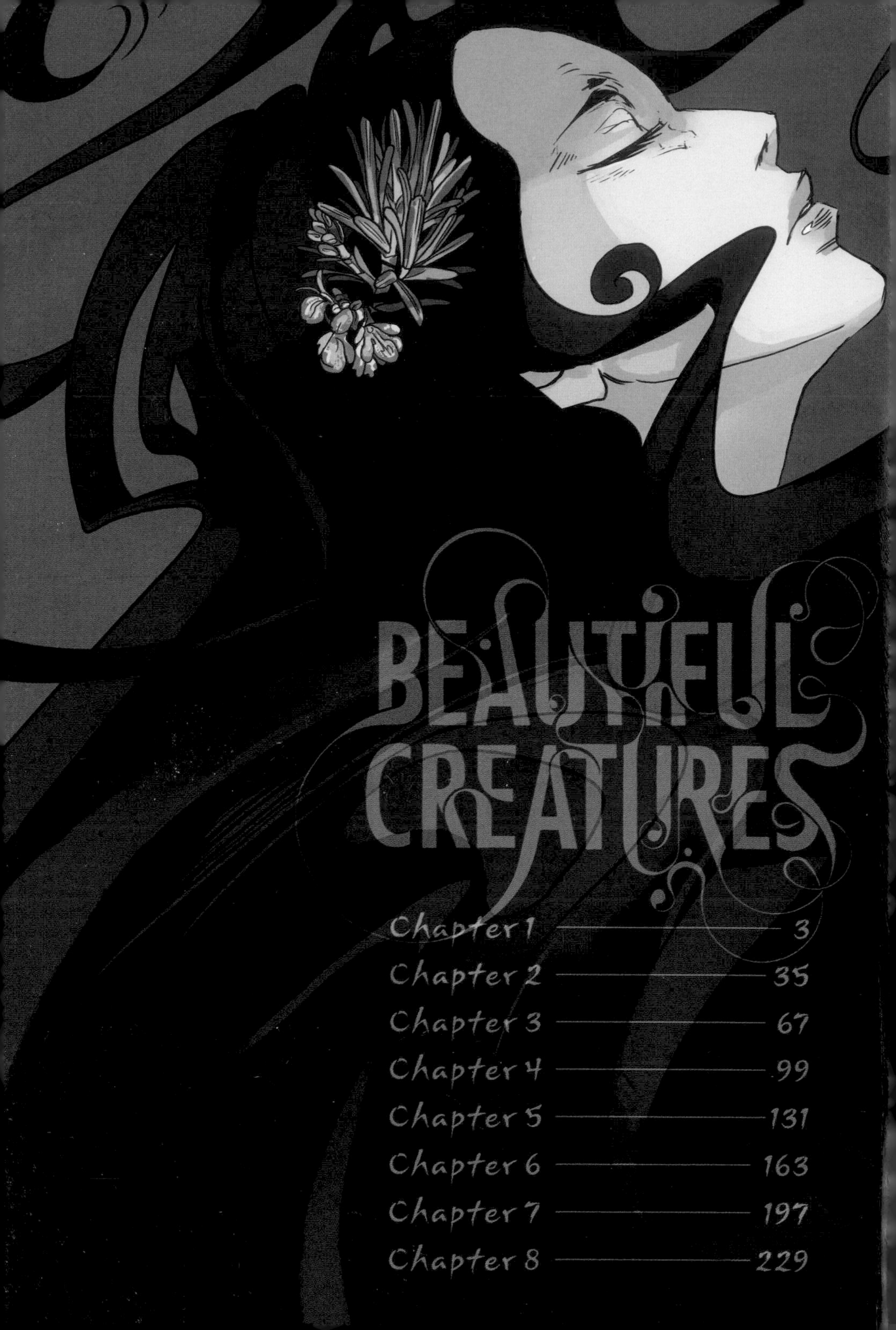

BEAUTIFUL CREATURES

CHAPTER 1

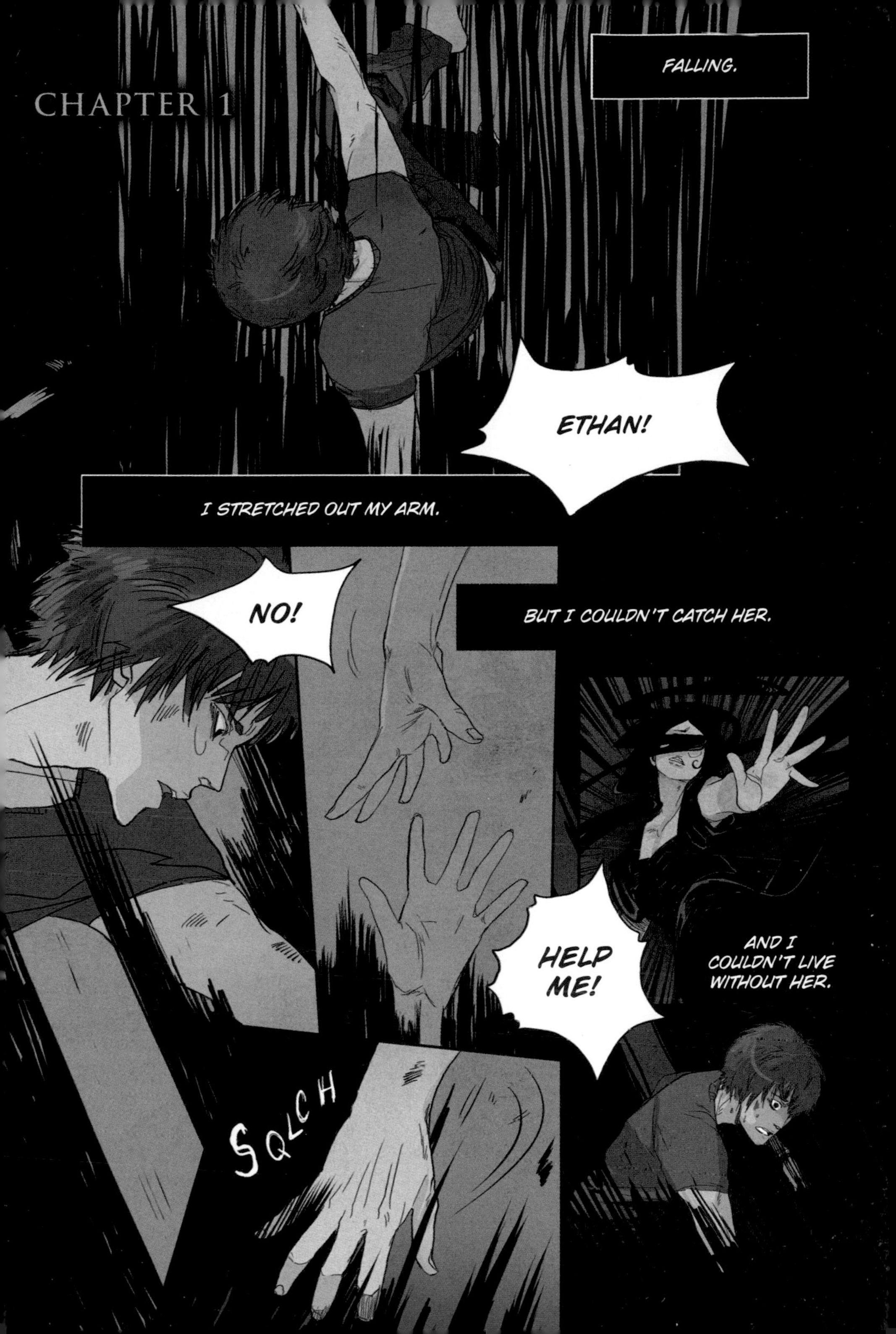
FALLING.
ETHAN!
I STRETCHED OUT MY ARM.
NO!
BUT I COULDN'T CATCH HER.
HELP ME!
AND I COULDN'T LIVE WITHOUT HER.
SQLCH

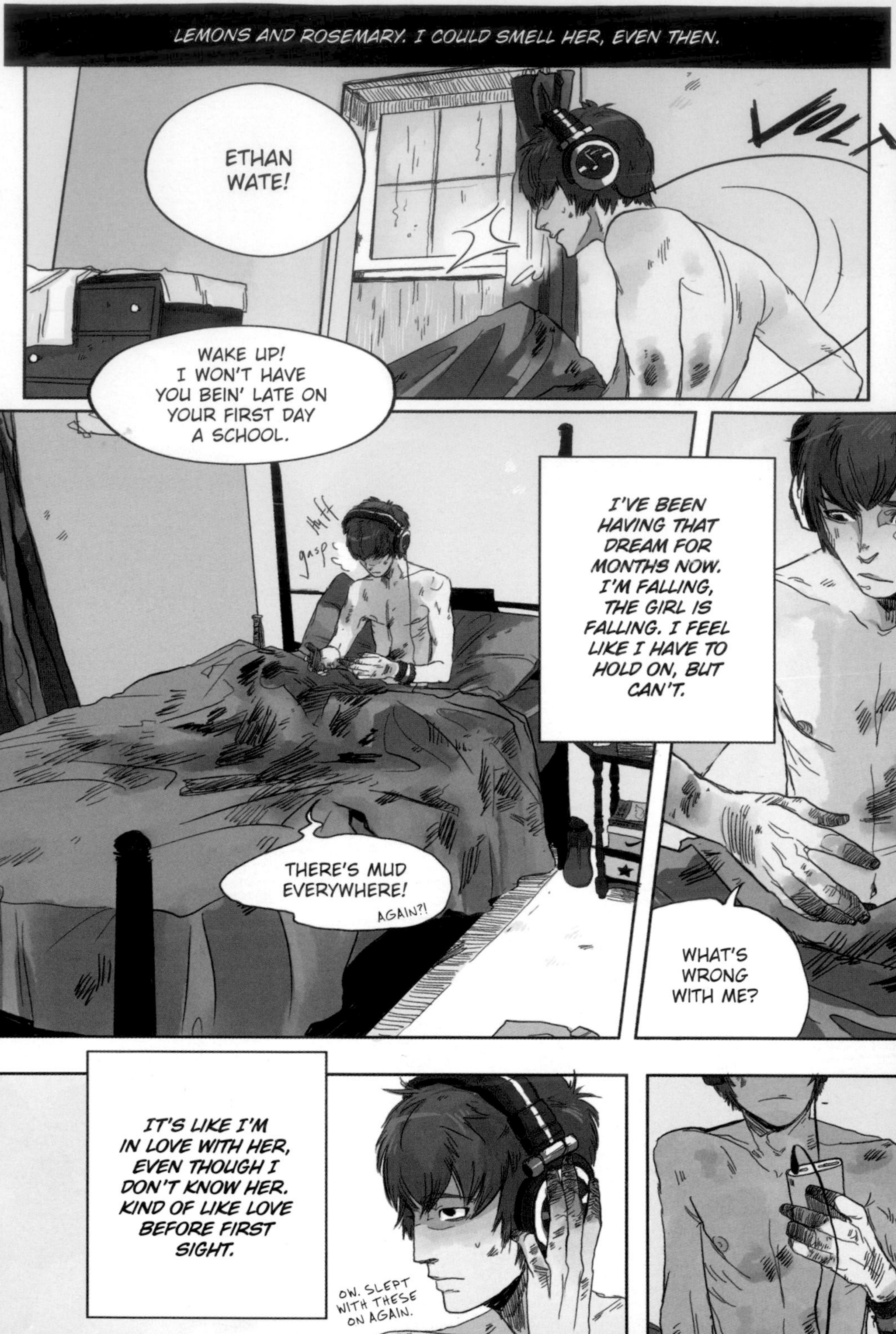
LEMONS AND ROSEMARY. I COULD SMELL HER, EVEN THEN.
ETHAN WATE!
VOLT
WAKE UP! I WON'T HAVE YOU BEIN' LATE ON YOUR FIRST DAY A SCHOOL.
huff
gasp
THERE'S MUD EVERYWHERE!
AGAIN?!
I'VE BEEN HAVING THAT DREAM FOR MONTHS NOW. I'M FALLING, THE GIRL IS FALLING. I FEEL LIKE I HAVE TO HOLD ON, BUT CAN'T.
WHAT'S WRONG WITH ME?
IT'S LIKE I'M IN LOVE WITH HER, EVEN THOUGH I DON'T KNOW HER. KIND OF LIKE LOVE BEFORE FIRST SIGHT.
OW. SLEPT WITH THESE ON AGAIN.

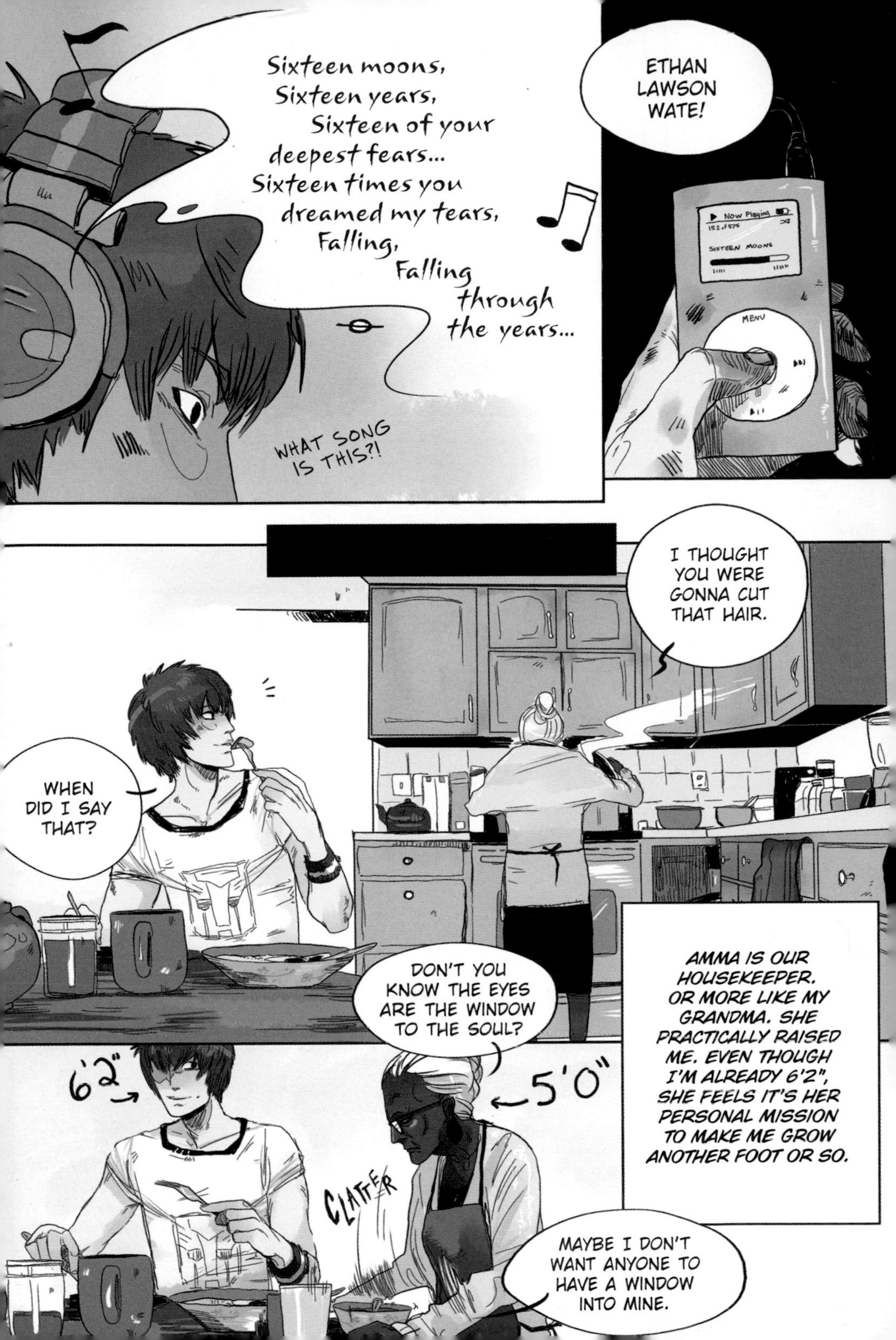

Sixteen moons,
Sixteen years,
Sixteen of your deepest fears...
Sixteen times you dreamed my tears,
Falling,
Falling through the years...
WHAT SONG IS THIS?!
ETHAN LAWSON WATE!
Now Playing
SIXTEEN MOONS
MENU
[redacted]
I THOUGHT YOU WERE GONNA CUT THAT HAIR.
WHEN DID I SAY THAT?
DON'T YOU KNOW THE EYES ARE THE WINDOW TO THE SOUL?
AMMA IS OUR HOUSEKEEPER. OR MORE LIKE MY GRANDMA. SHE PRACTICALLY RAISED ME. EVEN THOUGH I'M ALREADY 6'2", SHE FEELS IT'S HER PERSONAL MISSION TO MAKE ME GROW ANOTHER FOOT OR SO.
6'2"
5'0"
CLATTER
MAYBE I DON'T WANT ANYONE TO HAVE A WINDOW INTO MINE.

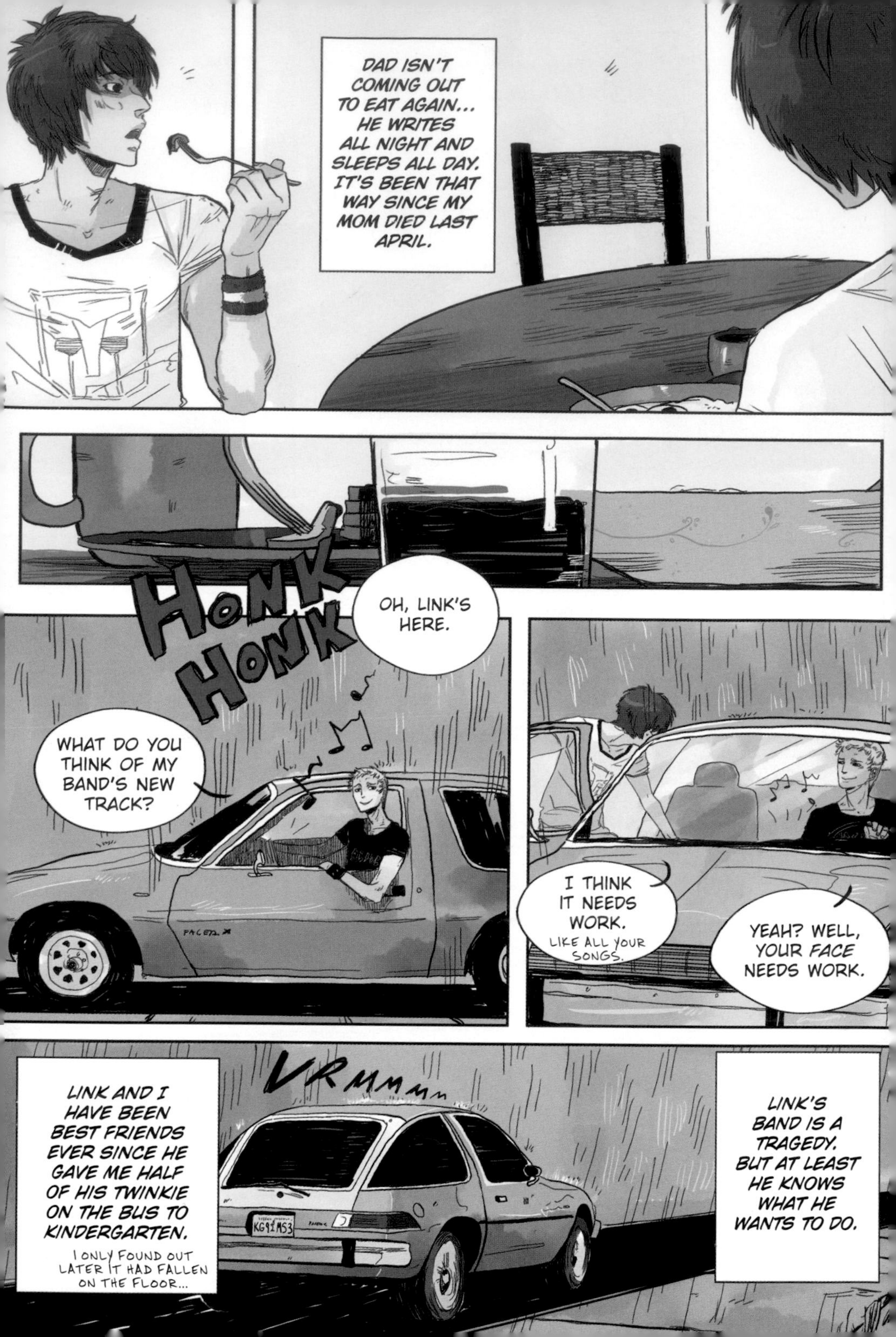
DAD ISN'T COMING OUT TO EAT AGAIN... HE WRITES ALL NIGHT AND SLEEPS ALL DAY. IT'S BEEN THAT WAY SINCE MY MOM DIED LAST APRIL.
HONK HONK
OH, LINK'S HERE.
WHAT DO YOU THINK OF MY BAND'S NEW TRACK?
I THINK IT NEEDS WORK.
LIKE ALL YOUR SONGS.
YEAH? WELL, YOUR FACE NEEDS WORK.
LINK AND I HAVE BEEN BEST FRIENDS EVER SINCE HE GAVE ME HALF OF HIS TWINKIE ON THE BUS TO KINDERGARTEN.
I ONLY FOUND OUT LATER IT HAD FALLEN ON THE FLOOR...
VRMMMMM
KG91MS3
LINK'S BAND IS A TRAGEDY. BUT AT LEAST HE KNOWS WHAT HE WANTS TO DO.

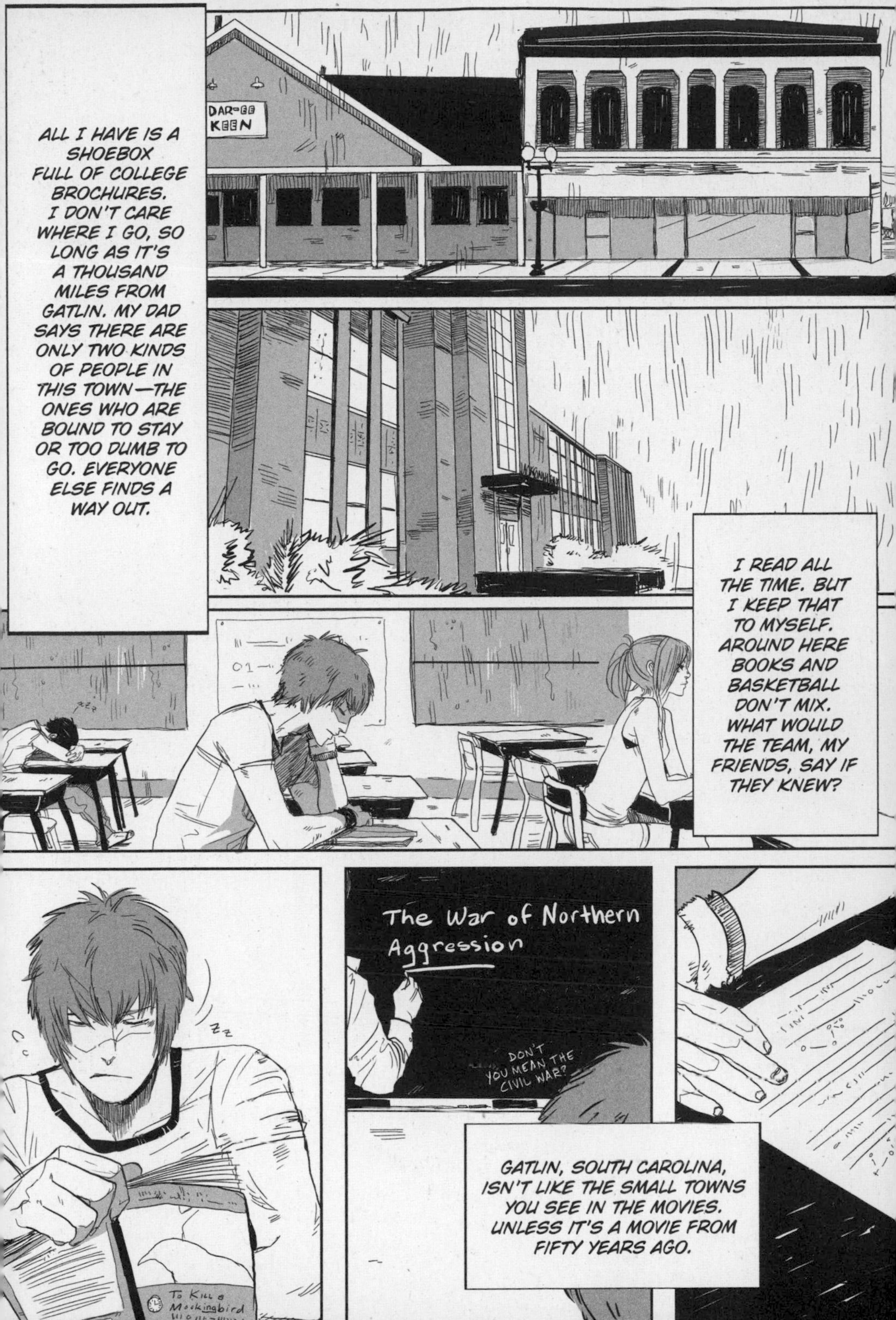
ALL I HAVE IS A SHOEBOX FULL OF COLLEGE BROCHURES. I DON'T CARE WHERE I GO, SO LONG AS IT'S A THOUSAND MILES FROM GATLIN. MY DAD SAYS THERE ARE ONLY TWO KINDS OF PEOPLE IN THIS TOWN—THE ONES WHO ARE BOUND TO STAY OR TOO DUMB TO GO. EVERYONE ELSE FINDS A WAY OUT.
DAR-EE KEEN
I READ ALL THE TIME. BUT I KEEP THAT TO MYSELF. AROUND HERE BOOKS AND BASKETBALL DON'T MIX. WHAT WOULD THE TEAM, MY FRIENDS, SAY IF THEY KNEW?
ZZ
To Kill a Mockingbird
The War of Northern Aggression
DON'T YOU MEAN THE CIVIL WAR?
GATLIN, SOUTH CAROLINA, ISN'T LIKE THE SMALL TOWNS YOU SEE IN THE MOVIES. UNLESS IT'S A MOVIE FROM FIFTY YEARS AGO.

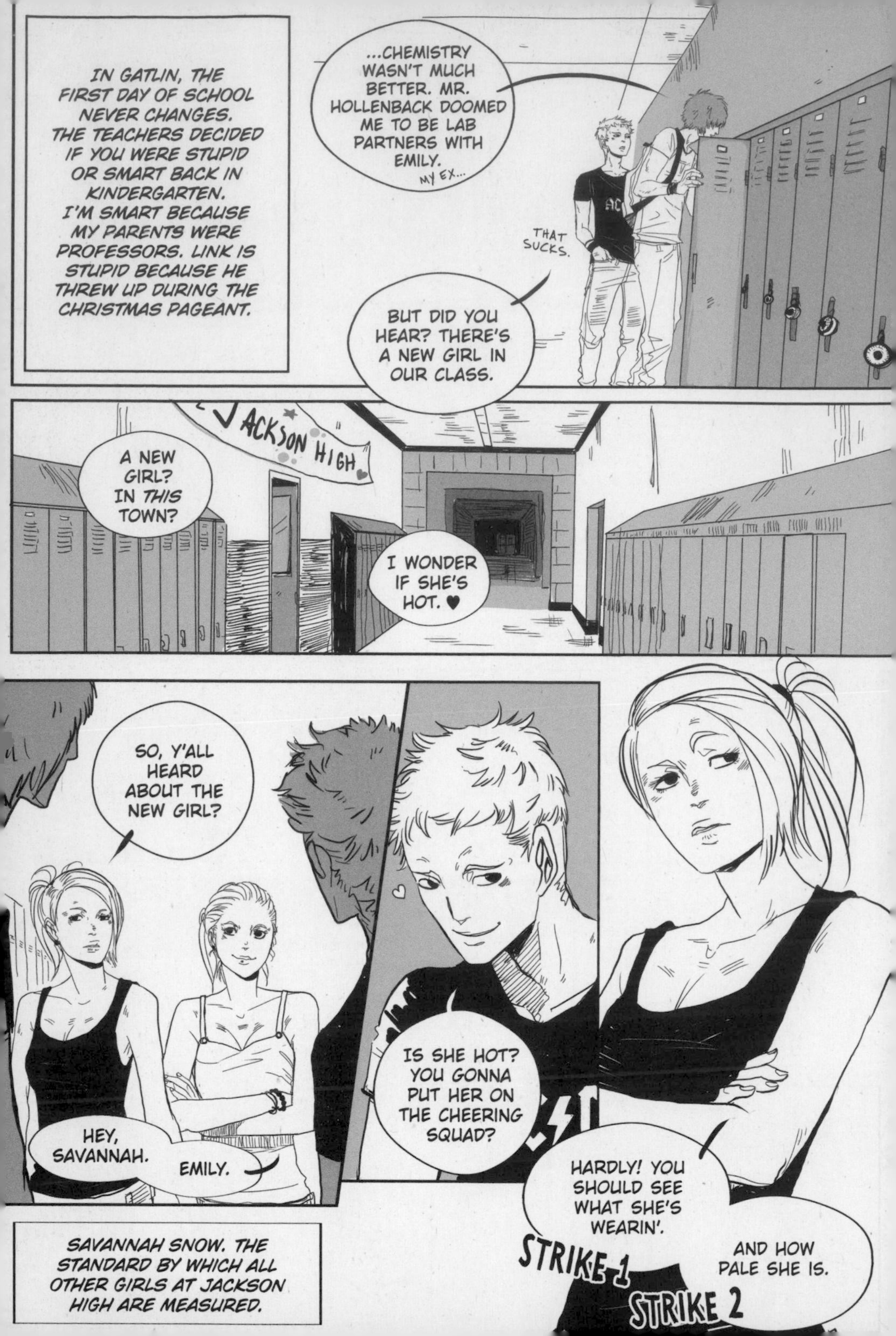
IN GATLIN, THE FIRST DAY OF SCHOOL NEVER CHANGES. THE TEACHERS DECIDED IF YOU WERE STUPID OR SMART BACK IN KINDERGARTEN. I'M SMART BECAUSE MY PARENTS WERE PROFESSORS. LINK IS STUPID BECAUSE HE THREW UP DURING THE CHRISTMAS PAGEANT.
...CHEMISTRY WASN'T MUCH BETTER. MR. HOLLENBACK DOOMED ME TO BE LAB PARTNERS WITH EMILY.
MY EX...
THAT SUCKS.
BUT DID YOU HEAR? THERE'S A NEW GIRL IN OUR CLASS.
JACKSON HIGH
A NEW GIRL? IN *THIS* TOWN?
I WONDER IF SHE'S HOT. ♥
SO, Y'ALL HEARD ABOUT THE NEW GIRL?
HEY, SAVANNAH.
EMILY.
SAVANNAH SNOW. THE STANDARD BY WHICH ALL OTHER GIRLS AT JACKSON HIGH ARE MEASURED.
IS SHE HOT? YOU GONNA PUT HER ON THE CHEERING SQUAD?
HARDLY! YOU SHOULD SEE WHAT SHE'S WEARIN'.
STRIKE 1
AND HOW PALE SHE IS.
STRIKE 2

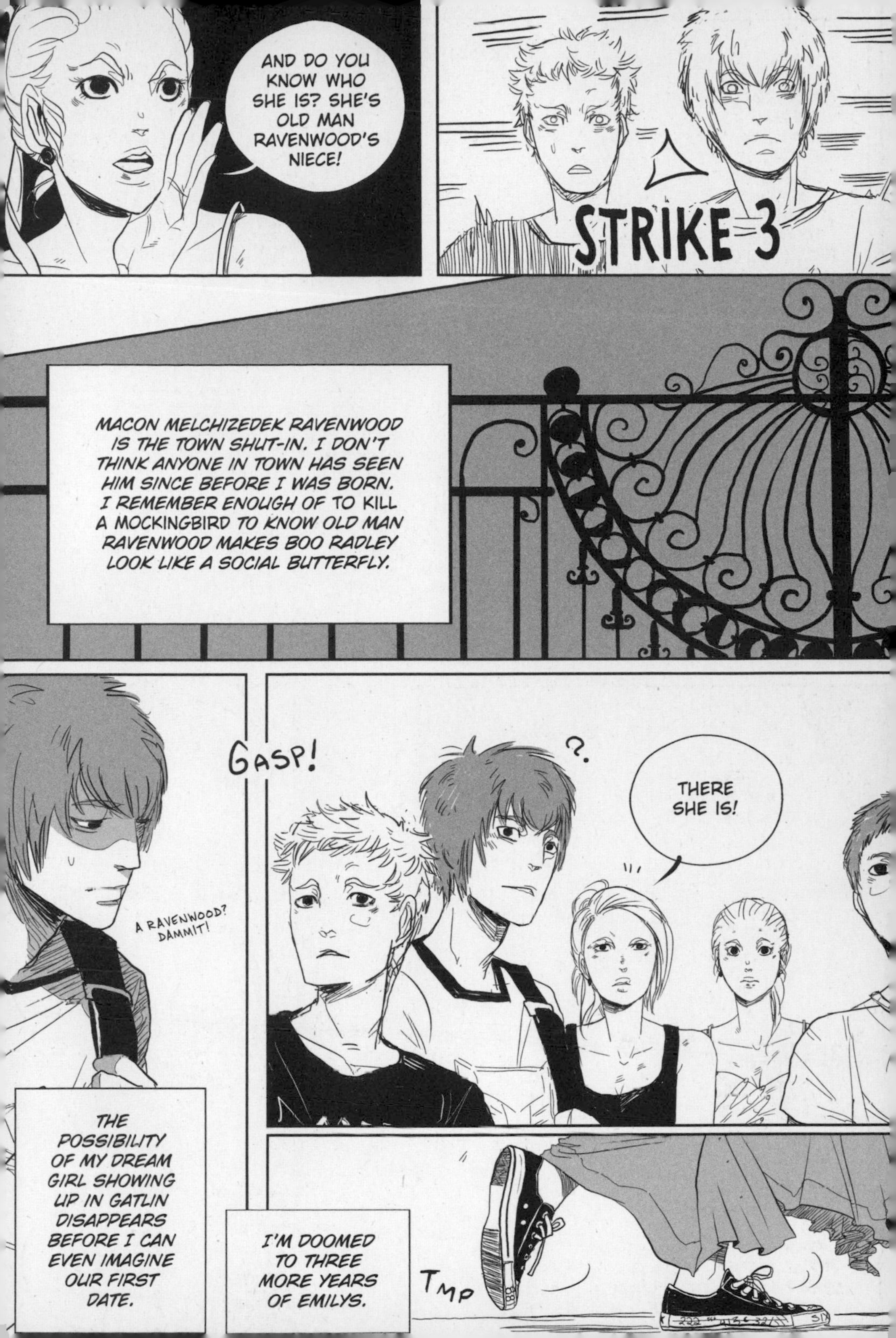
AND DO YOU KNOW WHO SHE IS? SHE'S OLD MAN RAVENWOOD'S NIECE!
STRIKE 3
MACON MELCHIZEDEK RAVENWOOD IS THE TOWN SHUT-IN. I DON'T THINK ANYONE IN TOWN HAS SEEN HIM SINCE BEFORE I WAS BORN. I REMEMBER ENOUGH OF TO KILL A MOCKINGBIRD TO KNOW OLD MAN RAVENWOOD MAKES BOO RADLEY LOOK LIKE A SOCIAL BUTTERFLY.
A RAVENWOOD? DAMMIT!
THE POSSIBILITY OF MY DREAM GIRL SHOWING UP IN GATLIN DISAPPEARS BEFORE I CAN EVEN IMAGINE OUR FIRST DATE.
GASP!
?
THERE SHE IS!
I'M DOOMED TO THREE MORE YEARS OF EMILYS.
TMP

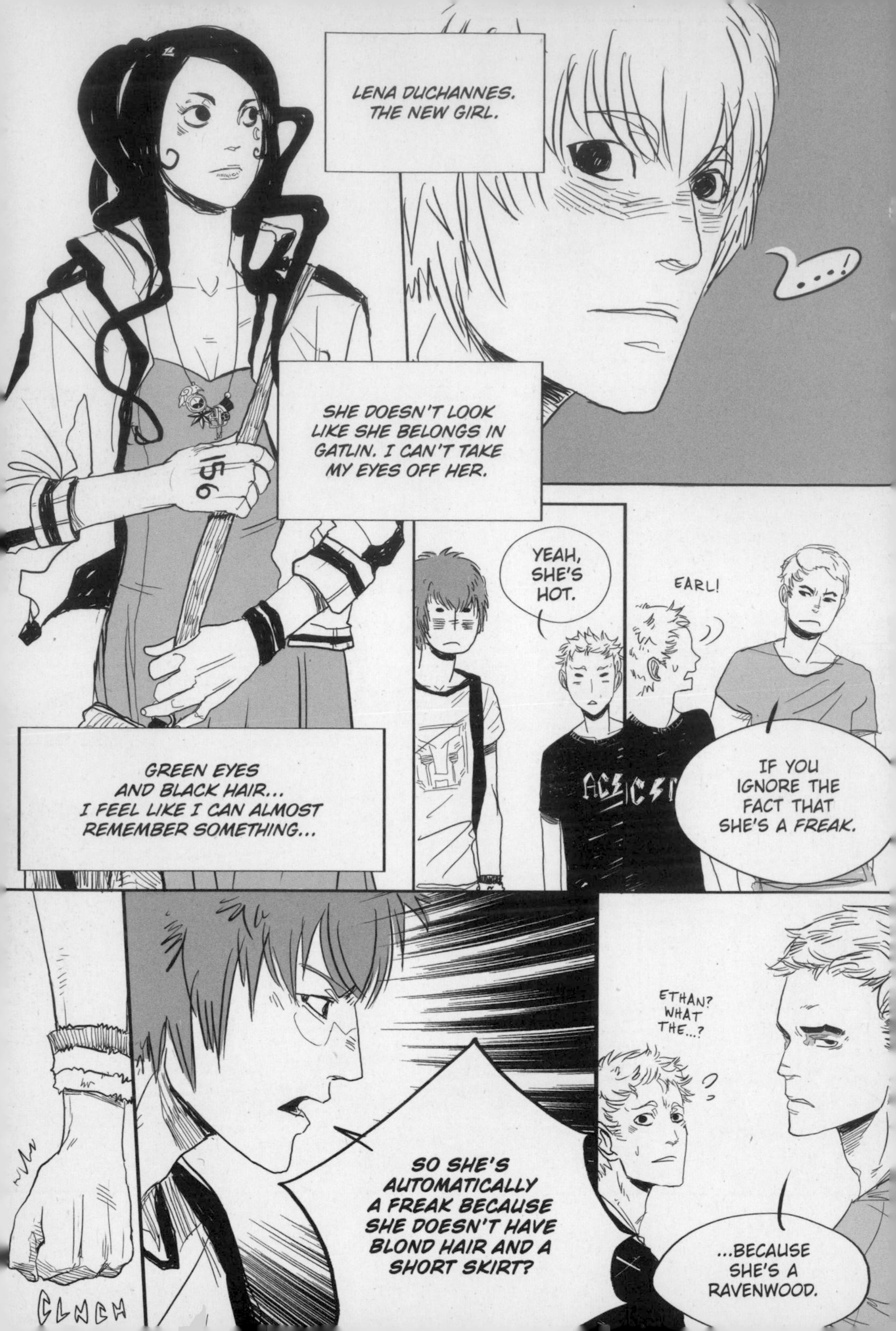
LENA DUCHANNES. THE NEW GIRL.
SHE DOESN'T LOOK LIKE SHE BELONGS IN GATLIN. I CAN'T TAKE MY EYES OFF HER.
156
GREEN EYES AND BLACK HAIR... I FEEL LIKE I CAN ALMOST REMEMBER SOMETHING...
...!
YEAH, SHE'S HOT.
EARL!
AC/DC
IF YOU IGNORE THE FACT THAT SHE'S A FREAK.
CLNCH
SO SHE'S AUTOMATICALLY A FREAK BECAUSE SHE DOESN'T HAVE BLOND HAIR AND A SHORT SKIRT?
ETHAN? WHAT THE...?
...BECAUSE SHE'S A RAVENWOOD.

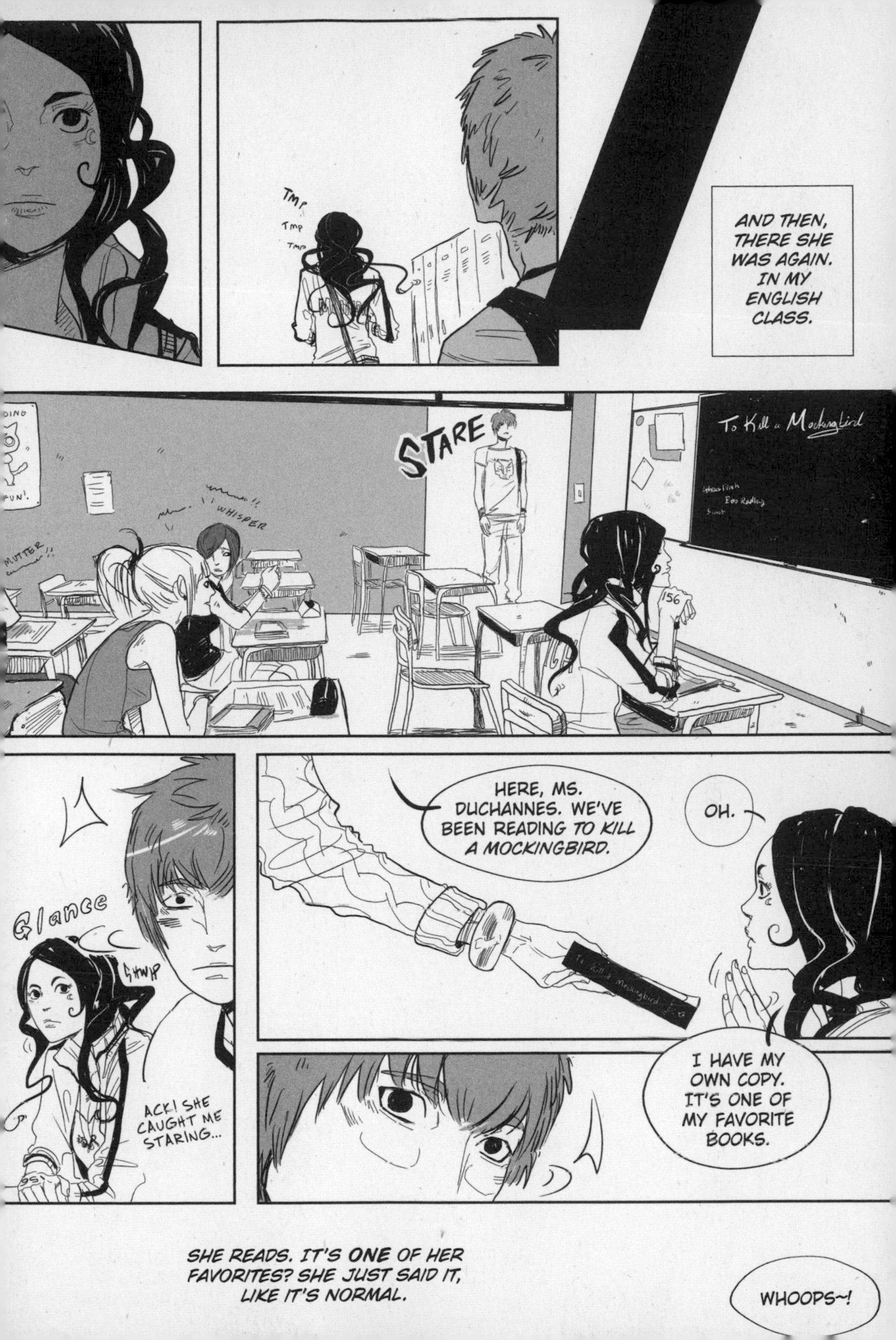

TMP
TMP
TMP
AND THEN, THERE SHE WAS AGAIN. IN MY ENGLISH CLASS.
FUN!
MUTTER
WHISPER
STARE
To Kill a Mockingbird
Glance
SHWIP
ACK! SHE CAUGHT ME STARING...
HERE, MS. DUCHANNES. WE'VE BEEN READING TO KILL A MOCKINGBIRD.
OH.
To Kill a Mockingbird
I HAVE MY OWN COPY. IT'S ONE OF MY FAVORITE BOOKS.
SHE READS. IT'S ONE OF HER FAVORITES? SHE JUST SAID IT, LIKE IT'S NORMAL.
WHOOPS~!

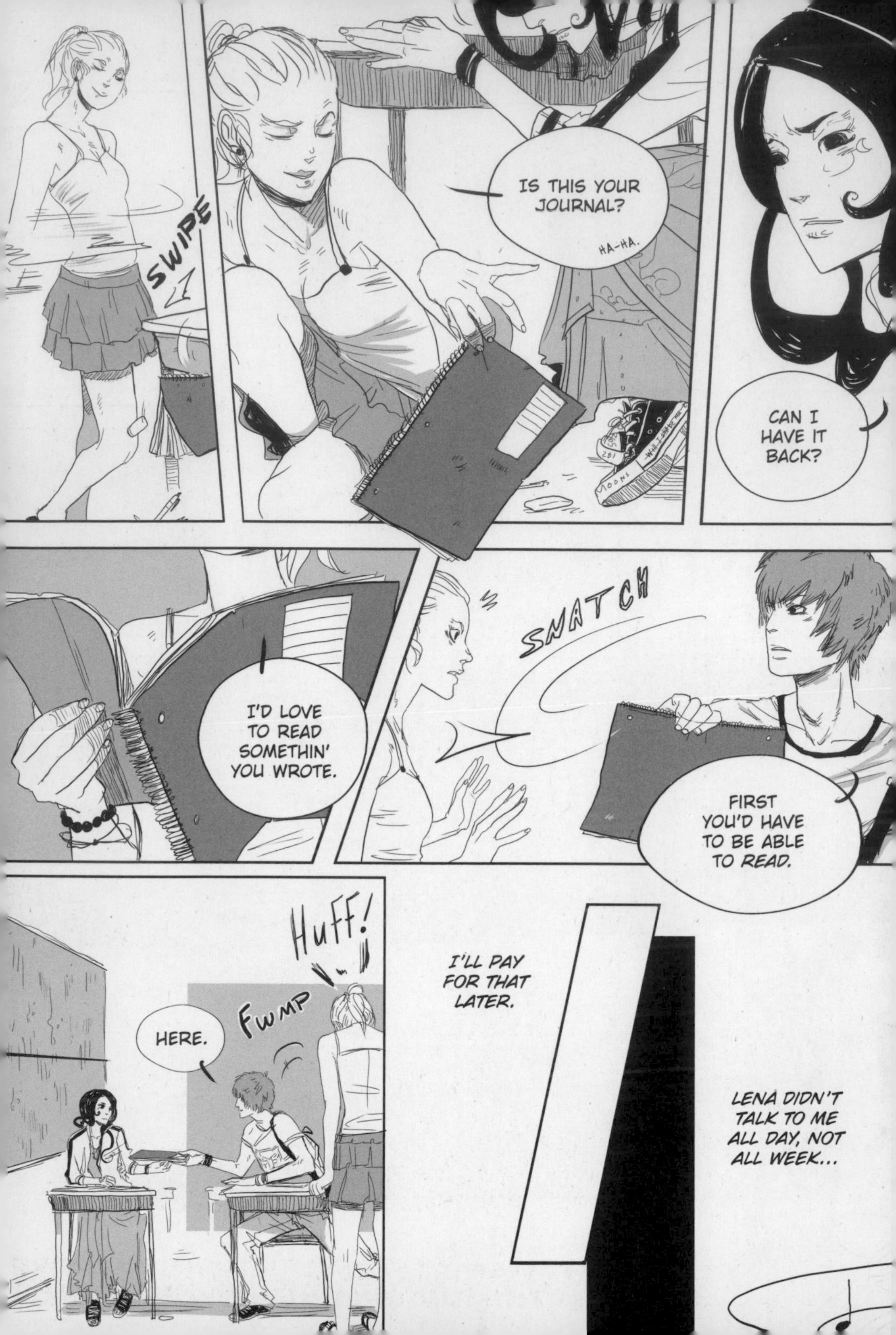
SWIPE
IS THIS YOUR JOURNAL?
HA-HA.
CAN I HAVE IT BACK?
I'D LOVE TO READ SOMETHIN' YOU WROTE.
SNATCH
FIRST YOU'D HAVE TO BE ABLE TO *READ.*
HUFF!
HERE.
FWMP
I'LL PAY FOR THAT LATER.
LENA DIDN'T TALK TO ME ALL DAY, NOT ALL WEEK...

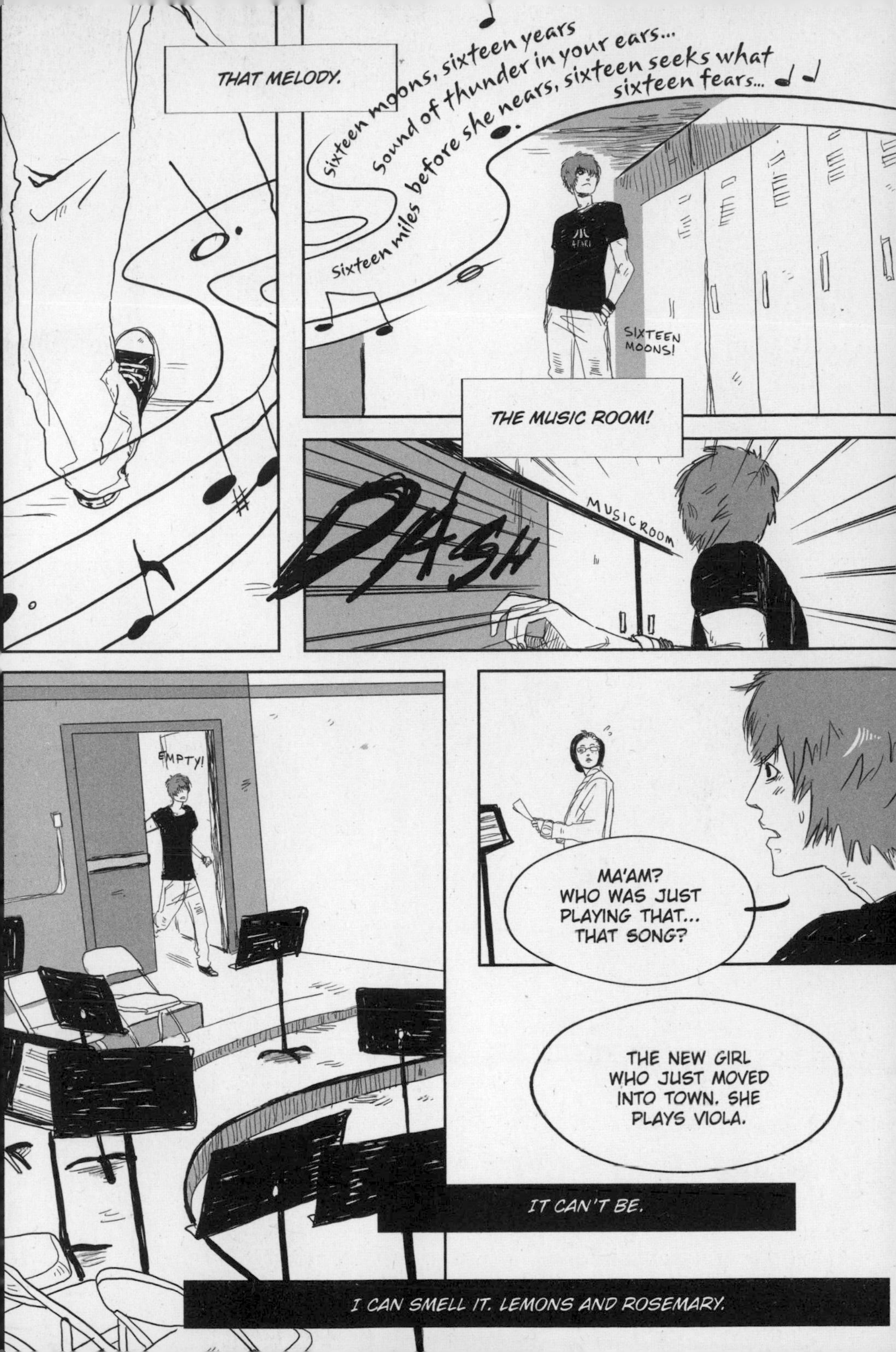
THAT MELODY.
Sixteen moons, sixteen years
Sound of thunder in your ears...
Sixteen miles before she nears, sixteen seeks what sixteen fears...
SIXTEEN MOONS!
THE MUSIC ROOM!
DASH
MUSIC ROOM
EMPTY!
MA'AM? WHO WAS JUST PLAYING THAT... THAT SONG?
THE NEW GIRL WHO JUST MOVED INTO TOWN. SHE PLAYS VIOLA.
IT CAN'T BE.
I CAN SMELL IT. LEMONS AND ROSEMARY.

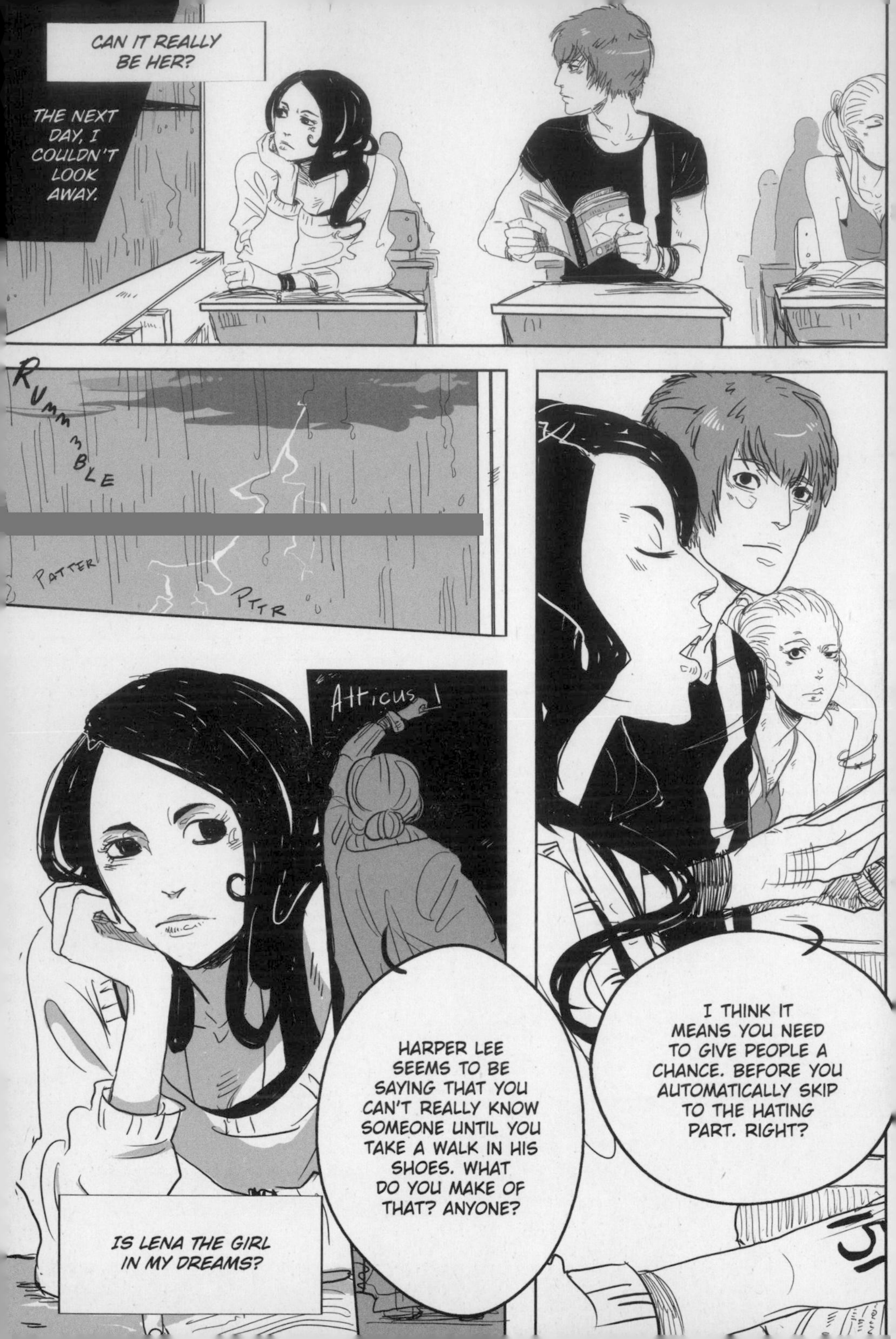
CAN IT REALLY BE HER?
THE NEXT DAY, I COULDN'T LOOK AWAY.
RUMMMBLE
PATTER
PTTR
Atticus!
HARPER LEE SEEMS TO BE SAYING THAT YOU CAN'T REALLY KNOW SOMEONE UNTIL YOU TAKE A WALK IN HIS SHOES. WHAT DO YOU MAKE OF THAT? ANYONE?
IS LENA THE GIRL IN MY DREAMS?
I THINK IT MEANS YOU NEED TO GIVE PEOPLE A CHANCE. BEFORE YOU AUTOMATICALLY SKIP TO THE HATING PART. RIGHT?

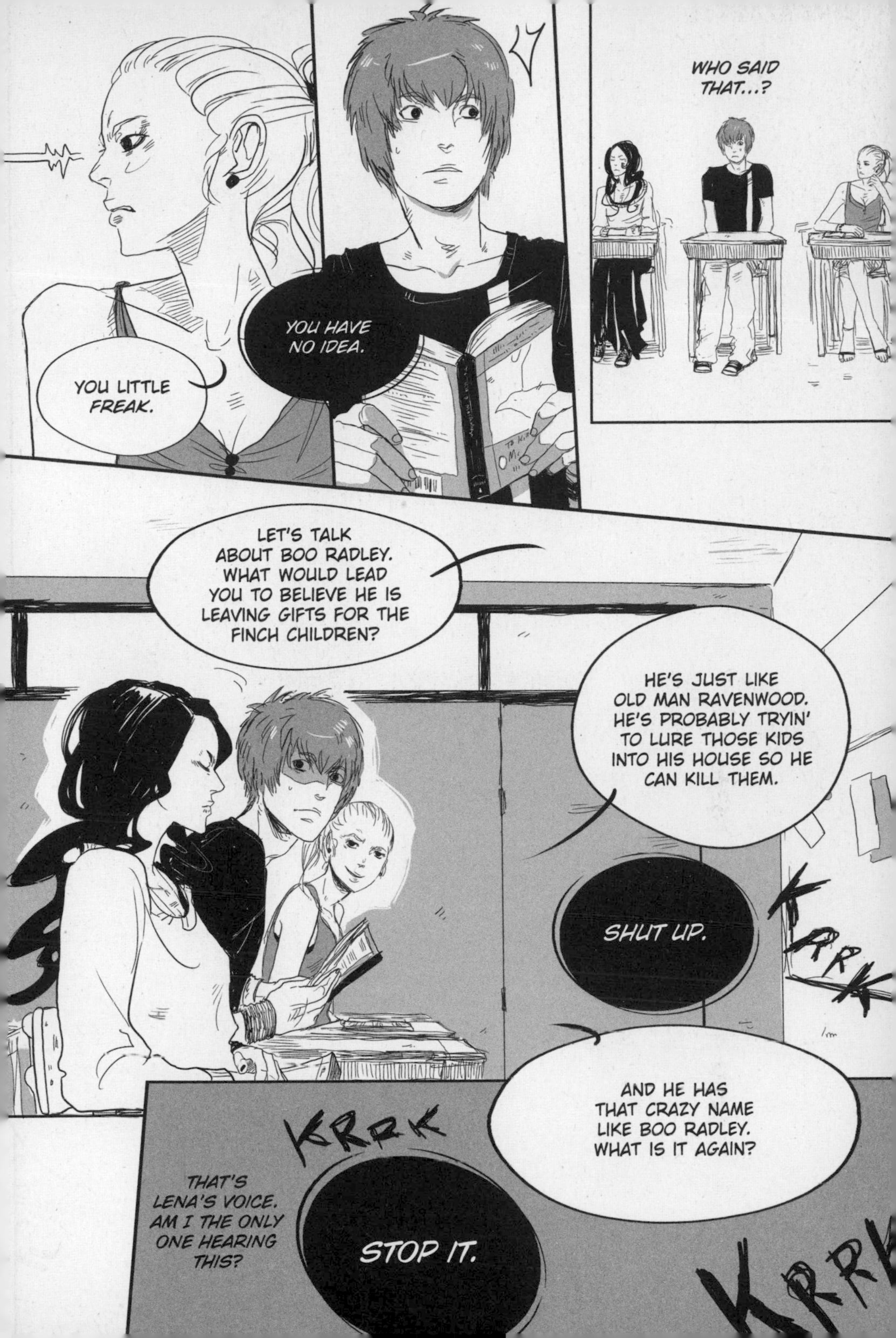

YOU LITTLE FREAK.
YOU HAVE NO IDEA.
WHO SAID THAT...?
LET'S TALK ABOUT BOO RADLEY. WHAT WOULD LEAD YOU TO BELIEVE HE IS LEAVING GIFTS FOR THE FINCH CHILDREN?
HE'S JUST LIKE OLD MAN RAVENWOOD. HE'S PROBABLY TRYIN' TO LURE THOSE KIDS INTO HIS HOUSE SO HE CAN KILL THEM.
SHUT UP.
KRRK
AND HE HAS THAT CRAZY NAME LIKE BOO RADLEY. WHAT IS IT AGAIN?
KRRK
THAT'S LENA'S VOICE. AM I THE ONLY ONE HEARING THIS?
STOP IT.
KRRK

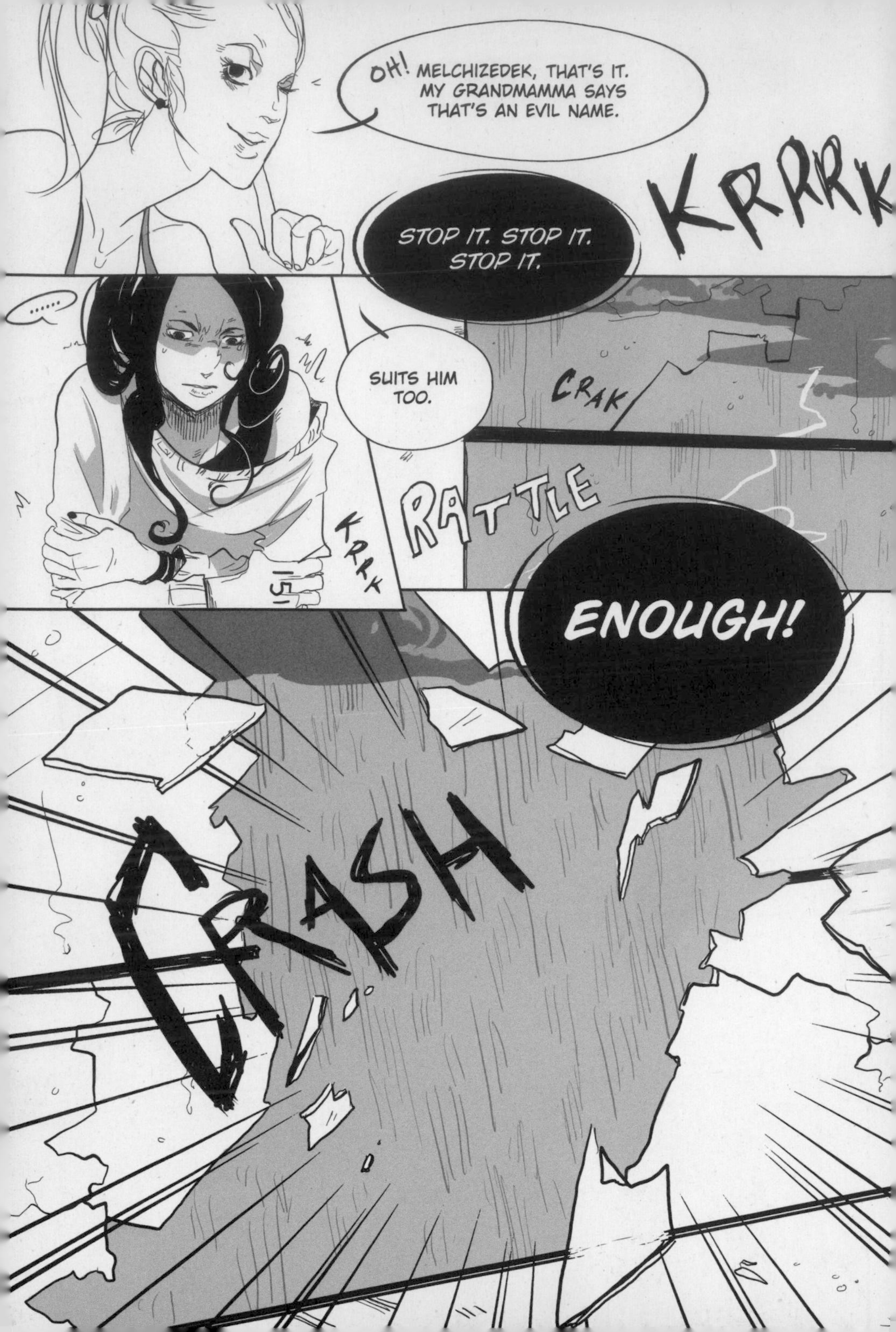
OH! MELCHIZEDEK, THAT'S IT. MY GRANDMAMMA SAYS THAT'S AN EVIL NAME.
STOP IT. STOP IT. STOP IT.
KRRRK
......
SUITS HIM TOO.
KRRRK
CRAK
RATTLE
ENOUGH!
CRASH

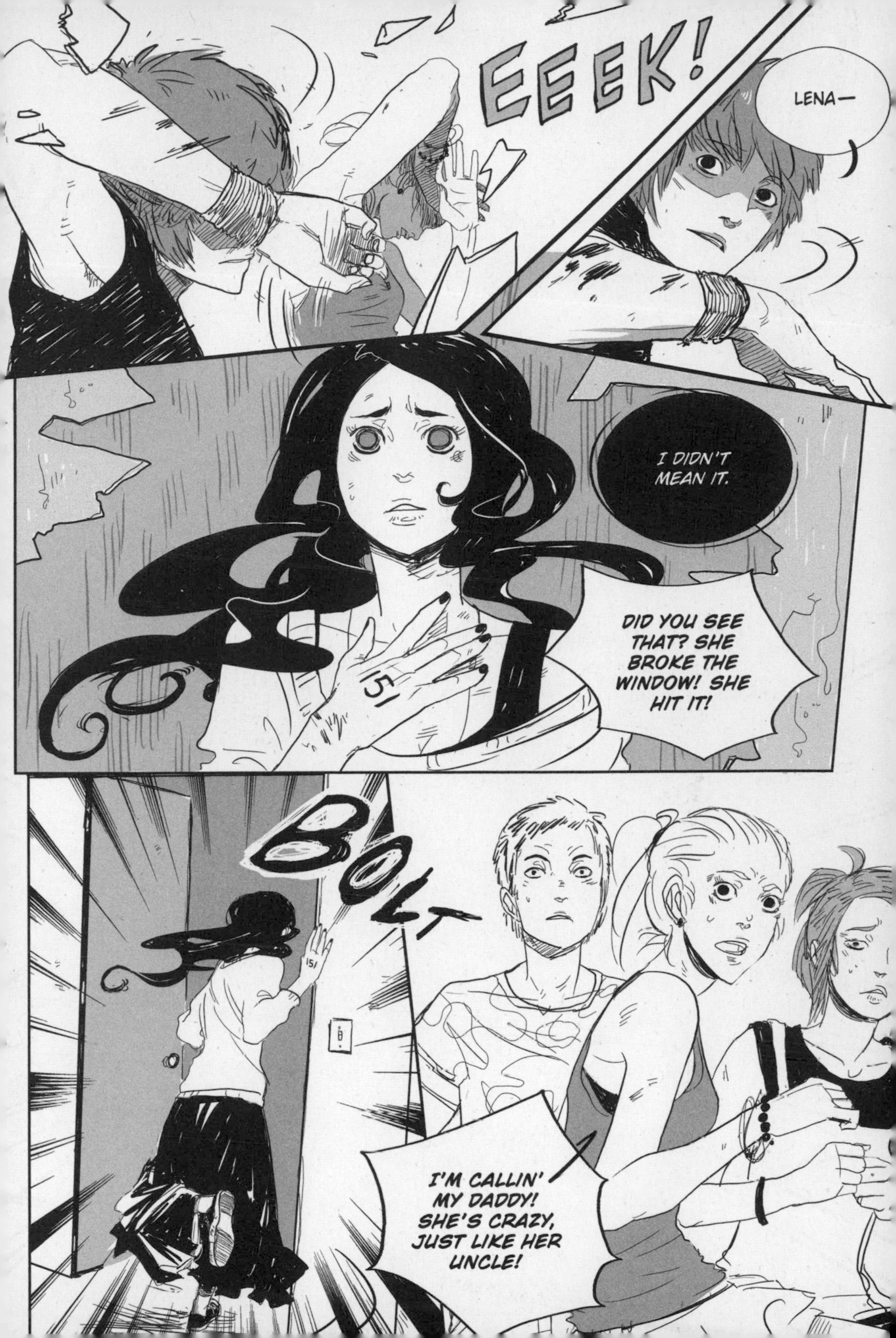
EEEK!
LENA—
I DIDN'T MEAN IT.
DID YOU SEE THAT? SHE BROKE THE WINDOW! SHE HIT IT!
151
BOLT
151
I'M CALLIN' MY DADDY! SHE'S CRAZY, JUST LIKE HER UNCLE!

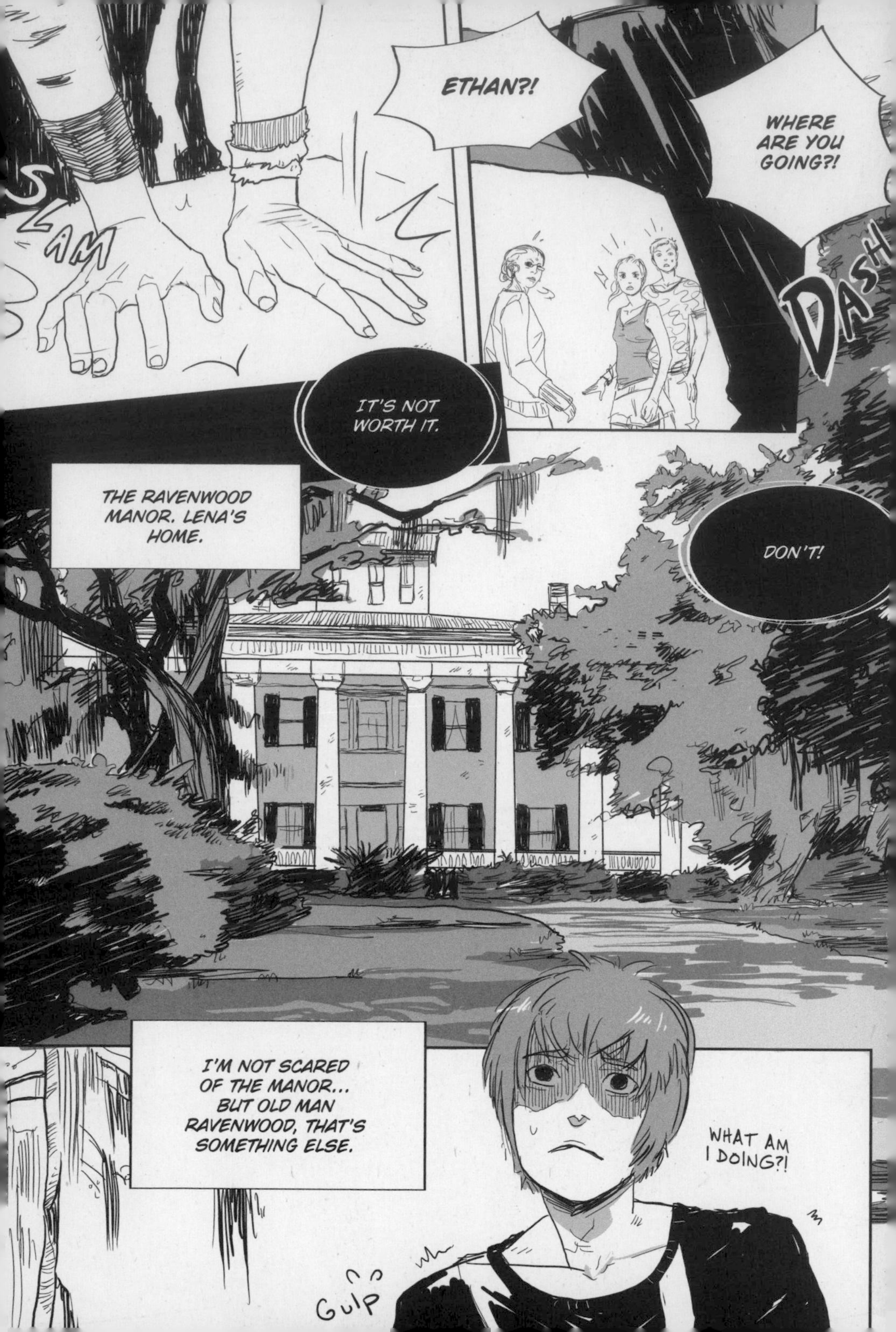
SLAM
ETHAN?!
WHERE ARE YOU GOING?!
DASH
IT'S NOT WORTH IT.
THE RAVENWOOD MANOR. LENA'S HOME.
DON'T!
I'M NOT SCARED OF THE MANOR... BUT OLD MAN RAVENWOOD, THAT'S SOMETHING ELSE.
WHAT AM I DOING?!
GULP

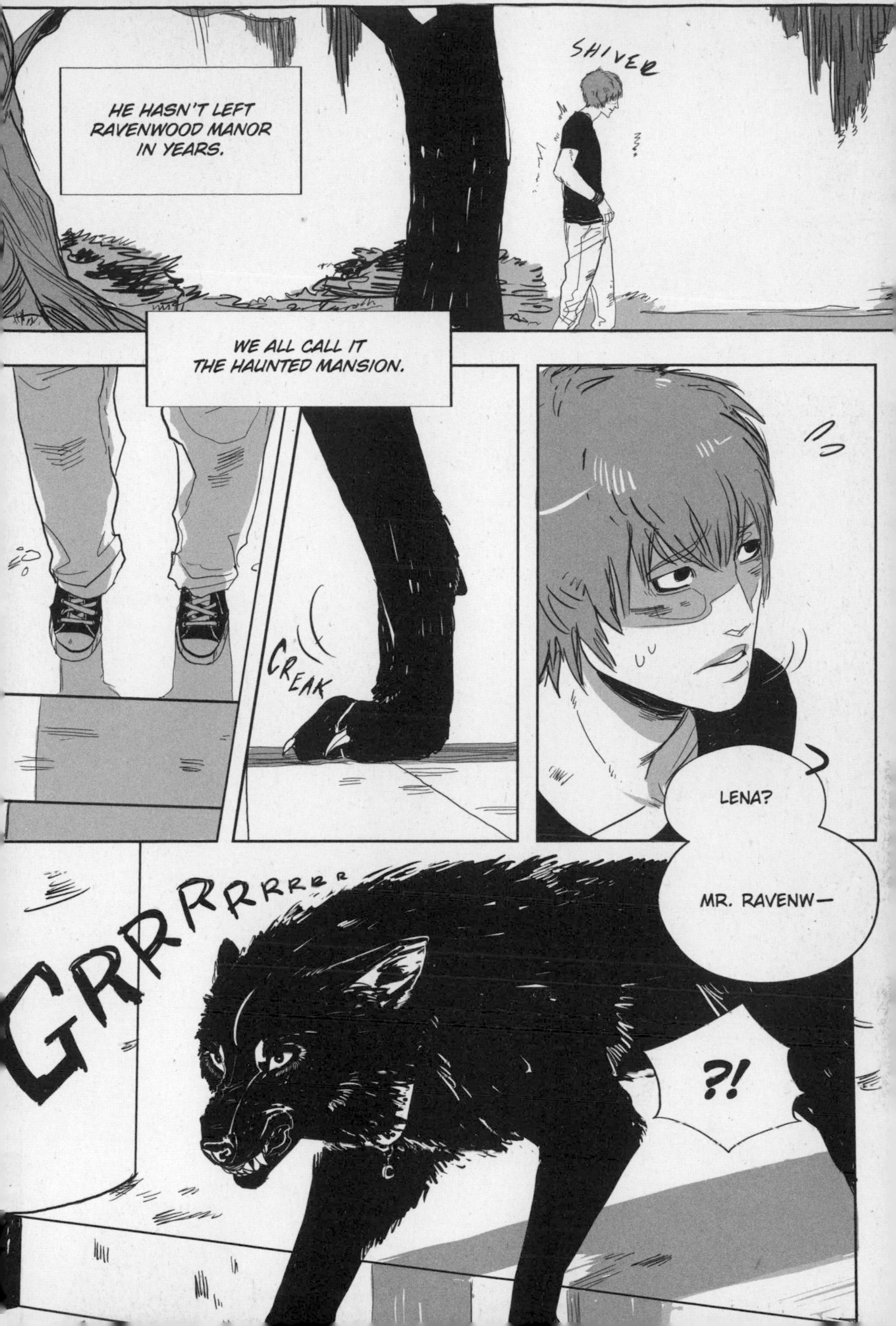
HE HASN'T LEFT RAVENWOOD MANOR IN YEARS.
SHIVER
WE ALL CALL IT THE HAUNTED MANSION.
CREAK
LENA?
MR. RAVENW—
GRRRRRRRR
?!

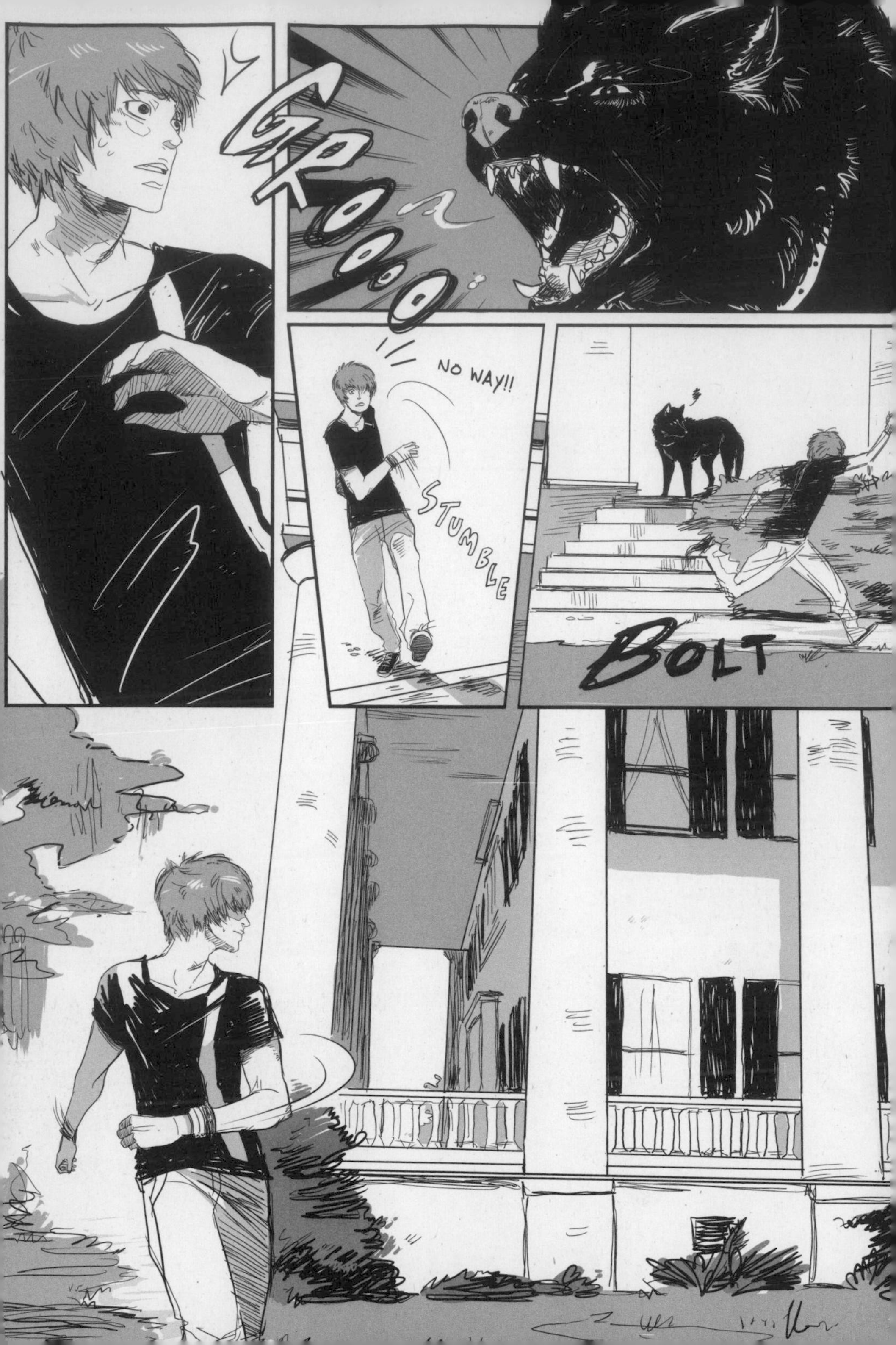
GROOOOOOO
NO WAY!!
STUMBLE
BOLT

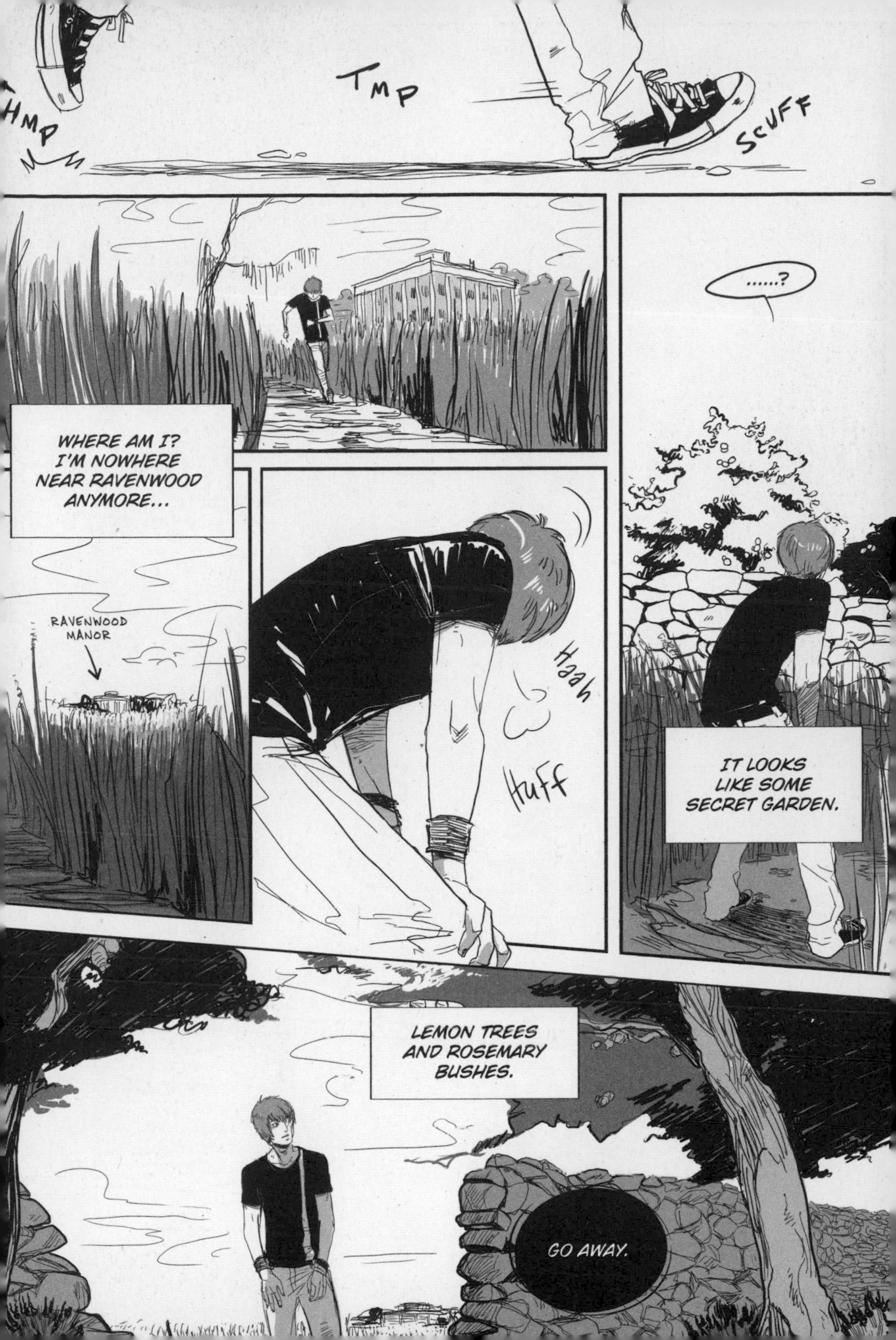
THMP
TMP
SCUFF
WHERE AM I? I'M NOWHERE NEAR RAVENWOOD ANYMORE...
RAVENWOOD MANOR
Haah
Huff
......?
IT LOOKS LIKE SOME SECRET GARDEN.
LEMON TREES AND ROSEMARY BUSHES.
GO AWAY.

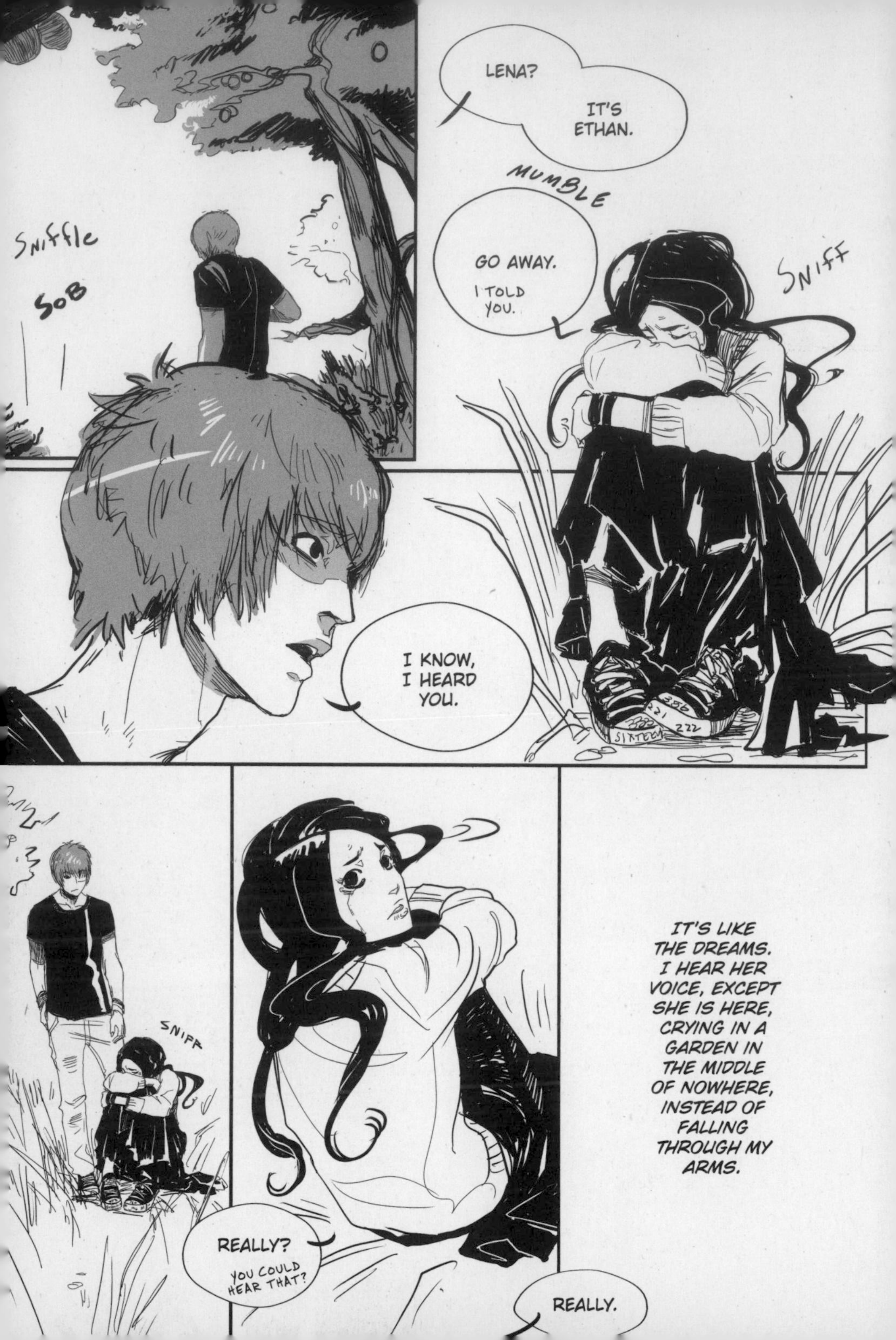
SNIFFLE
SOB
LENA?
IT'S ETHAN.
MUMBLE
GO AWAY.
I TOLD YOU.
SNIFF
I KNOW, I HEARD YOU.
SNIFF
REALLY?
YOU COULD HEAR THAT?
IT'S LIKE THE DREAMS. I HEAR HER VOICE, EXCEPT SHE IS HERE, CRYING IN A GARDEN IN THE MIDDLE OF NOWHERE, INSTEAD OF FALLING THROUGH MY ARMS.
REALLY.

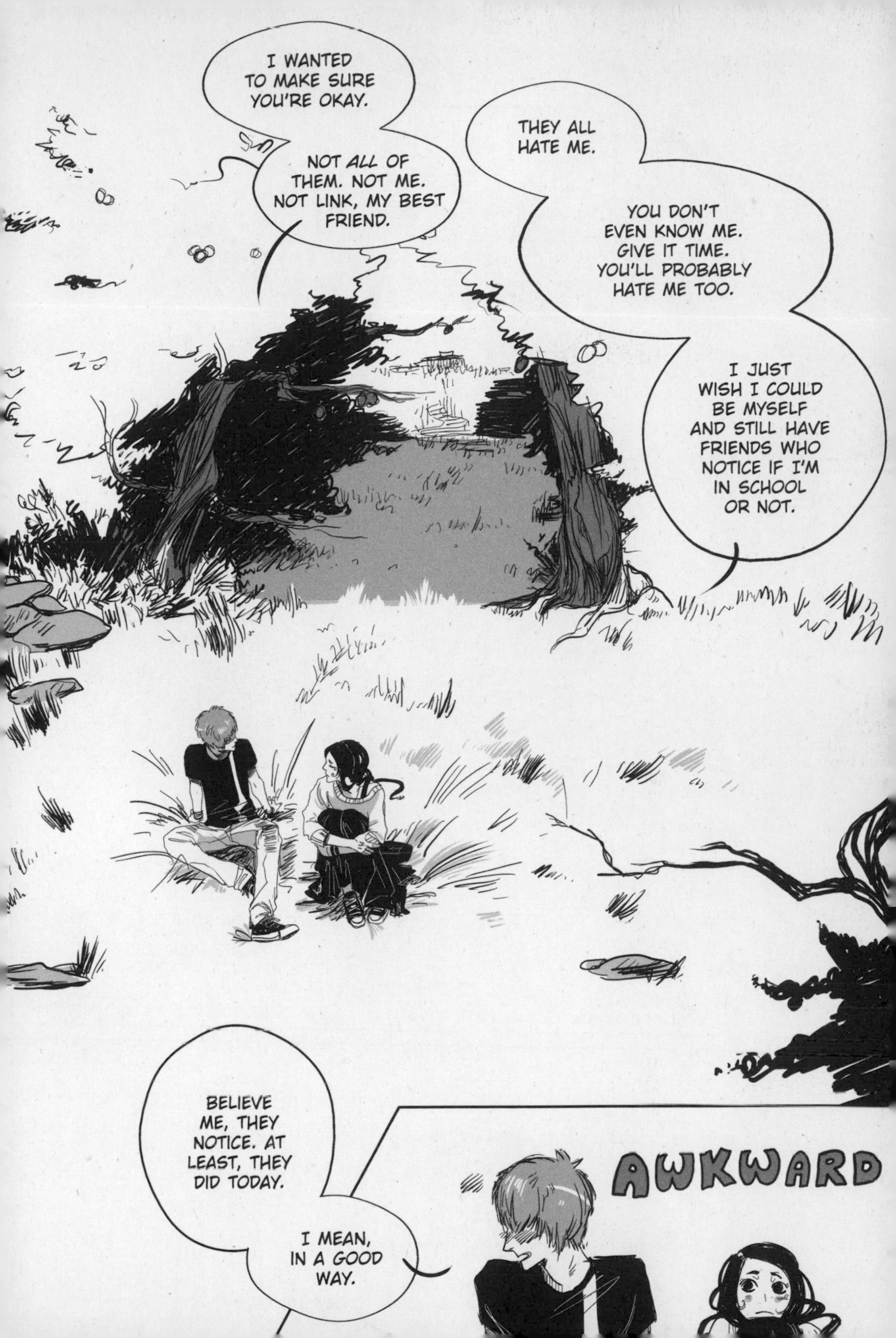
I WANTED TO MAKE SURE YOU'RE OKAY.
THEY ALL HATE ME.
NOT *ALL* OF THEM. NOT ME. NOT LINK, MY BEST FRIEND.
YOU DON'T EVEN KNOW ME. GIVE IT TIME. YOU'LL PROBABLY HATE ME TOO.
I JUST WISH I COULD BE MYSELF AND STILL HAVE FRIENDS WHO NOTICE IF I'M IN SCHOOL OR NOT.
BELIEVE ME, THEY NOTICE. AT LEAST, THEY DID TODAY.
I MEAN, IN A GOOD WAY.
AWKWARD

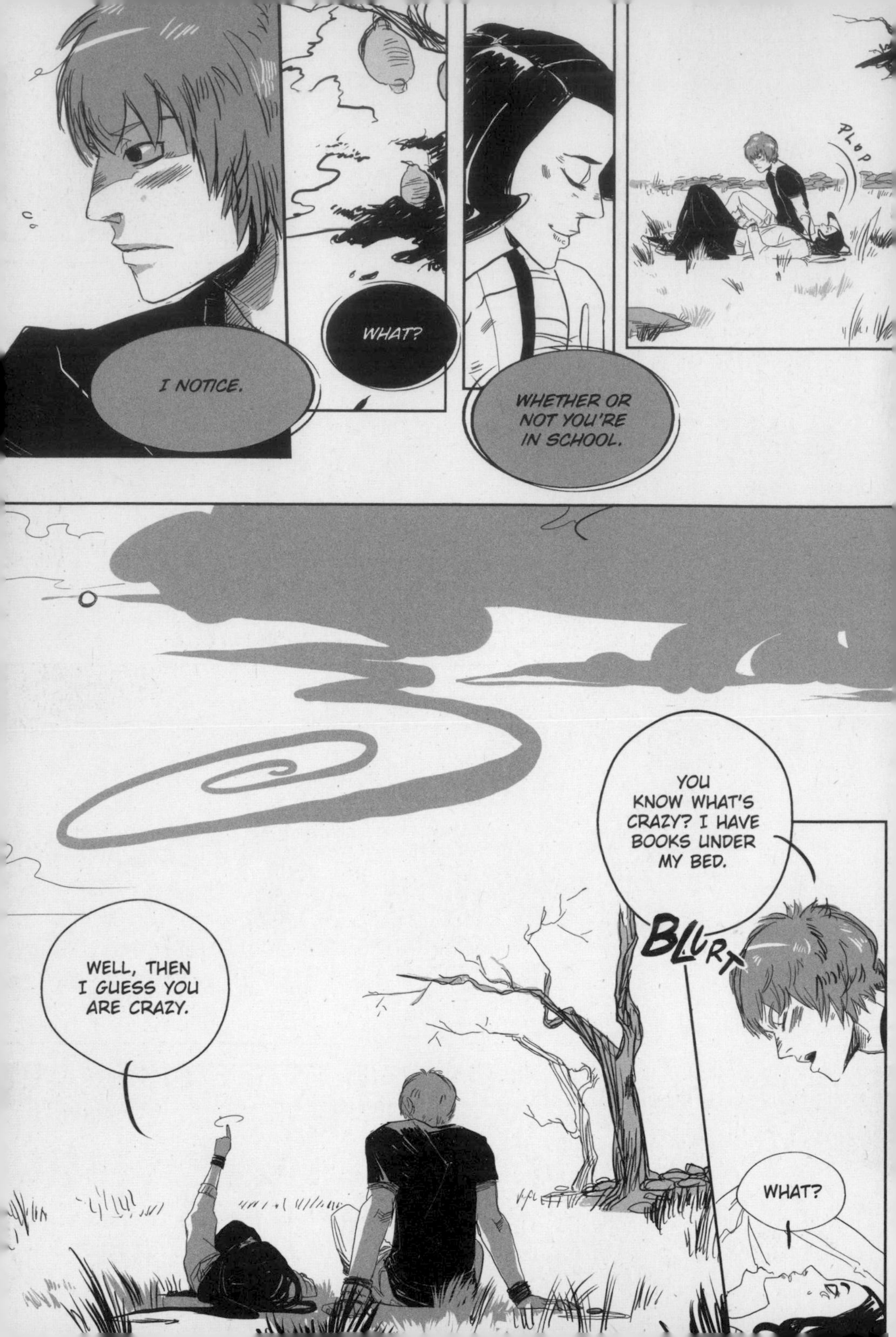
I NOTICE.
WHAT?
WHETHER OR NOT YOU'RE IN SCHOOL.
PLOP
YOU KNOW WHAT'S CRAZY? I HAVE BOOKS UNDER MY BED.
BLURT
WELL, THEN I GUESS YOU ARE CRAZY.
WHAT?

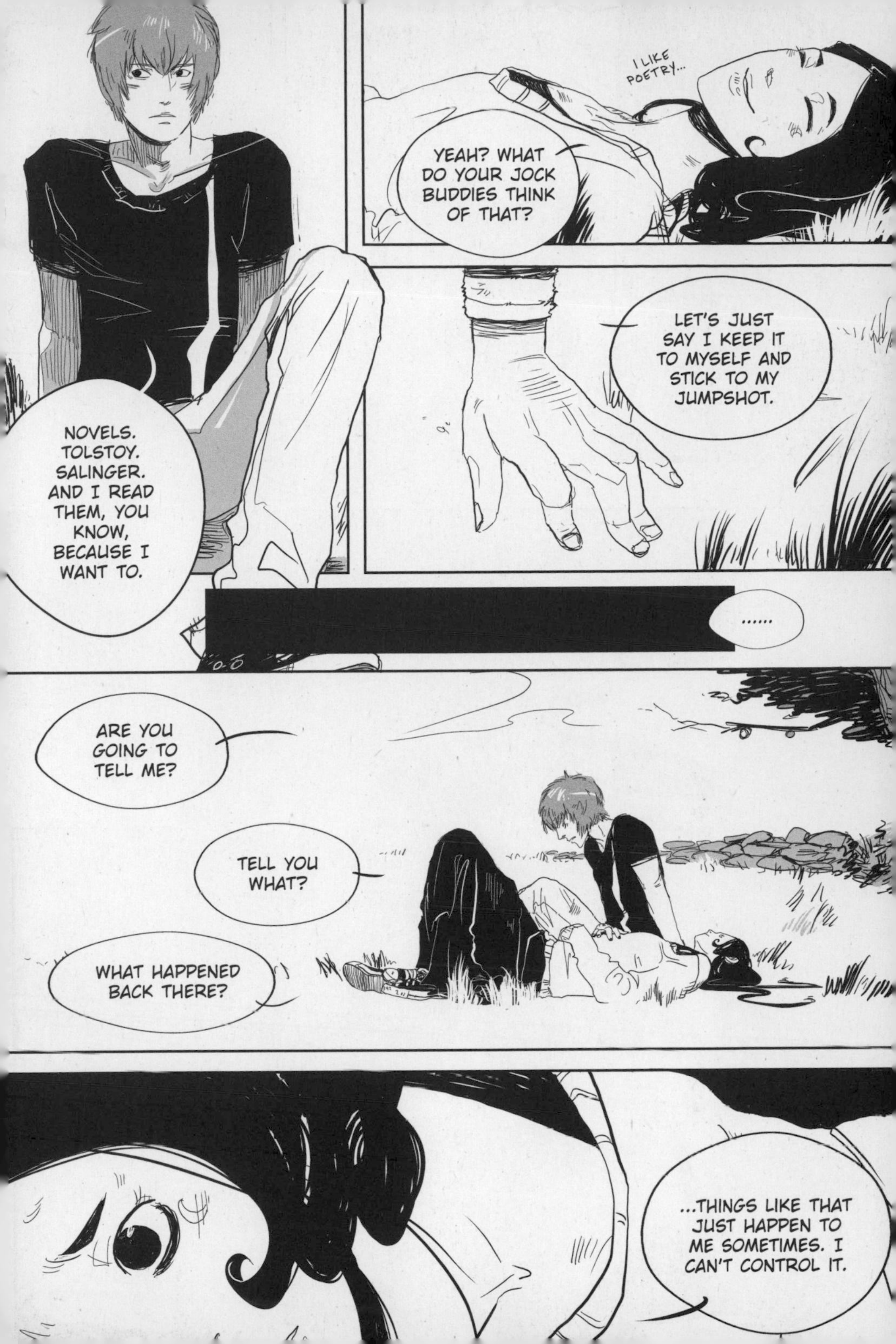
NOVELS. TOLSTOY. SALINGER. AND I READ THEM, YOU KNOW, BECAUSE I WANT TO.
I LIKE POETRY...
YEAH? WHAT DO YOUR JOCK BUDDIES THINK OF THAT?
LET'S JUST SAY I KEEP IT TO MYSELF AND STICK TO MY JUMPSHOT.
......
ARE YOU GOING TO TELL ME?
TELL YOU WHAT?
WHAT HAPPENED BACK THERE?
...THINGS LIKE THAT JUST HAPPEN TO ME SOMETIMES. I CAN'T CONTROL IT.

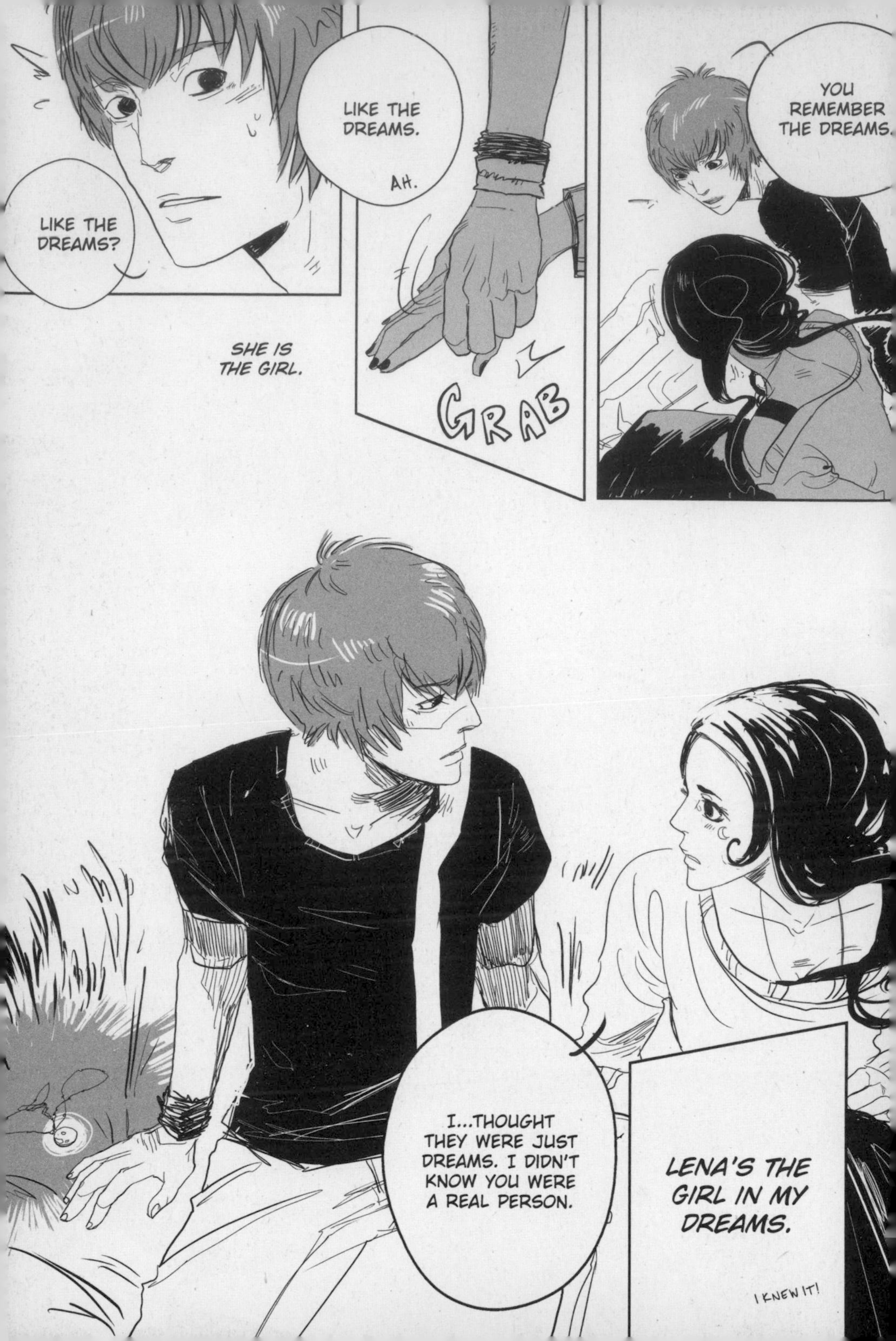
LIKE THE DREAMS?
SHE IS THE GIRL.
LIKE THE DREAMS.
AH.
GRAB
YOU REMEMBER THE DREAMS.
I...THOUGHT THEY WERE JUST DREAMS. I DIDN'T KNOW YOU WERE A REAL PERSON.
LENA'S THE GIRL IN MY DREAMS.
I KNEW IT!

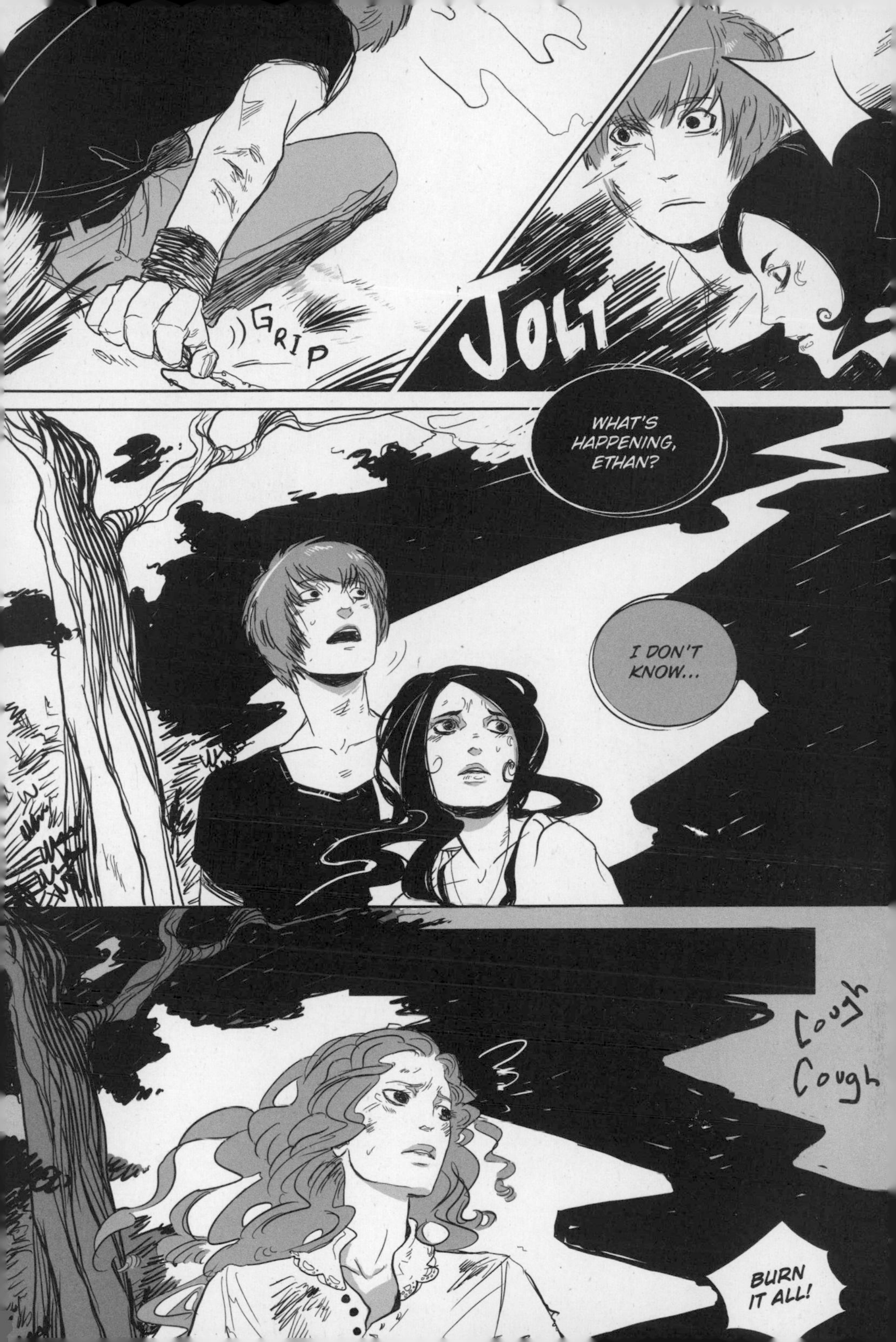
GRIP
JOLT
WHAT'S HAPPENING, ETHAN?
I DON'T KNOW...
Cough
Cough
BURN IT ALL!

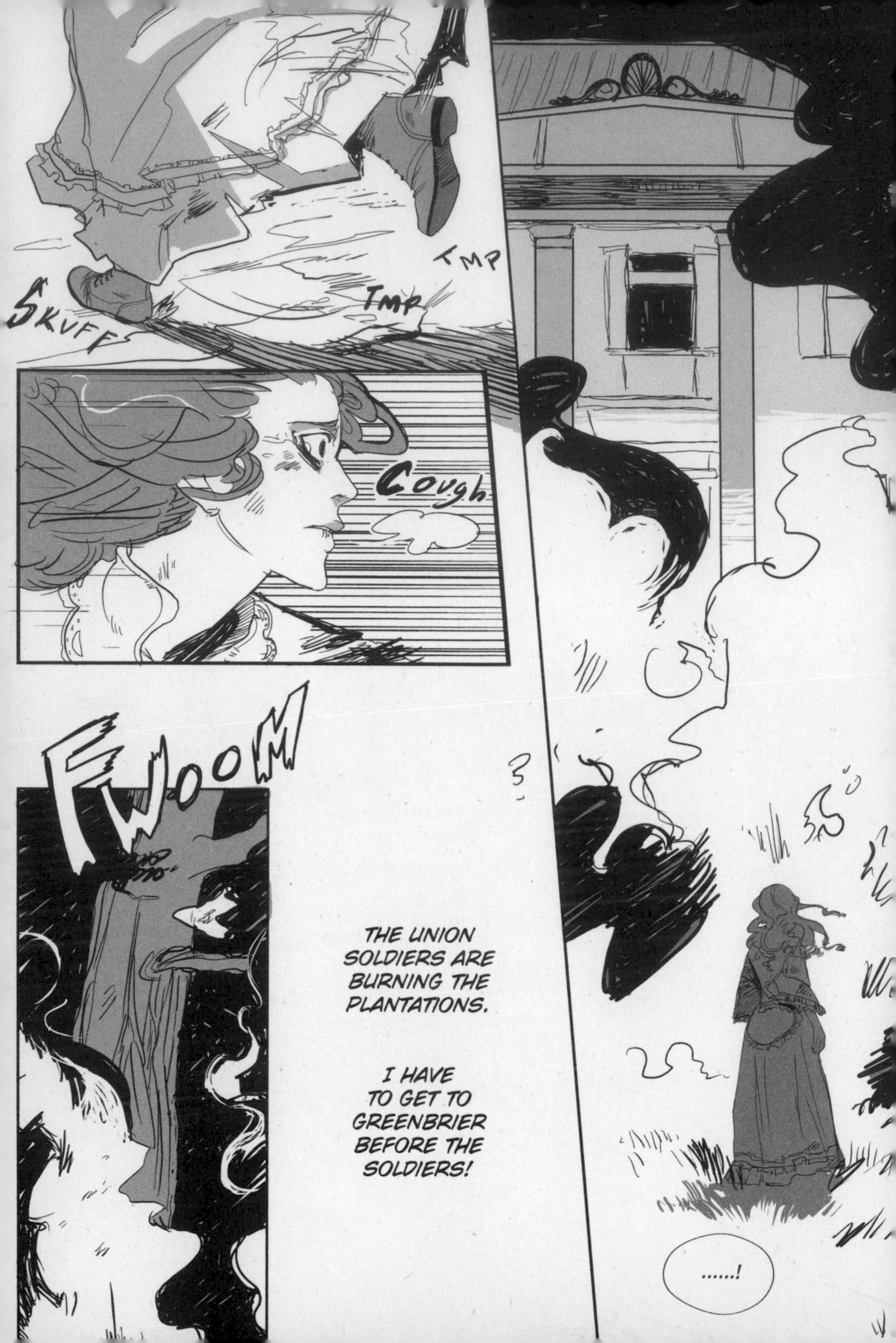
SKUFF
TMP
TMP
COUGH
FWOOM
THE UNION SOLDIERS ARE BURNING THE PLANTATIONS.
I HAVE TO GET TO GREENBRIER BEFORE THE SOLDIERS!
......!

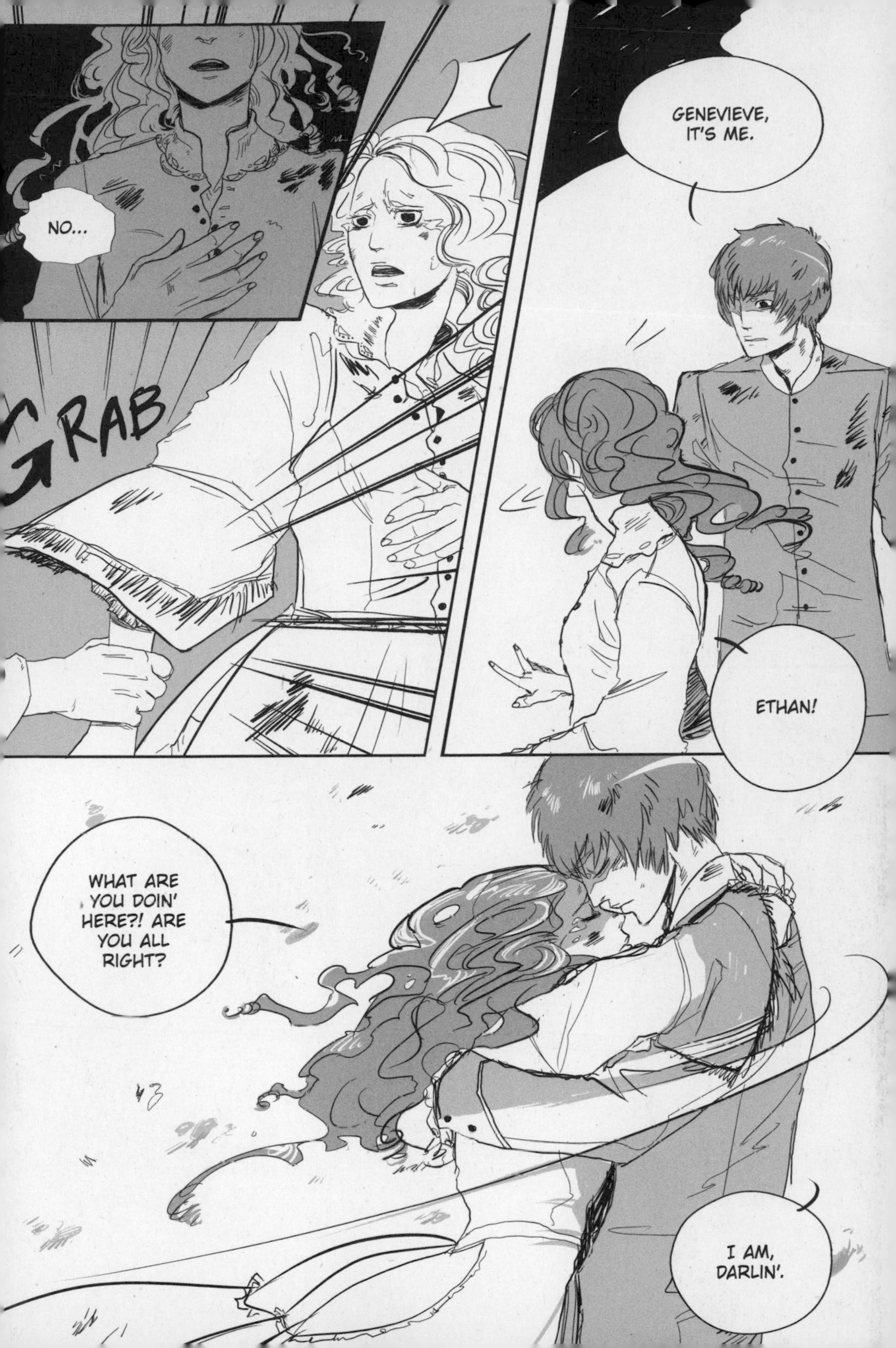
NO...
GRAB
GENEVIEVE, IT'S ME.
ETHAN!
WHAT ARE YOU DOIN' HERE?! ARE YOU ALL RIGHT?
I AM, DARLIN'.

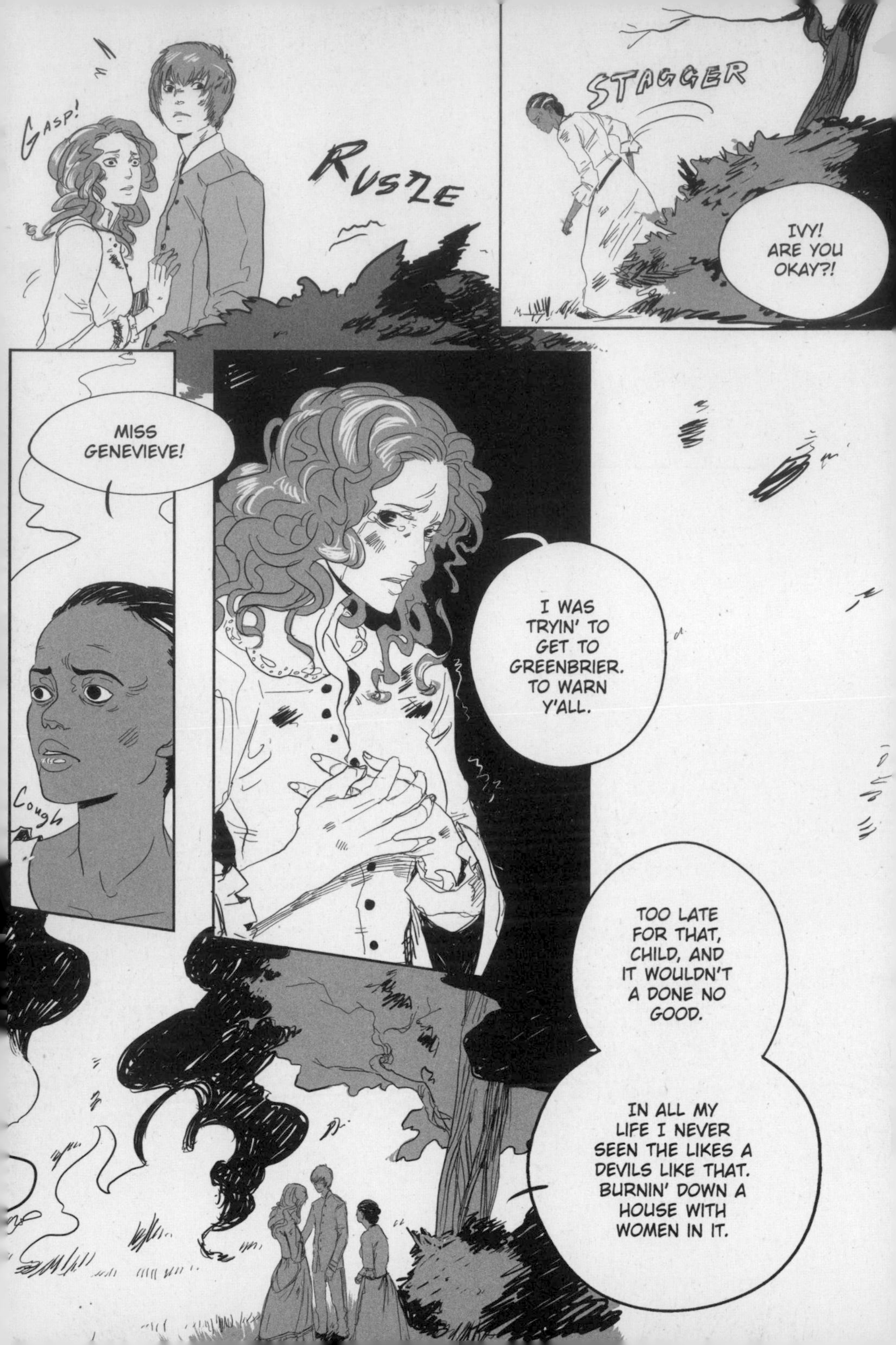
GASP!
RUSTLE
STAGGER
IVY! ARE YOU OKAY?!
MISS GENEVIEVE!
COUGH
I WAS TRYIN' TO GET TO GREENBRIER. TO WARN Y'ALL.
TOO LATE FOR THAT, CHILD, AND IT WOULDN'T A DONE NO GOOD.
IN ALL MY LIFE I NEVER SEEN THE LIKES A DEVILS LIKE THAT. BURNIN' DOWN A HOUSE WITH WOMEN IN IT.

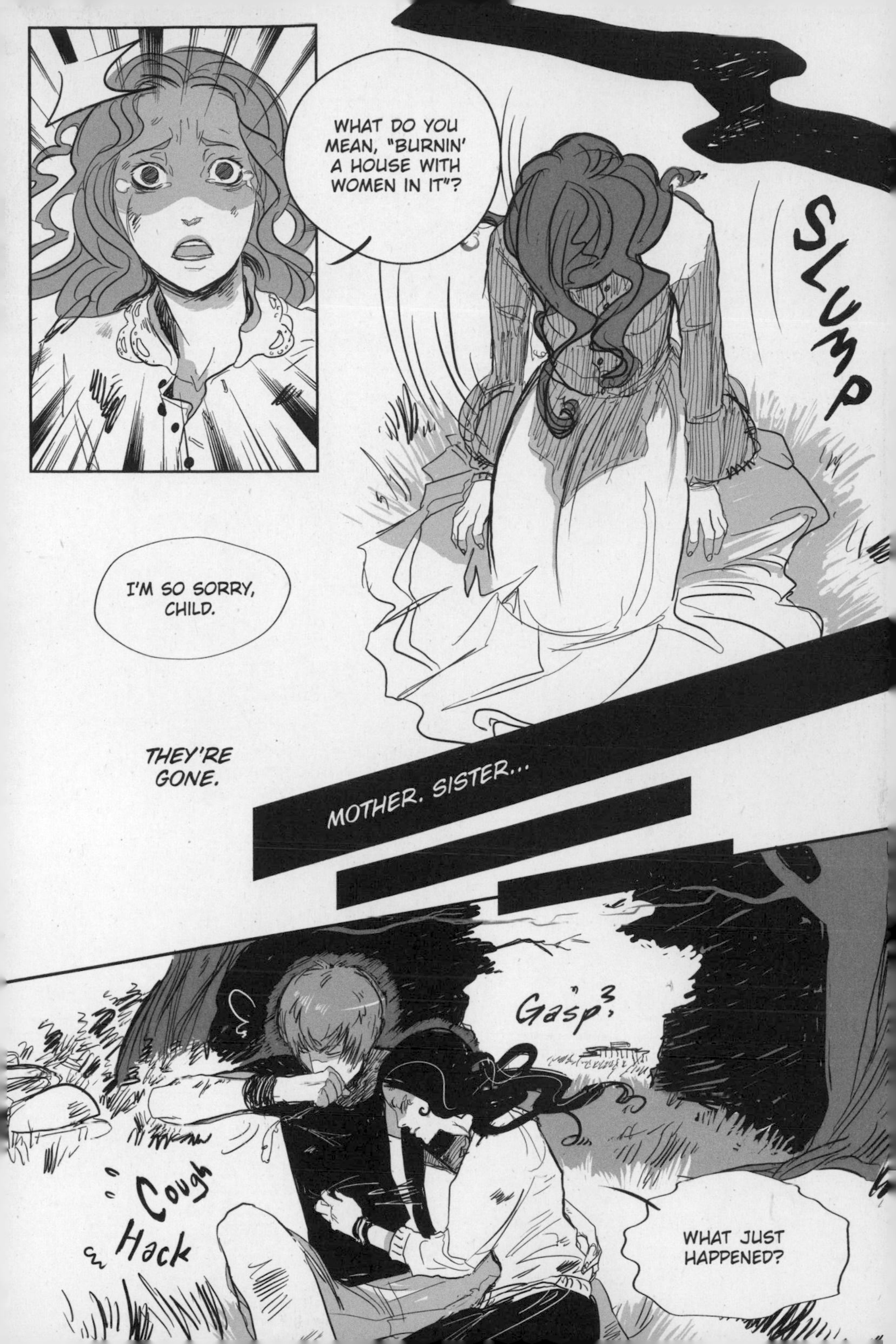
WHAT DO YOU MEAN, "BURNIN' A HOUSE WITH WOMEN IN IT"?
SLUMP
I'M SO SORRY, CHILD.
THEY'RE GONE.
MOTHER. SISTER...
Gasp
Cough
Hack
WHAT JUST HAPPENED?

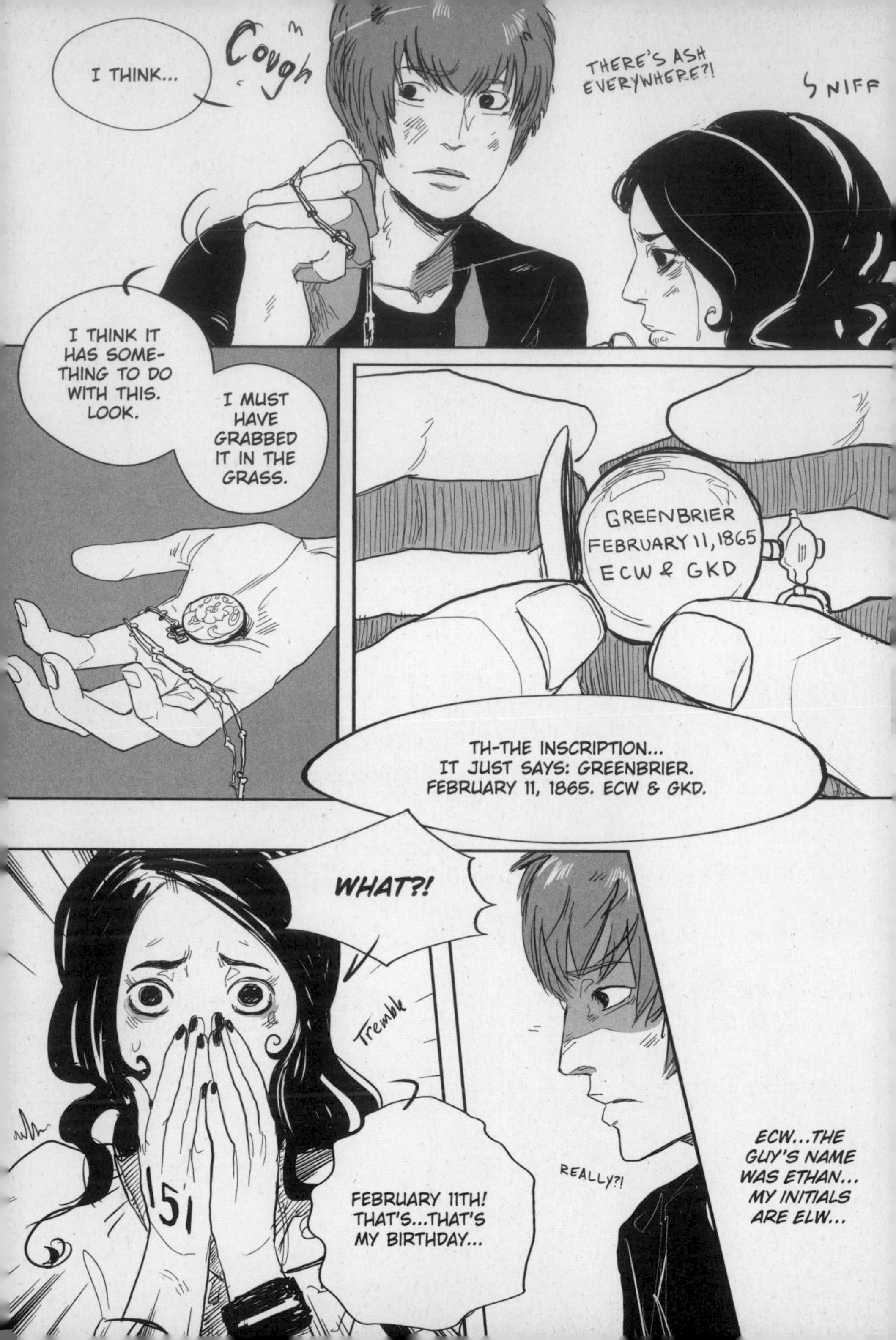
I THINK...
Cough
THERE'S ASH EVERYWHERE?!
SNIFF
I THINK IT HAS SOME-THING TO DO WITH THIS. LOOK.
I MUST HAVE GRABBED IT IN THE GRASS.
GREENBRIER FEBRUARY 11, 1865 ECW & GKD
TH-THE INSCRIPTION... IT JUST SAYS: GREENBRIER. FEBRUARY 11, 1865. ECW & GKD.
WHAT?!
Tremble
FEBRUARY 11TH! THAT'S...THAT'S MY BIRTHDAY...
REALLY?!
ECW...THE GUY'S NAME WAS ETHAN... MY INITIALS ARE ELW...
151

BEAUTIFUL CREATURES

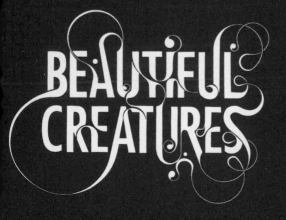

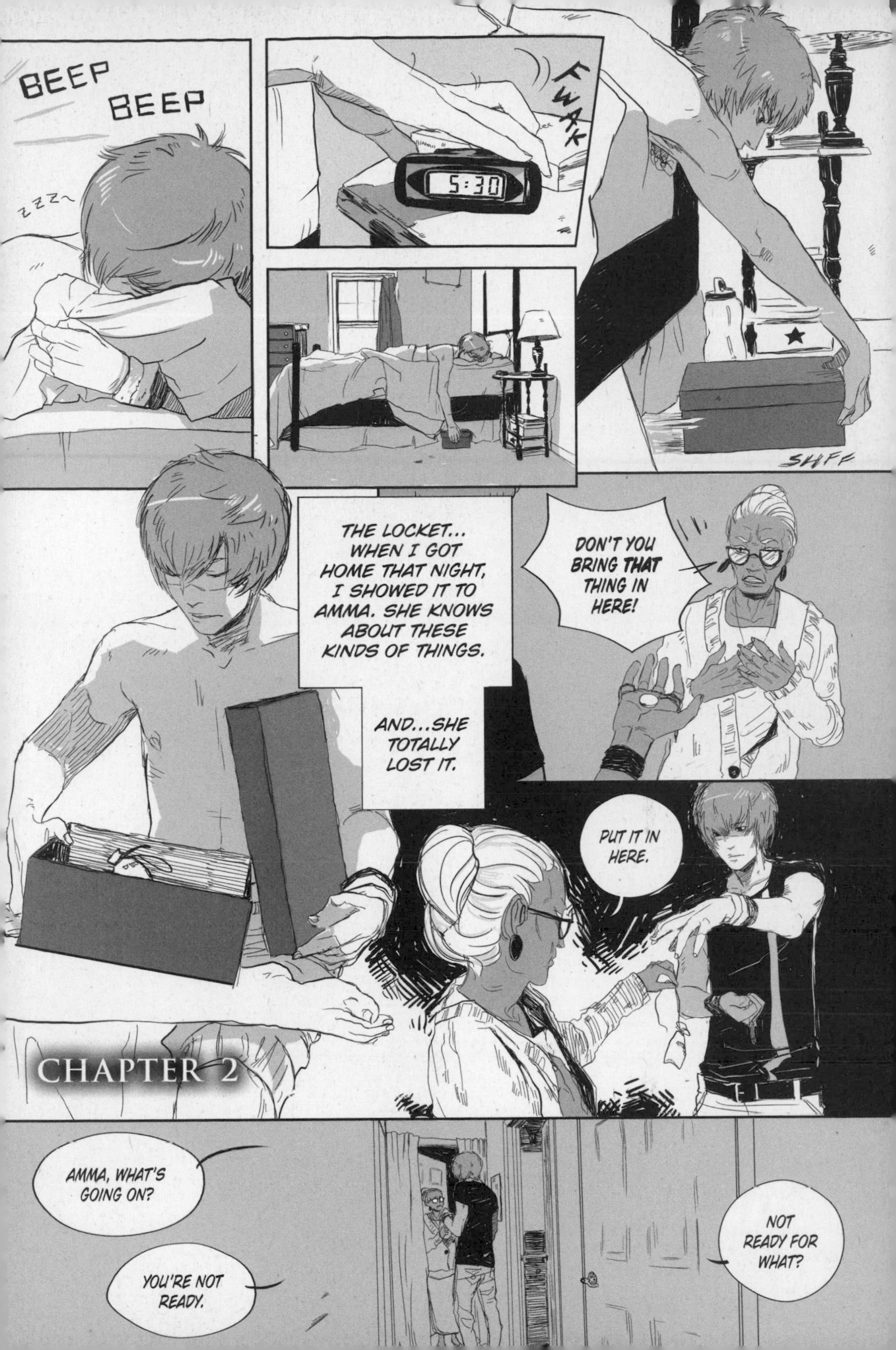
BEEP
BEEP
ZZZ~
FWAK
5:30
SHFF
THE LOCKET... WHEN I GOT HOME THAT NIGHT, I SHOWED IT TO AMMA. SHE KNOWS ABOUT THESE KINDS OF THINGS.
AND...SHE TOTALLY LOST IT.
DON'T YOU BRING THAT THING IN HERE!
PUT IT IN HERE.
CHAPTER 2
AMMA, WHAT'S GOING ON?
YOU'RE NOT READY.
NOT READY FOR WHAT?

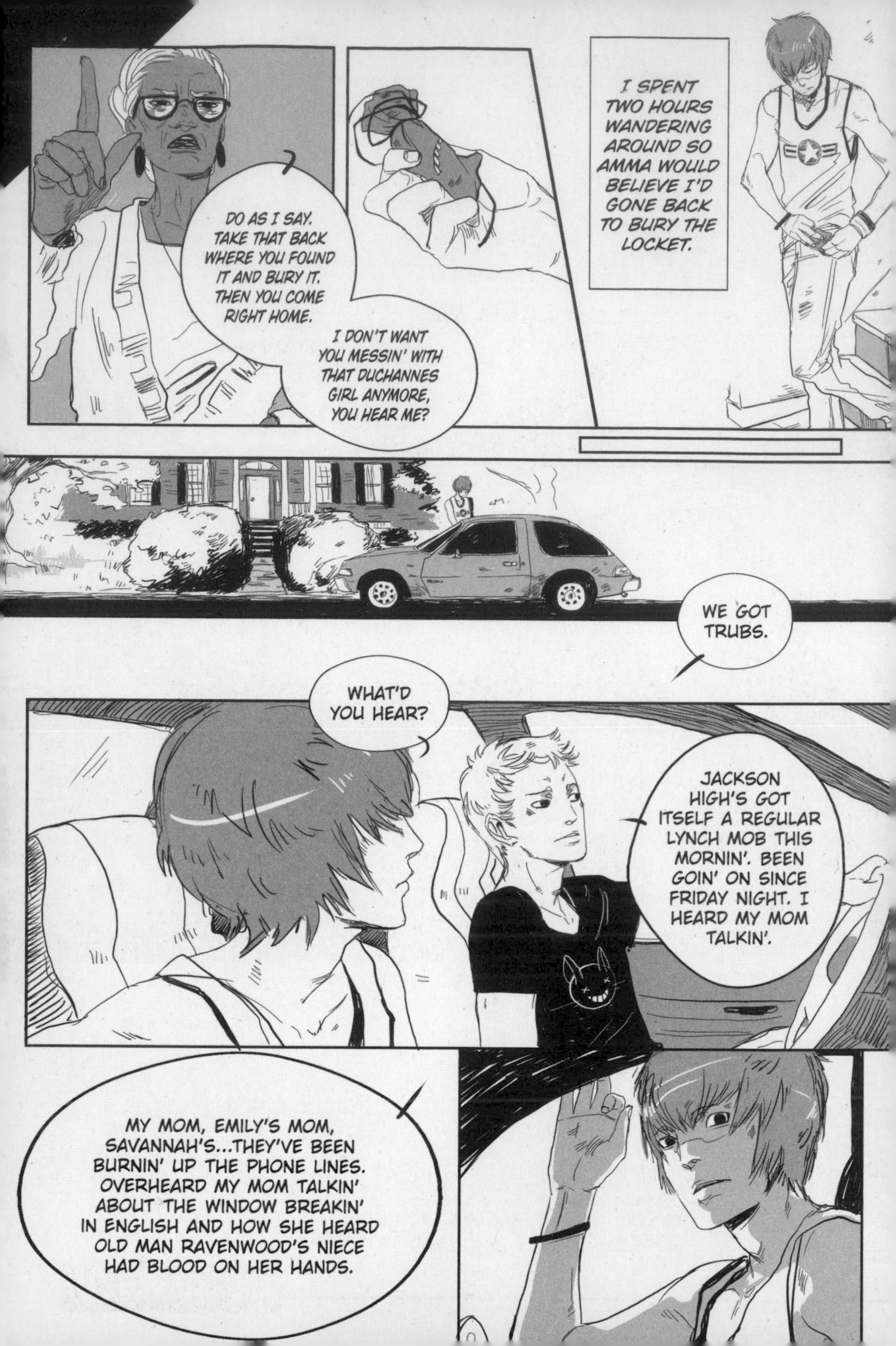
DO AS I SAY. TAKE THAT BACK WHERE YOU FOUND IT AND BURY IT. THEN YOU COME RIGHT HOME.
I DON'T WANT YOU MESSIN' WITH THAT DUCHANNES GIRL ANYMORE, YOU HEAR ME?
I SPENT TWO HOURS WANDERING AROUND SO AMMA WOULD BELIEVE I'D GONE BACK TO BURY THE LOCKET.
WE GOT TRUBS.
WHAT'D YOU HEAR?
JACKSON HIGH'S GOT ITSELF A REGULAR LYNCH MOB THIS MORNIN'. BEEN GOIN' ON SINCE FRIDAY NIGHT. I HEARD MY MOM TALKIN'.
MY MOM, EMILY'S MOM, SAVANNAH'S...THEY'VE BEEN BURNIN' UP THE PHONE LINES. OVERHEARD MY MOM TALKIN' ABOUT THE WINDOW BREAKIN' IN ENGLISH AND HOW SHE HEARD OLD MAN RAVENWOOD'S NIECE HAD BLOOD ON HER HANDS.

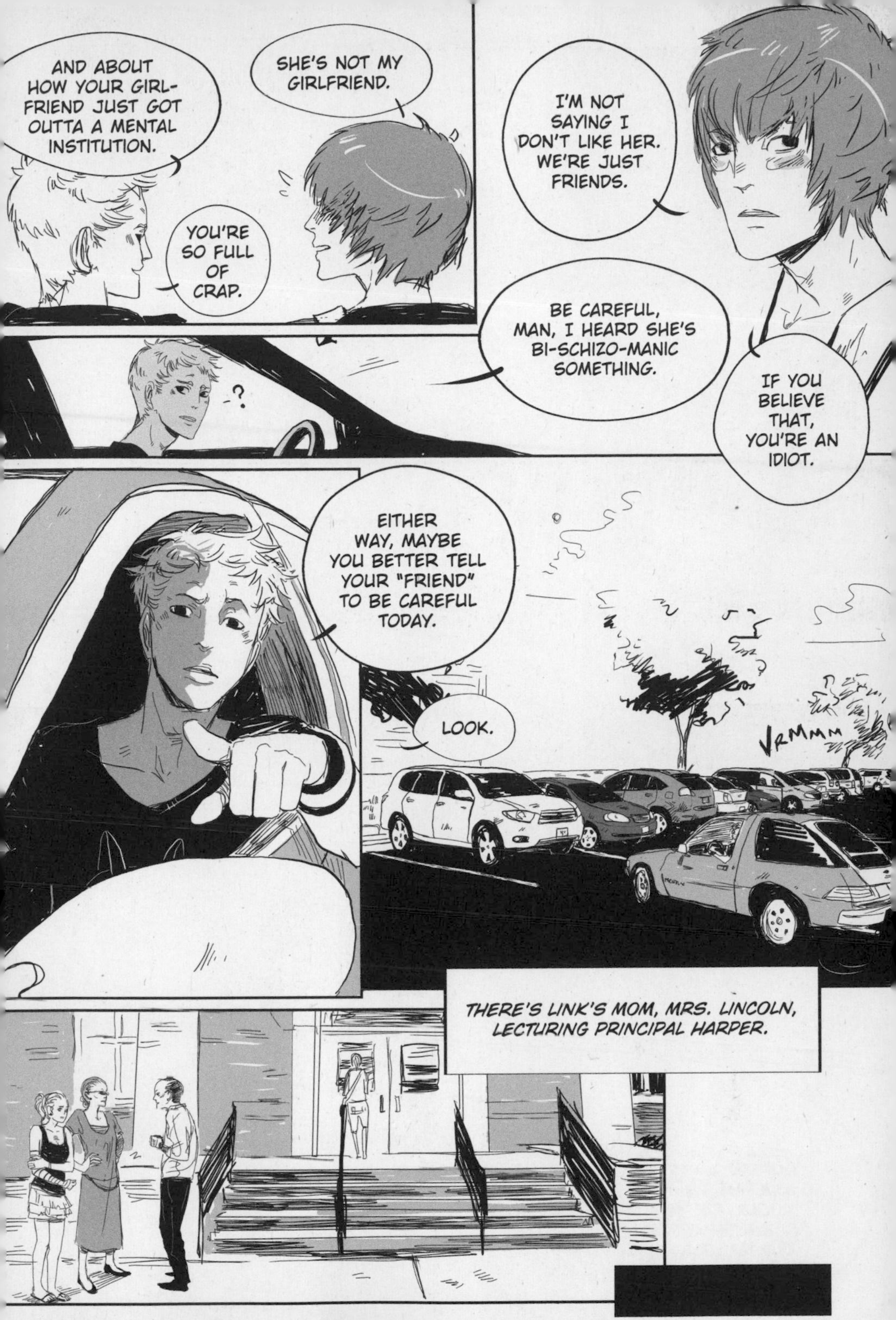
AND ABOUT HOW YOUR GIRL-FRIEND JUST GOT OUTTA A MENTAL INSTITUTION.
SHE'S NOT MY GIRLFRIEND.
YOU'RE SO FULL OF CRAP.
I'M NOT SAYING I DON'T LIKE HER. WE'RE JUST FRIENDS.
?
BE CAREFUL, MAN, I HEARD SHE'S BI-SCHIZO-MANIC SOMETHING.
IF YOU BELIEVE THAT, YOU'RE AN IDIOT.
EITHER WAY, MAYBE YOU BETTER TELL YOUR "FRIEND" TO BE CAREFUL TODAY.
LOOK.
VRMMM
THERE'S LINK'S MOM, MRS. LINCOLN, LECTURING PRINCIPAL HARPER.

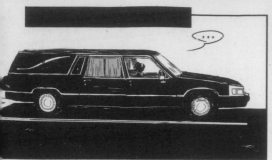

WHAT ARE YOU DOING?

WAITING.

IT'S GONNA BE A LONG WAIT.

I'VE GOT TIME.

sigh

DID ANYONE EVER TELL YOU YOU'RE CRAZY?

NOT AS CRAZY AS YOU, I HEAR.

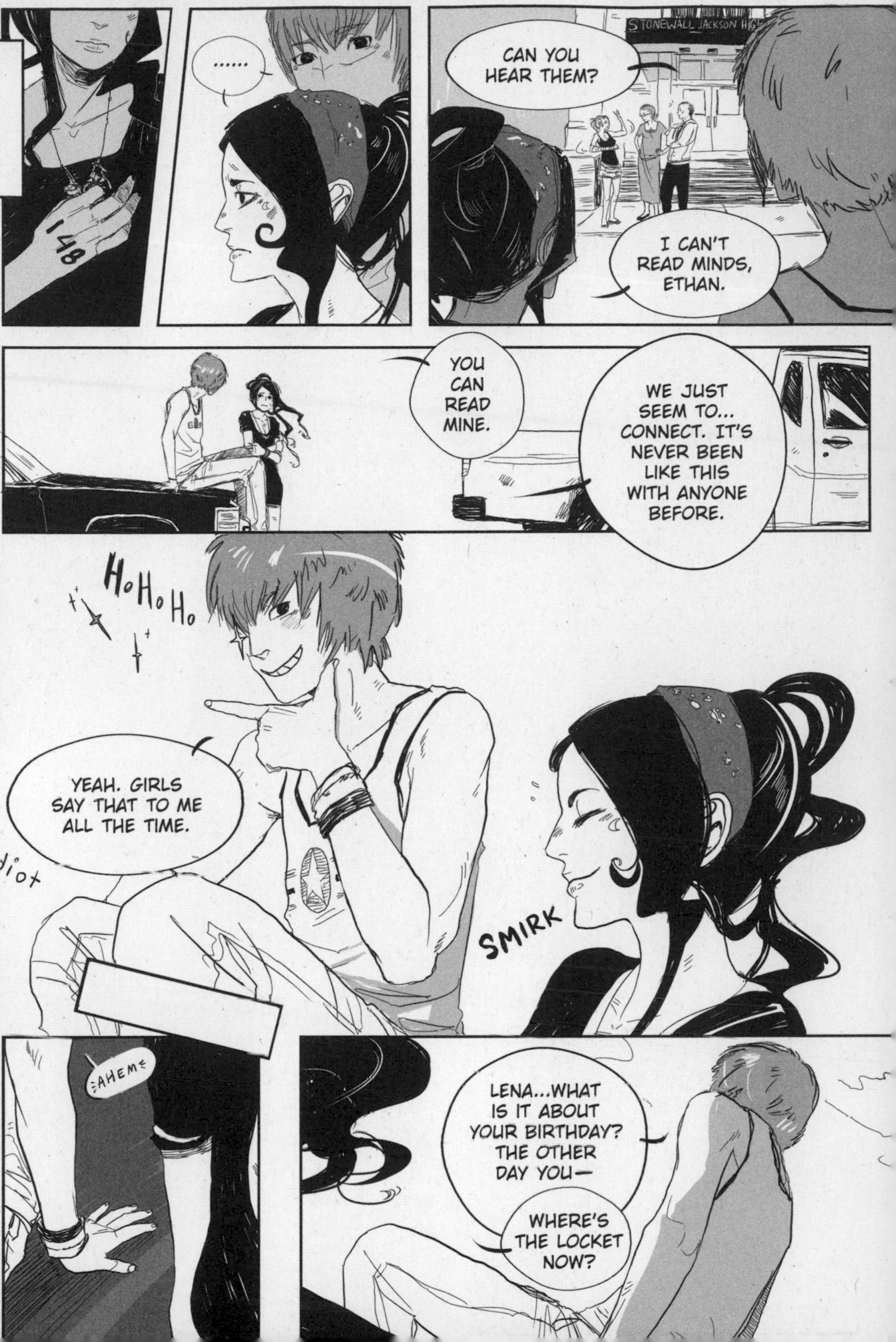
148
......
STONEWALL JACKSON HIG
CAN YOU HEAR THEM?
I CAN'T READ MINDS, ETHAN.
YOU CAN READ MINE.
WE JUST SEEM TO... CONNECT. IT'S NEVER BEEN LIKE THIS WITH ANYONE BEFORE.
HoHoHo
YEAH. GIRLS SAY THAT TO ME ALL THE TIME.
Idiot
SMIRK
AHEM
LENA...WHAT IS IT ABOUT YOUR BIRTHDAY? THE OTHER DAY YOU—
WHERE'S THE LOCKET NOW?

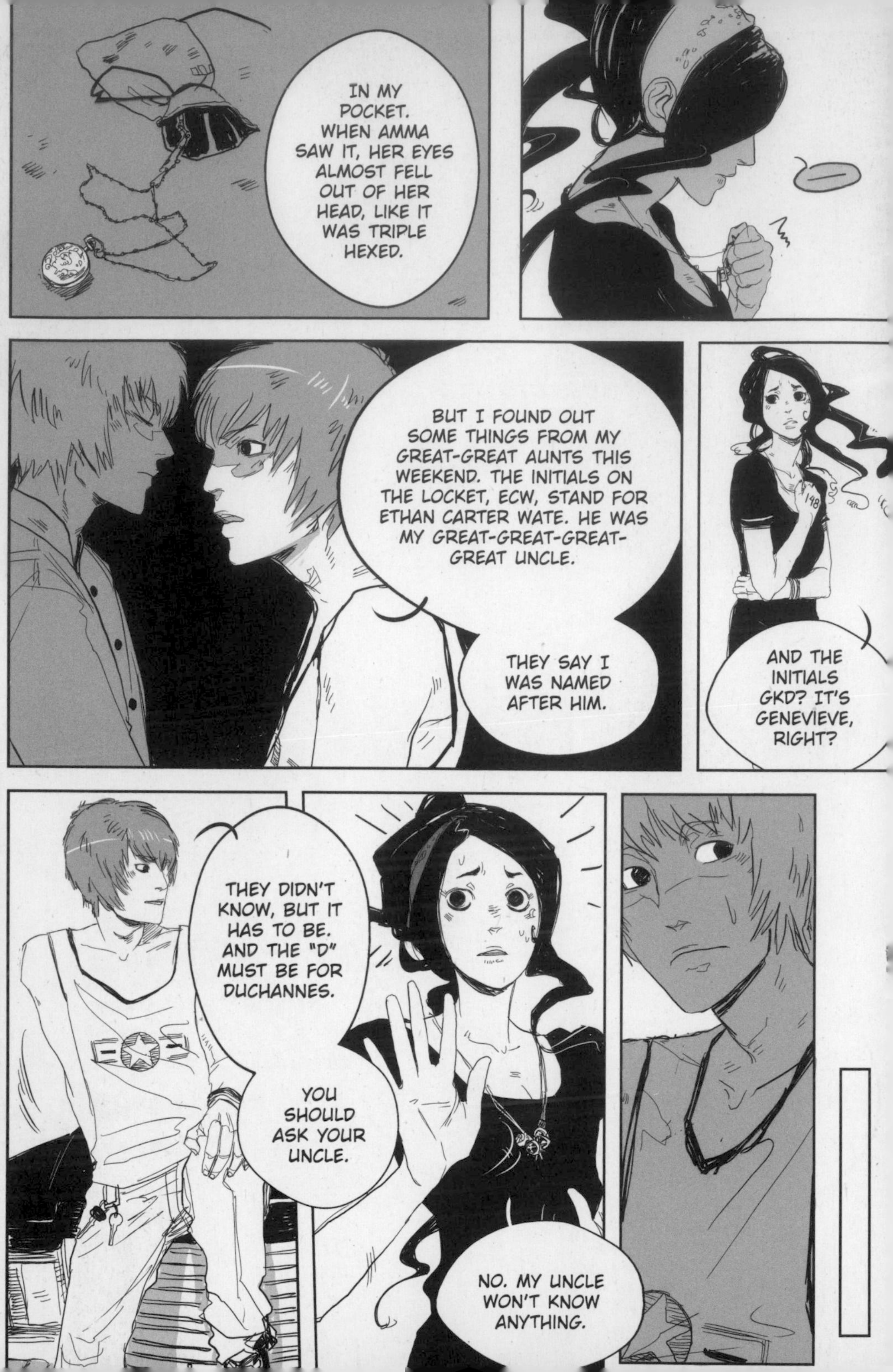
IN MY POCKET. WHEN AMMA SAW IT, HER EYES ALMOST FELL OUT OF HER HEAD, LIKE IT WAS TRIPLE HEXED.
BUT I FOUND OUT SOME THINGS FROM MY GREAT-GREAT AUNTS THIS WEEKEND. THE INITIALS ON THE LOCKET, ECW, STAND FOR ETHAN CARTER WATE. HE WAS MY GREAT-GREAT-GREAT-GREAT UNCLE.
THEY SAY I WAS NAMED AFTER HIM.
148
AND THE INITIALS GKD? IT'S GENEVIEVE, RIGHT?
THEY DIDN'T KNOW, BUT IT HAS TO BE. AND THE "D" MUST BE FOR DUCHANNES.
YOU SHOULD ASK YOUR UNCLE.
NO. MY UNCLE WON'T KNOW ANYTHING.

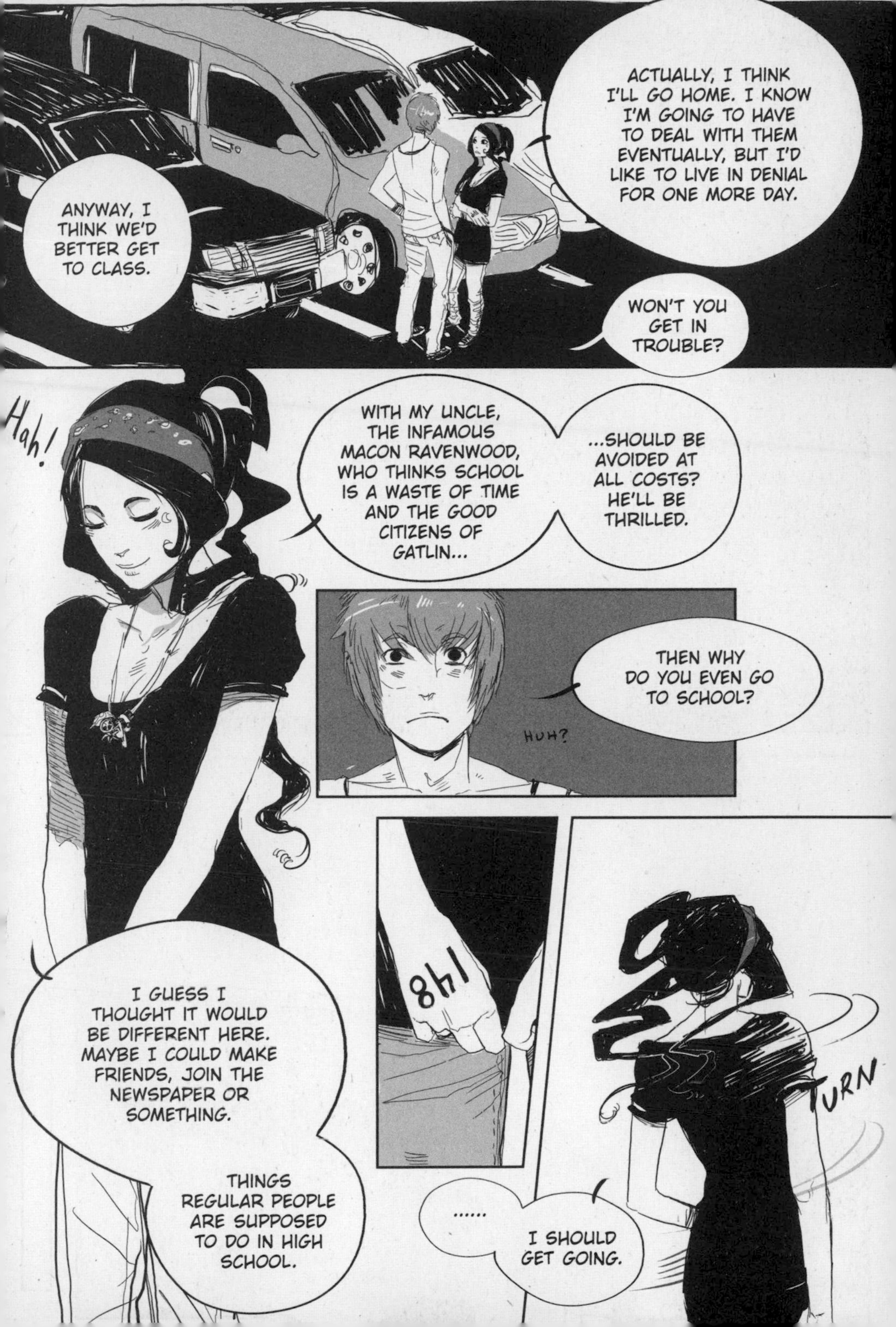
ANYWAY, I THINK WE'D BETTER GET TO CLASS.
ACTUALLY, I THINK I'LL GO HOME. I KNOW I'M GOING TO HAVE TO DEAL WITH THEM EVENTUALLY, BUT I'D LIKE TO LIVE IN DENIAL FOR ONE MORE DAY.
WON'T YOU GET IN TROUBLE?
Hah!
WITH MY UNCLE, THE INFAMOUS MACON RAVENWOOD, WHO THINKS SCHOOL IS A WASTE OF TIME AND THE GOOD CITIZENS OF GATLIN...
...SHOULD BE AVOIDED AT ALL COSTS? HE'LL BE THRILLED.
THEN WHY DO YOU EVEN GO TO SCHOOL?
HUH?
I GUESS I THOUGHT IT WOULD BE DIFFERENT HERE. MAYBE I COULD MAKE FRIENDS, JOIN THE NEWSPAPER OR SOMETHING.
THINGS REGULAR PEOPLE ARE SUPPOSED TO DO IN HIGH SCHOOL.
148
......
I SHOULD GET GOING.
TURN

VRMᴍ-

WOOF

RAVENWOOD'S DOG!!

GRᴿᴿ

......!!

WILD DOGS CARRY RABIES. SOMEONE SHOULD NOTIFY THE COUNTY.

MRS. LINCOLN?!

PRINCIPAL HARPER WAS JUST TELLIN' ME HE'S PLANNIN' ON OFFERIN' THAT RAVEN-WOOD GIRL A TRANSFER. SHE CAN TAKE HER PICK OF ANY SCHOOL. AS LONG AS IT'S NOT JACKSON.

GʀRR..

GRᴿRowl

IT'S OUR RESPONSIBILITY, ETHAN. WE HAVE TO KEEP THE YOUNG PEOPLE IN THIS TOWN SAFE. AND AWAY FROM THE WRONG SORTA PEOPLE.

WHICH MEANS ANYONE WHO ISN'T LIKE YOU?

I'M SURE YOU UNDERSTAND MY MEANIN'. AFTER ALL, YOU'RE ONE OF US. YOUR DADDY WAS BORN HERE AND YOUR MAMMA WAS BURIED HERE. YOU BELONG HERE. NOT *EVERYONE* DOES.

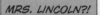

ONCE I GOT TO CLASS, THE DAY BECAME ABNORMALLY NORMAL.

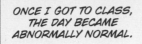
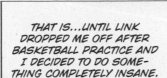

THAT IS...UNTIL LINK DROPPED ME OFF AFTER BASKETBALL PRACTICE AND I DECIDED TO DO SOMETHING COMPLETELY INSANE.

I LIED TO AMMA. I TOLD HER I WAS GOING TO THE LIBRARY TO VISIT MARIAN, A FAMILY FRIEND, AND TO WORK ON A PROJECT, BUT...

...NOW I'M BACK AT RAVENWOOD MANOR.

THIS IS INSANE.

I SHOULDN'T DO THIS.

WHAT AM I DOING?!

!!

BARK

WOOF

GRRROWL

BARK

BUT I HAVE A FEELING LENA'S UNCLE MIGHT KNOW SOMETHING THAT COULD HELP US...

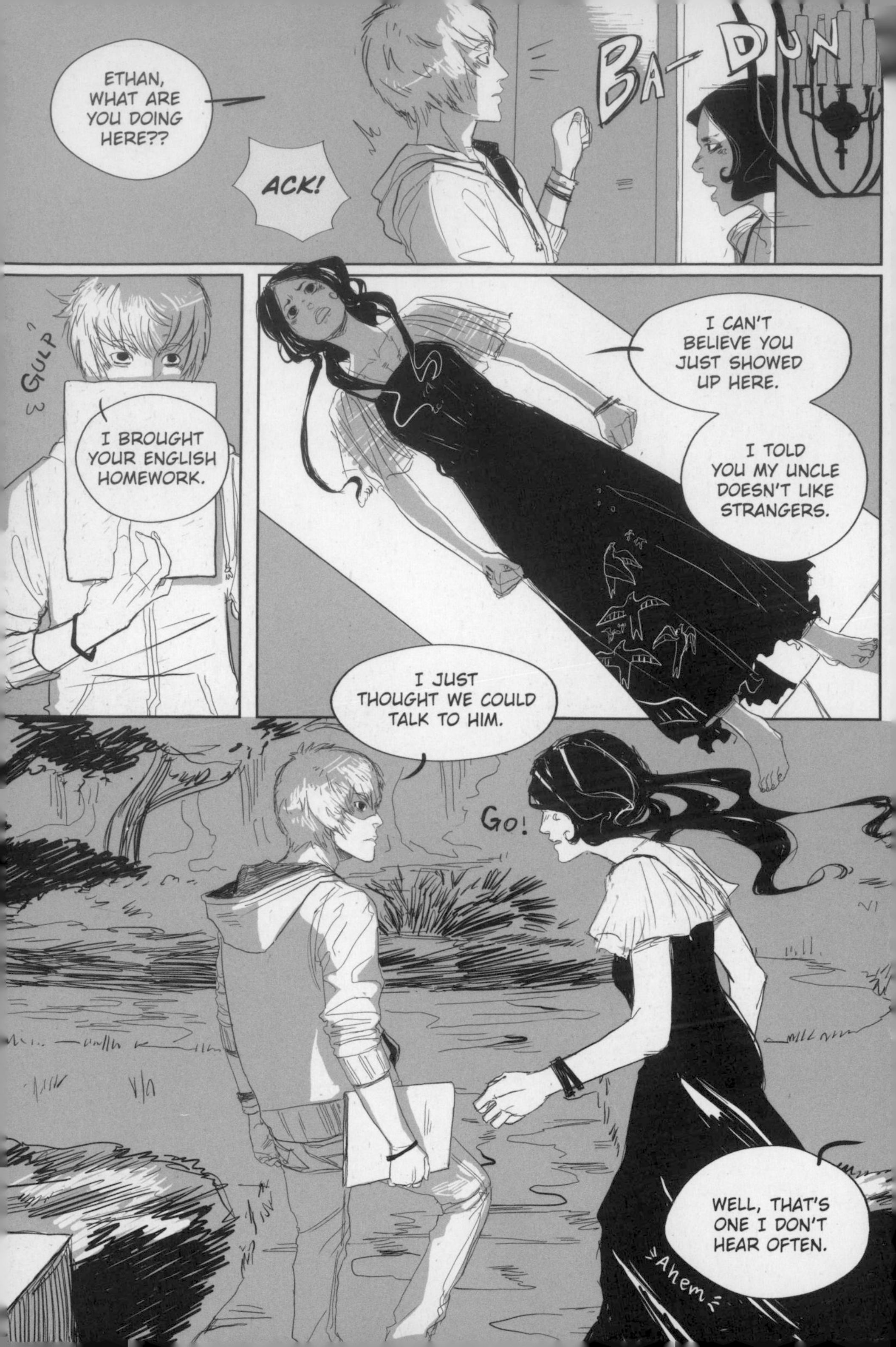
ETHAN, WHAT ARE YOU DOING HERE??
ACK!
BA-DUN
GULP
I BROUGHT YOUR ENGLISH HOMEWORK.
I CAN'T BELIEVE YOU JUST SHOWED UP HERE.
I TOLD YOU MY UNCLE DOESN'T LIKE STRANGERS.
I JUST THOUGHT WE COULD TALK TO HIM.
GO!
WELL, THAT'S ONE I DON'T HEAR OFTEN.
Ahem

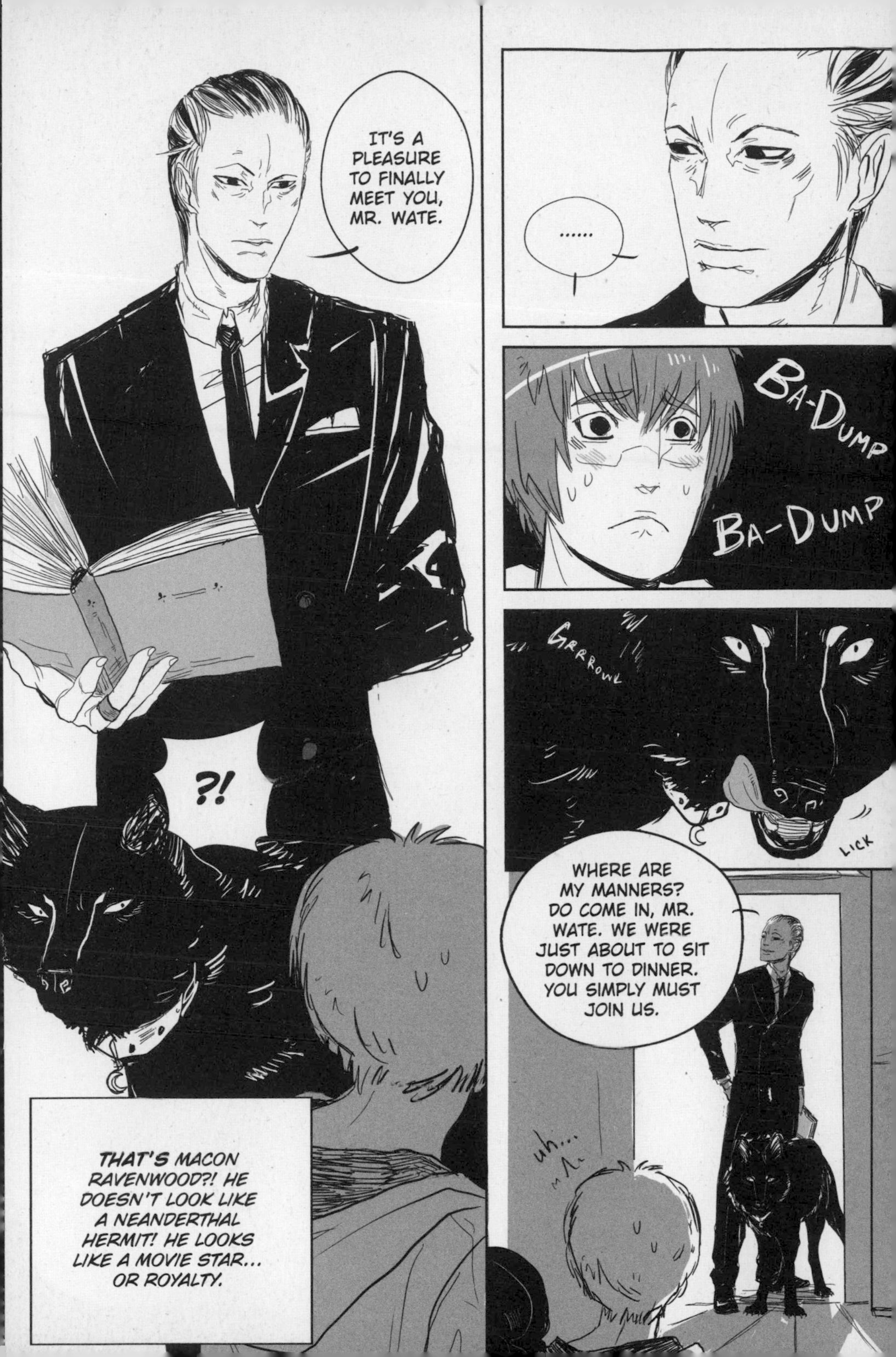
IT'S A PLEASURE TO FINALLY MEET YOU, MR. WATE.
?!
THAT'S MACON RAVENWOOD?! HE DOESN'T LOOK LIKE A NEANDERTHAL HERMIT! HE LOOKS LIKE A MOVIE STAR... OR ROYALTY.
......
BA-DUMP
BA-DUMP
GRRROWL
LICK
WHERE ARE MY MANNERS? DO COME IN, MR. WATE. WE WERE JUST ABOUT TO SIT DOWN TO DINNER. YOU SIMPLY MUST JOIN US.
uh...

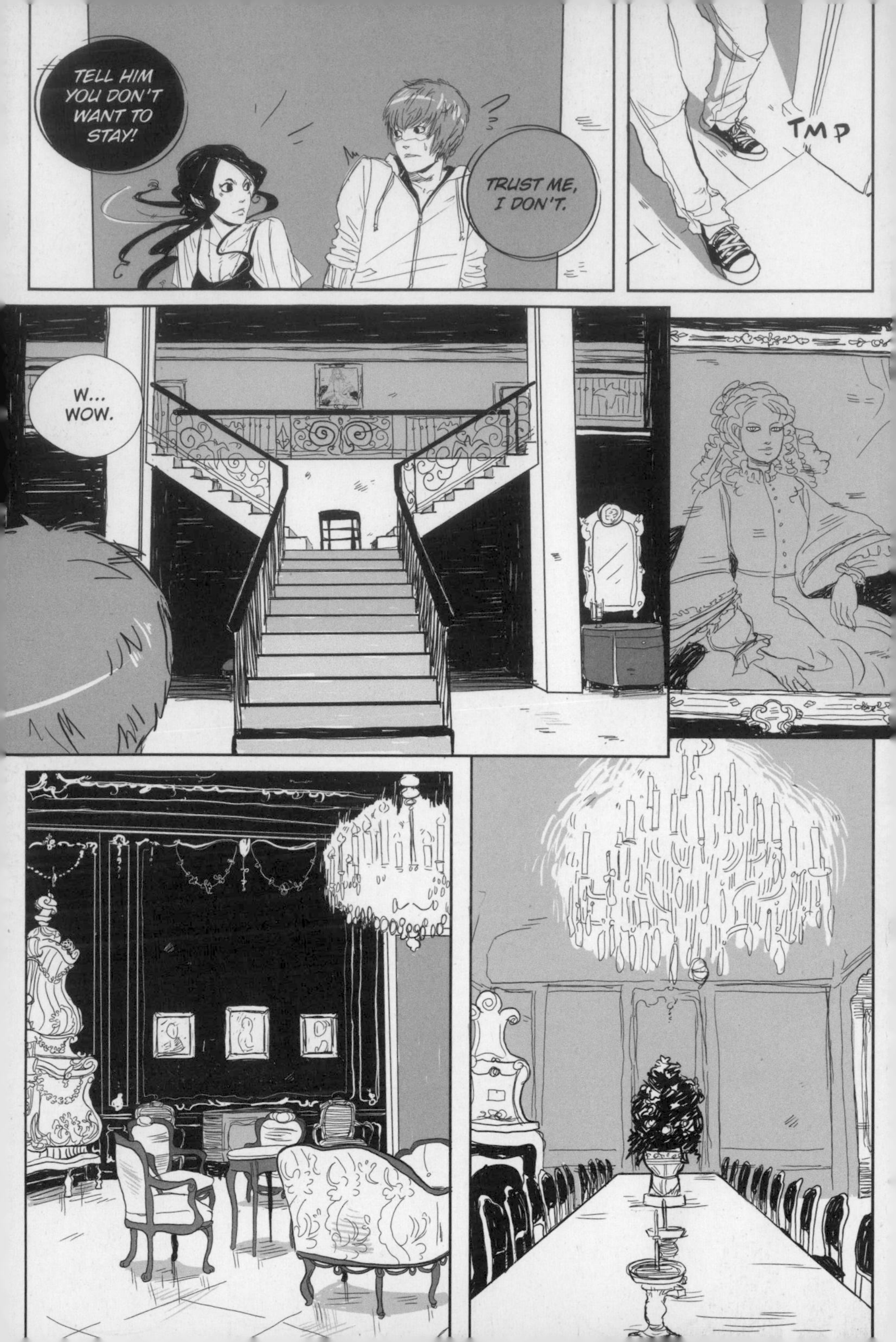
TELL HIM YOU DON'T WANT TO STAY!
TRUST ME, I DON'T.
TMP
W... WOW.

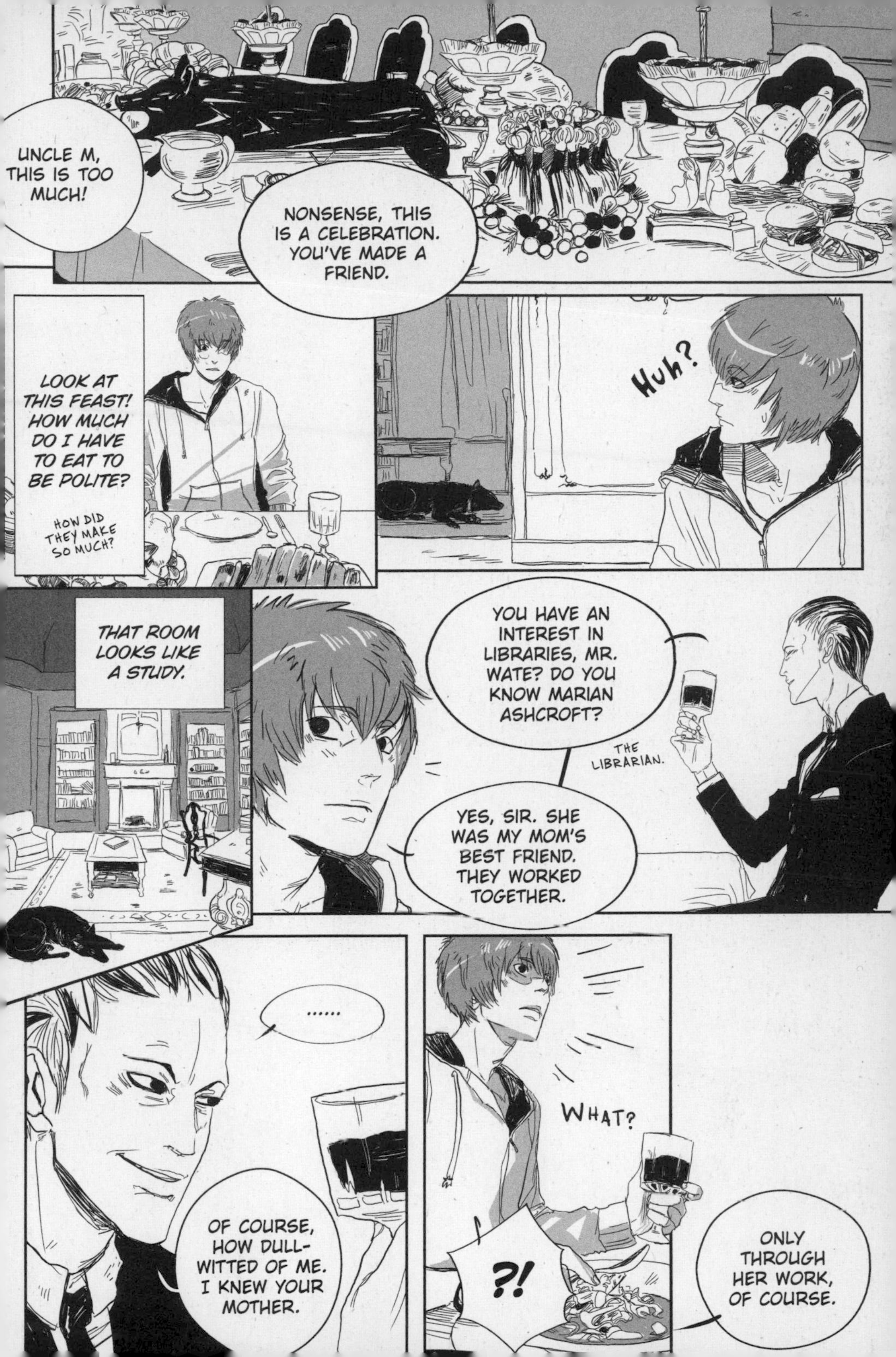
UNCLE M, THIS IS TOO MUCH!
NONSENSE, THIS IS A CELEBRATION. YOU'VE MADE A FRIEND.
LOOK AT THIS FEAST! HOW MUCH DO I HAVE TO EAT TO BE POLITE?
HOW DID THEY MAKE SO MUCH?
HUH?
THAT ROOM LOOKS LIKE A STUDY.
YOU HAVE AN INTEREST IN LIBRARIES, MR. WATE? DO YOU KNOW MARIAN ASHCROFT?
THE LIBRARIAN.
YES, SIR. SHE WAS MY MOM'S BEST FRIEND. THEY WORKED TOGETHER.
......
OF COURSE, HOW DULL-WITTED OF ME. I KNEW YOUR MOTHER.
WHAT?
?!
ONLY THROUGH HER WORK, OF COURSE.

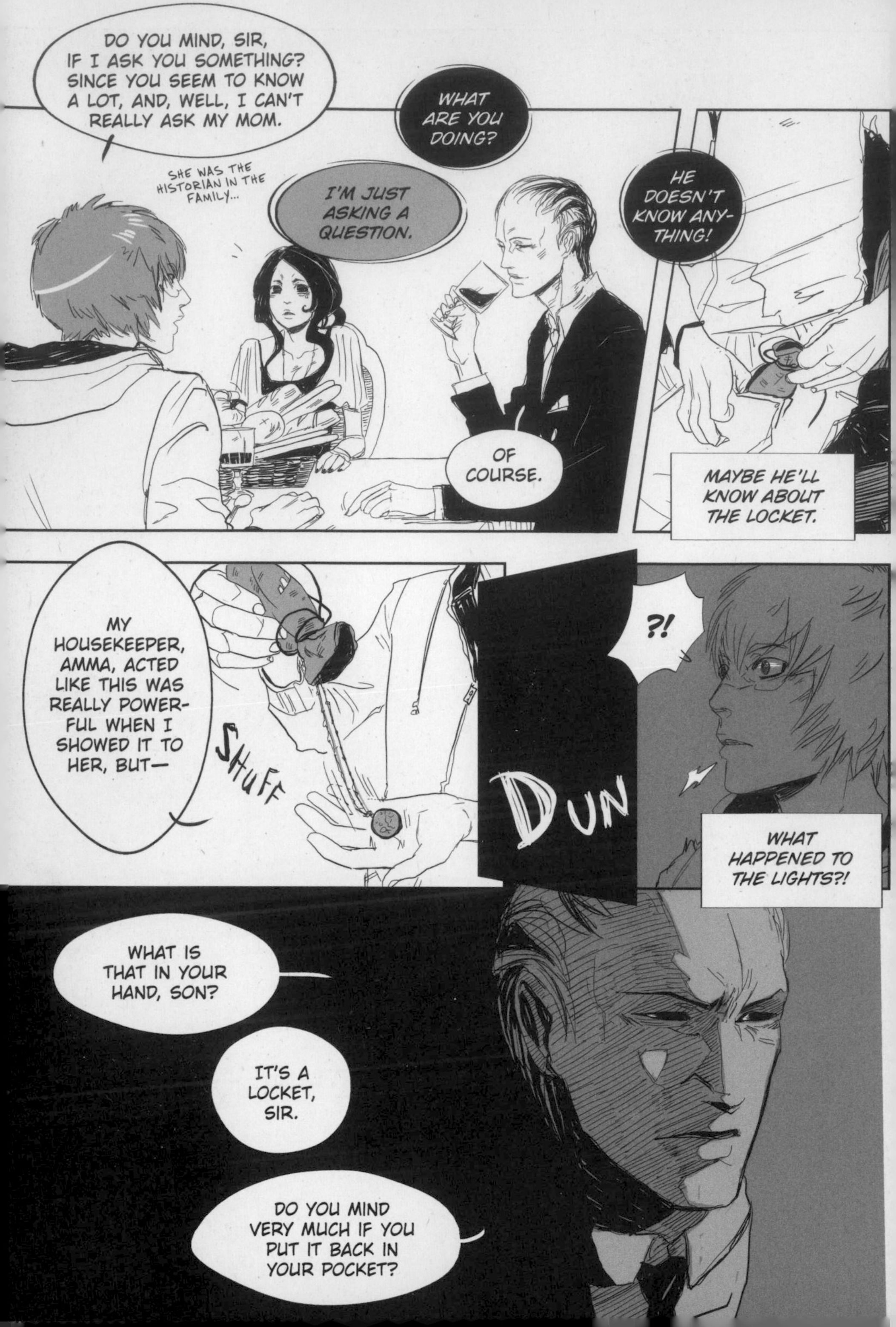
DO YOU MIND, SIR, IF I ASK YOU SOMETHING? SINCE YOU SEEM TO KNOW A LOT, AND, WELL, I CAN'T REALLY ASK MY MOM.
WHAT ARE YOU DOING?
SHE WAS THE HISTORIAN IN THE FAMILY...
I'M JUST ASKING A QUESTION.
OF COURSE.
HE DOESN'T KNOW ANY-THING!
MAYBE HE'LL KNOW ABOUT THE LOCKET.
MY HOUSEKEEPER, AMMA, ACTED LIKE THIS WAS REALLY POWER-FUL WHEN I SHOWED IT TO HER, BUT—
SHUFF
DUN
?!
WHAT HAPPENED TO THE LIGHTS?!
WHAT IS THAT IN YOUR HAND, SON?
IT'S A LOCKET, SIR.
DO YOU MIND VERY MUCH IF YOU PUT IT BACK IN YOUR POCKET?

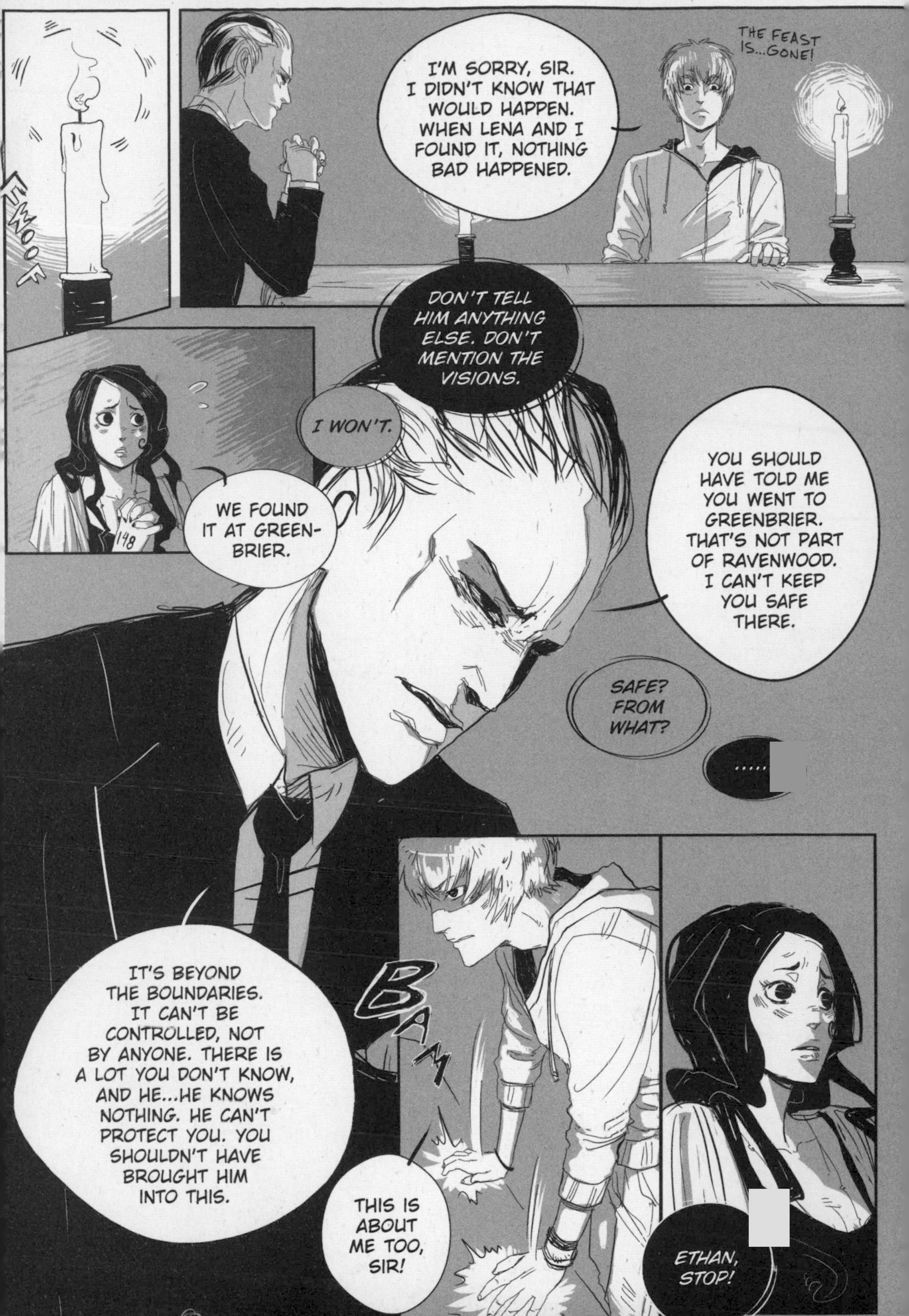
FWOOF
I'M SORRY, SIR. I DIDN'T KNOW THAT WOULD HAPPEN. WHEN LENA AND I FOUND IT, NOTHING BAD HAPPENED.
THE FEAST IS...GONE!
WE FOUND IT AT GREEN-BRIER.
DON'T TELL HIM ANYTHING ELSE. DON'T MENTION THE VISIONS.
I WON'T.
YOU SHOULD HAVE TOLD ME YOU WENT TO GREENBRIER. THAT'S NOT PART OF RAVENWOOD. I CAN'T KEEP YOU SAFE THERE.
SAFE? FROM WHAT?
......
IT'S BEYOND THE BOUNDARIES. IT CAN'T BE CONTROLLED, NOT BY ANYONE. THERE IS A LOT YOU DON'T KNOW, AND HE...HE KNOWS NOTHING. HE CAN'T PROTECT YOU. YOU SHOULDN'T HAVE BROUGHT HIM INTO THIS.
BAM
THIS IS ABOUT ME TOO, SIR!
ETHAN, STOP!

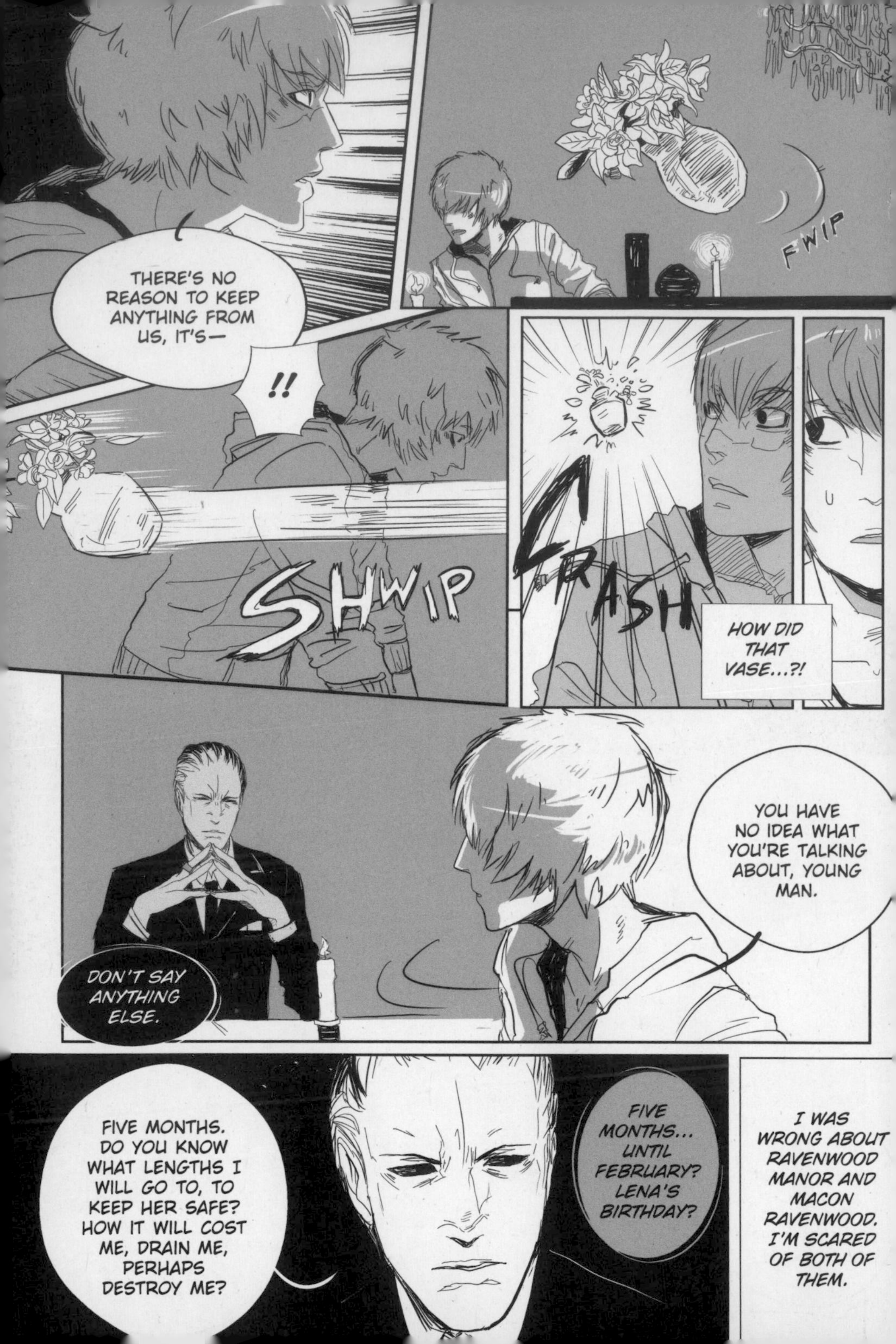
FWIP
THERE'S NO REASON TO KEEP ANYTHING FROM US, IT'S—
!!
SHWIP
CRASH
HOW DID THAT VASE...?!
YOU HAVE NO IDEA WHAT YOU'RE TALKING ABOUT, YOUNG MAN.
DON'T SAY ANYTHING ELSE.
FIVE MONTHS. DO YOU KNOW WHAT LENGTHS I WILL GO TO, TO KEEP HER SAFE? HOW IT WILL COST ME, DRAIN ME, PERHAPS DESTROY ME?
FIVE MONTHS... UNTIL FEBRUARY? LENA'S BIRTHDAY?
I WAS WRONG ABOUT RAVENWOOD MANOR AND MACON RAVENWOOD. I'M SCARED OF BOTH OF THEM.

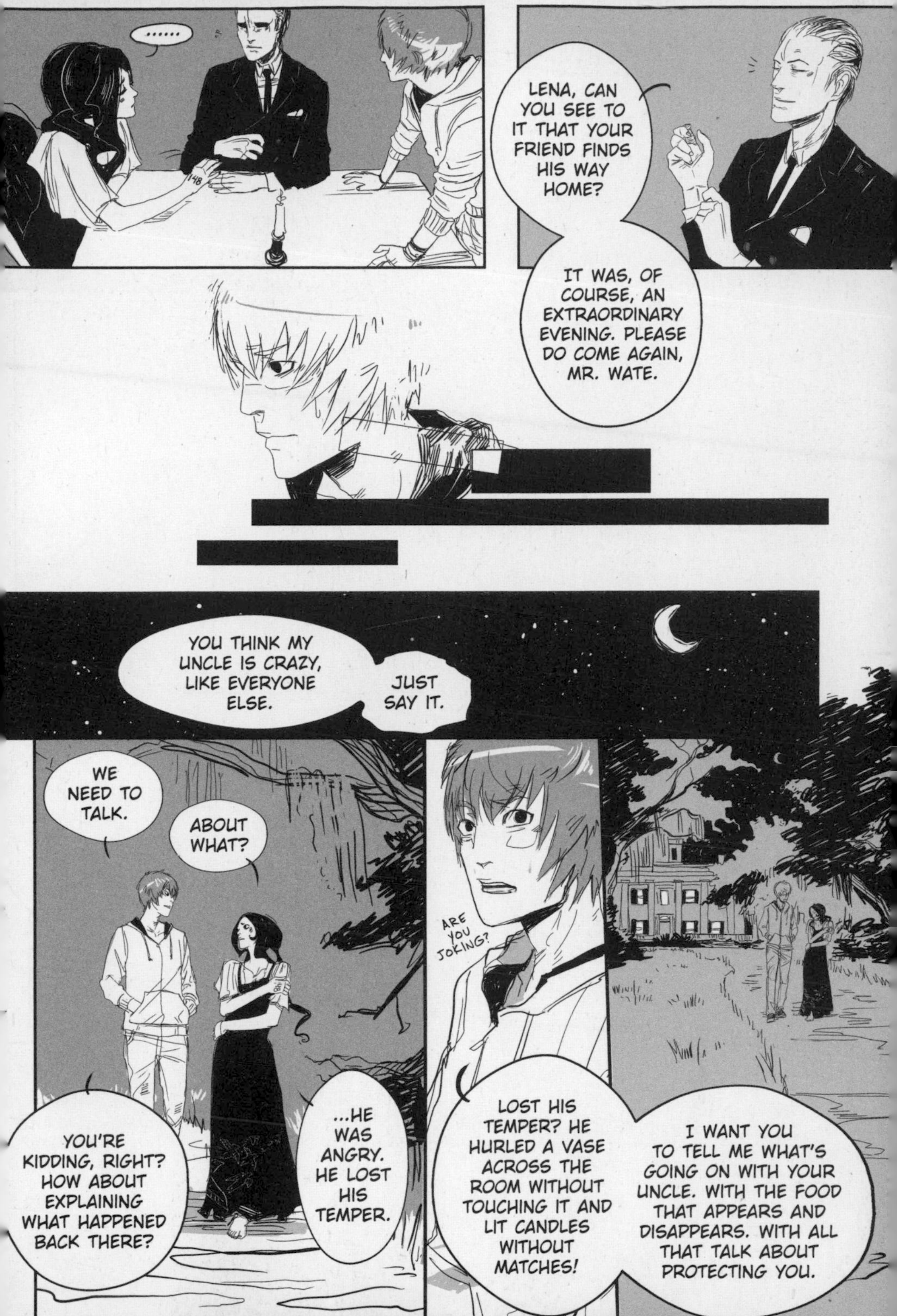

......
148
LENA, CAN YOU SEE TO IT THAT YOUR FRIEND FINDS HIS WAY HOME?
IT WAS, OF COURSE, AN EXTRAORDINARY EVENING. PLEASE DO COME AGAIN, MR. WATE.
YOU THINK MY UNCLE IS CRAZY, LIKE EVERYONE ELSE.
JUST SAY IT.
WE NEED TO TALK.
ABOUT WHAT?
YOU'RE KIDDING, RIGHT? HOW ABOUT EXPLAINING WHAT HAPPENED BACK THERE?
...HE WAS ANGRY. HE LOST HIS TEMPER.
ARE YOU JOKING?
LOST HIS TEMPER? HE HURLED A VASE ACROSS THE ROOM WITHOUT TOUCHING IT AND LIT CANDLES WITHOUT MATCHES!
I WANT YOU TO TELL ME WHAT'S GOING ON WITH YOUR UNCLE. WITH THE FOOD THAT APPEARS AND DISAPPEARS. WITH ALL THAT TALK ABOUT PROTECTING YOU.

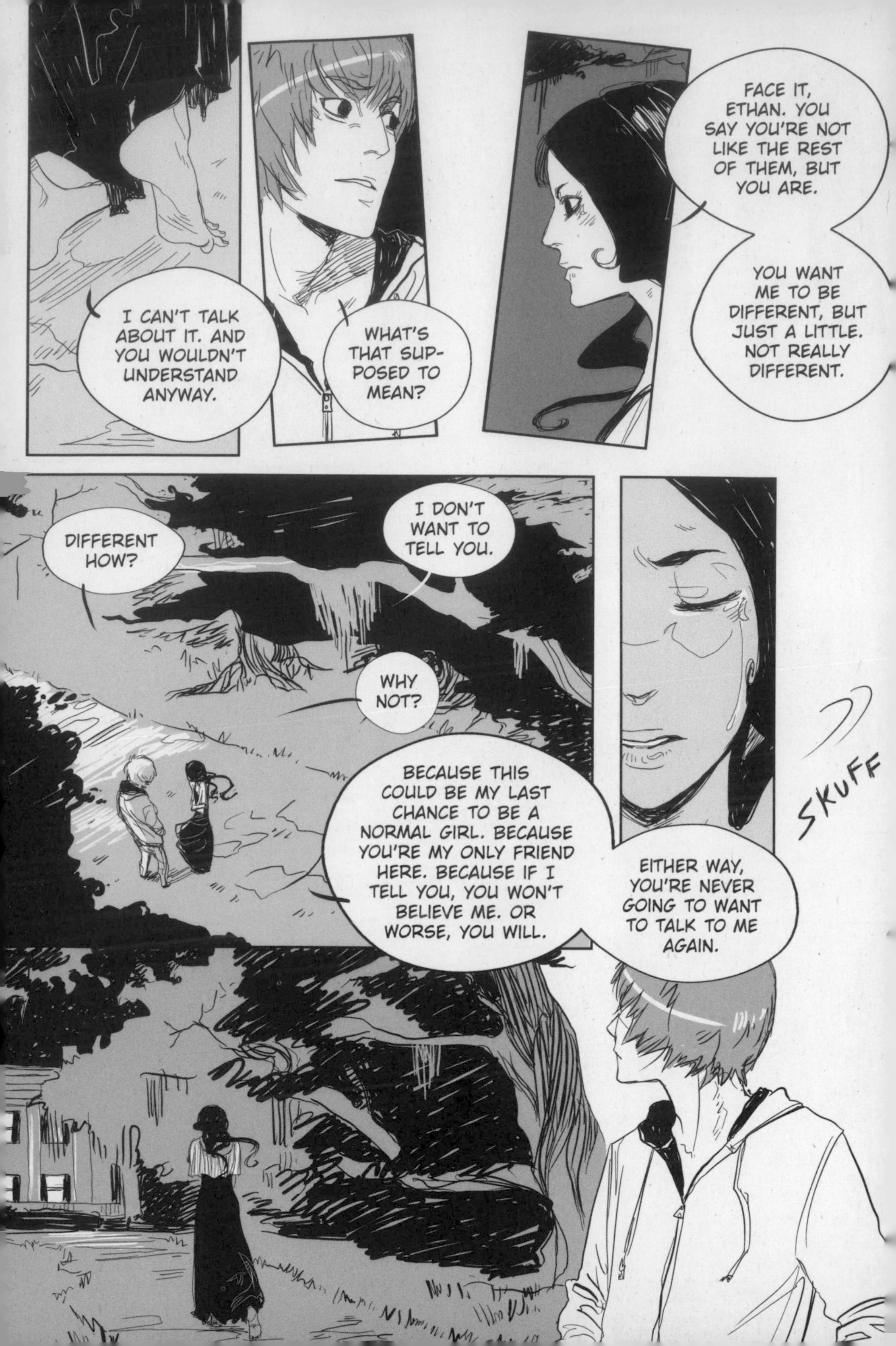
I CAN'T TALK ABOUT IT. AND YOU WOULDN'T UNDERSTAND ANYWAY.
WHAT'S THAT SUP-POSED TO MEAN?
FACE IT, ETHAN. YOU SAY YOU'RE NOT LIKE THE REST OF THEM, BUT YOU ARE.
YOU WANT ME TO BE DIFFERENT, BUT JUST A LITTLE. NOT REALLY DIFFERENT.
DIFFERENT HOW?
I DON'T WANT TO TELL YOU.
WHY NOT?
BECAUSE THIS COULD BE MY LAST CHANCE TO BE A NORMAL GIRL. BECAUSE YOU'RE MY ONLY FRIEND HERE. BECAUSE IF I TELL YOU, YOU WON'T BELIEVE ME. OR WORSE, YOU WILL.
EITHER WAY, YOU'RE NEVER GOING TO WANT TO TALK TO ME AGAIN.
SKUFF

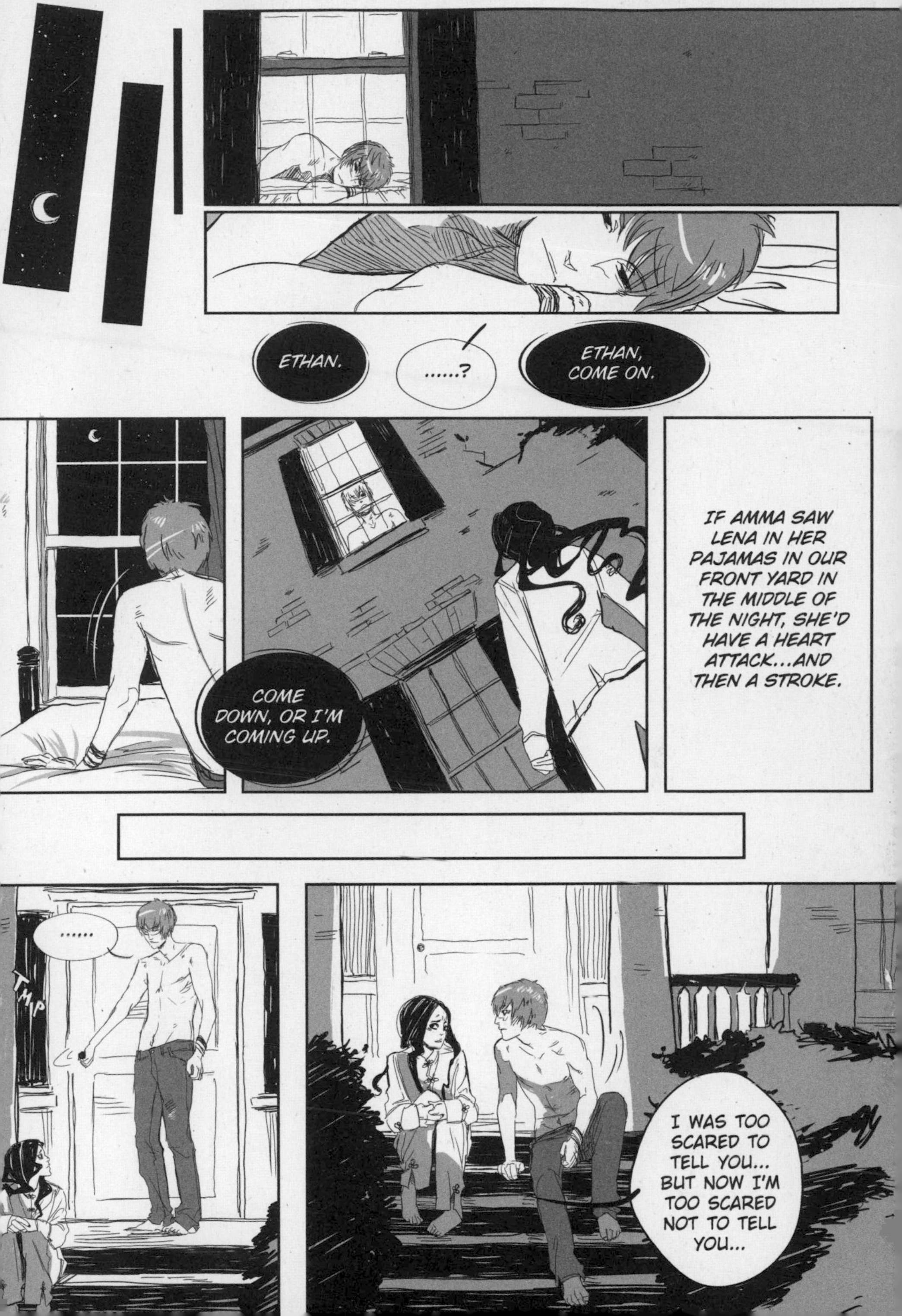
ETHAN.
......?
ETHAN, COME ON.
COME DOWN, OR I'M COMING UP.
IF AMMA SAW LENA IN HER PAJAMAS IN OUR FRONT YARD IN THE MIDDLE OF THE NIGHT, SHE'D HAVE A HEART ATTACK...AND THEN A STROKE.
......
TMIP
I WAS TOO SCARED TO TELL YOU... BUT NOW I'M TOO SCARED NOT TO TELL YOU...

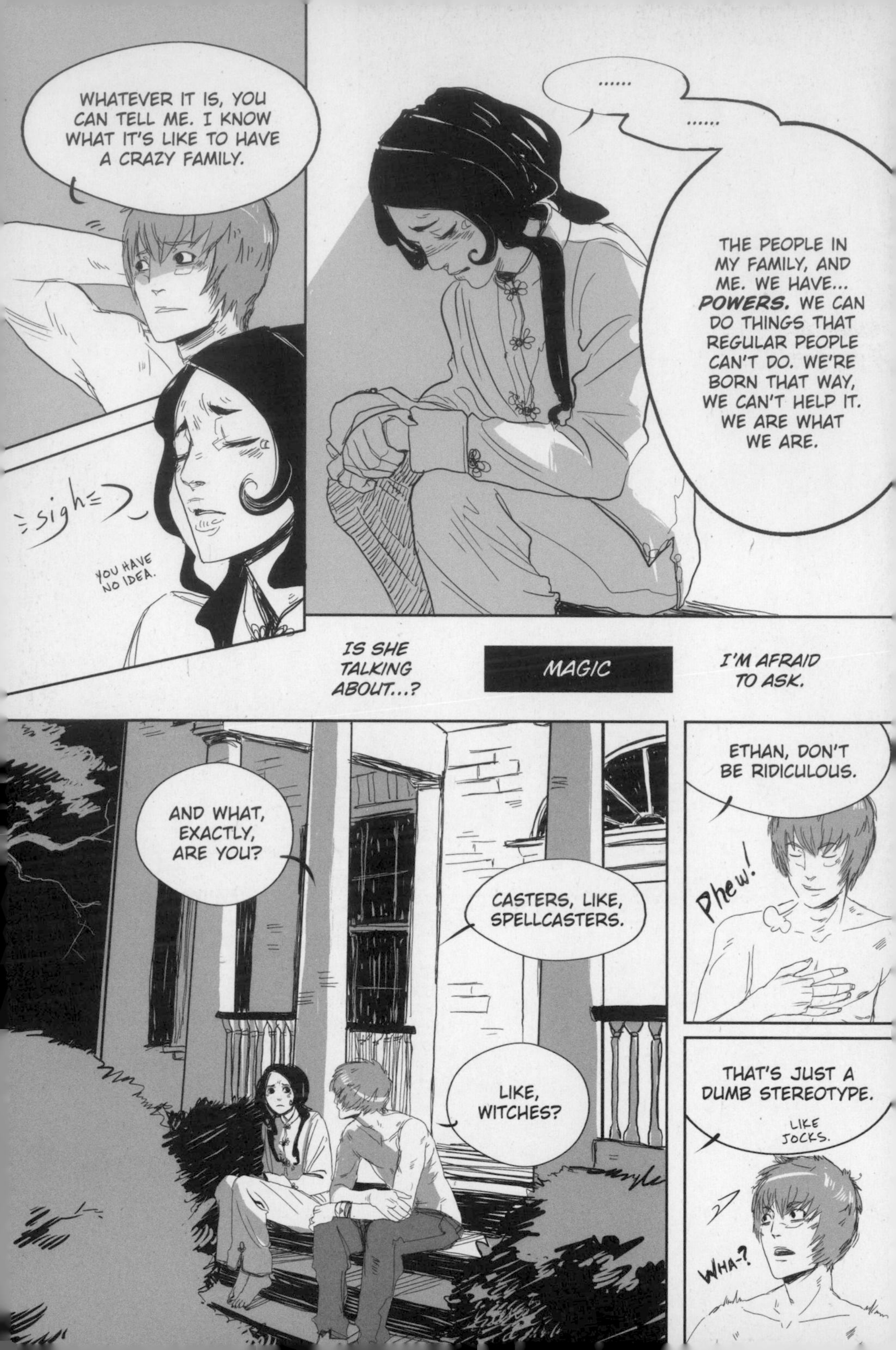
WHATEVER IT IS, YOU CAN TELL ME. I KNOW WHAT IT'S LIKE TO HAVE A CRAZY FAMILY.
SIGH
YOU HAVE NO IDEA.
......
......
THE PEOPLE IN MY FAMILY, AND ME. WE HAVE... **POWERS.** WE CAN DO THINGS THAT REGULAR PEOPLE CAN'T DO. WE'RE BORN THAT WAY, WE CAN'T HELP IT. WE ARE WHAT WE ARE.
IS SHE TALKING ABOUT...?
MAGIC
I'M AFRAID TO ASK.
AND WHAT, EXACTLY, ARE YOU?
CASTERS, LIKE, SPELLCASTERS.
LIKE, WITCHES?
ETHAN, DON'T BE RIDICULOUS.
PHEW!
THAT'S JUST A DUMB STEREOTYPE.
LIKE JOCKS.
WHA-?

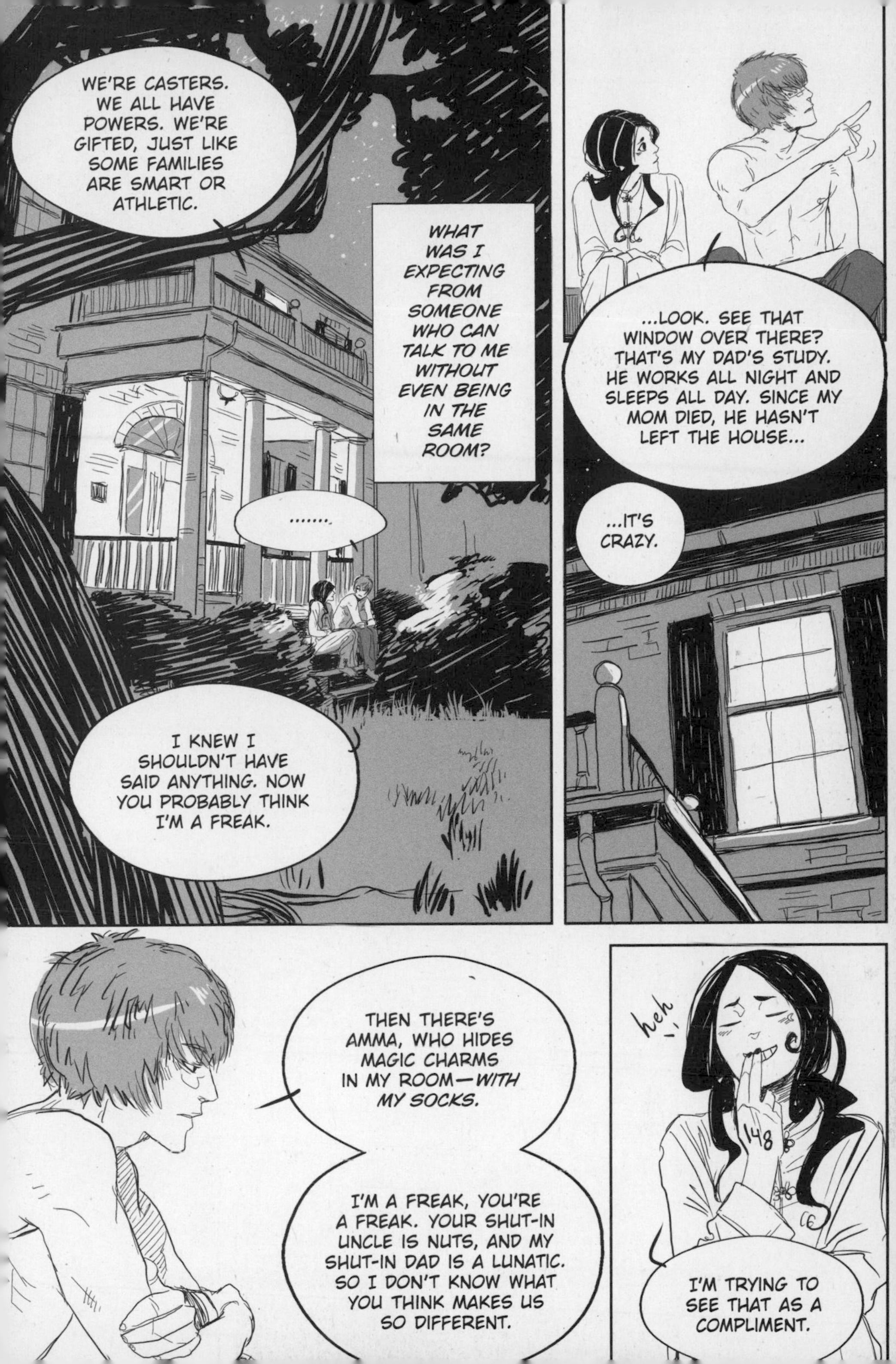
WE'RE CASTERS. WE ALL HAVE POWERS. WE'RE GIFTED, JUST LIKE SOME FAMILIES ARE SMART OR ATHLETIC.
WHAT WAS I EXPECTING FROM SOMEONE WHO CAN TALK TO ME WITHOUT EVEN BEING IN THE SAME ROOM?
....
I KNEW I SHOULDN'T HAVE SAID ANYTHING. NOW YOU PROBABLY THINK I'M A FREAK.
...LOOK. SEE THAT WINDOW OVER THERE? THAT'S MY DAD'S STUDY. HE WORKS ALL NIGHT AND SLEEPS ALL DAY. SINCE MY MOM DIED, HE HASN'T LEFT THE HOUSE...
...IT'S CRAZY.
THEN THERE'S AMMA, WHO HIDES MAGIC CHARMS IN MY ROOM—*WITH MY SOCKS.*
I'M A FREAK, YOU'RE A FREAK. YOUR SHUT-IN UNCLE IS NUTS, AND MY SHUT-IN DAD IS A LUNATIC. SO I DON'T KNOW WHAT YOU THINK MAKES US SO DIFFERENT.
heh
148
I'M TRYING TO SEE THAT AS A COMPLIMENT.

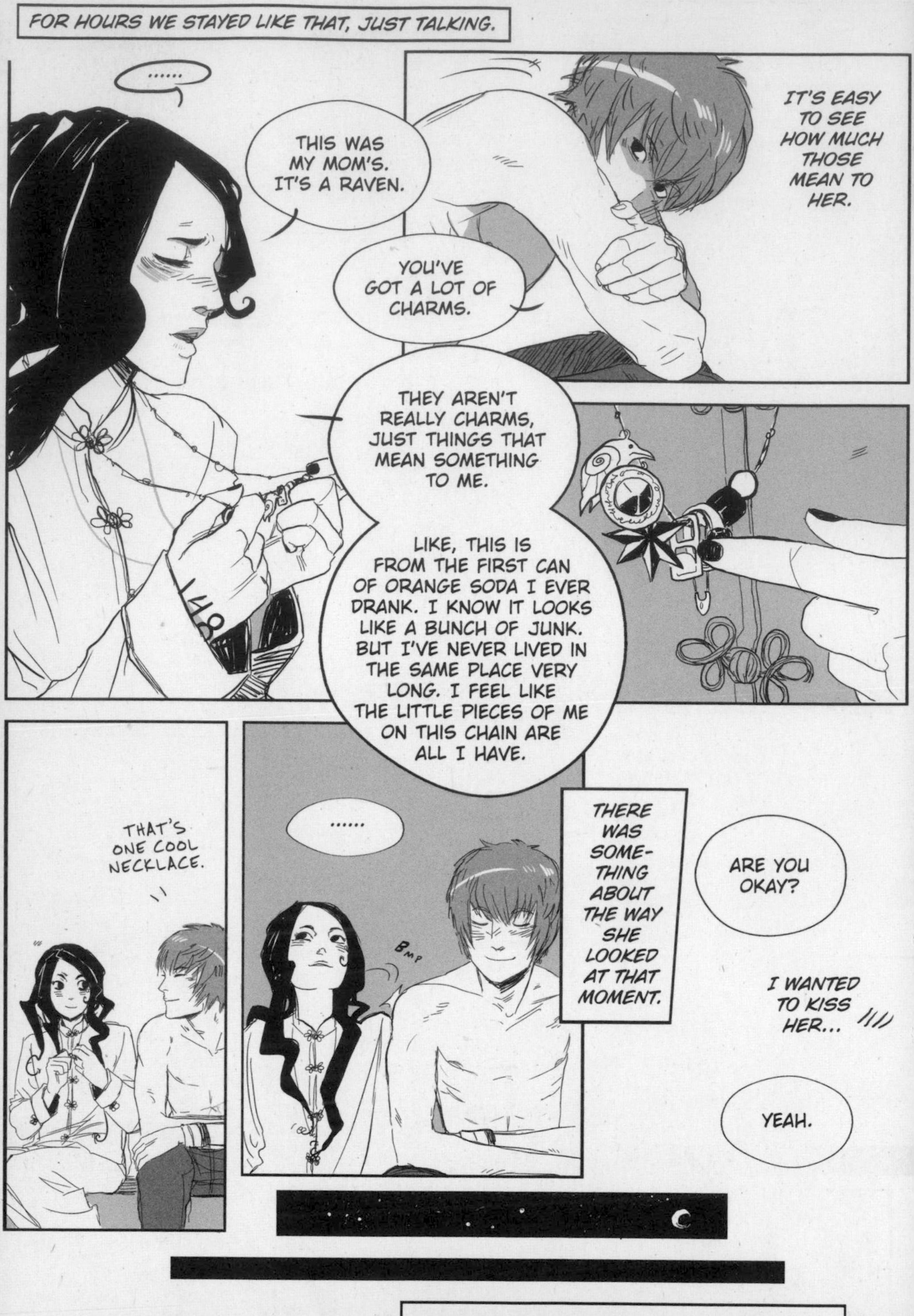
FOR HOURS WE STAYED LIKE THAT, JUST TALKING.
......
THIS WAS MY MOM'S. IT'S A RAVEN.
YOU'VE GOT A LOT OF CHARMS.
IT'S EASY TO SEE HOW MUCH THOSE MEAN TO HER.
THEY AREN'T REALLY CHARMS, JUST THINGS THAT MEAN SOMETHING TO ME.
LIKE, THIS IS FROM THE FIRST CAN OF ORANGE SODA I EVER DRANK. I KNOW IT LOOKS LIKE A BUNCH OF JUNK. BUT I'VE NEVER LIVED IN THE SAME PLACE VERY LONG. I FEEL LIKE THE LITTLE PIECES OF ME ON THIS CHAIN ARE ALL I HAVE.
THAT'S ONE COOL NECKLACE.
......
Bmp
THERE WAS SOME-THING ABOUT THE WAY SHE LOOKED AT THAT MOMENT.
ARE YOU OKAY?
I WANTED TO KISS HER...
YEAH.

I TOLD LENA IT WAS NO BIG DEAL THAT SHE WAS — WHAT? A WITCH? A CASTER?

YEAH, NO BIG DEAL.

I'M A BIG LIAR.

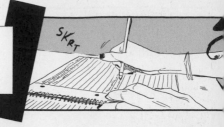

SKRT

BUT EVER SINCE THEN, I ONLY EVER WANT TO BE WITH LENA.

SHE ISN'T MY GIRLFRIEND, I DON'T EVEN KNOW HOW SHE FEELS ABOUT ME. WE DON'T DATE. BUT I WANT TO.

IT DIDN'T TAKE LONG FOR WORD TO GET OUT THAT "OLD MAN RAVENWOOD'S NIECE" WAS HANGING OUT WITH "ETHAN WATE WHOSE MAMMA DIED JUST LAST YEAR."

SHDING

STOP&SHOP

NO WAY!

Huh?

WHAT?

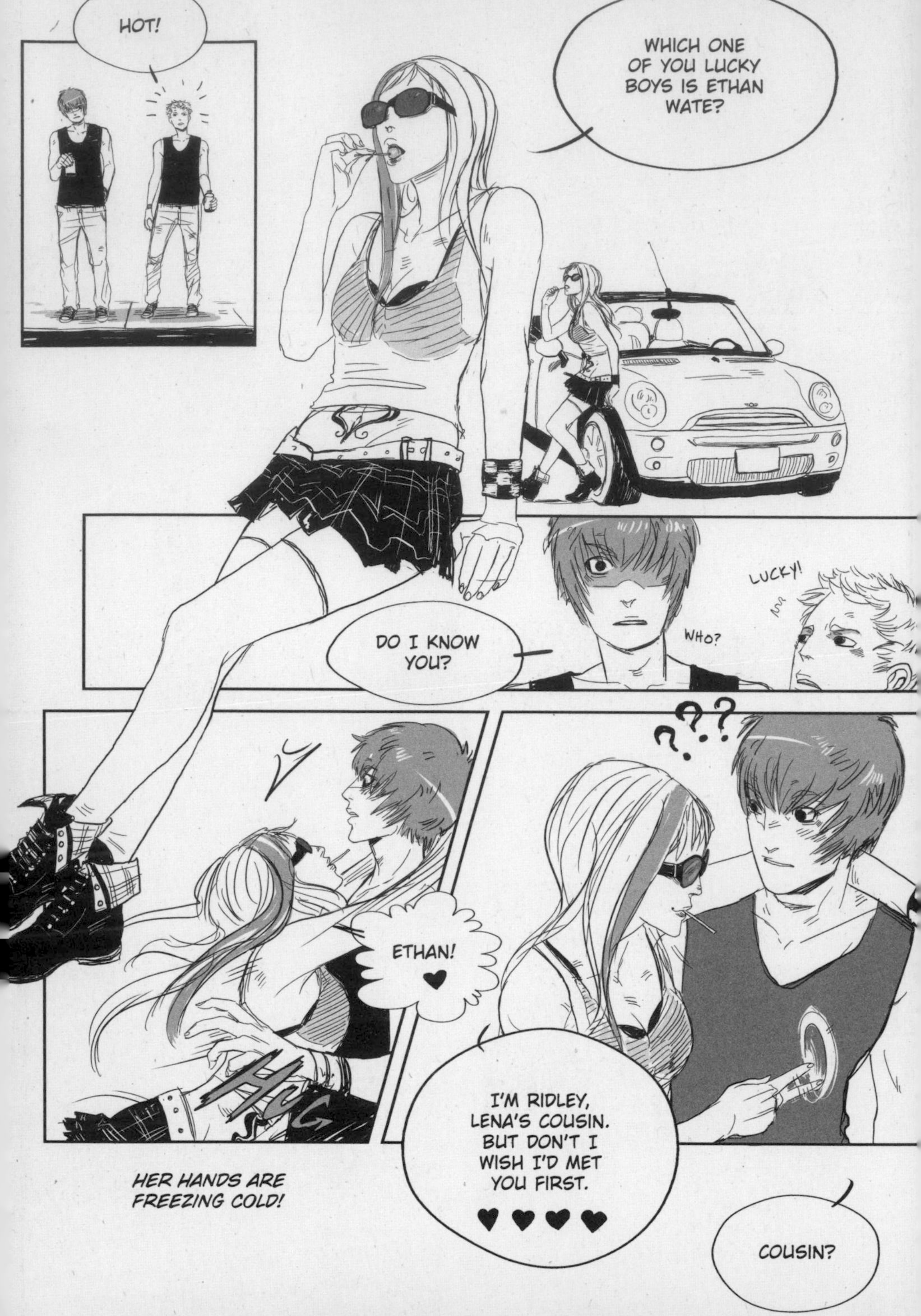
HOT!
WHICH ONE OF YOU LUCKY BOYS IS ETHAN WATE?
DO I KNOW YOU?
WHO?
LUCKY!
ETHAN! ♥
HUG
HER HANDS ARE FREEZING COLD!
I'M RIDLEY, LENA'S COUSIN. BUT DON'T I WISH I'D MET YOU FIRST. ♥♥♥♥
COUSIN?

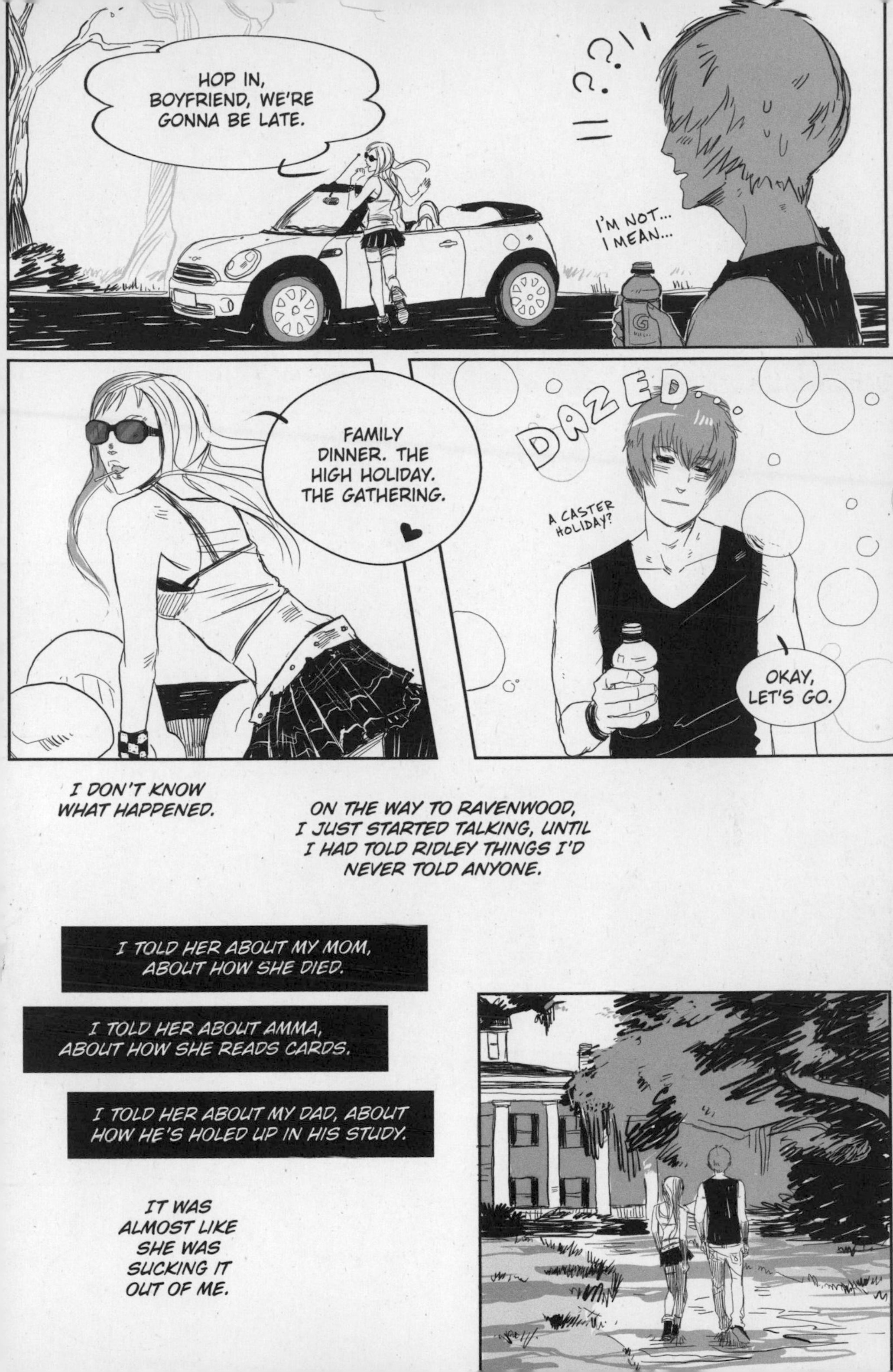
HOP IN, BOYFRIEND, WE'RE GONNA BE LATE.
I'M NOT... I MEAN...
FAMILY DINNER. THE HIGH HOLIDAY. THE GATHERING.
DAZED
A CASTER HOLIDAY?
OKAY, LET'S GO.
I DON'T KNOW WHAT HAPPENED.
ON THE WAY TO RAVENWOOD, I JUST STARTED TALKING, UNTIL I HAD TOLD RIDLEY THINGS I'D NEVER TOLD ANYONE.
I TOLD HER ABOUT MY MOM, ABOUT HOW SHE DIED.
I TOLD HER ABOUT AMMA, ABOUT HOW SHE READS CARDS.
I TOLD HER ABOUT MY DAD, ABOUT HOW HE'S HOLED UP IN HIS STUDY.
IT WAS ALMOST LIKE SHE WAS SUCKING IT OUT OF ME.

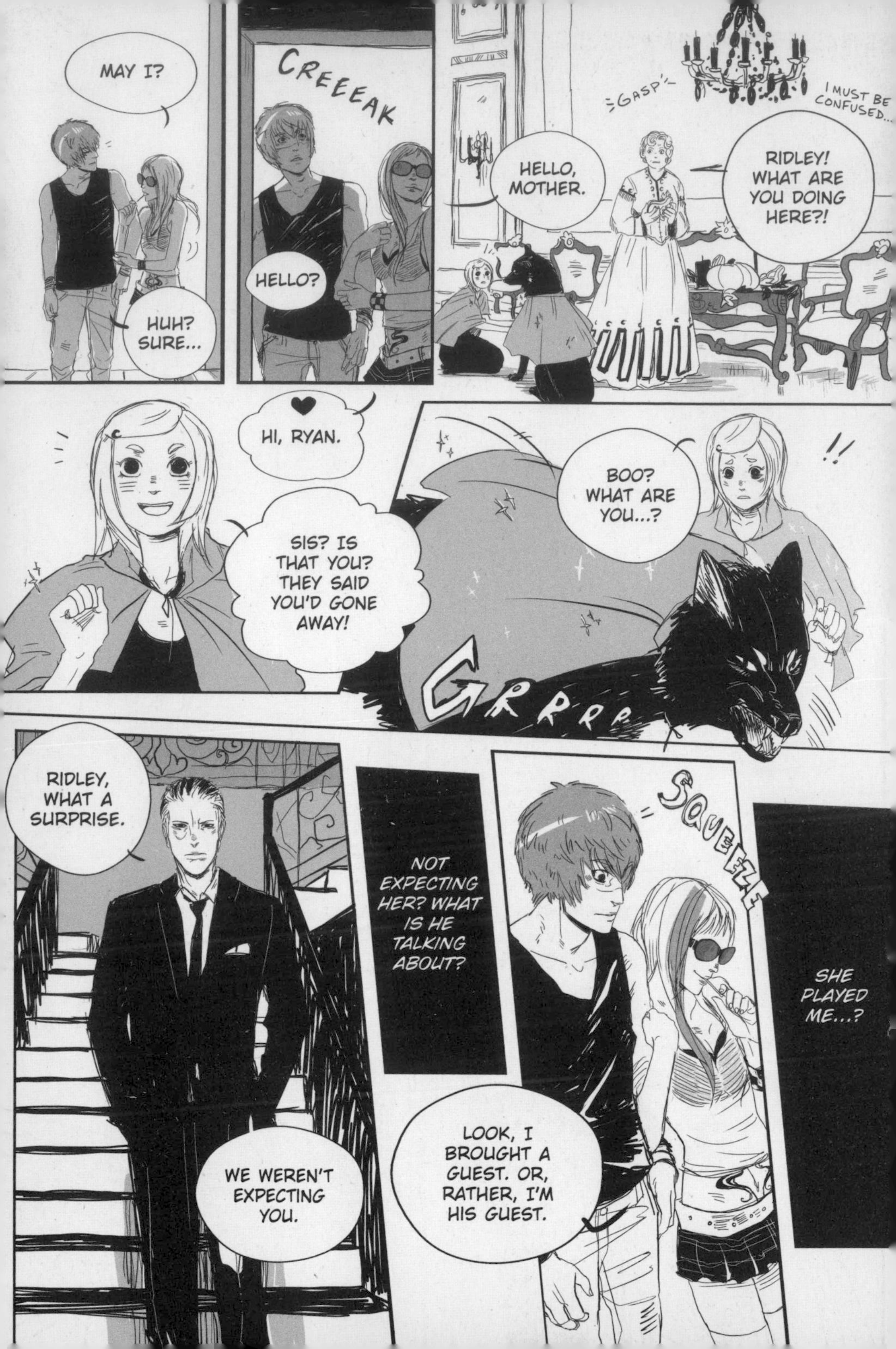
MAY I?
HUH? SURE...
CREEEEAK
HELLO?
HELLO, MOTHER.
GASP
I MUST BE CONFUSED...
RIDLEY! WHAT ARE YOU DOING HERE?!
HI, RYAN.
SIS? IS THAT YOU? THEY SAID YOU'D GONE AWAY!
BOO? WHAT ARE YOU...?
!!
GRRRR
RIDLEY, WHAT A SURPRISE.
WE WEREN'T EXPECTING YOU.
NOT EXPECTING HER? WHAT IS HE TALKING ABOUT?
SQUEEZE
LOOK, I BROUGHT A GUEST. OR, RATHER, I'M HIS GUEST.
SHE PLAYED ME...?

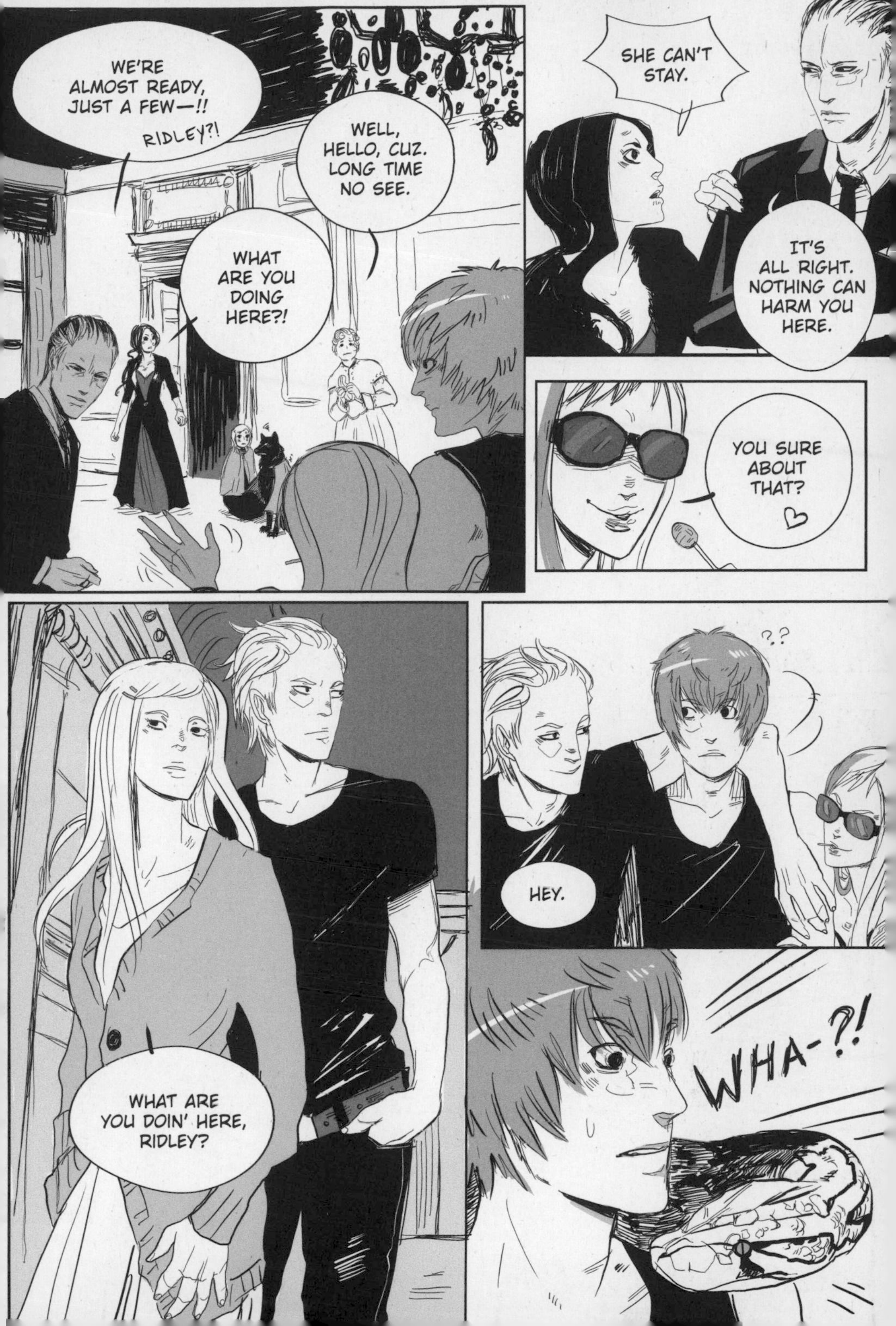
WE'RE ALMOST READY, JUST A FEW—!!
RIDLEY?!
WELL, HELLO, CUZ. LONG TIME NO SEE.
WHAT ARE YOU DOING HERE?!
SHE CAN'T STAY.
IT'S ALL RIGHT. NOTHING CAN HARM YOU HERE.
YOU SURE ABOUT THAT? ♡
WHAT ARE YOU DOIN' HERE, RIDLEY?
HEY.
??
WHA-?!

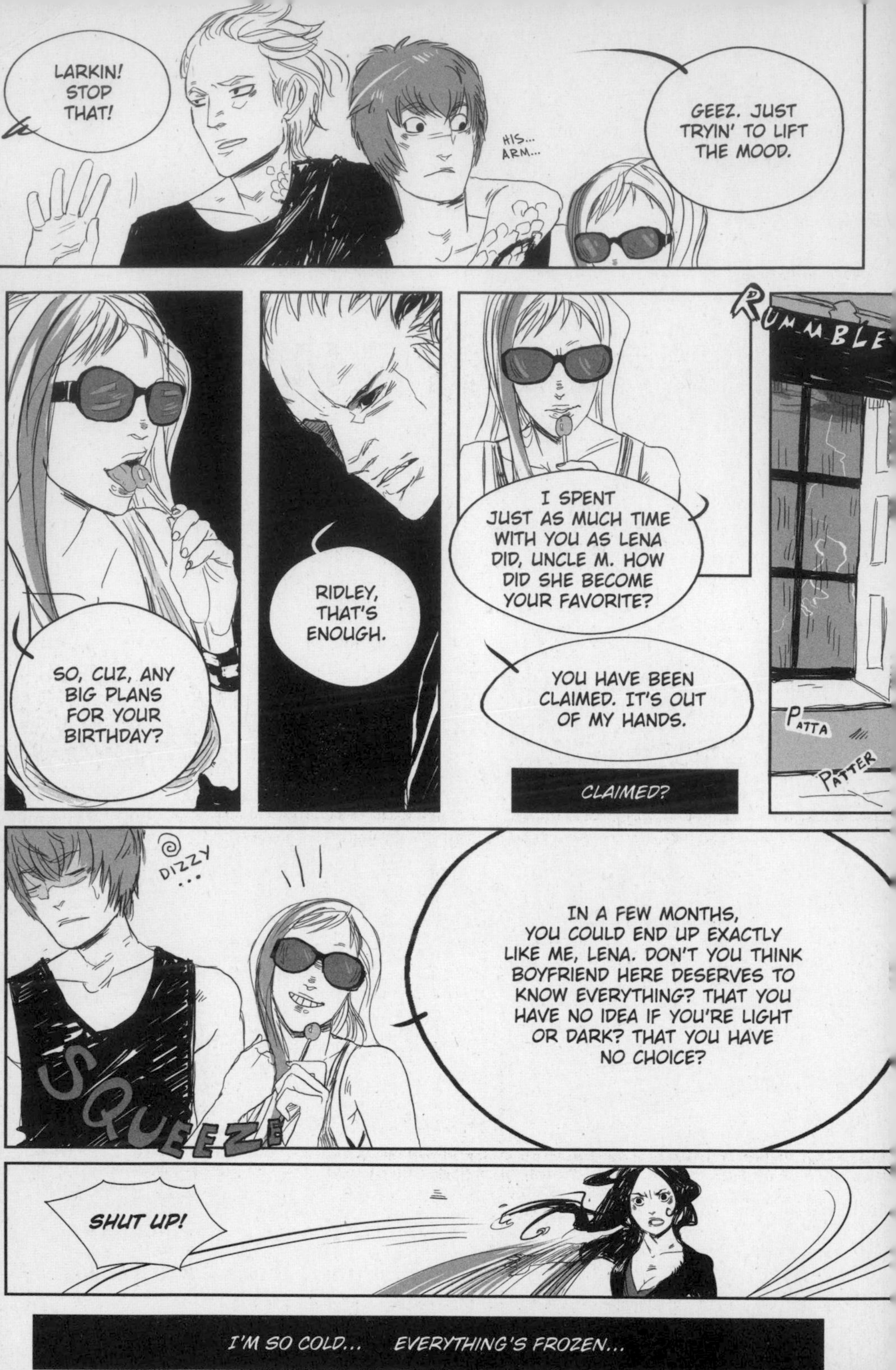
LARKIN! STOP THAT!
HIS... ARM...
GEEZ. JUST TRYIN' TO LIFT THE MOOD.
SO, CUZ, ANY BIG PLANS FOR YOUR BIRTHDAY?
RIDLEY, THAT'S ENOUGH.
I SPENT JUST AS MUCH TIME WITH YOU AS LENA DID, UNCLE M. HOW DID SHE BECOME YOUR FAVORITE?
YOU HAVE BEEN CLAIMED. IT'S OUT OF MY HANDS.
CLAIMED?
RUMMBLE
PATTA
PATTER
DIZZY...
SQUEEEZE
IN A FEW MONTHS, YOU COULD END UP EXACTLY LIKE ME, LENA. DON'T YOU THINK BOYFRIEND HERE DESERVES TO KNOW EVERYTHING? THAT YOU HAVE NO IDEA IF YOU'RE LIGHT OR DARK? THAT YOU HAVE NO CHOICE?
SHUT UP!
I'M SO COLD... EVERYTHING'S FROZEN...

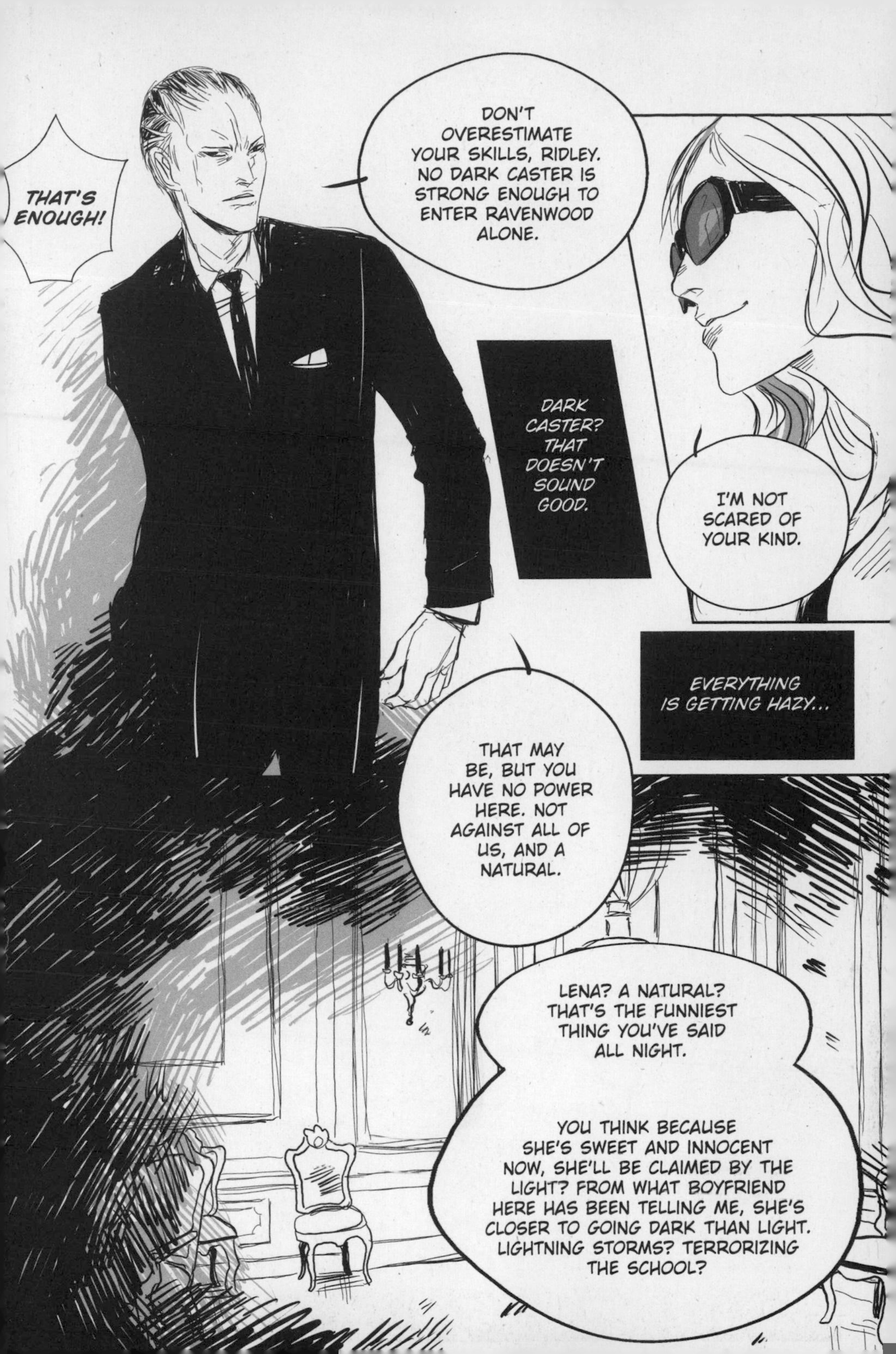
THAT'S ENOUGH!
DON'T OVERESTIMATE YOUR SKILLS, RIDLEY. NO DARK CASTER IS STRONG ENOUGH TO ENTER RAVENWOOD ALONE.
DARK CASTER? THAT DOESN'T SOUND GOOD.
I'M NOT SCARED OF YOUR KIND.
EVERYTHING IS GETTING HAZY...
THAT MAY BE, BUT YOU HAVE NO POWER HERE. NOT AGAINST ALL OF US, AND A NATURAL.
LENA? A NATURAL? THAT'S THE FUNNIEST THING YOU'VE SAID ALL NIGHT.
YOU THINK BECAUSE SHE'S SWEET AND INNOCENT NOW, SHE'LL BE CLAIMED BY THE LIGHT? FROM WHAT BOYFRIEND HERE HAS BEEN TELLING ME, SHE'S CLOSER TO GOING DARK THAN LIGHT. LIGHTNING STORMS? TERRORIZING THE SCHOOL?

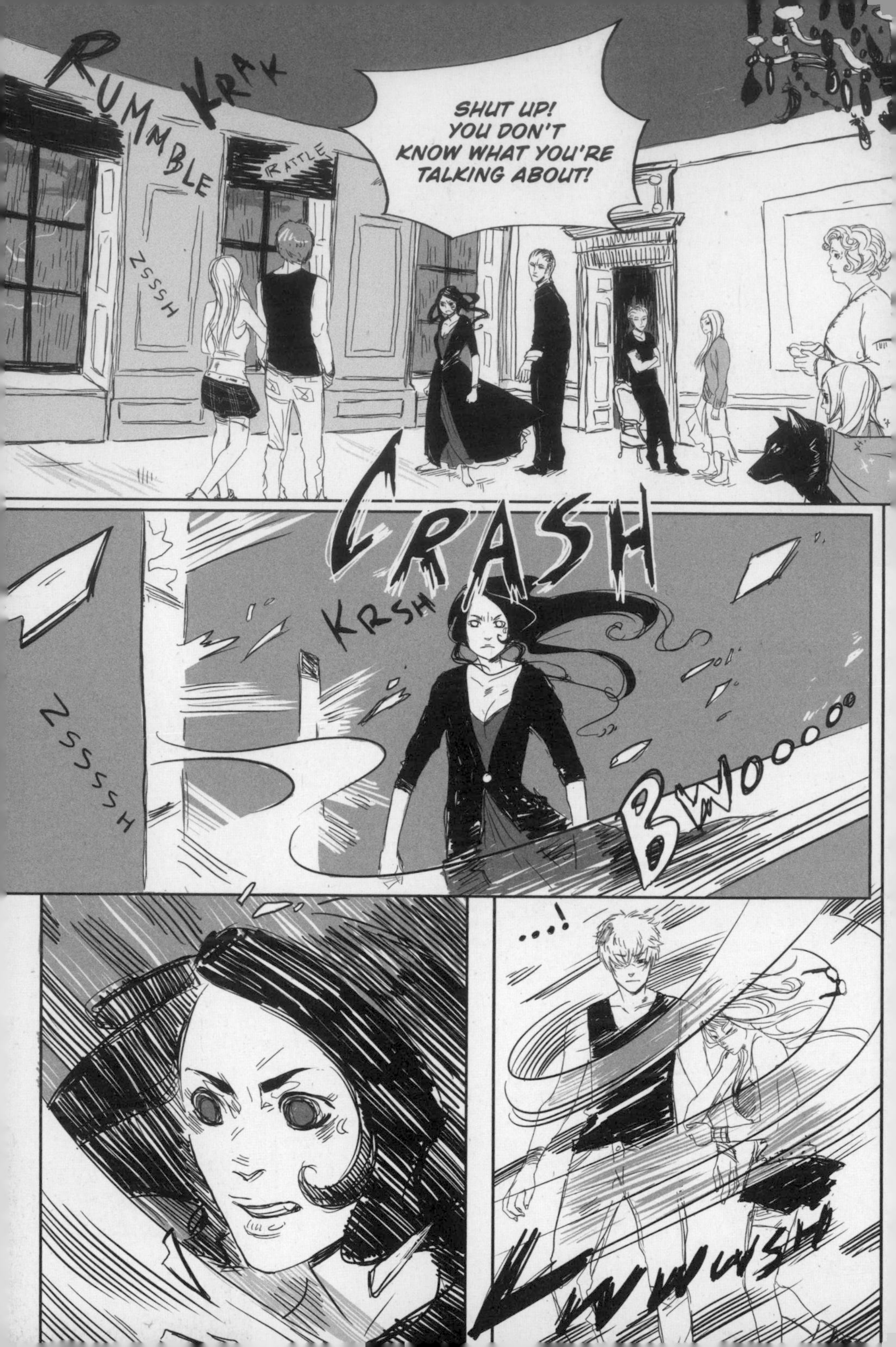

RUMMBLE
KRAK
RATTLE
SHUT UP! YOU DON'T KNOW WHAT YOU'RE TALKING ABOUT!
ZSSSH
CRASH
KRSH
ZSSSSH
BWOOOOO
...!
WWWUSH

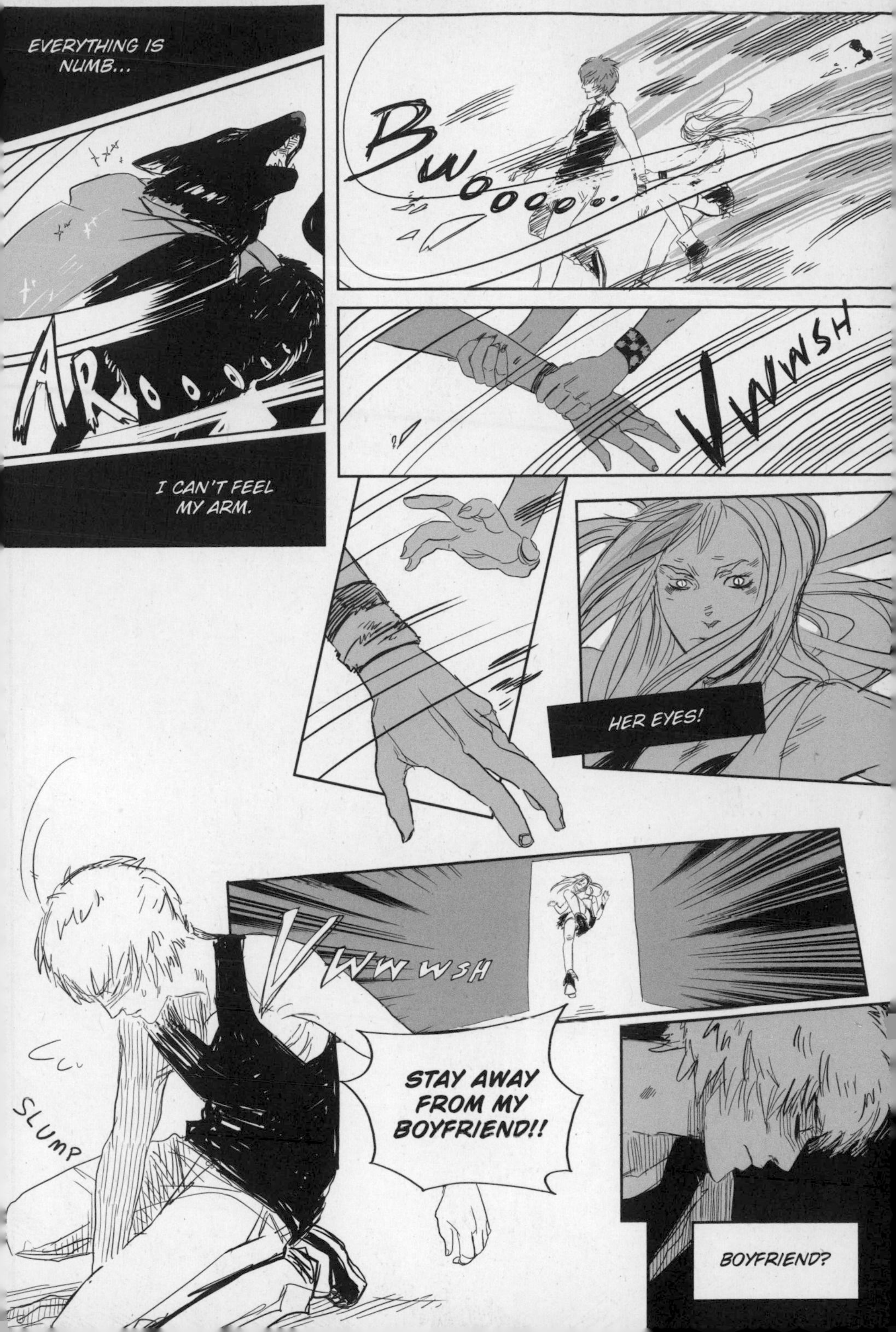

EVERYTHING IS NUMB...
AROOOOO
I CAN'T FEEL MY ARM.
BWOOOOO..
VWWWSH
HER EYES!
SLUMP
VWWWSH
STAY AWAY FROM MY BOYFRIEND!!
BOYFRIEND?

BEAUTIFUL
CREATURES

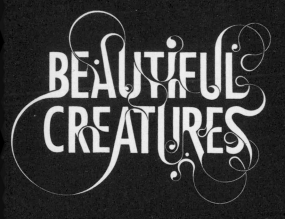

CHAPTER 3

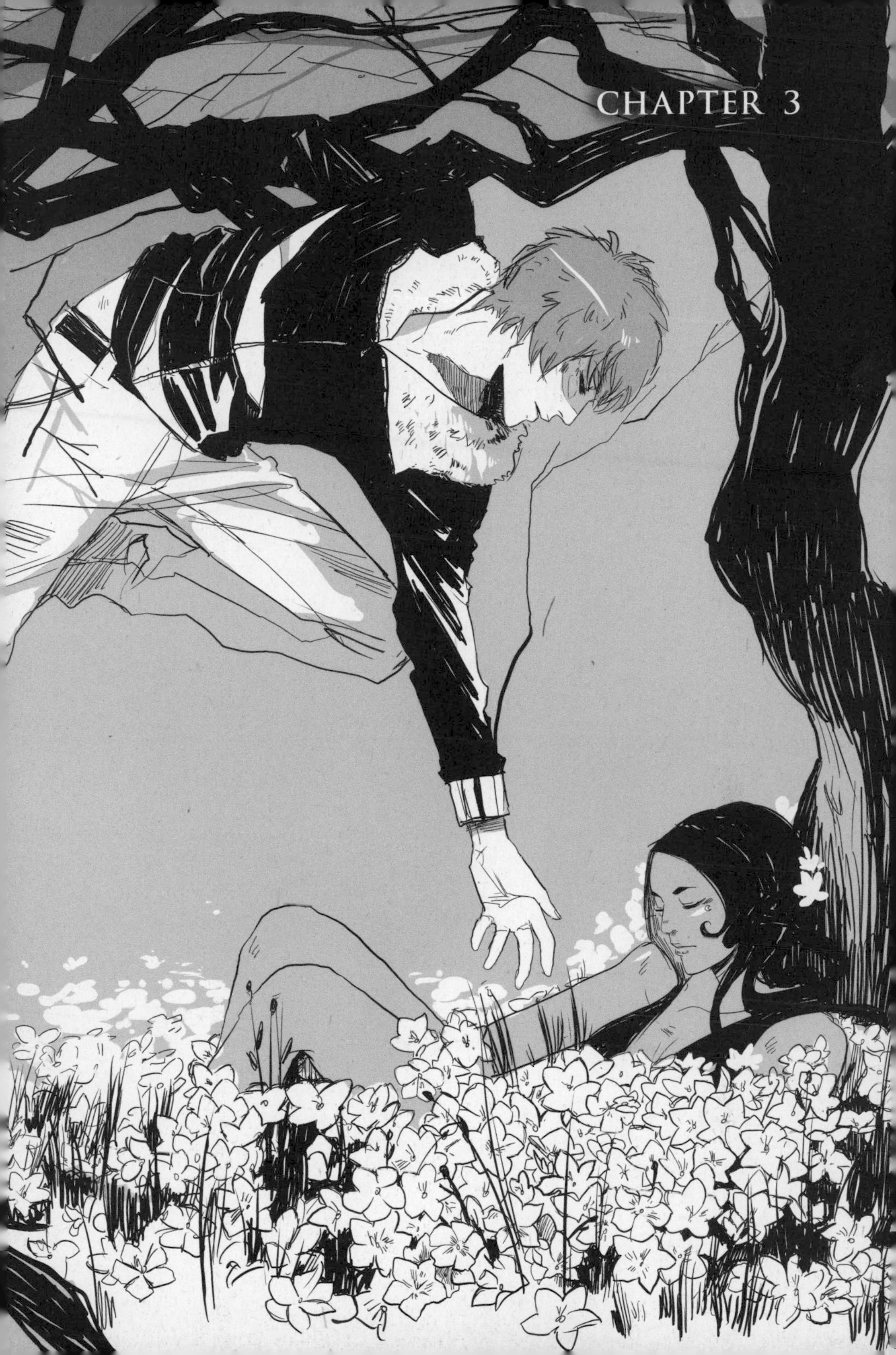

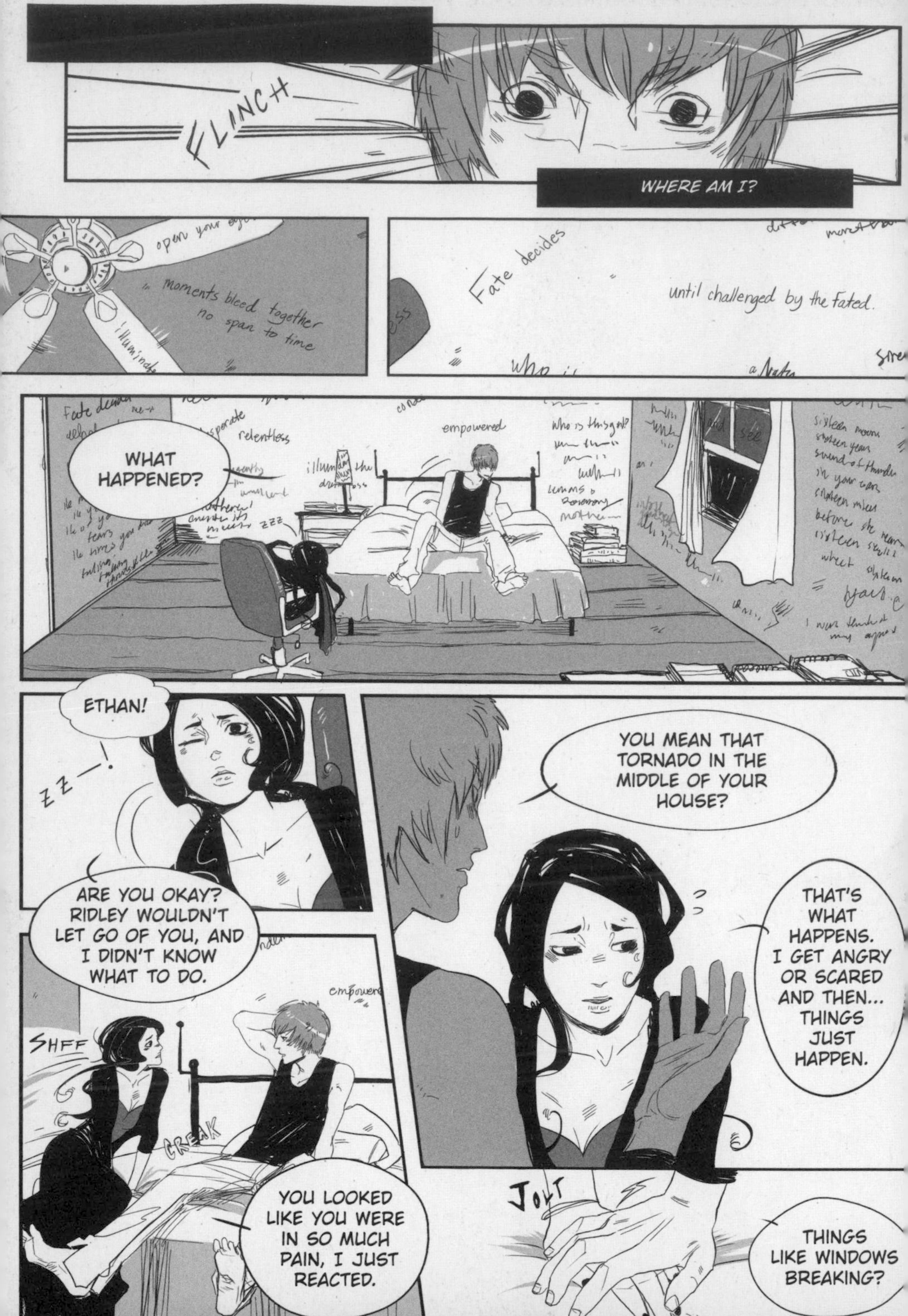
FLINCH
WHERE AM I?
moments bleed together
no span to time
Fate decides
until challenged by the Fated.
WHAT HAPPENED?
relentless
empowered
ETHAN!
Z Z —!
ARE YOU OKAY? RIDLEY WOULDN'T LET GO OF YOU, AND I DIDN'T KNOW WHAT TO DO.
SHFF
CREAK
YOU LOOKED LIKE YOU WERE IN SO MUCH PAIN, I JUST REACTED.
YOU MEAN THAT TORNADO IN THE MIDDLE OF YOUR HOUSE?
THAT'S WHAT HAPPENS. I GET ANGRY OR SCARED AND THEN... THINGS JUST HAPPEN.
JOLT
THINGS LIKE WINDOWS BREAKING?

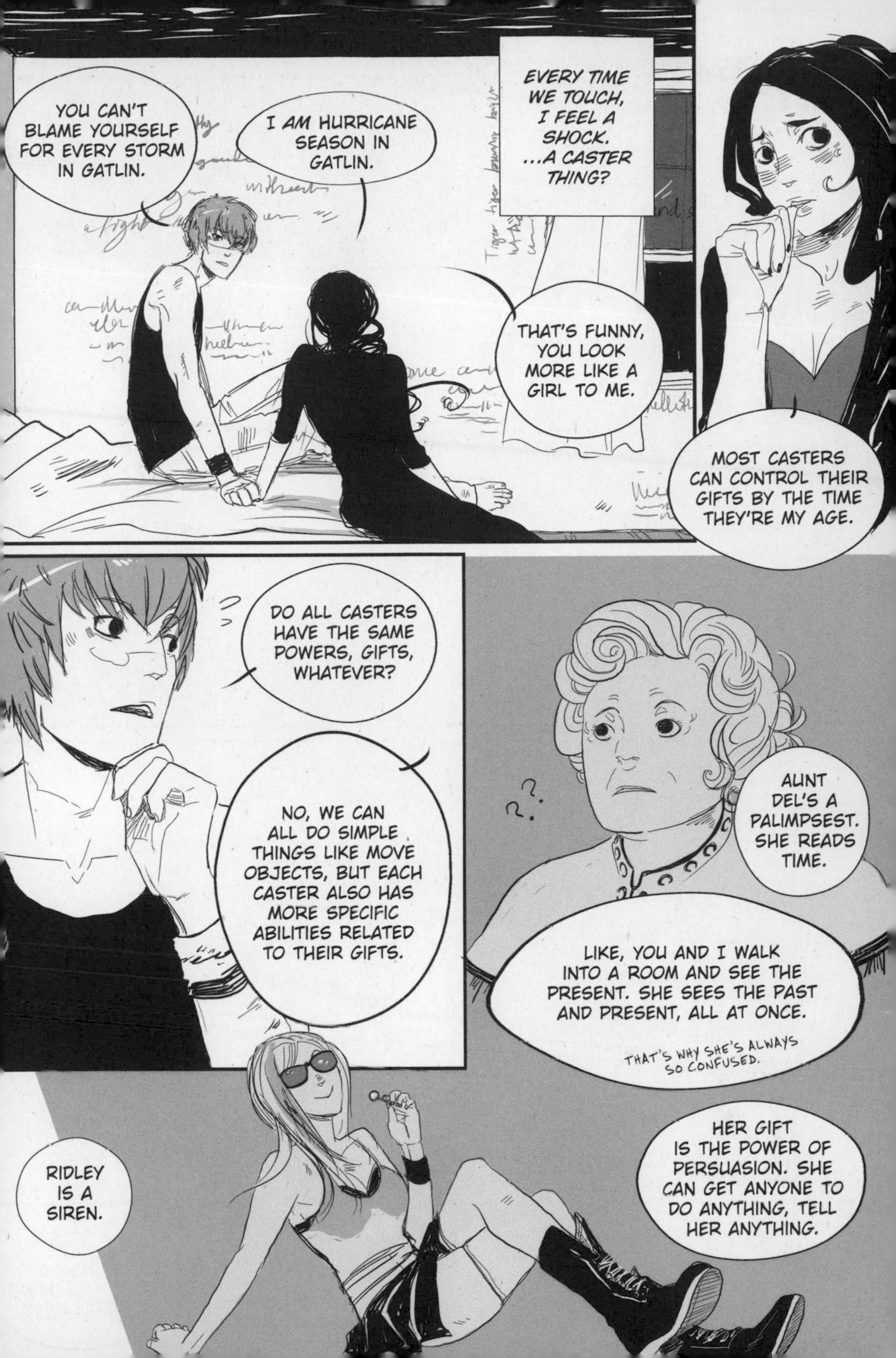
YOU CAN'T BLAME YOURSELF FOR EVERY STORM IN GATLIN.
I AM HURRICANE SEASON IN GATLIN.
THAT'S FUNNY, YOU LOOK MORE LIKE A GIRL TO ME.
EVERY TIME WE TOUCH, I FEEL A SHOCK. ...A CASTER THING?
MOST CASTERS CAN CONTROL THEIR GIFTS BY THE TIME THEY'RE MY AGE.
DO ALL CASTERS HAVE THE SAME POWERS, GIFTS, WHATEVER?
NO, WE CAN ALL DO SIMPLE THINGS LIKE MOVE OBJECTS, BUT EACH CASTER ALSO HAS MORE SPECIFIC ABILITIES RELATED TO THEIR GIFTS.
AUNT DEL'S A PALIMPSEST. SHE READS TIME.
LIKE, YOU AND I WALK INTO A ROOM AND SEE THE PRESENT. SHE SEES THE PAST AND PRESENT, ALL AT ONCE.
THAT'S WHY SHE'S ALWAYS SO CONFUSED.
RIDLEY IS A SIREN.
HER GIFT IS THE POWER OF PERSUASION. SHE CAN GET ANYONE TO DO ANYTHING, TELL HER ANYTHING.

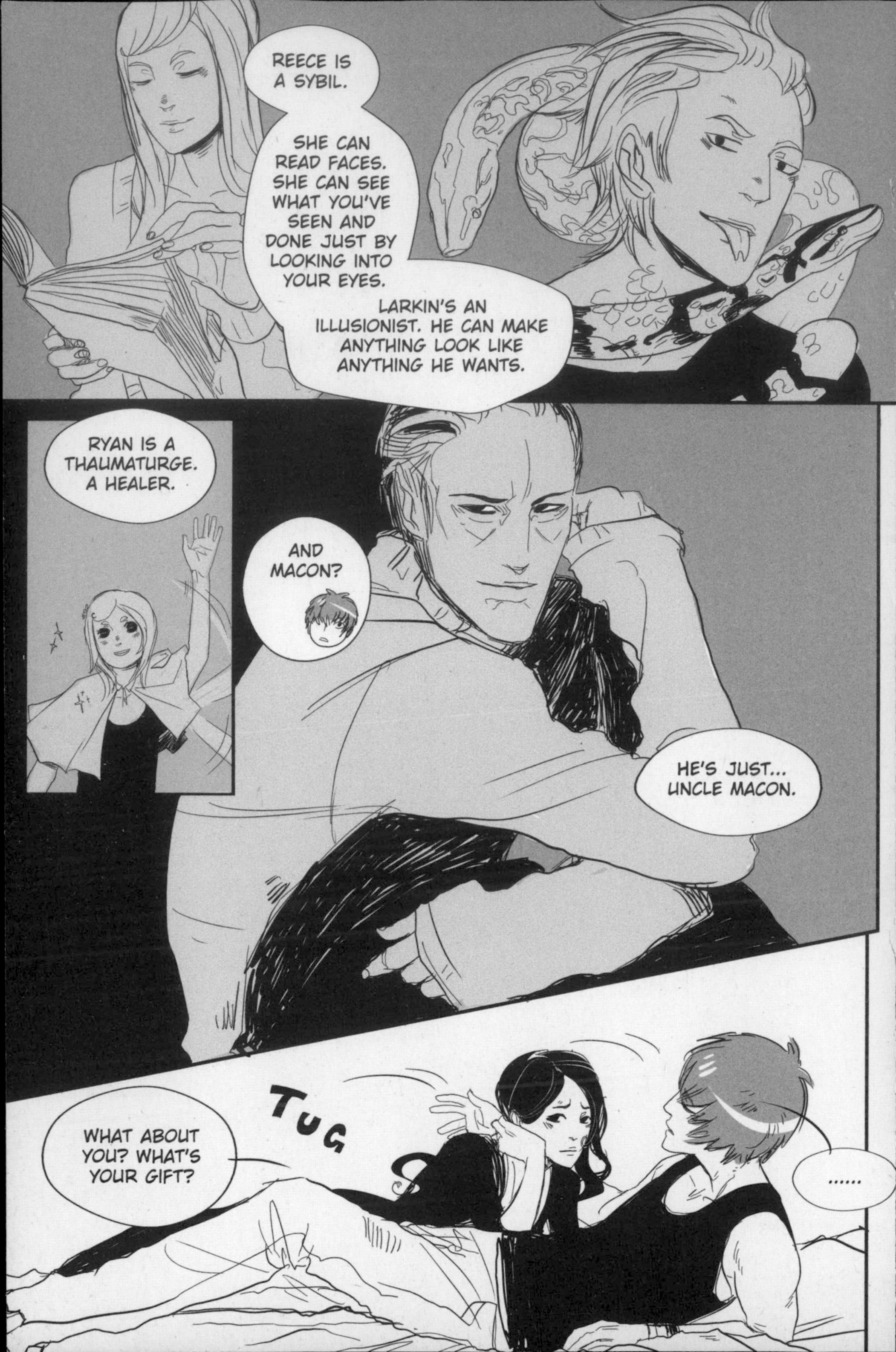
REECE IS A SYBIL.
SHE CAN READ FACES. SHE CAN SEE WHAT YOU'VE SEEN AND DONE JUST BY LOOKING INTO YOUR EYES.
LARKIN'S AN ILLUSIONIST. HE CAN MAKE ANYTHING LOOK LIKE ANYTHING HE WANTS.
RYAN IS A THAUMATURGE. A HEALER.
AND MACON?
HE'S JUST... UNCLE MACON.
WHAT ABOUT YOU? WHAT'S YOUR GIFT?
TUG
......

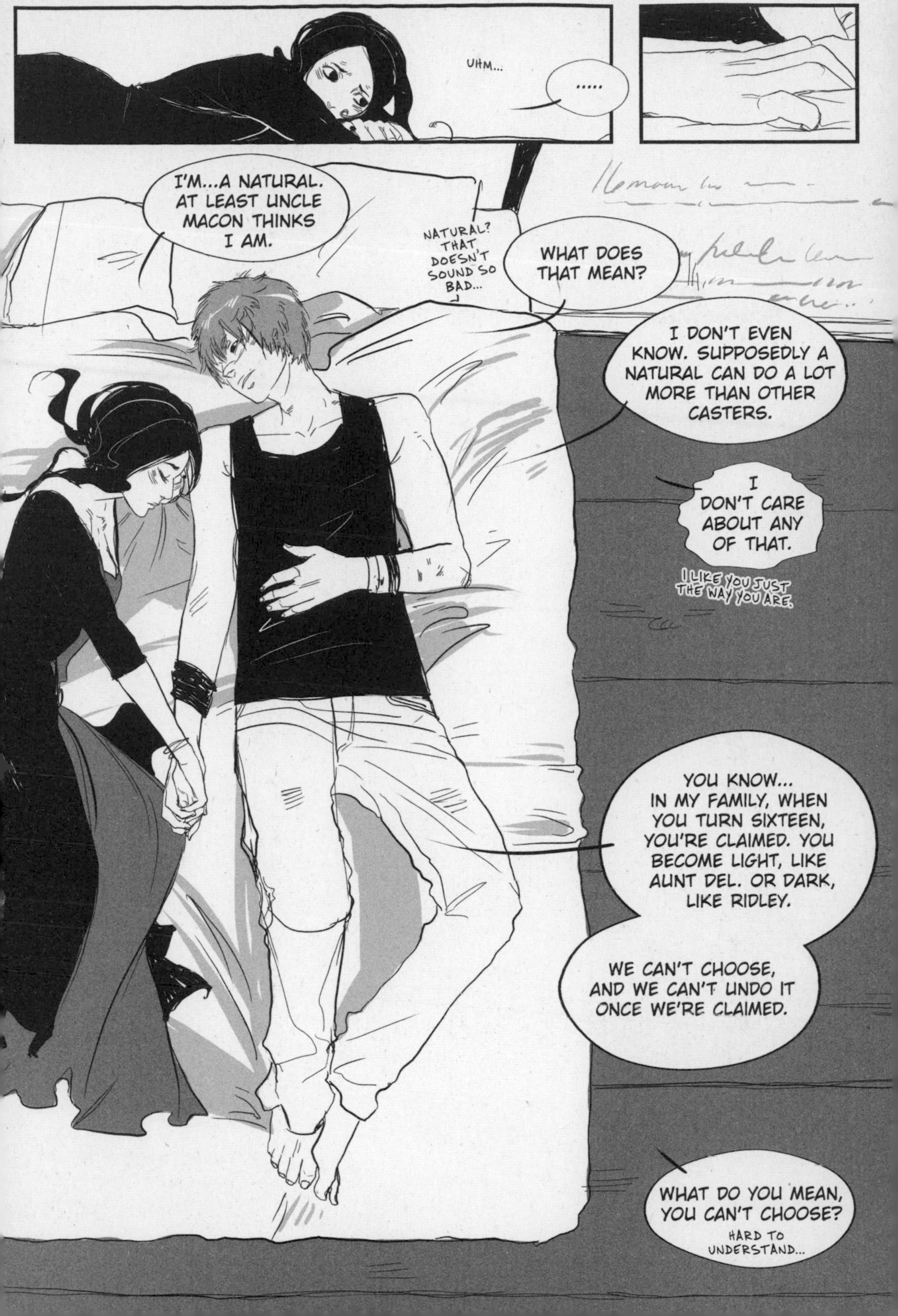
UHM...
.....
I'M...A NATURAL. AT LEAST UNCLE MACON THINKS I AM.
NATURAL? THAT DOESN'T SOUND SO BAD...
WHAT DOES THAT MEAN?
I DON'T EVEN KNOW. SUPPOSEDLY A NATURAL CAN DO A LOT MORE THAN OTHER CASTERS.
I DON'T CARE ABOUT ANY OF THAT.
I LIKE YOU JUST THE WAY YOU ARE.
YOU KNOW... IN MY FAMILY, WHEN YOU TURN SIXTEEN, YOU'RE CLAIMED. YOU BECOME LIGHT, LIKE AUNT DEL. OR DARK, LIKE RIDLEY.
WE CAN'T CHOOSE, AND WE CAN'T UNDO IT ONCE WE'RE CLAIMED.
WHAT DO YOU MEAN, YOU CAN'T CHOOSE?
HARD TO UNDERSTAND...

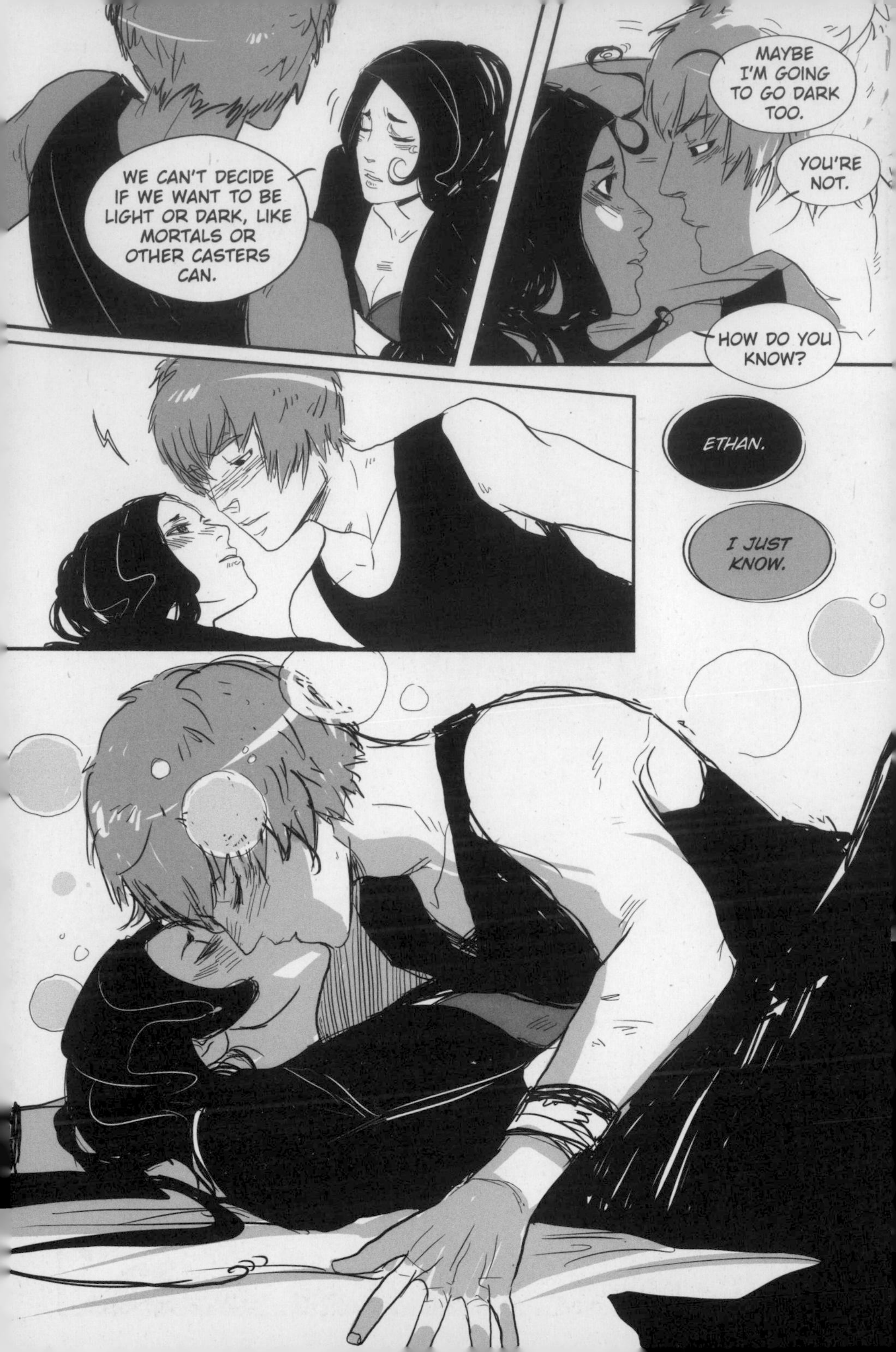
WE CAN'T DECIDE IF WE WANT TO BE LIGHT OR DARK, LIKE MORTALS OR OTHER CASTERS CAN.
MAYBE I'M GOING TO GO DARK TOO.
YOU'RE NOT.
HOW DO YOU KNOW?
ETHAN.
I JUST KNOW.

WE'LL FIGURE SOMETHING OUT.

AFTER LEAVING RAVENWOOD MANOR, ALL I WANT IS TO RETURN TO LENA.

THMP

UGH, I CAN'T SLEEP.

Tmp
Tmp
Tmp

WHAT?

SNEAK

WHERE IS AMMA GOING IN THE MIDDLE OF THE NIGHT?

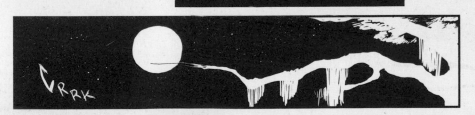

CRRK

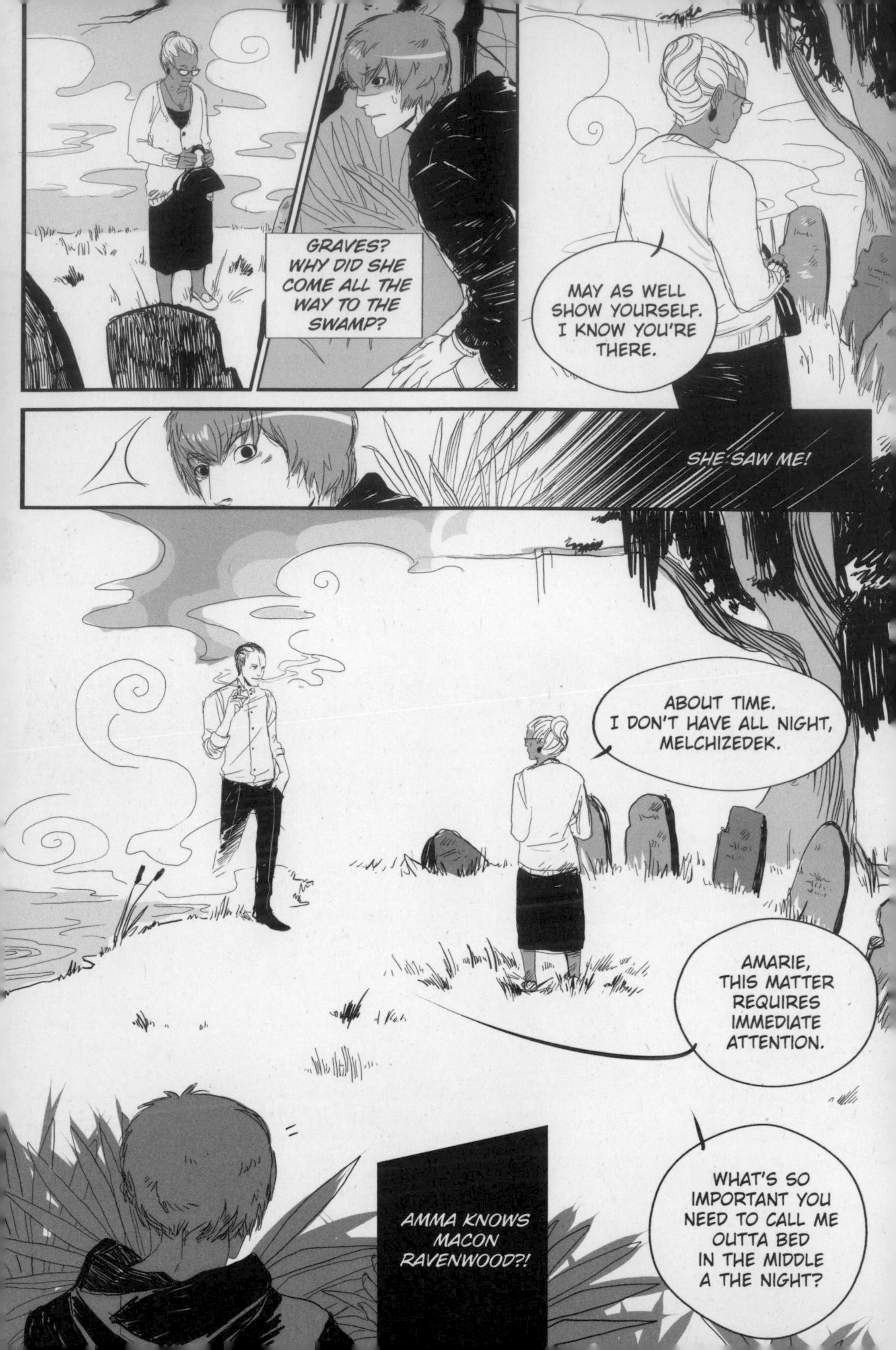
GRAVES? WHY DID SHE COME ALL THE WAY TO THE SWAMP?
MAY AS WELL SHOW YOURSELF. I KNOW YOU'RE THERE.
SHE SAW ME!
ABOUT TIME. I DON'T HAVE ALL NIGHT, MELCHIZEDEK.
AMARIE, THIS MATTER REQUIRES IMMEDIATE ATTENTION.
AMMA KNOWS MACON RAVENWOOD?!
WHAT'S SO IMPORTANT YOU NEED TO CALL ME OUTTA BED IN THE MIDDLE A THE NIGHT?

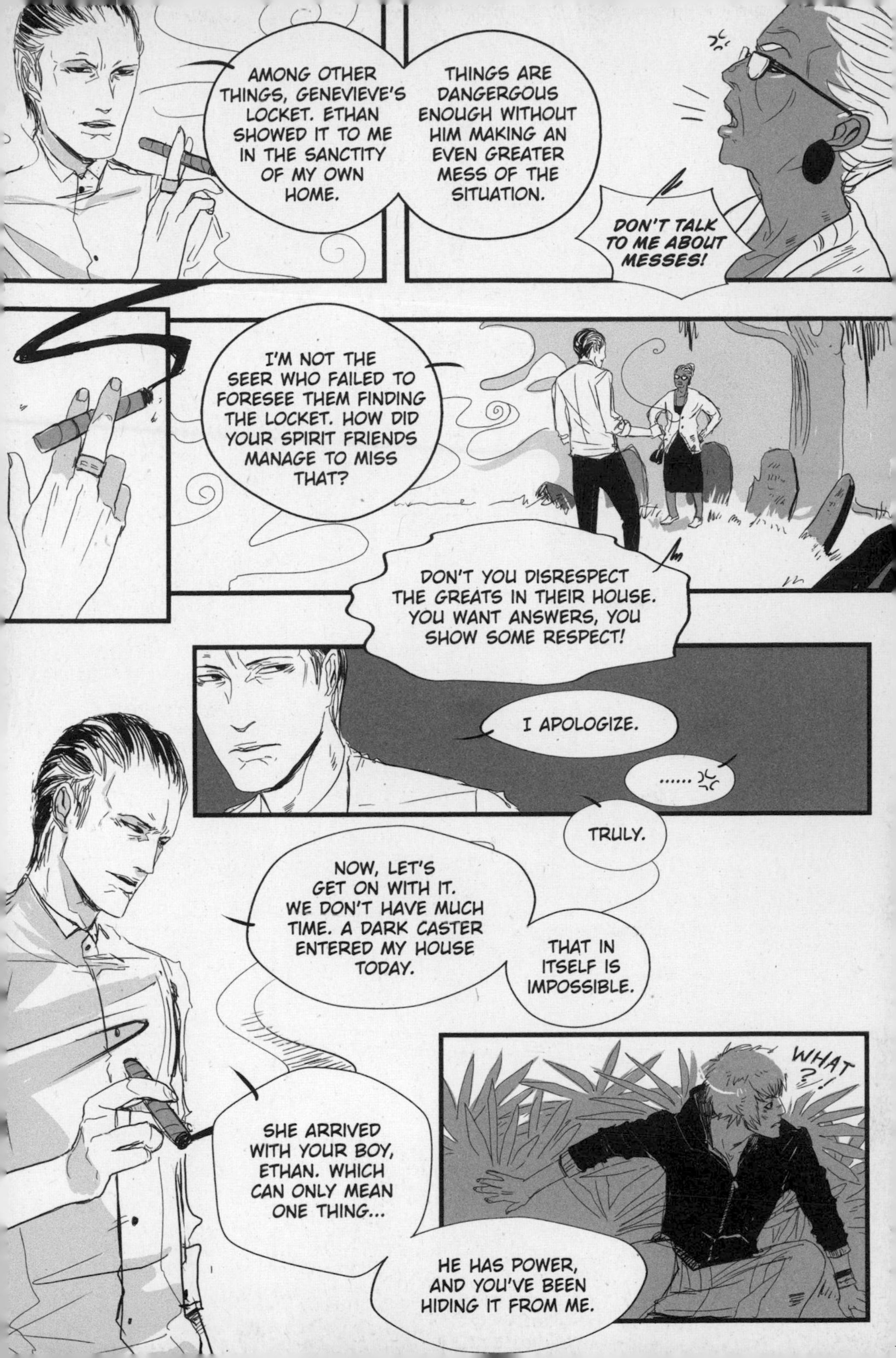
AMONG OTHER THINGS, GENEVIEVE'S LOCKET. ETHAN SHOWED IT TO ME IN THE SANCTITY OF MY OWN HOME.
THINGS ARE DANGERGOUS ENOUGH WITHOUT HIM MAKING AN EVEN GREATER MESS OF THE SITUATION.
DON'T TALK TO ME ABOUT MESSES!
I'M NOT THE SEER WHO FAILED TO FORESEE THEM FINDING THE LOCKET. HOW DID YOUR SPIRIT FRIENDS MANAGE TO MISS THAT?
DON'T YOU DISRESPECT THE GREATS IN THEIR HOUSE. YOU WANT ANSWERS, YOU SHOW SOME RESPECT!
I APOLOGIZE.
......
TRULY.
NOW, LET'S GET ON WITH IT. WE DON'T HAVE MUCH TIME. A DARK CASTER ENTERED MY HOUSE TODAY.
THAT IN ITSELF IS IMPOSSIBLE.
SHE ARRIVED WITH YOUR BOY, ETHAN. WHICH CAN ONLY MEAN ONE THING...
HE HAS POWER, AND YOU'VE BEEN HIDING IT FROM ME.
WHAT?!

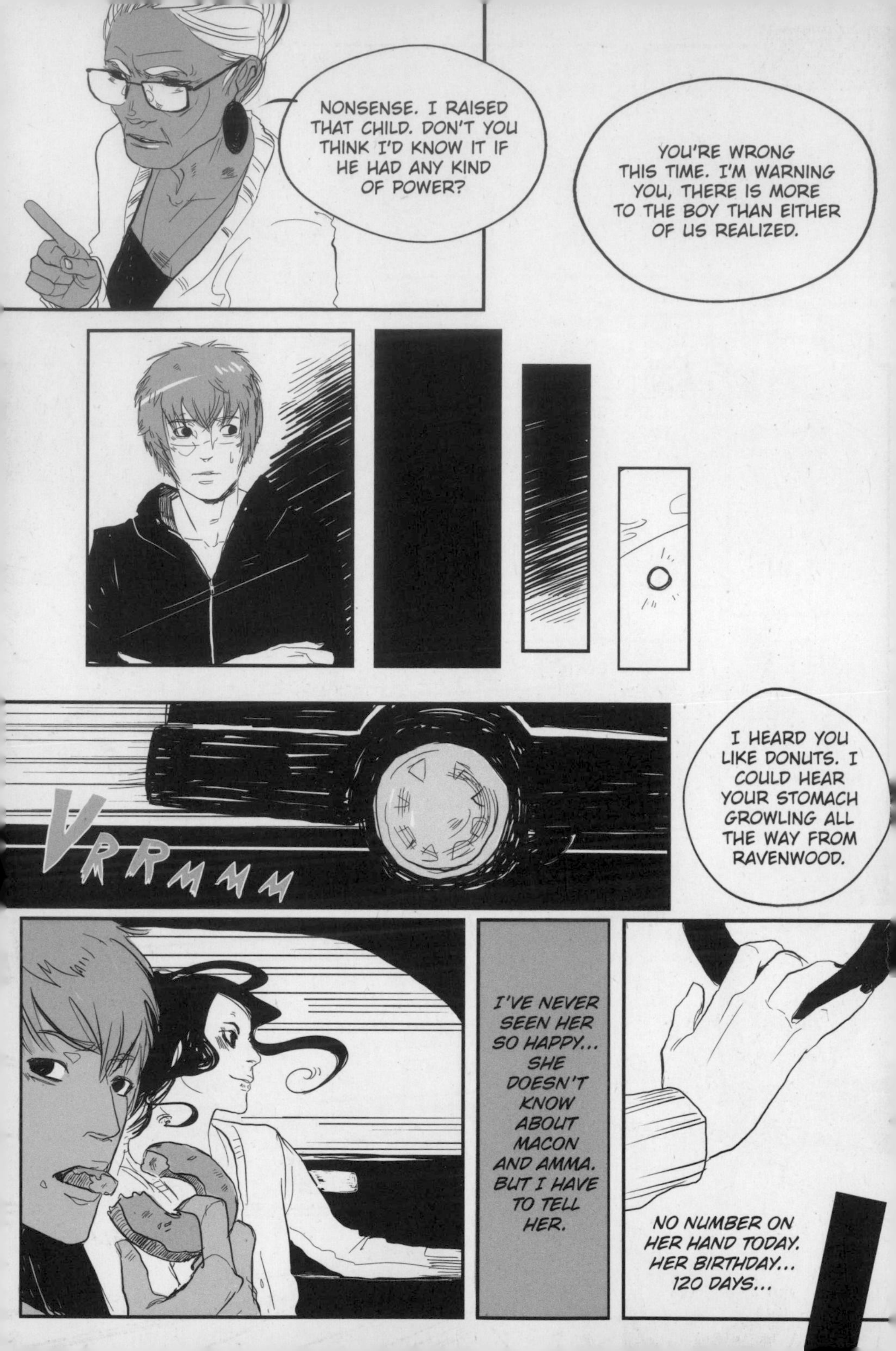
NONSENSE. I RAISED THAT CHILD. DON'T YOU THINK I'D KNOW IT IF HE HAD ANY KIND OF POWER?
YOU'RE WRONG THIS TIME. I'M WARNING YOU, THERE IS MORE TO THE BOY THAN EITHER OF US REALIZED.
VRRMMM
I HEARD YOU LIKE DONUTS. I COULD HEAR YOUR STOMACH GROWLING ALL THE WAY FROM RAVENWOOD.
I'VE NEVER SEEN HER SO HAPPY... SHE DOESN'T KNOW ABOUT MACON AND AMMA. BUT I HAVE TO TELL HER.
NO NUMBER ON HER HAND TODAY. HER BIRTHDAY... 120 DAYS...

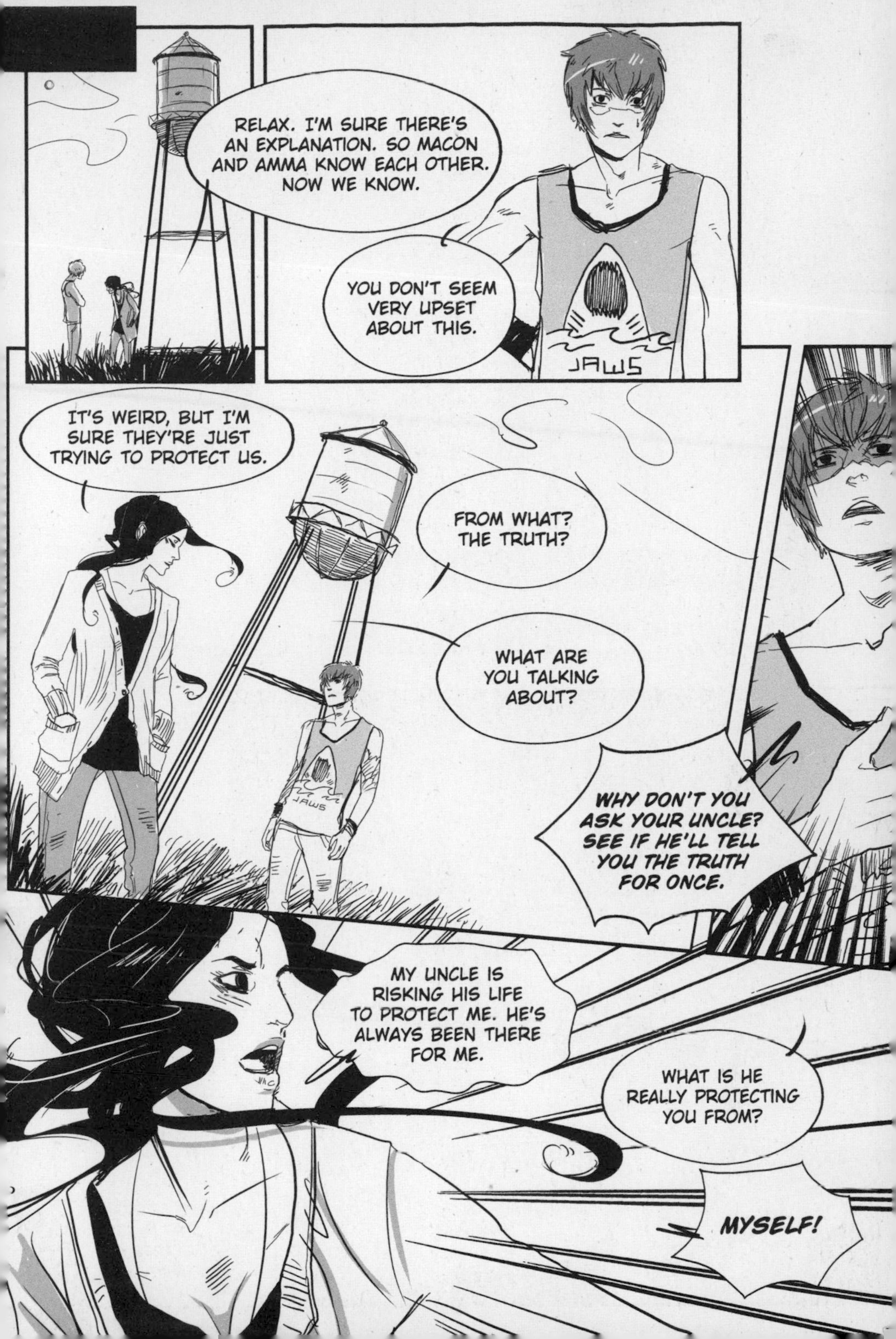
RELAX. I'M SURE THERE'S AN EXPLANATION. SO MACON AND AMMA KNOW EACH OTHER. NOW WE KNOW.
YOU DON'T SEEM VERY UPSET ABOUT THIS.
JAWS
IT'S WEIRD, BUT I'M SURE THEY'RE JUST TRYING TO PROTECT US.
FROM WHAT? THE TRUTH?
WHAT ARE YOU TALKING ABOUT?
JAWS
WHY DON'T YOU ASK YOUR UNCLE? SEE IF HE'LL TELL YOU THE TRUTH FOR ONCE.
MY UNCLE IS RISKING HIS LIFE TO PROTECT ME. HE'S ALWAYS BEEN THERE FOR ME.
WHAT IS HE REALLY PROTECTING YOU FROM?
MYSELF!

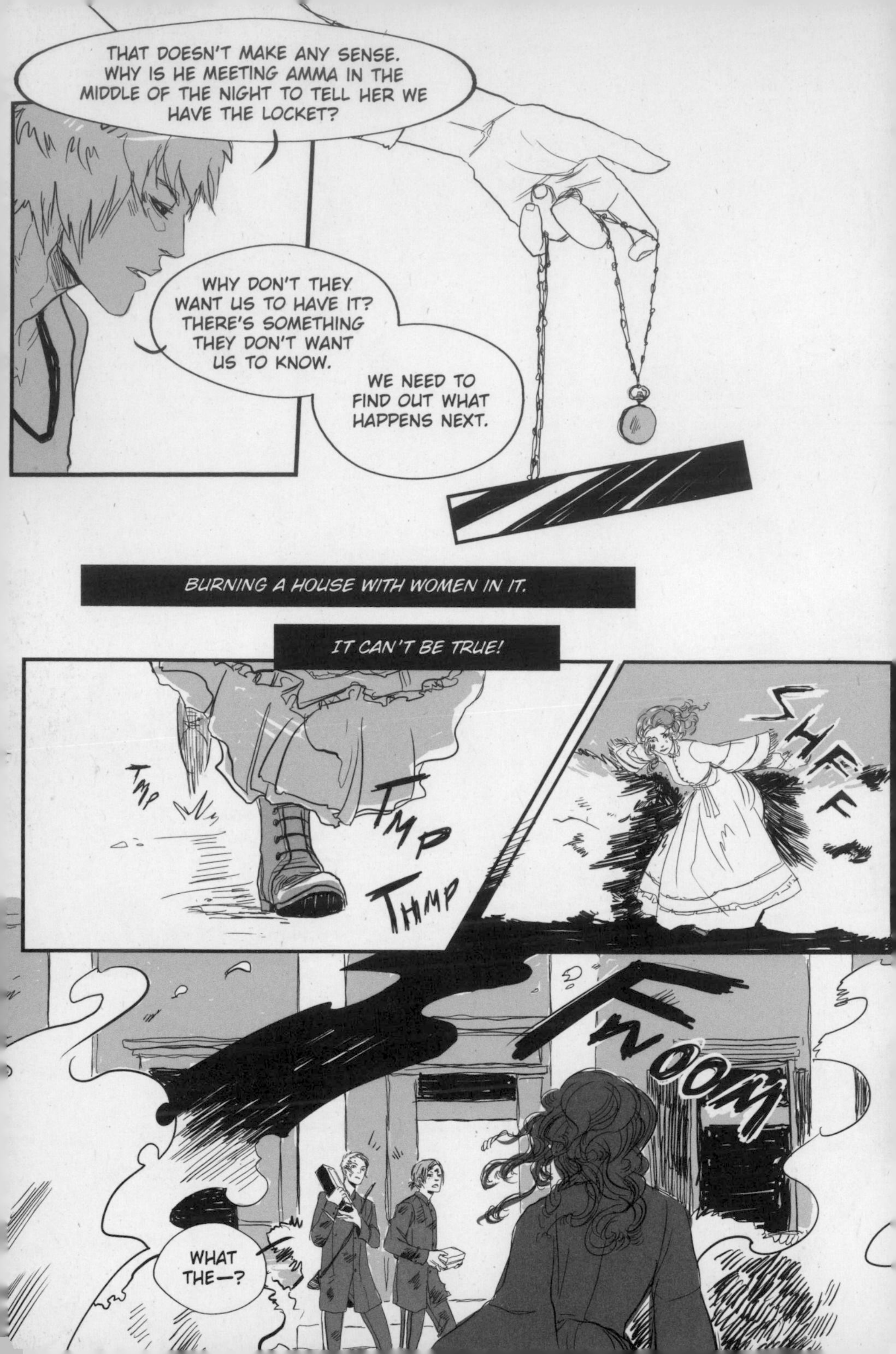
THAT DOESN'T MAKE ANY SENSE. WHY IS HE MEETING AMMA IN THE MIDDLE OF THE NIGHT TO TELL HER WE HAVE THE LOCKET?
WHY DON'T THEY WANT US TO HAVE IT? THERE'S SOMETHING THEY DON'T WANT US TO KNOW.
WE NEED TO FIND OUT WHAT HAPPENS NEXT.
BURNING A HOUSE WITH WOMEN IN IT.
IT CAN'T BE TRUE!
TMP
TMP
THMP
SHFF
WOOM
WHAT THE—?

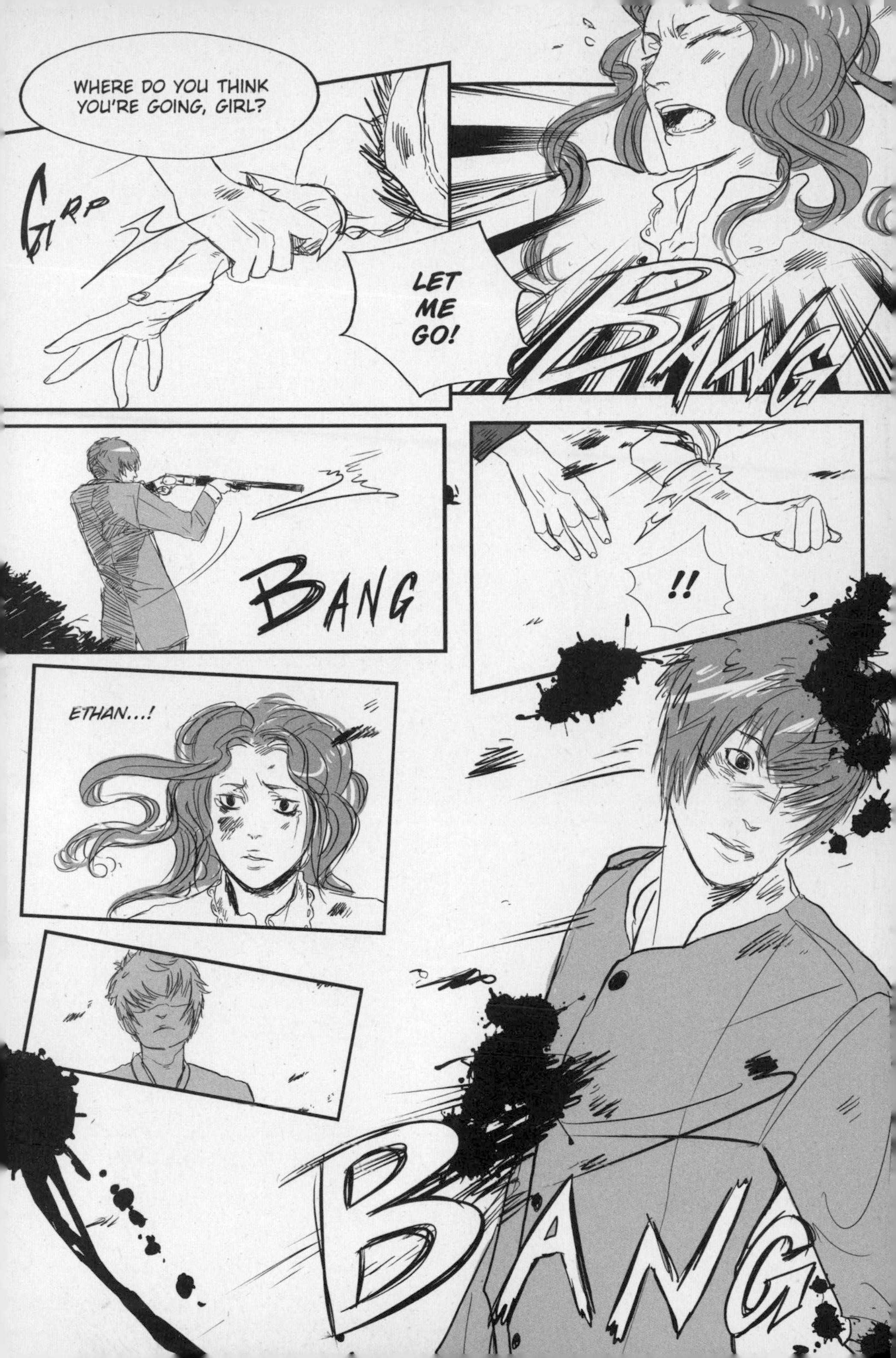
WHERE DO YOU THINK YOU'RE GOING, GIRL?
GRP
LET ME GO!
BANG
BANG
!!
ETHAN...!
BANG

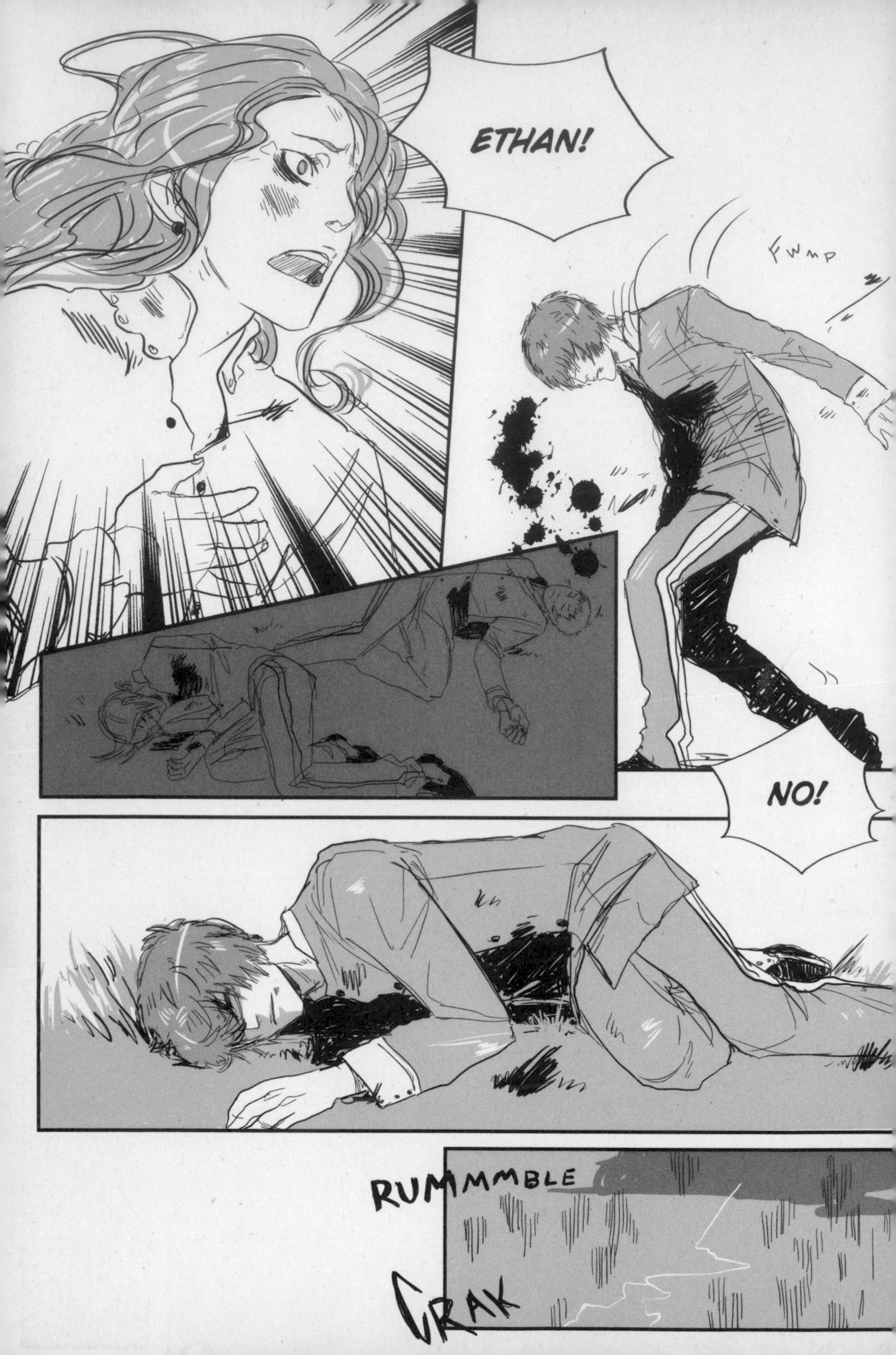
ETHAN!
FWMP
NO!
RUMMMBLE
CRAK

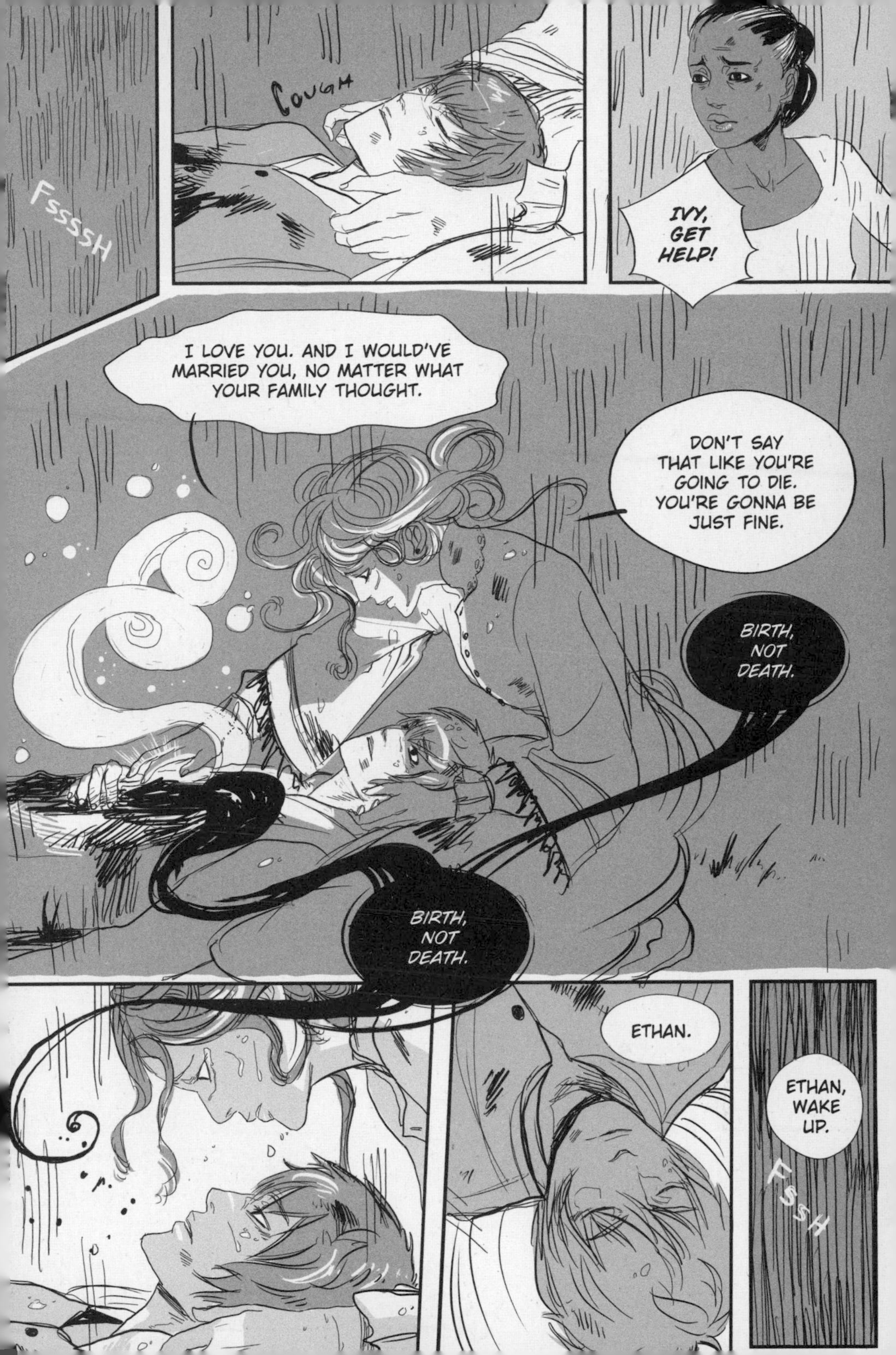
FSSSSH
COUGH
IVY, GET HELP!
I LOVE YOU. AND I WOULD'VE MARRIED YOU, NO MATTER WHAT YOUR FAMILY THOUGHT.
DON'T SAY THAT LIKE YOU'RE GOING TO DIE. YOU'RE GONNA BE JUST FINE.
BIRTH, NOT DEATH.
BIRTH, NOT DEATH.
ETHAN.
ETHAN, WAKE UP.
FSSH

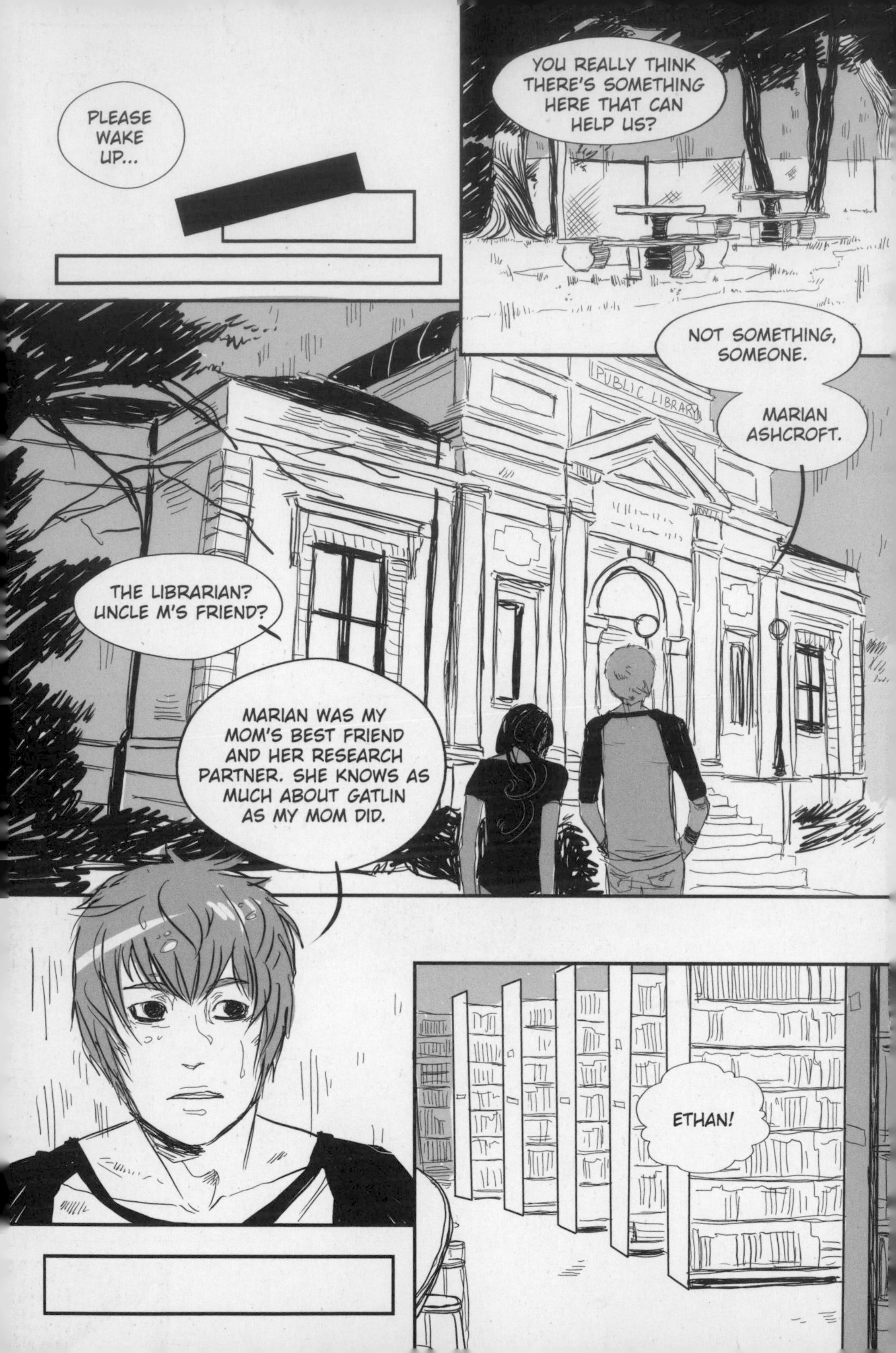
PLEASE WAKE UP...
YOU REALLY THINK THERE'S SOMETHING HERE THAT CAN HELP US?
NOT SOMETHING, SOMEONE.
MARIAN ASHCROFT.
PUBLIC LIBRARY
THE LIBRARIAN? UNCLE M'S FRIEND?
MARIAN WAS MY MOM'S BEST FRIEND AND HER RESEARCH PARTNER. SHE KNOWS AS MUCH ABOUT GATLIN AS MY MOM DID.
ETHAN!

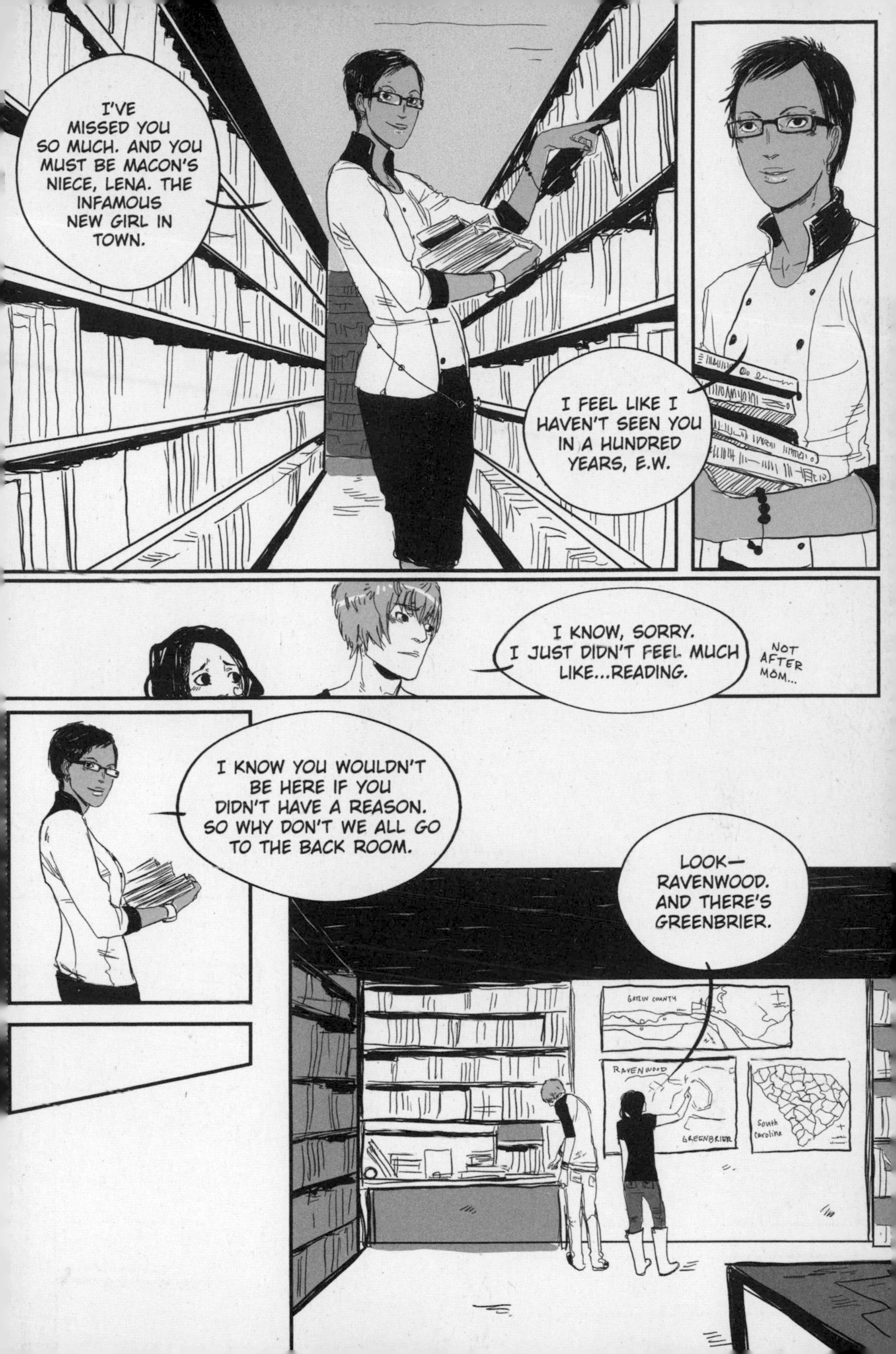
I'VE MISSED YOU SO MUCH. AND YOU MUST BE MACON'S NIECE, LENA. THE INFAMOUS NEW GIRL IN TOWN.
I FEEL LIKE I HAVEN'T SEEN YOU IN A HUNDRED YEARS, E.W.
I KNOW, SORRY. I JUST DIDN'T FEEL MUCH LIKE...READING.
NOT AFTER MOM...
I KNOW YOU WOULDN'T BE HERE IF YOU DIDN'T HAVE A REASON. SO WHY DON'T WE ALL GO TO THE BACK ROOM.
LOOK— RAVENWOOD. AND THERE'S GREENBRIER.
GATLIN COUNTY
RAVENWOOD
GREENBRIER
South Carolina

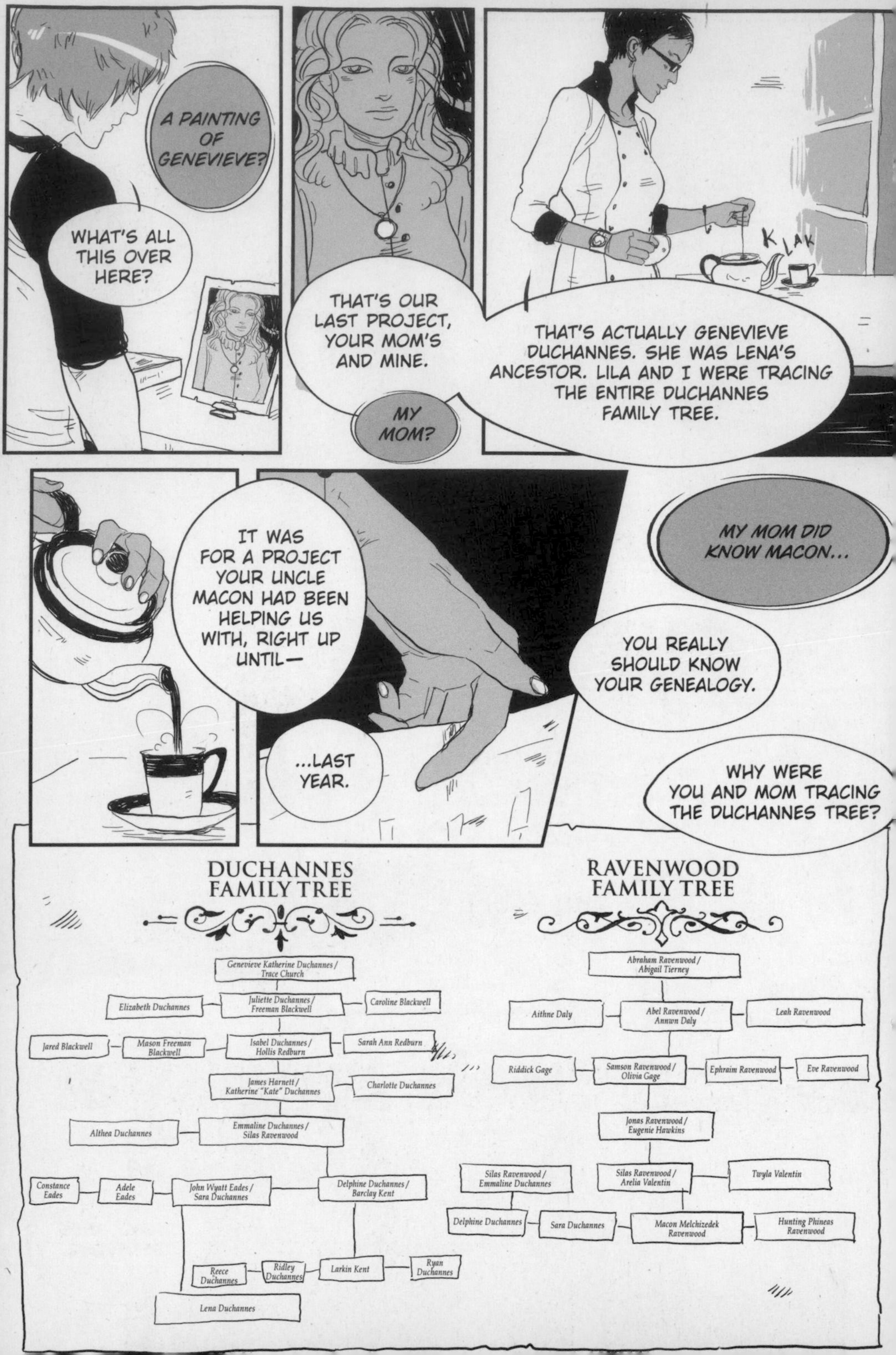
A PAINTING OF GENEVIEVE?
WHAT'S ALL THIS OVER HERE?
THAT'S OUR LAST PROJECT, YOUR MOM'S AND MINE.
MY MOM?
THAT'S ACTUALLY GENEVIEVE DUCHANNES. SHE WAS LENA'S ANCESTOR. LILA AND I WERE TRACING THE ENTIRE DUCHANNES FAMILY TREE.
KLAK
IT WAS FOR A PROJECT YOUR UNCLE MACON HAD BEEN HELPING US WITH, RIGHT UP UNTIL—
...LAST YEAR.
MY MOM DID KNOW MACON...
YOU REALLY SHOULD KNOW YOUR GENEALOGY.
WHY WERE YOU AND MOM TRACING THE DUCHANNES TREE?
DUCHANNES FAMILY TREE
Genevieve Katherine Duchannes / Trace Church
Elizabeth Duchannes
Juliette Duchannes / Freeman Blackwell
Caroline Blackwell
Jared Blackwell
Mason Freeman Blackwell
Isabel Duchannes / Hollis Redburn
Sarah Ann Redburn
James Harnett / Katherine "Kate" Duchannes
Charlotte Duchannes
Althea Duchannes
Emmaline Duchannes / Silas Ravenwood
Constance Eades
Adele Eades
John Wyatt Eades / Sara Duchannes
Delphine Duchannes / Barclay Kent
Reece Duchannes
Ridley Duchannes
Larkin Kent
Ryan Duchannes
Lena Duchannes
RAVENWOOD FAMILY TREE
Abraham Ravenwood / Abigail Tierney
Aithne Daly
Abel Ravenwood / Annwn Daly
Leah Ravenwood
Riddick Gage
Samson Ravenwood / Olivia Gage
Ephraim Ravenwood
Eve Ravenwood
Jonas Ravenwood / Eugenie Hawkins
Silas Ravenwood / Emmaline Duchannes
Silas Ravenwood / Arelia Valentin
Twyla Valentin
Delphine Duchannes
Sara Duchannes
Macon Melchizedek Ravenwood
Hunting Phineas Ravenwood

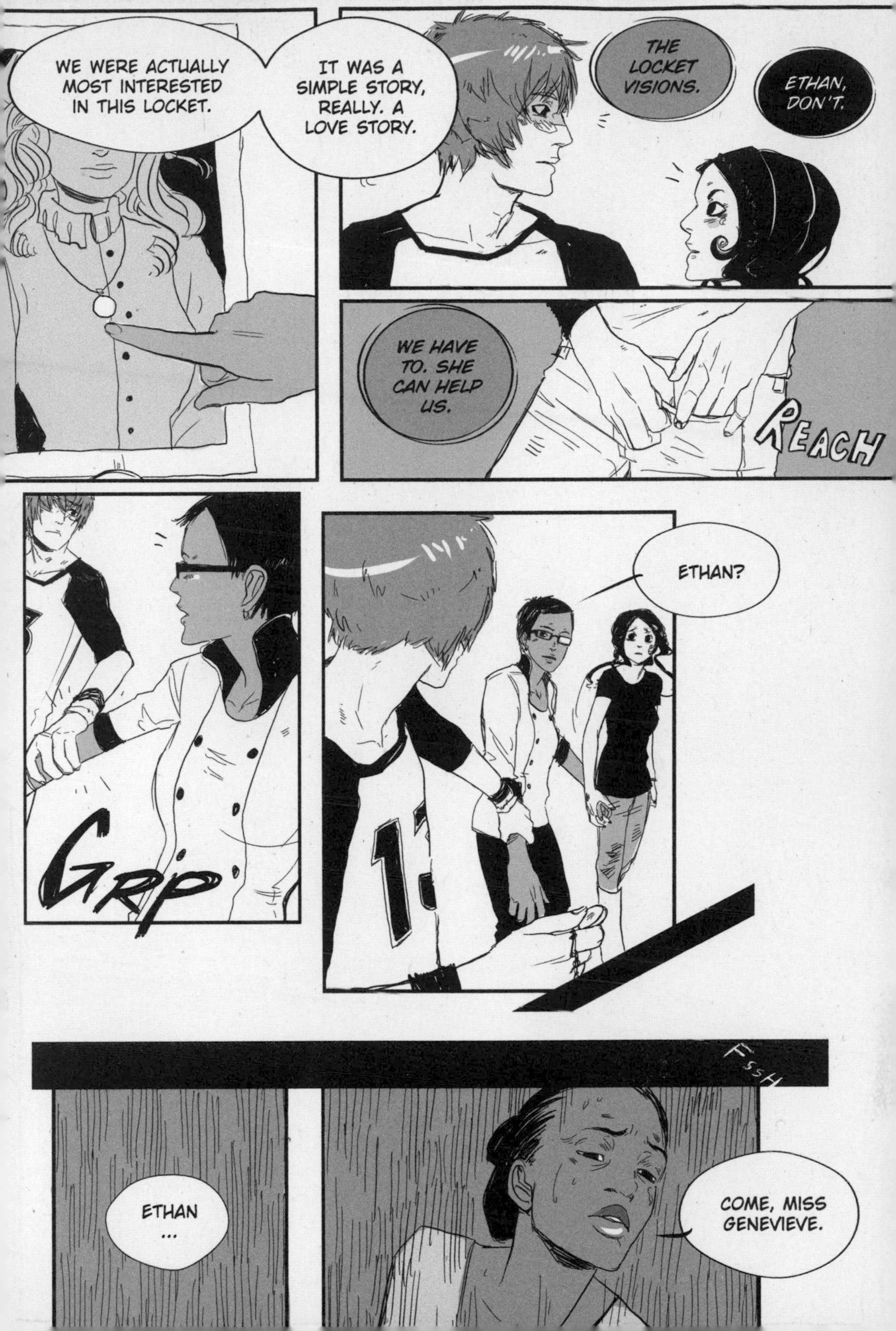

WE WERE ACTUALLY MOST INTERESTED IN THIS LOCKET.
IT WAS A SIMPLE STORY, REALLY. A LOVE STORY.
THE LOCKET VISIONS.
ETHAN, DON'T.
WE HAVE TO. SHE CAN HELP US.
REACH
GRP
ETHAN?
FSSH
ETHAN ...
COME, MISS GENEVIEVE.

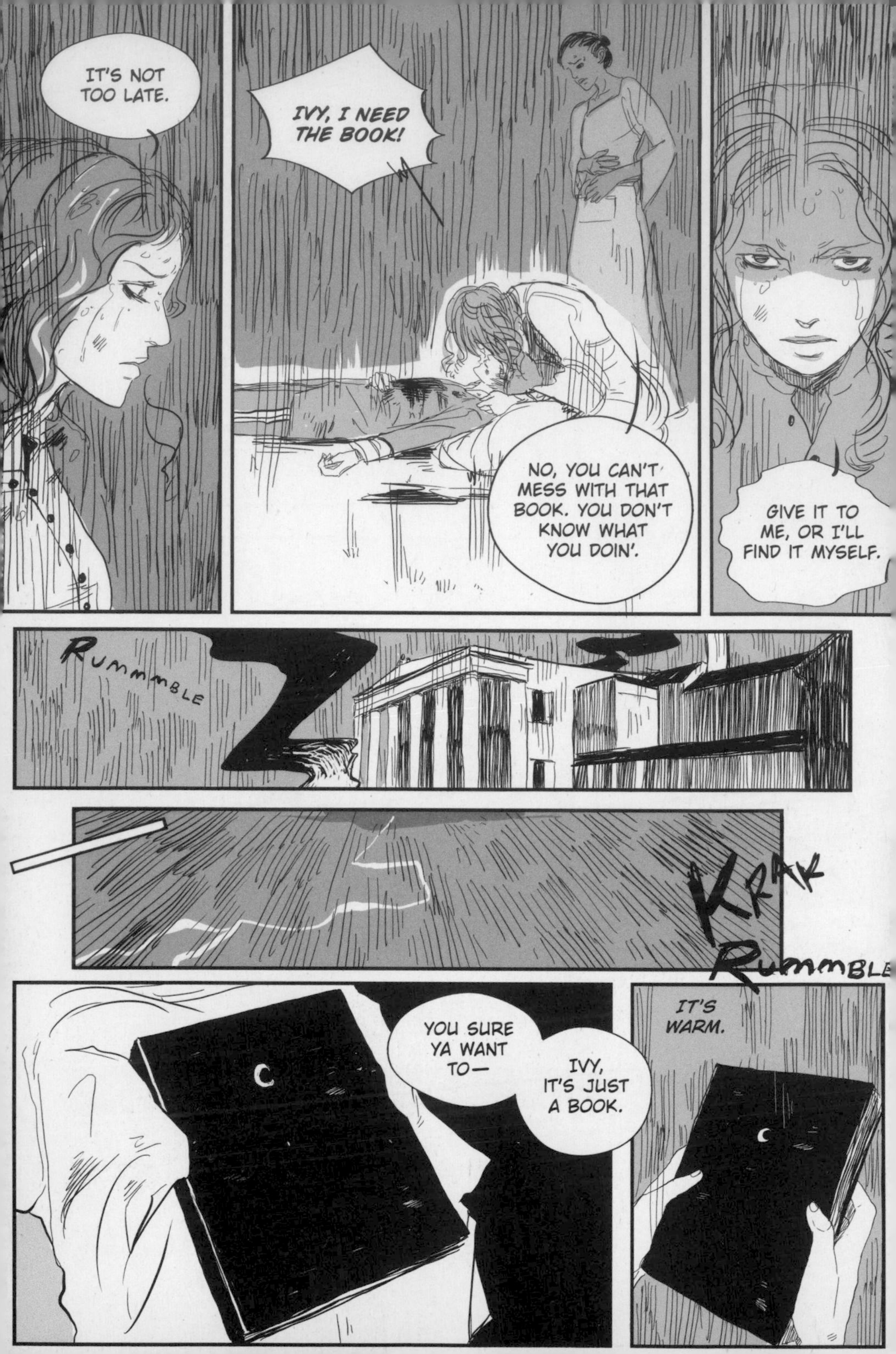
IT'S NOT TOO LATE.
IVY, I NEED THE BOOK!
NO, YOU CAN'T MESS WITH THAT BOOK. YOU DON'T KNOW WHAT YOU DOIN'.
GIVE IT TO ME, OR I'LL FIND IT MYSELF.
RUMMMBLE
KRAK
RUMMMBLE
YOU SURE YA WANT TO—
IVY, IT'S JUST A BOOK.
IT'S WARM.

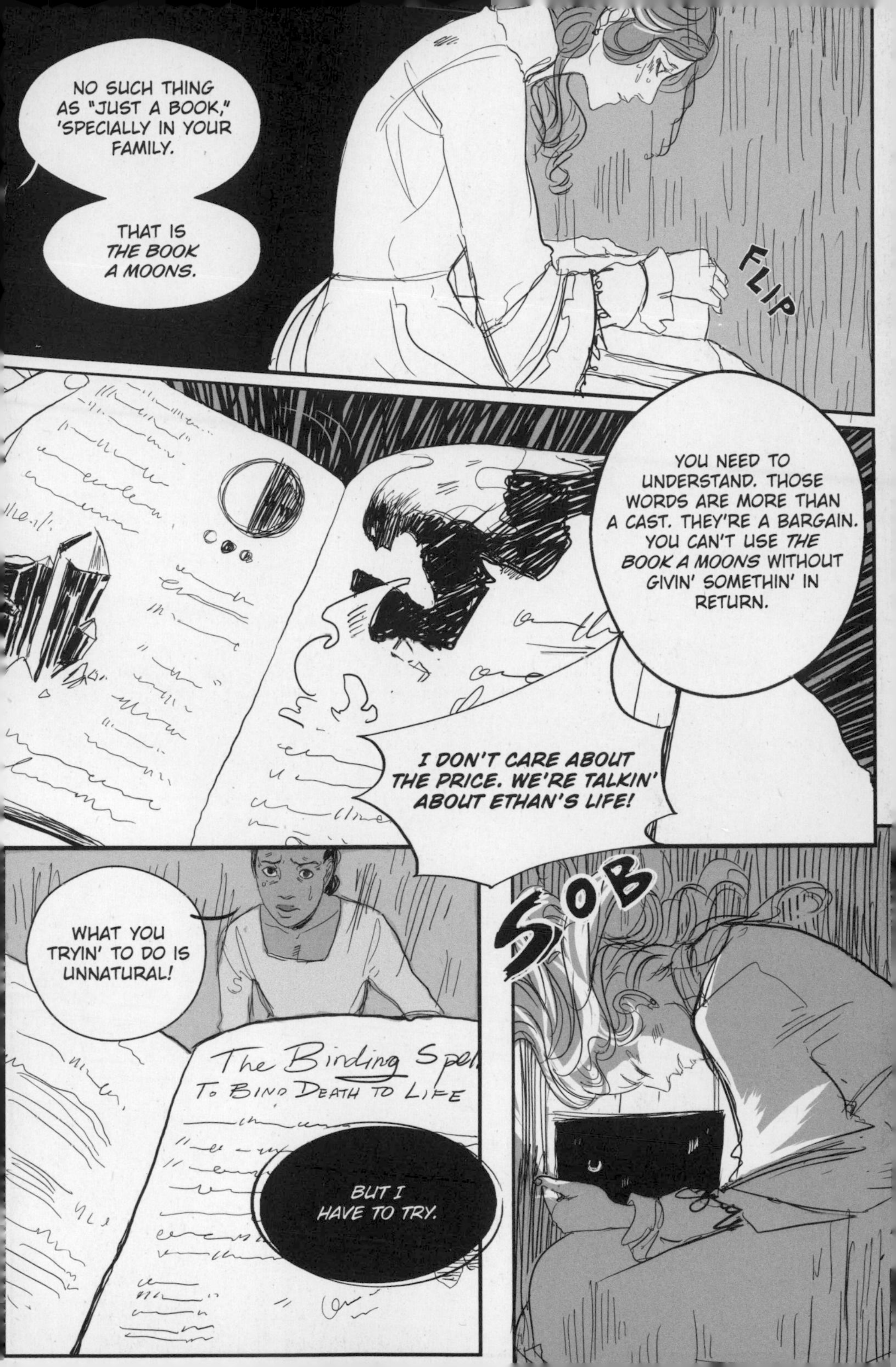
NO SUCH THING AS "JUST A BOOK," 'SPECIALLY IN YOUR FAMILY.
THAT IS *THE BOOK A MOONS.*
FLIP
YOU NEED TO UNDERSTAND. THOSE WORDS ARE MORE THAN A CAST. THEY'RE A BARGAIN. YOU CAN'T USE *THE BOOK A MOONS* WITHOUT GIVIN' SOMETHIN' IN RETURN.
I DON'T CARE ABOUT THE PRICE. WE'RE TALKIN' ABOUT ETHAN'S LIFE!
WHAT YOU TRYIN' TO DO IS UNNATURAL!
The Binding Spel
TO BIND DEATH TO LIFE
BUT I HAVE TO TRY.
SOB

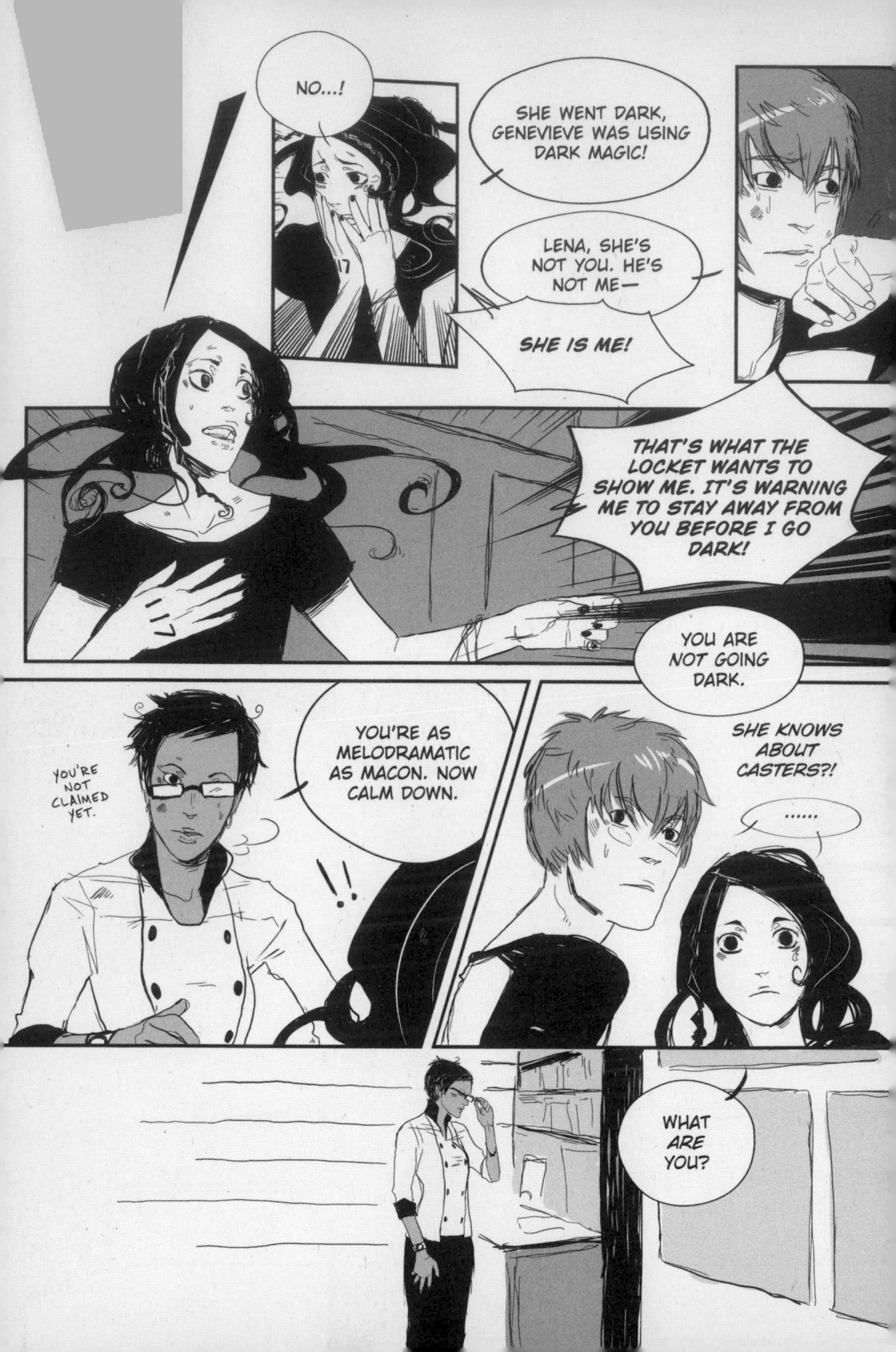
NO...!
SHE WENT DARK, GENEVIEVE WAS USING DARK MAGIC!
LENA, SHE'S NOT YOU. HE'S NOT ME—
SHE IS ME!
THAT'S WHAT THE LOCKET WANTS TO SHOW ME. IT'S WARNING ME TO STAY AWAY FROM YOU BEFORE I GO DARK!
YOU ARE NOT GOING DARK.
YOU'RE NOT CLAIMED YET.
YOU'RE AS MELODRAMATIC AS MACON. NOW CALM DOWN.
!!
SHE KNOWS ABOUT CASTERS?!
......
WHAT ARE YOU?

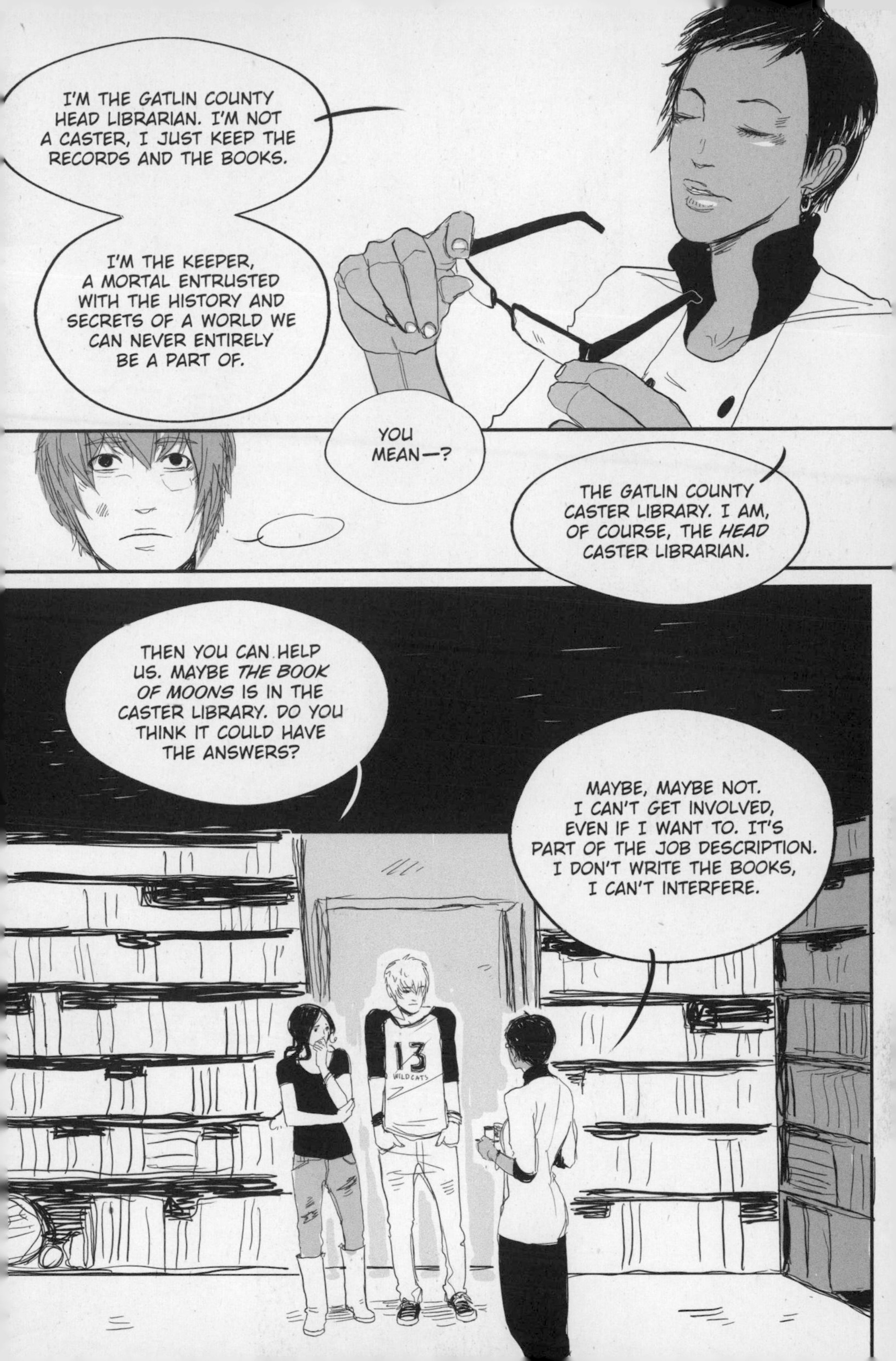
I'M THE GATLIN COUNTY HEAD LIBRARIAN. I'M NOT A CASTER, I JUST KEEP THE RECORDS AND THE BOOKS.
I'M THE KEEPER, A MORTAL ENTRUSTED WITH THE HISTORY AND SECRETS OF A WORLD WE CAN NEVER ENTIRELY BE A PART OF.
YOU MEAN—?
THE GATLIN COUNTY CASTER LIBRARY. I AM, OF COURSE, THE *HEAD* CASTER LIBRARIAN.
THEN YOU CAN HELP US. MAYBE *THE BOOK OF MOONS* IS IN THE CASTER LIBRARY. DO YOU THINK IT COULD HAVE THE ANSWERS?
MAYBE, MAYBE NOT. I CAN'T GET INVOLVED, EVEN IF I WANT TO. IT'S PART OF THE JOB DESCRIPTION. I DON'T WRITE THE BOOKS, I CAN'T INTERFERE.
13
WILDCATS

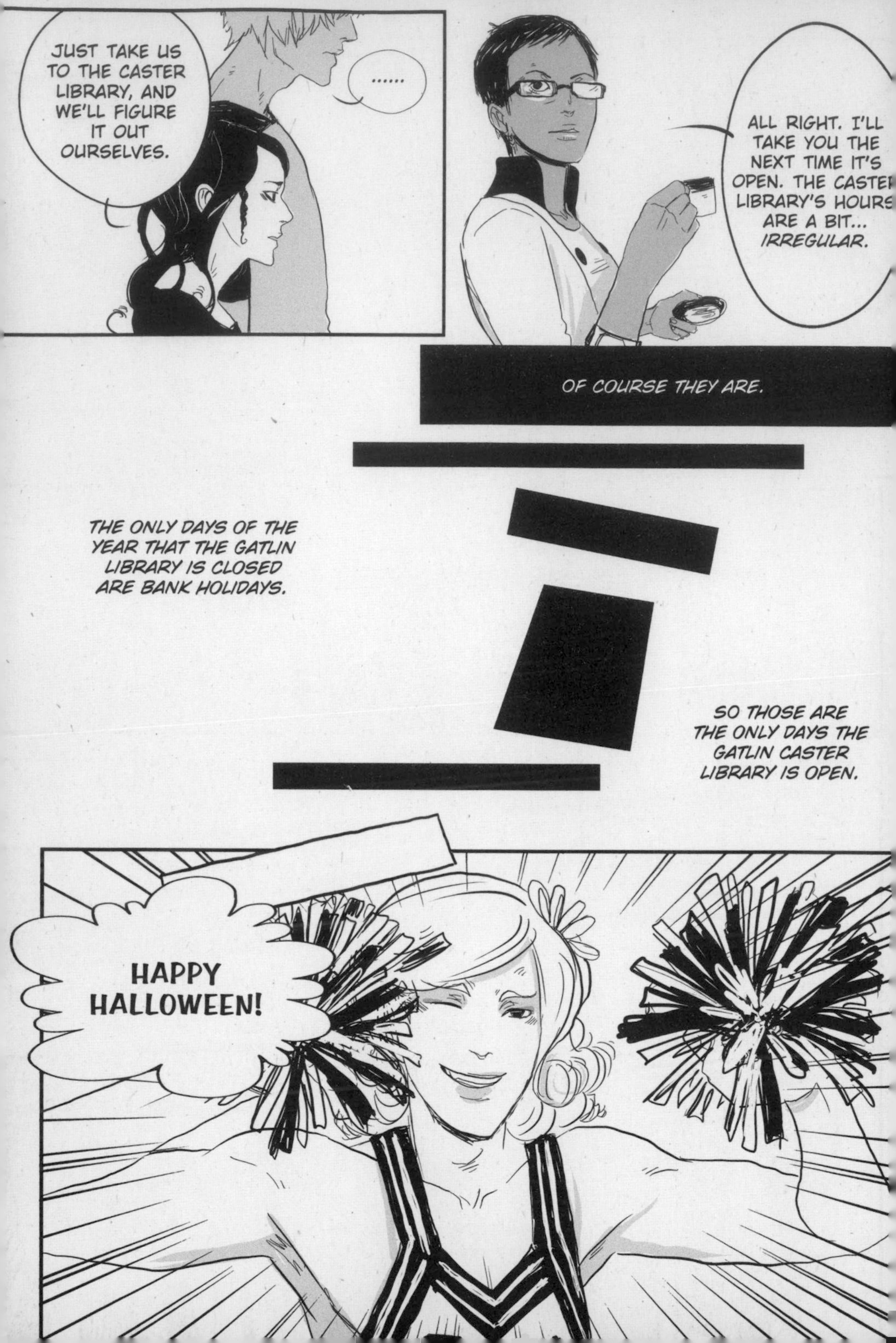
JUST TAKE US TO THE CASTER LIBRARY, AND WE'LL FIGURE IT OUT OURSELVES.
......
ALL RIGHT. I'LL TAKE YOU THE NEXT TIME IT'S OPEN. THE CASTER LIBRARY'S HOURS ARE A BIT... *IRREGULAR.*
OF COURSE THEY ARE.
THE ONLY DAYS OF THE YEAR THAT THE GATLIN LIBRARY IS CLOSED ARE BANK HOLIDAYS.
SO THOSE ARE THE ONLY DAYS THE GATLIN CASTER LIBRARY IS OPEN.
HAPPY HALLOWEEN!

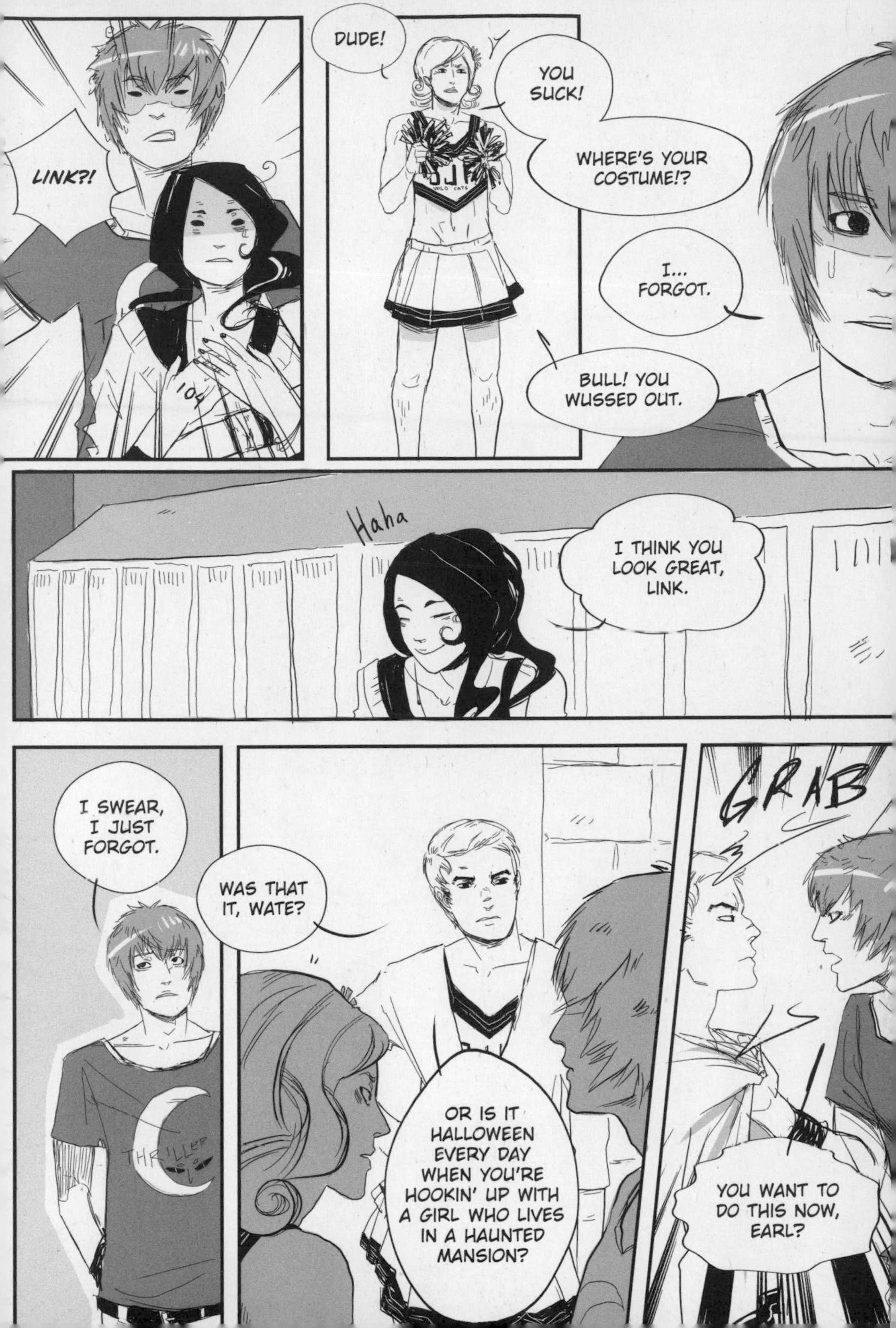

LINK?!
DUDE!
YOU SUCK!
WHERE'S YOUR COSTUME!?
I... FORGOT.
BULL! YOU WUSSED OUT.
Haha
I THINK YOU LOOK GREAT, LINK.
I SWEAR, I JUST FORGOT.
WAS THAT IT, WATE?
OR IS IT HALLOWEEN EVERY DAY WHEN YOU'RE HOOKIN' UP WITH A GIRL WHO LIVES IN A HAUNTED MANSION?
GRAB
YOU WANT TO DO THIS NOW, EARL?

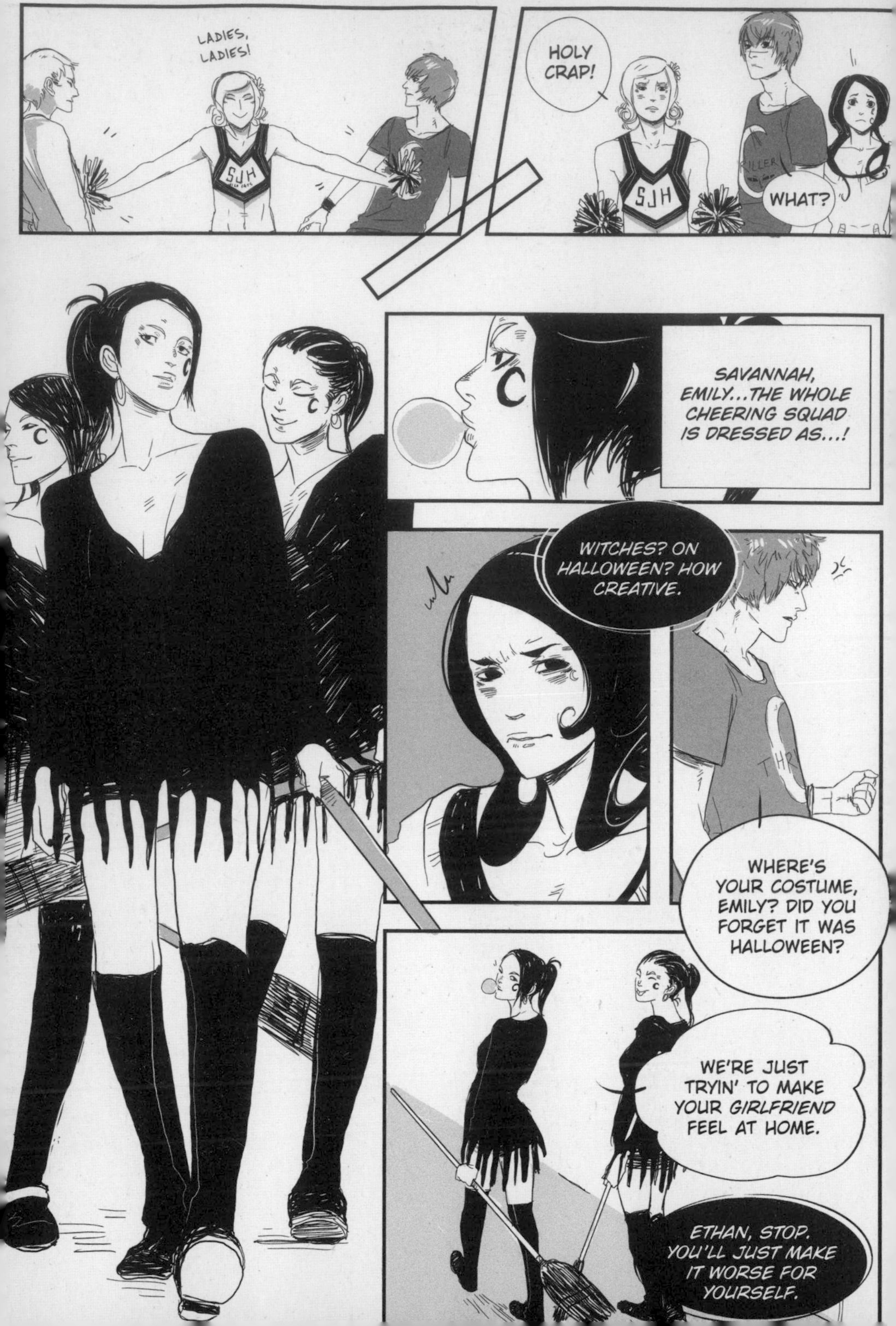

LADIES, LADIES!
HOLY CRAP!
WHAT?
SAVANNAH, EMILY...THE WHOLE CHEERING SQUAD IS DRESSED AS...!
WITCHES? ON HALLOWEEN? HOW CREATIVE.
WHERE'S YOUR COSTUME, EMILY? DID YOU FORGET IT WAS HALLOWEEN?
WE'RE JUST TRYIN' TO MAKE YOUR *GIRLFRIEND* FEEL AT HOME.
ETHAN, STOP. YOU'LL JUST MAKE IT WORSE FOR YOURSELF.

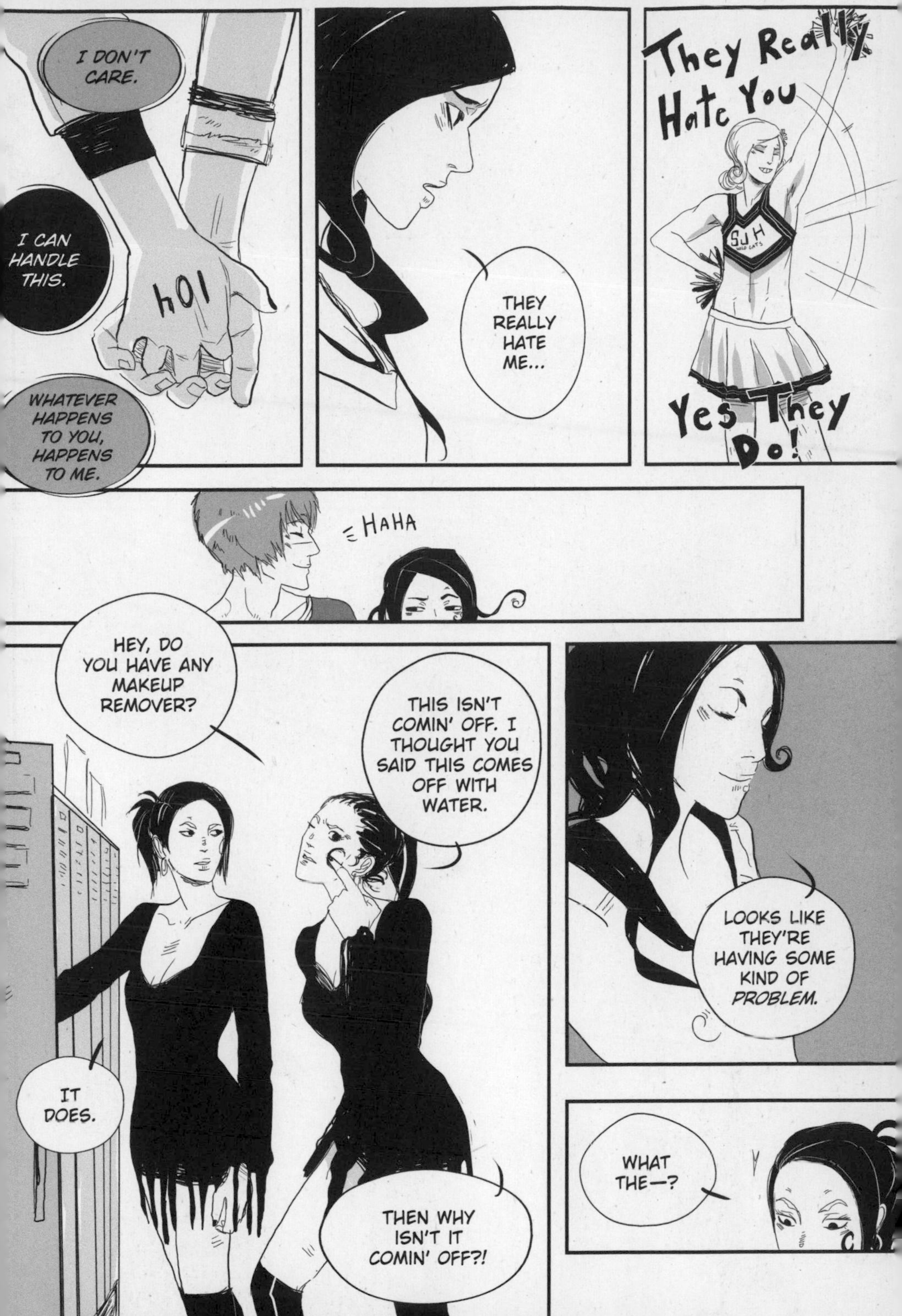
I DON'T CARE.
I CAN HANDLE THIS.
h01
WHATEVER HAPPENS TO YOU, HAPPENS TO ME.
THEY REALLY HATE ME...
They Really Hate You
SJH
Yes They Do!
HAHA
HEY, DO YOU HAVE ANY MAKEUP REMOVER?
THIS ISN'T COMIN' OFF. I THOUGHT YOU SAID THIS COMES OFF WITH WATER.
IT DOES.
THEN WHY ISN'T IT COMIN' OFF?!
LOOKS LIKE THEY'RE HAVING SOME KIND OF *PROBLEM.*
WHAT THE—?

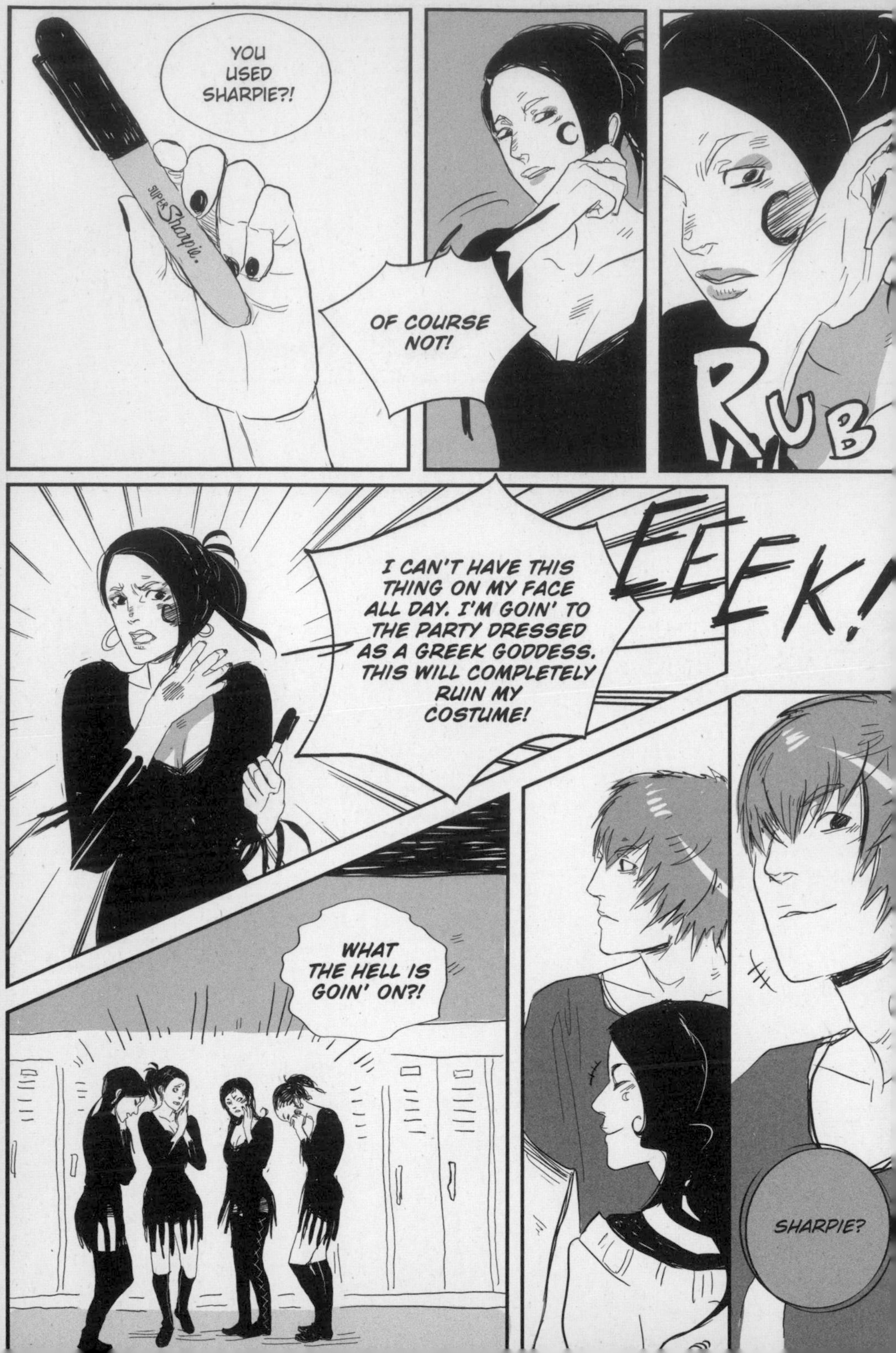
YOU USED SHARPIE?!
SUPER Sharpie.
OF COURSE NOT!
RUB
I CAN'T HAVE THIS THING ON MY FACE ALL DAY. I'M GOIN' TO THE PARTY DRESSED AS A GREEK GODDESS. THIS WILL COMPLETELY RUIN MY COSTUME!
EEEK!
WHAT THE HELL IS GOIN' ON?!
SHARPIE?

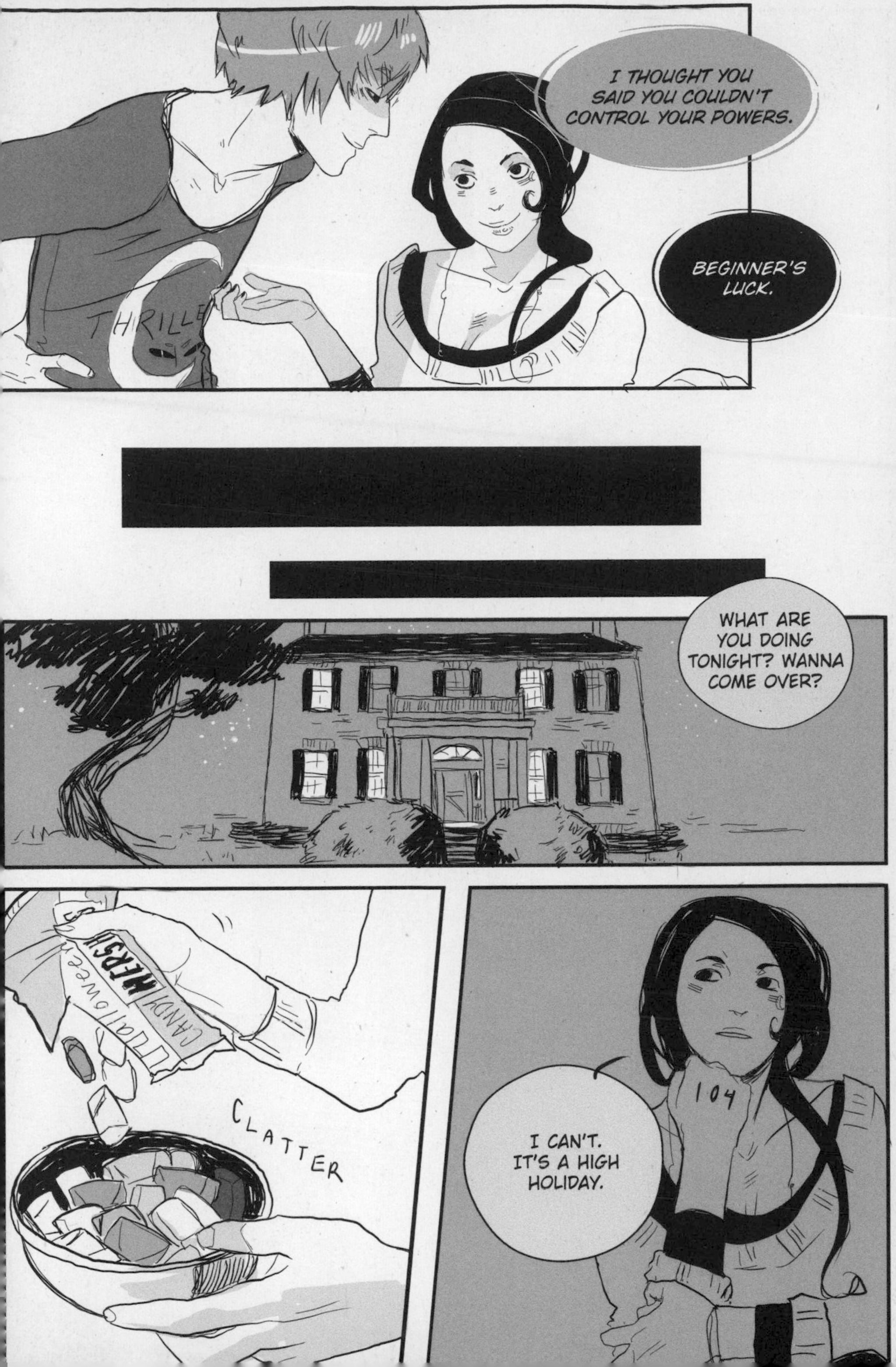
I THOUGHT YOU SAID YOU COULDN'T CONTROL YOUR POWERS.
BEGINNER'S LUCK.
[redacted]
[redacted]
WHAT ARE YOU DOING TONIGHT? WANNA COME OVER?
CANDY
CLATTER
104
I CAN'T. IT'S A HIGH HOLIDAY.

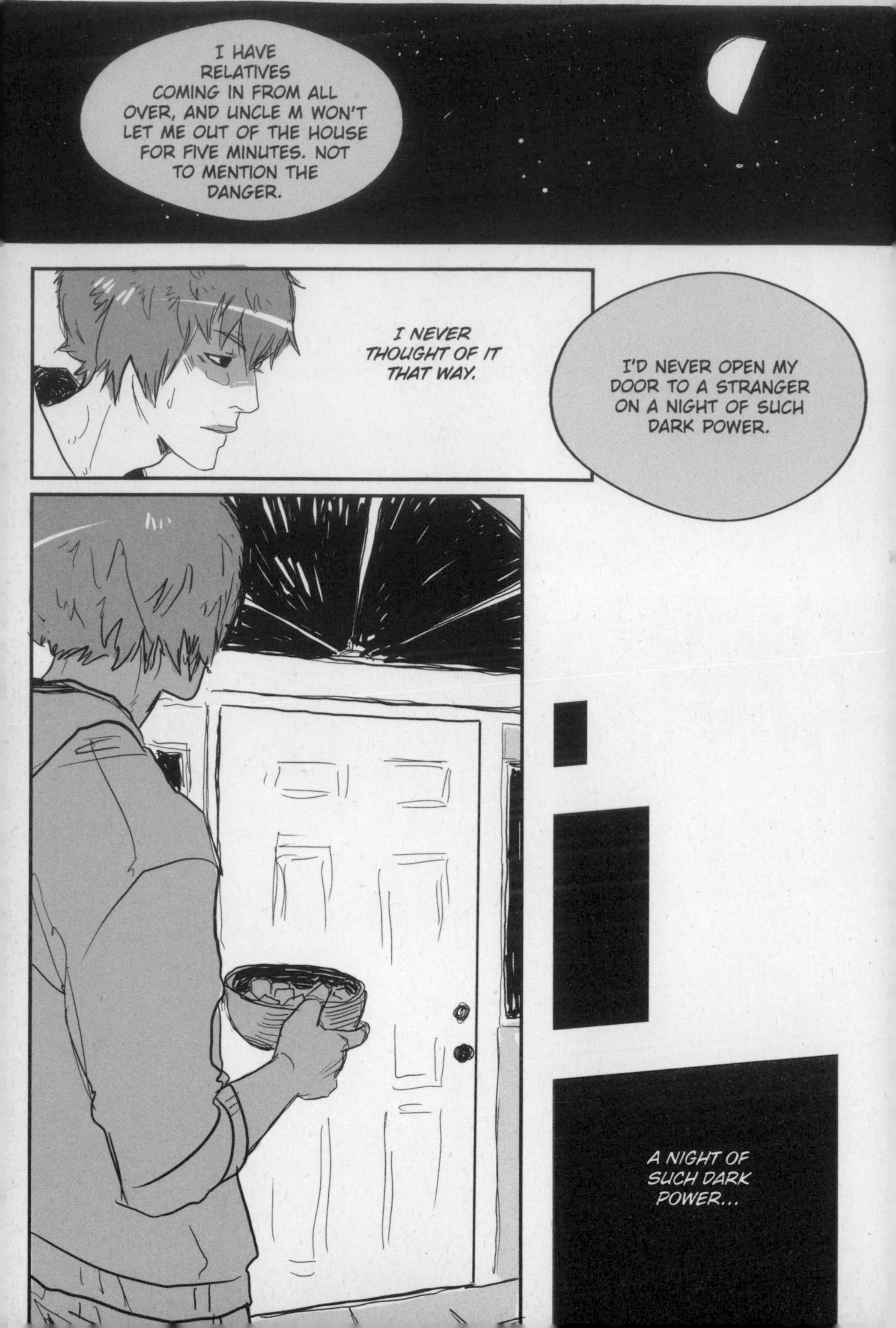
I HAVE RELATIVES COMING IN FROM ALL OVER, AND UNCLE M WON'T LET ME OUT OF THE HOUSE FOR FIVE MINUTES. NOT TO MENTION THE DANGER.
I NEVER THOUGHT OF IT THAT WAY.
I'D NEVER OPEN MY DOOR TO A STRANGER ON A NIGHT OF SUCH DARK POWER.
A NIGHT OF SUCH DARK POWER...

BEAUTIFUL CREATURES

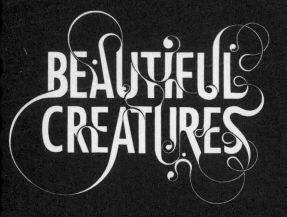

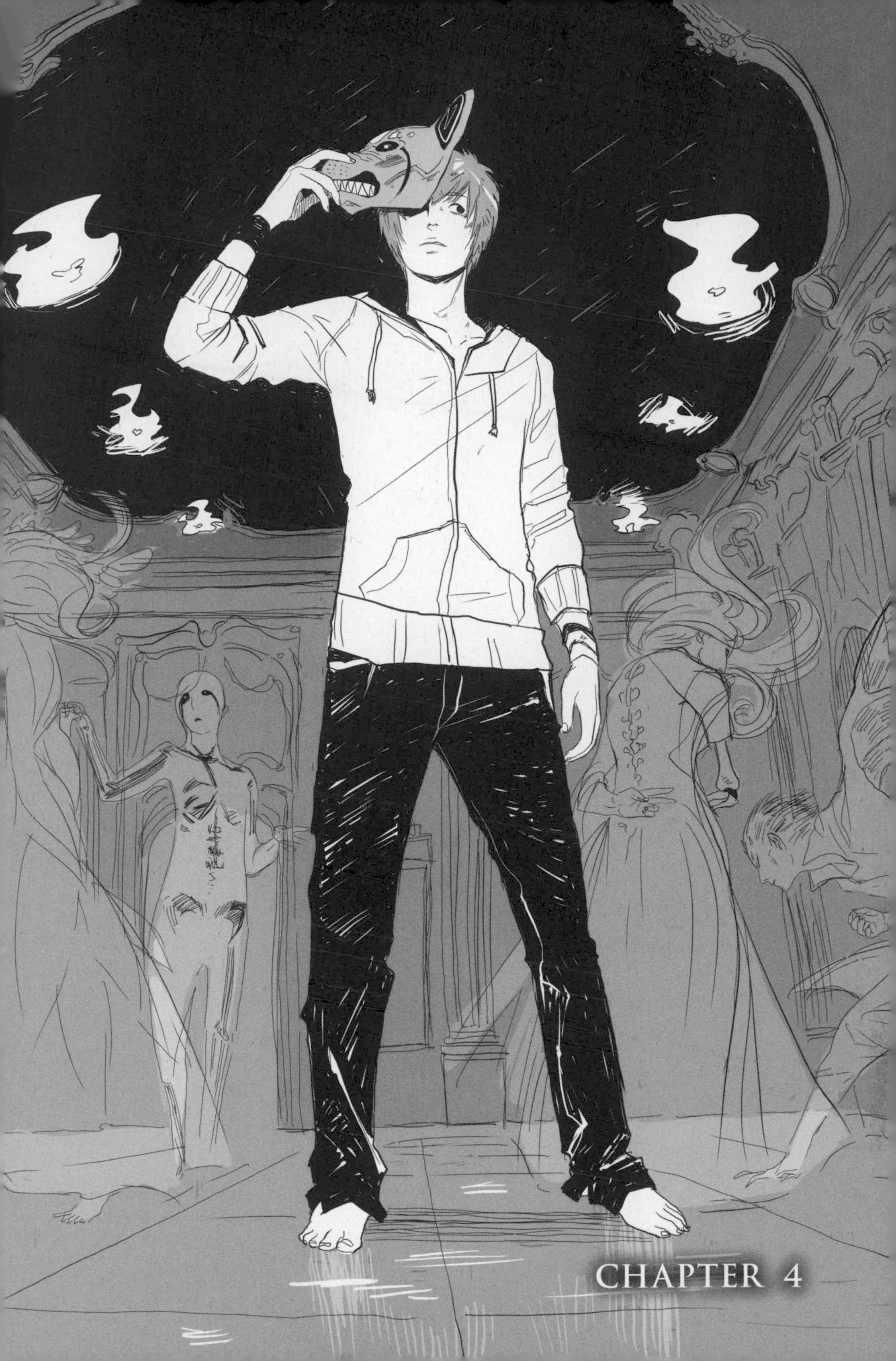

CHAPTER 4

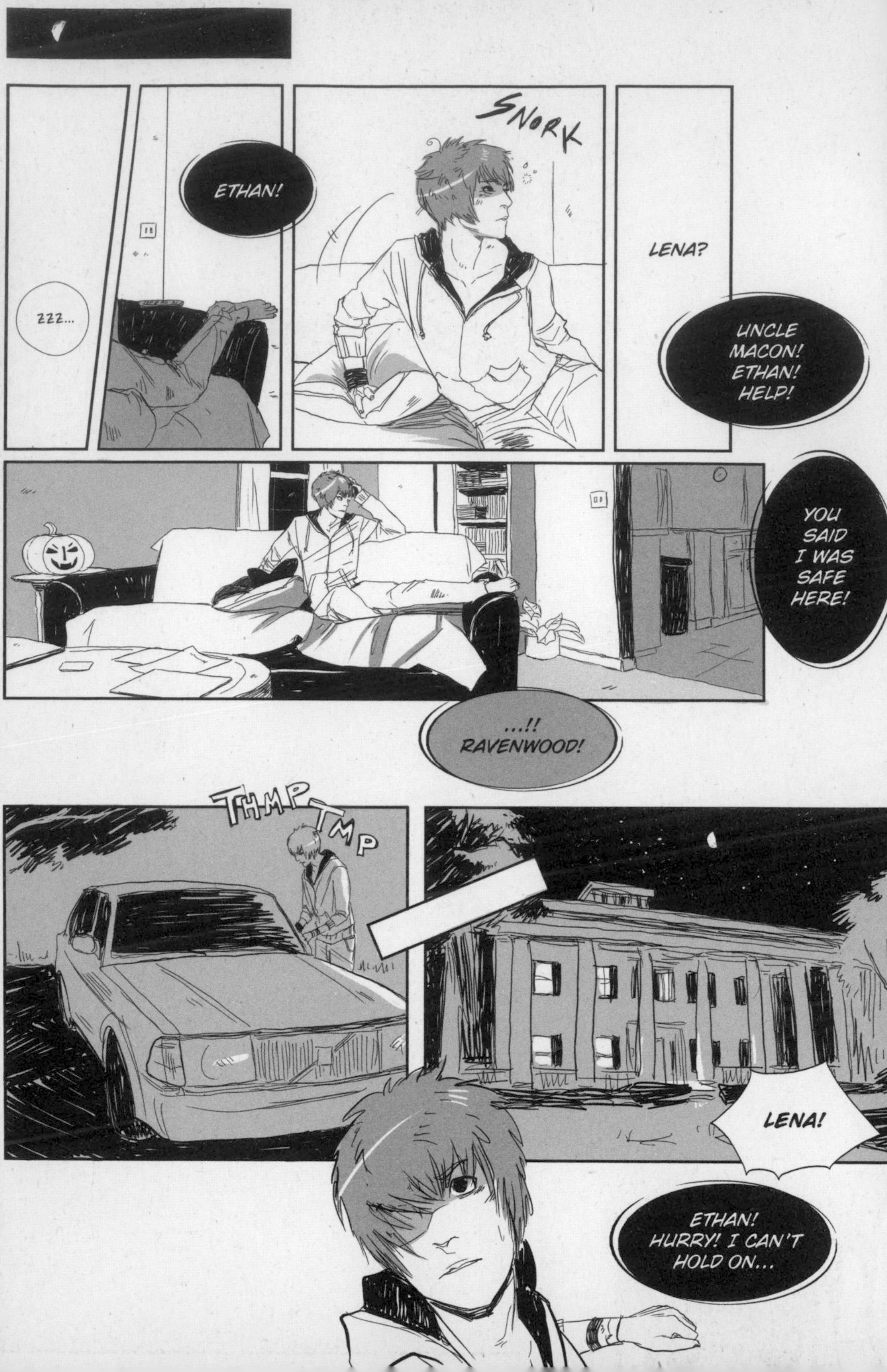

SNORK
ETHAN!
ZZZ...
LENA?
UNCLE MACON! ETHAN! HELP!
YOU SAID I WAS SAFE HERE!
...!! RAVENWOOD!
THMP TMP
LENA!
ETHAN! HURRY! I CAN'T HOLD ON...

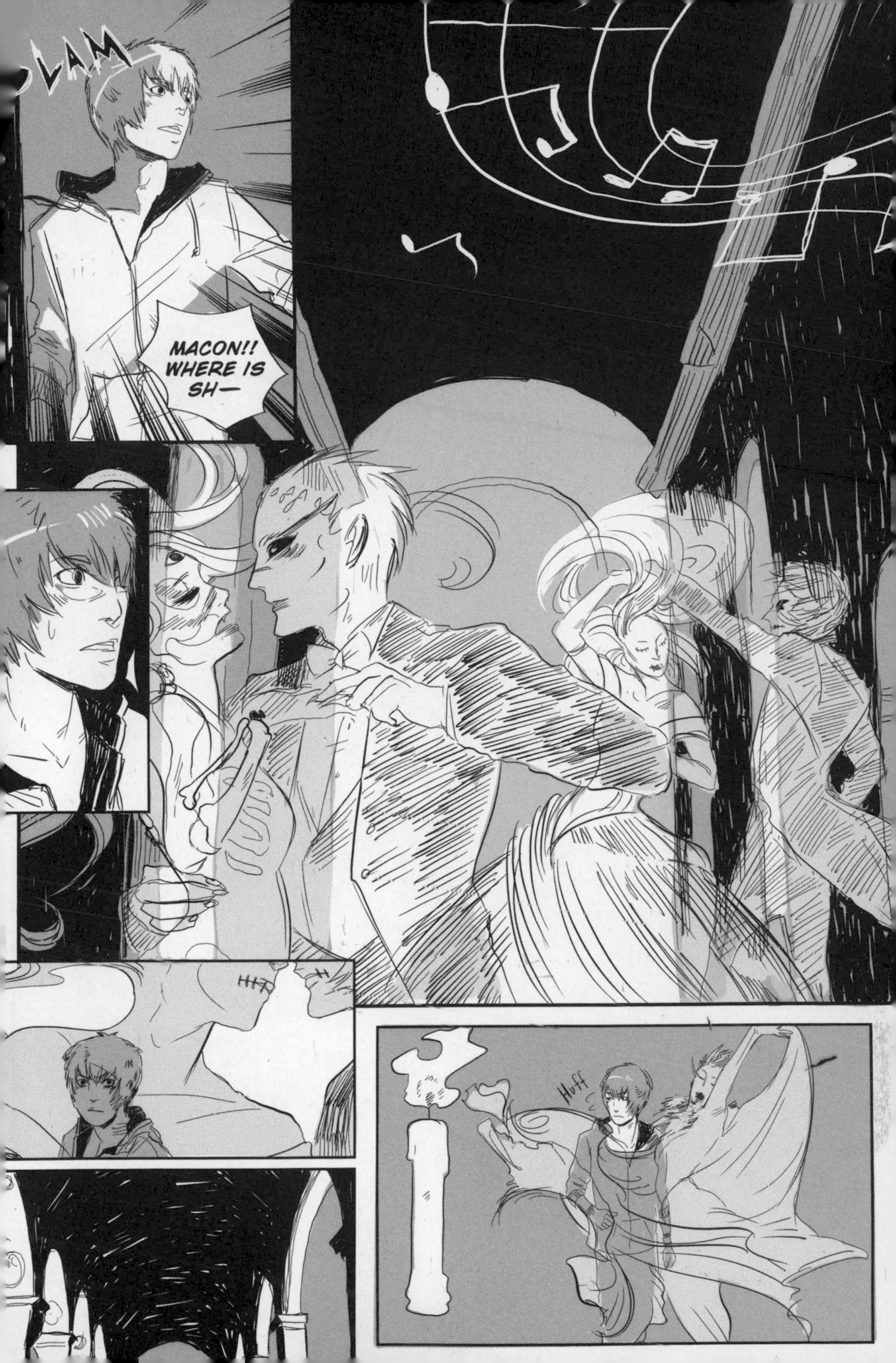
SLAM
MACON!! WHERE IS SH—
Huff

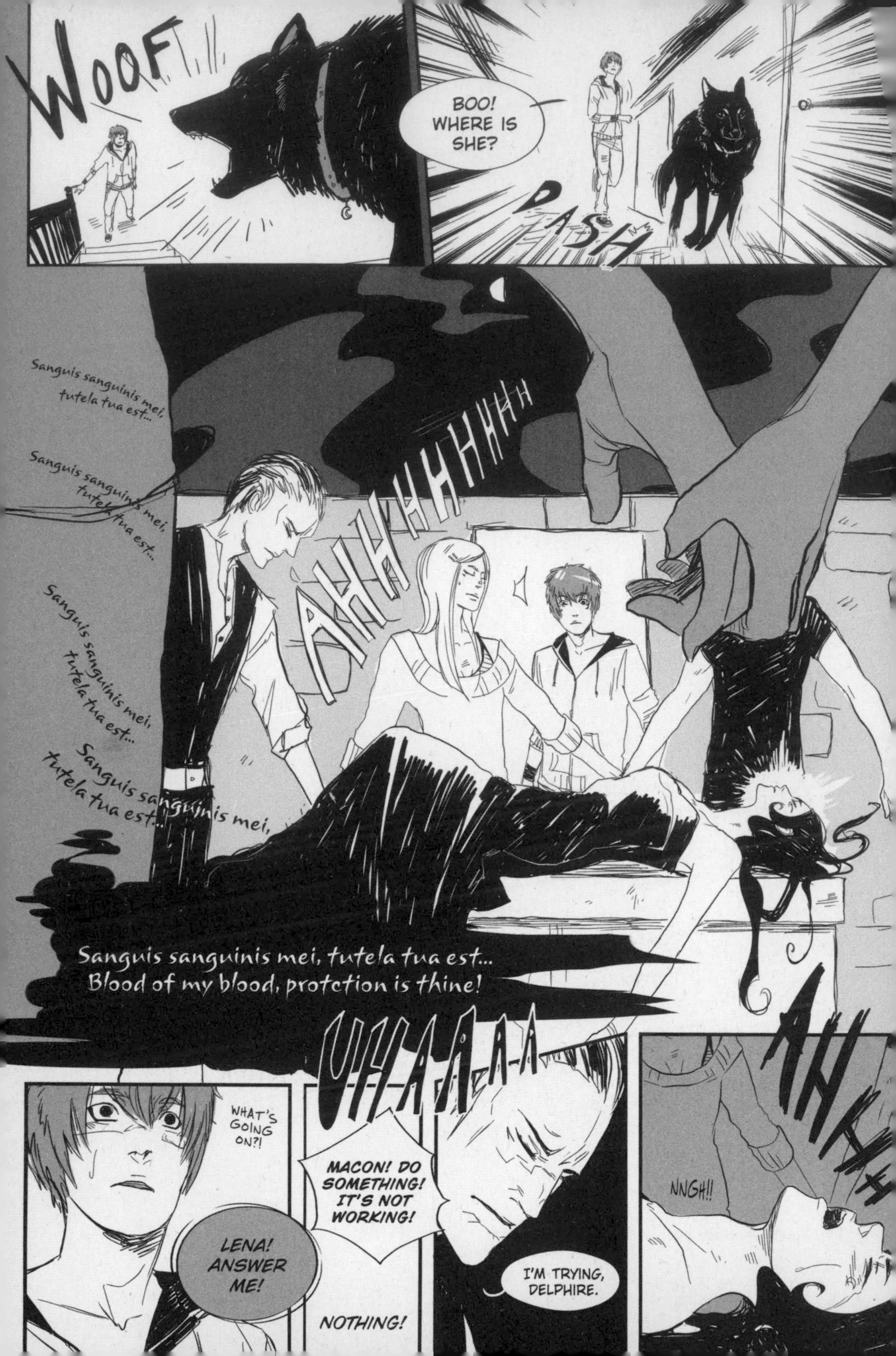
WOOF
BOO! WHERE IS SHE?
DASH
Sanguis sanguinis mei, tutela tua est...
Sanguis sanguinis mei, tutela tua est...
Sanguis sanguinis mei, tutela tua est...
Sanguis sanguinis mei, tutela tua est...
AHHHHHHHHHHHH
Sanguis sanguinis mei, tutela tua est...
Blood of my blood, protection is thine!
UHAAAAAA
WHAT'S GOING ON?!
LENA! ANSWER ME!
MACON! DO SOMETHING! IT'S NOT WORKING!
I'M TRYING, DELPHIRE.
NOTHING!
AHHHH
NNGH!!

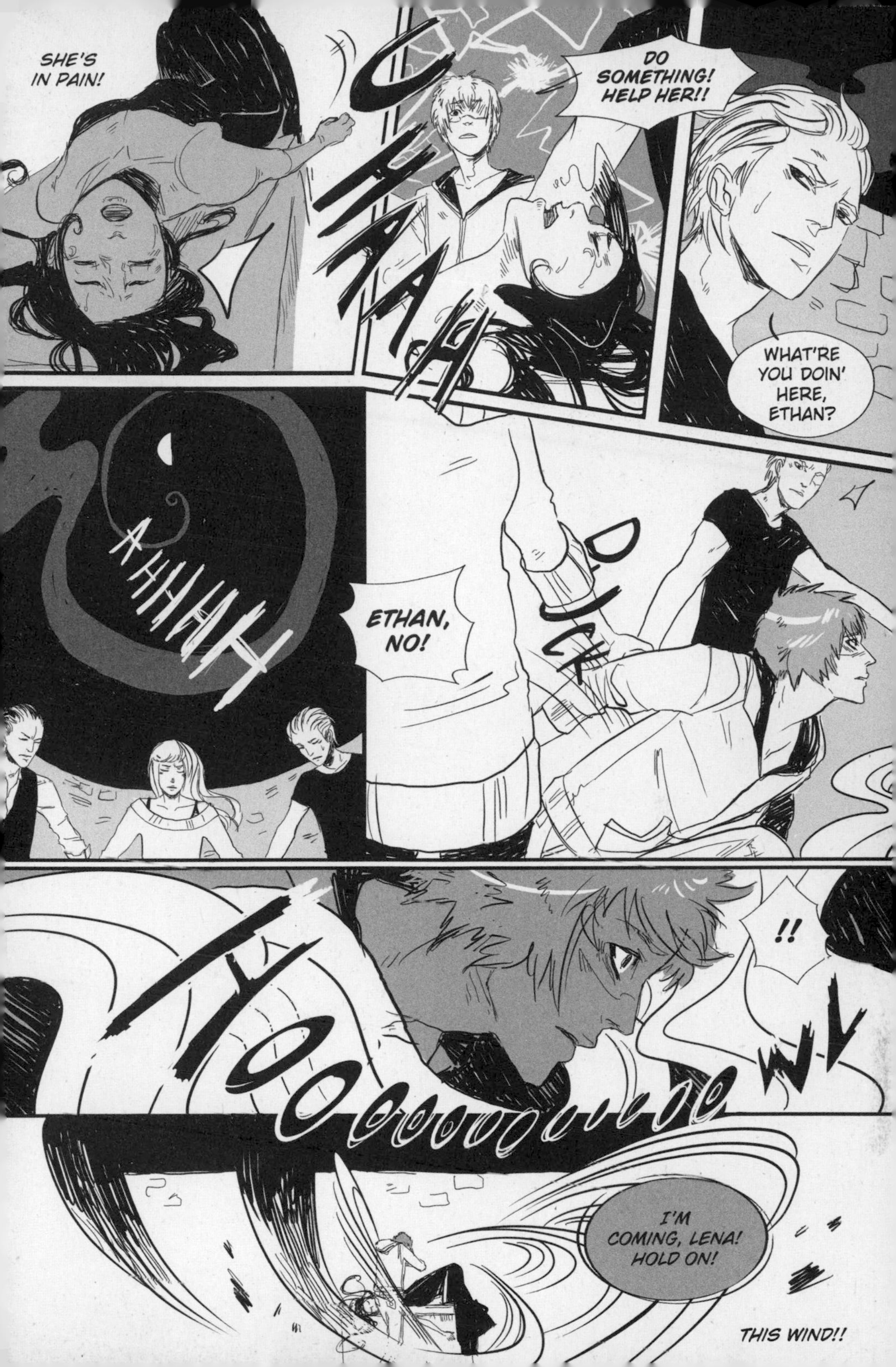
SHE'S IN PAIN!
UHAAH
DO SOMETHING! HELP HER!!
WHAT'RE YOU DOIN' HERE, ETHAN?
AHHAHH
ETHAN, NO!
DUCK
HOOOOOOOOOOOOOW
!!
I'M COMING, LENA! HOLD ON!
THIS WIND!!

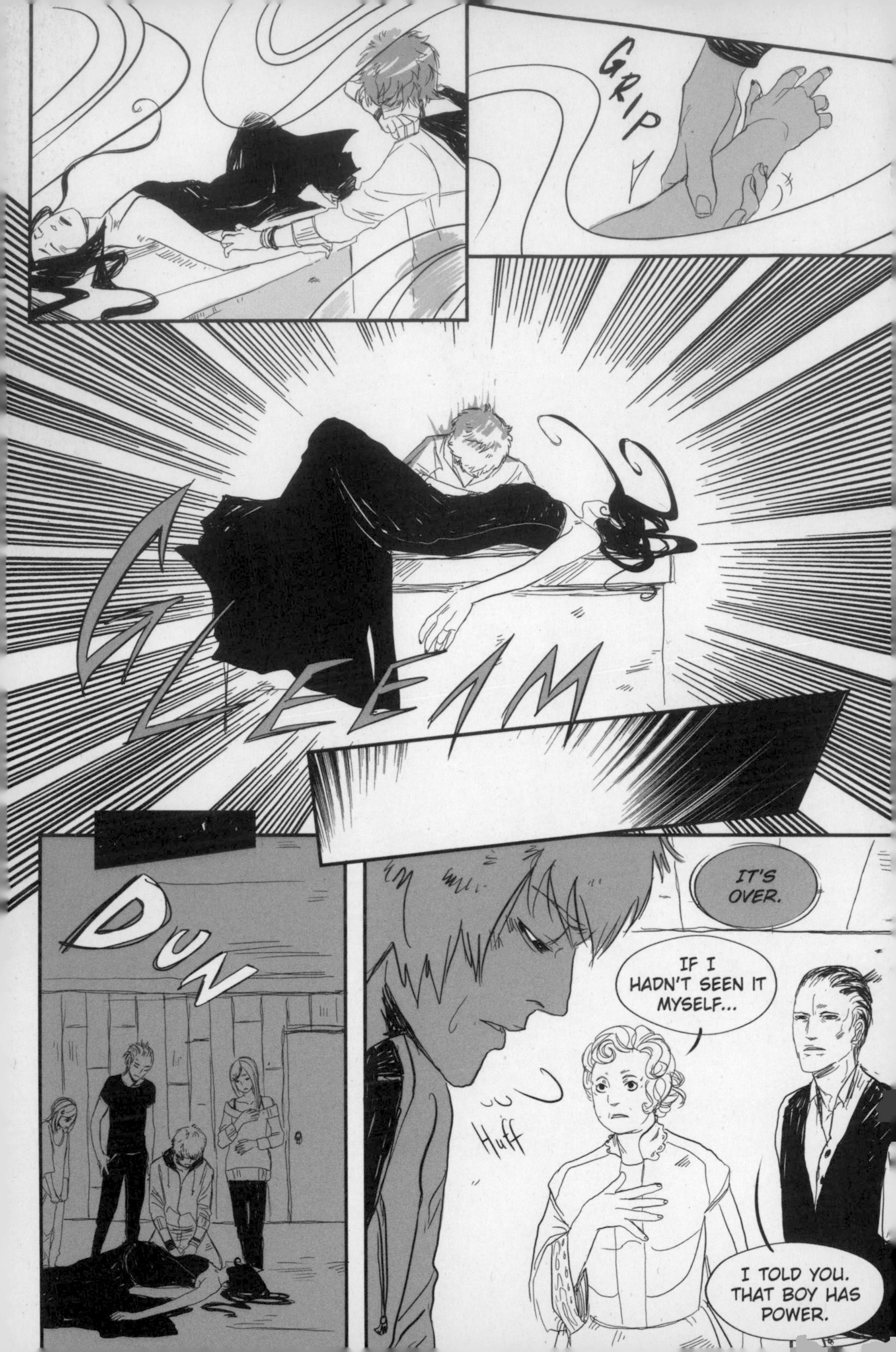
GRIP
GLEEAM
DUN
IT'S OVER.
Huff
IF I HADN'T SEEN IT MYSELF...
I TOLD YOU. THAT BOY HAS POWER.

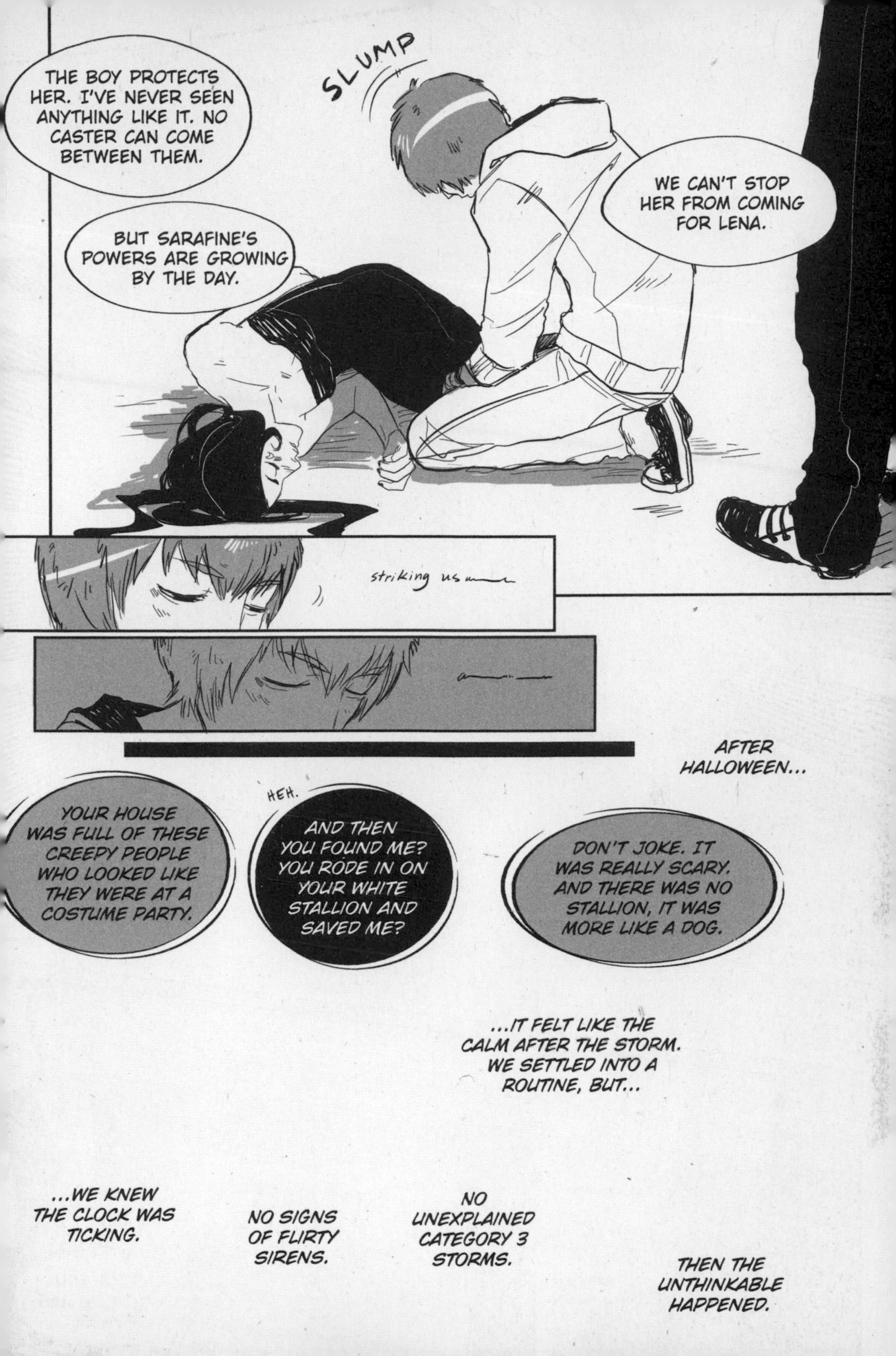
THE BOY PROTECTS HER. I'VE NEVER SEEN ANYTHING LIKE IT. NO CASTER CAN COME BETWEEN THEM.
SLUMP
BUT SARAFINE'S POWERS ARE GROWING BY THE DAY.
WE CAN'T STOP HER FROM COMING FOR LENA.
striking us
AFTER HALLOWEEN...
YOUR HOUSE WAS FULL OF THESE CREEPY PEOPLE WHO LOOKED LIKE THEY WERE AT A COSTUME PARTY.
HEH.
AND THEN YOU FOUND ME? YOU RODE IN ON YOUR WHITE STALLION AND SAVED ME?
DON'T JOKE. IT WAS REALLY SCARY. AND THERE WAS NO STALLION, IT WAS MORE LIKE A DOG.
...IT FELT LIKE THE CALM AFTER THE STORM. WE SETTLED INTO A ROUTINE, BUT...
...WE KNEW THE CLOCK WAS TICKING.
NO SIGNS OF FLIRTY SIRENS.
NO UNEXPLAINED CATEGORY 3 STORMS.
THEN THE UNTHINKABLE HAPPENED.

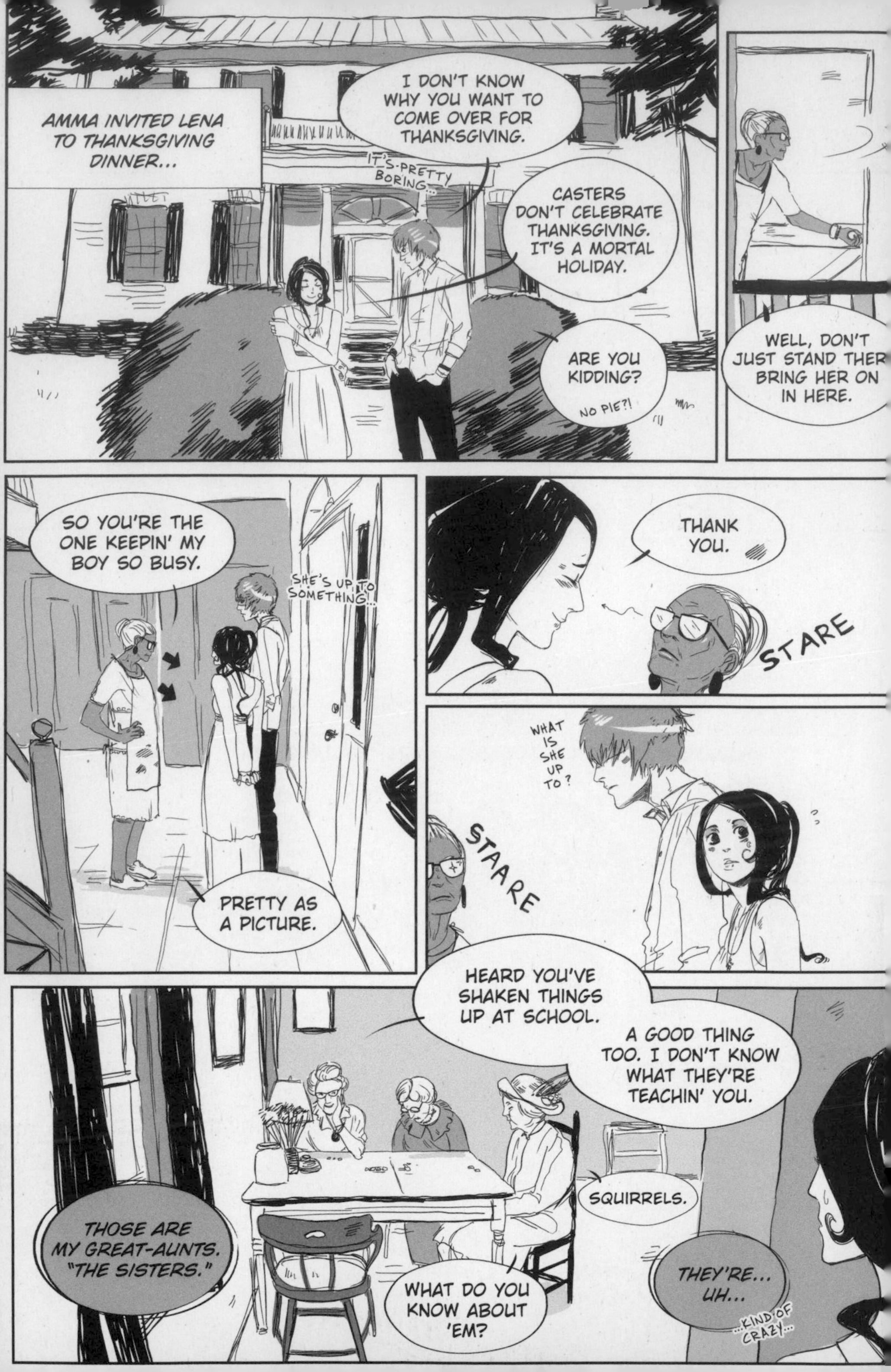
AMMA INVITED LENA TO THANKSGIVING DINNER...
I DON'T KNOW WHY YOU WANT TO COME OVER FOR THANKSGIVING.
IT'S PRETTY BORING...
CASTERS DON'T CELEBRATE THANKSGIVING. IT'S A MORTAL HOLIDAY.
ARE YOU KIDDING?
NO PIE?!
WELL, DON'T JUST STAND THER BRING HER ON IN HERE.
SO YOU'RE THE ONE KEEPIN' MY BOY SO BUSY.
SHE'S UP TO SOMETHING...
PRETTY AS A PICTURE.
THANK YOU.
STARE
WHAT IS SHE UP TO?
STAARE
HEARD YOU'VE SHAKEN THINGS UP AT SCHOOL.
A GOOD THING TOO. I DON'T KNOW WHAT THEY'RE TEACHIN' YOU.
SQUIRRELS.
THOSE ARE MY GREAT-AUNTS. "THE SISTERS."
WHAT DO YOU KNOW ABOUT 'EM?
THEY'RE... UH...
...KIND OF CRAZY...

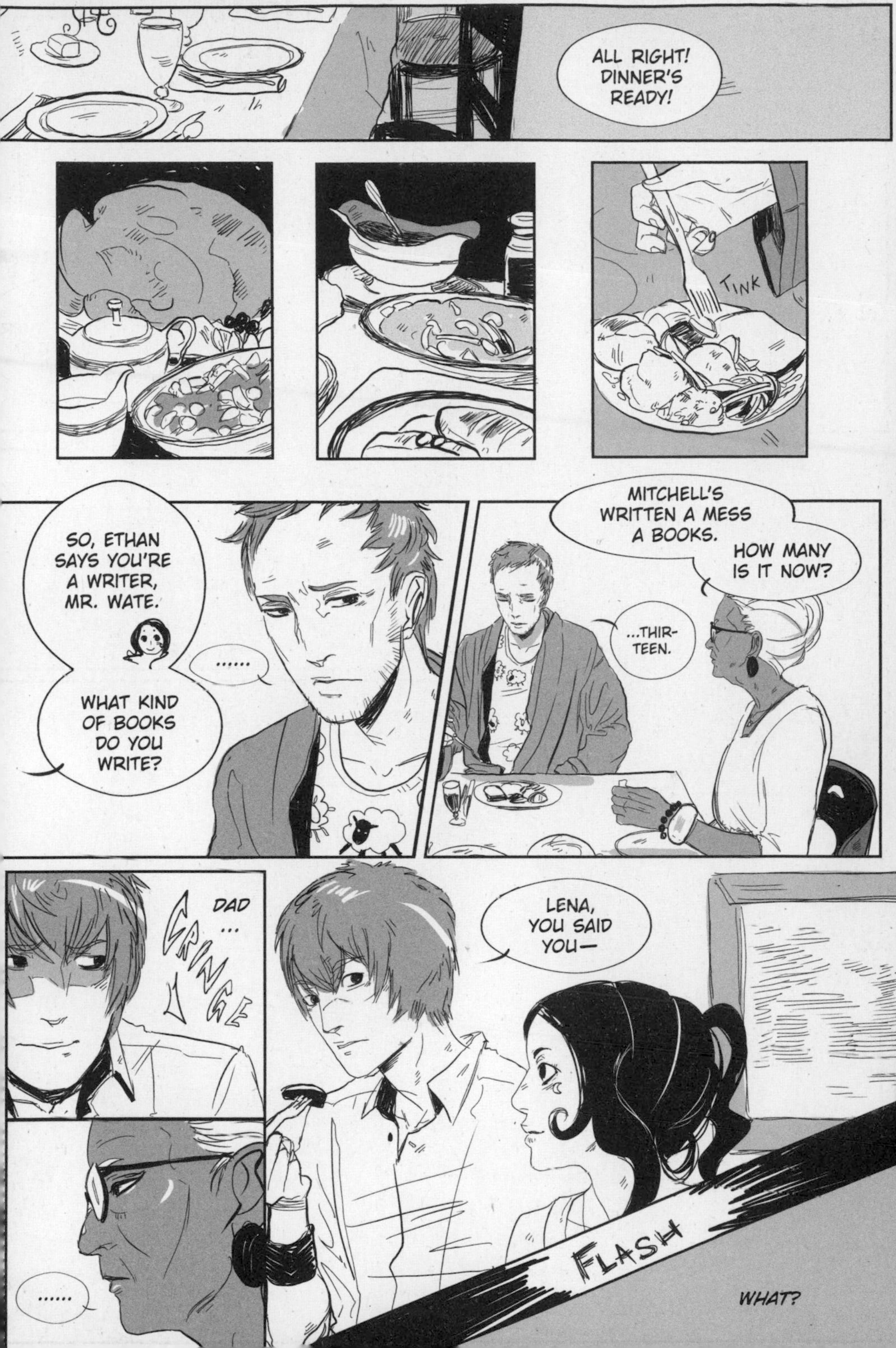
ALL RIGHT! DINNER'S READY!
TINK
SO, ETHAN SAYS YOU'RE A WRITER, MR. WATE.
......
WHAT KIND OF BOOKS DO YOU WRITE?
MITCHELL'S WRITTEN A MESS A BOOKS.
HOW MANY IS IT NOW?
...THIR-TEEN.
DAD ...
CRINGE
LENA, YOU SAID YOU—
......
FLASH
WHAT?

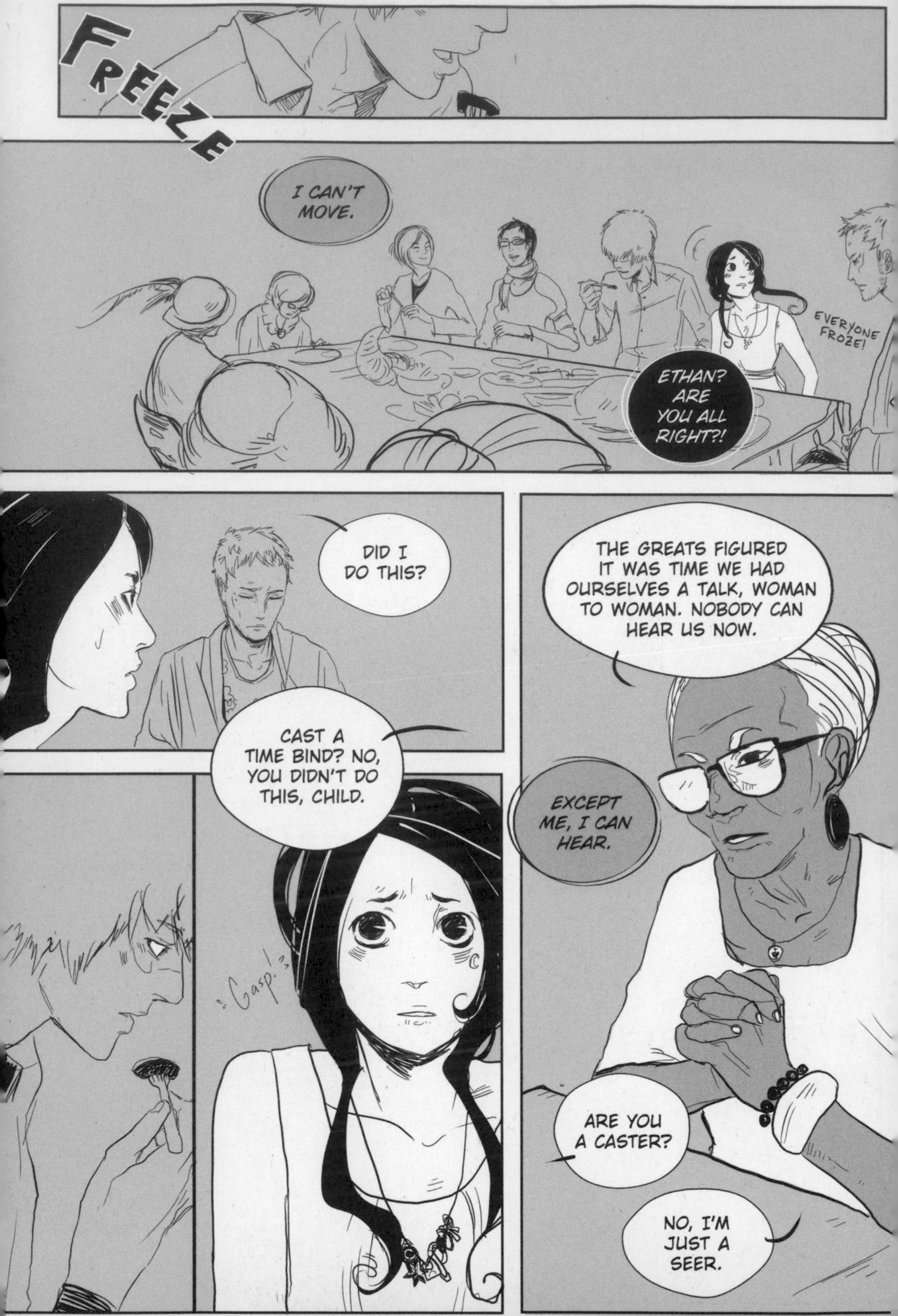
FREEZE
I CAN'T MOVE.
EVERYONE FROZE!
ETHAN? ARE YOU ALL RIGHT?!
DID I DO THIS?
CAST A TIME BIND? NO, YOU DIDN'T DO THIS, CHILD.
Gasp!
THE GREATS FIGURED IT WAS TIME WE HAD OURSELVES A TALK, WOMAN TO WOMAN. NOBODY CAN HEAR US NOW.
EXCEPT ME, I CAN HEAR.
ARE YOU A CASTER?
NO, I'M JUST A SEER.

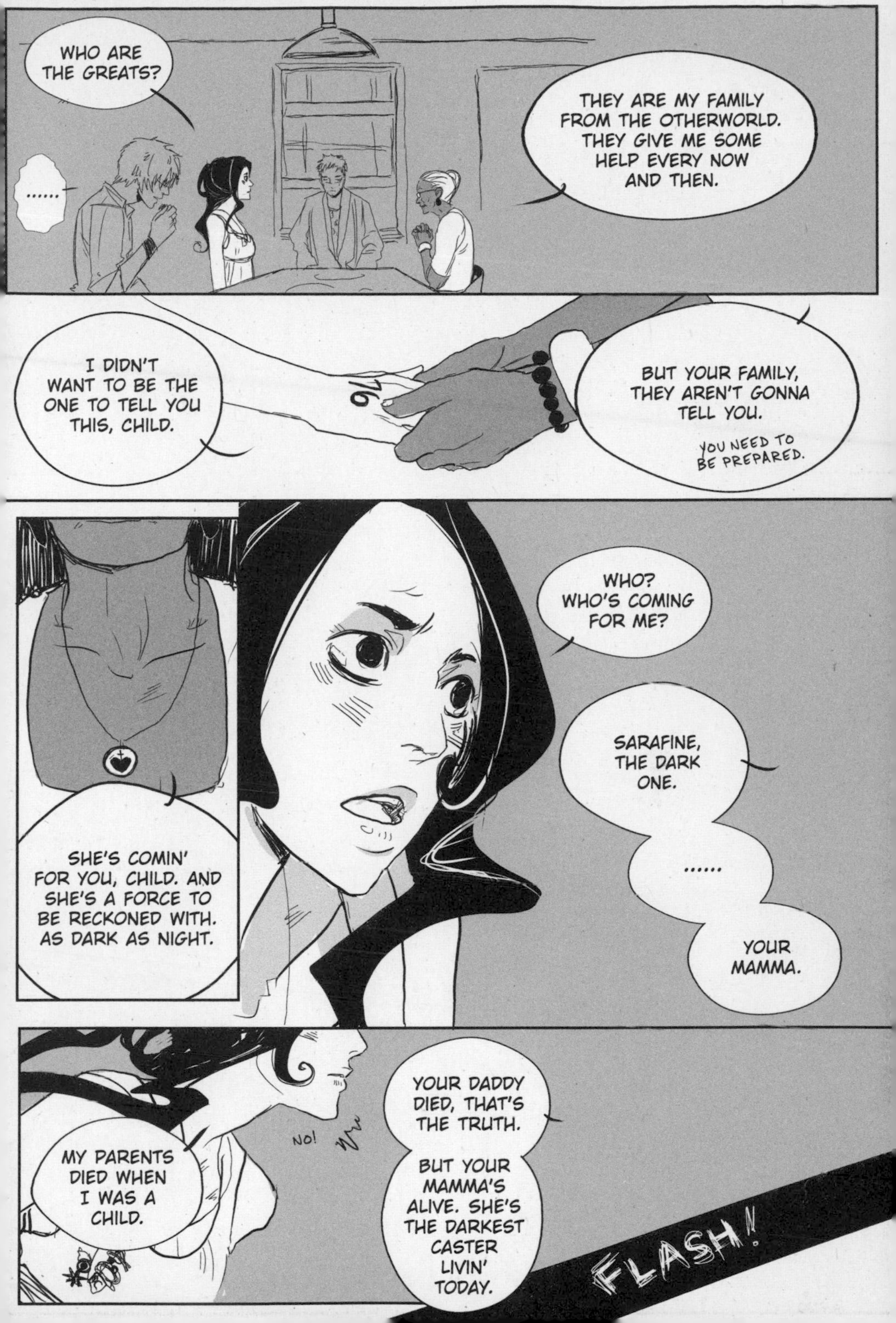
WHO ARE THE GREATS?
......
THEY ARE MY FAMILY FROM THE OTHERWORLD. THEY GIVE ME SOME HELP EVERY NOW AND THEN.
I DIDN'T WANT TO BE THE ONE TO TELL YOU THIS, CHILD.
BUT YOUR FAMILY, THEY AREN'T GONNA TELL YOU.
YOU NEED TO BE PREPARED.
SHE'S COMIN' FOR YOU, CHILD. AND SHE'S A FORCE TO BE RECKONED WITH. AS DARK AS NIGHT.
WHO? WHO'S COMING FOR ME?
SARAFINE, THE DARK ONE.
......
YOUR MAMMA.
MY PARENTS DIED WHEN I WAS A CHILD.
NO!
YOUR DADDY DIED, THAT'S THE TRUTH.
BUT YOUR MAMMA'S ALIVE. SHE'S THE DARKEST CASTER LIVIN' TODAY.
FLASH!

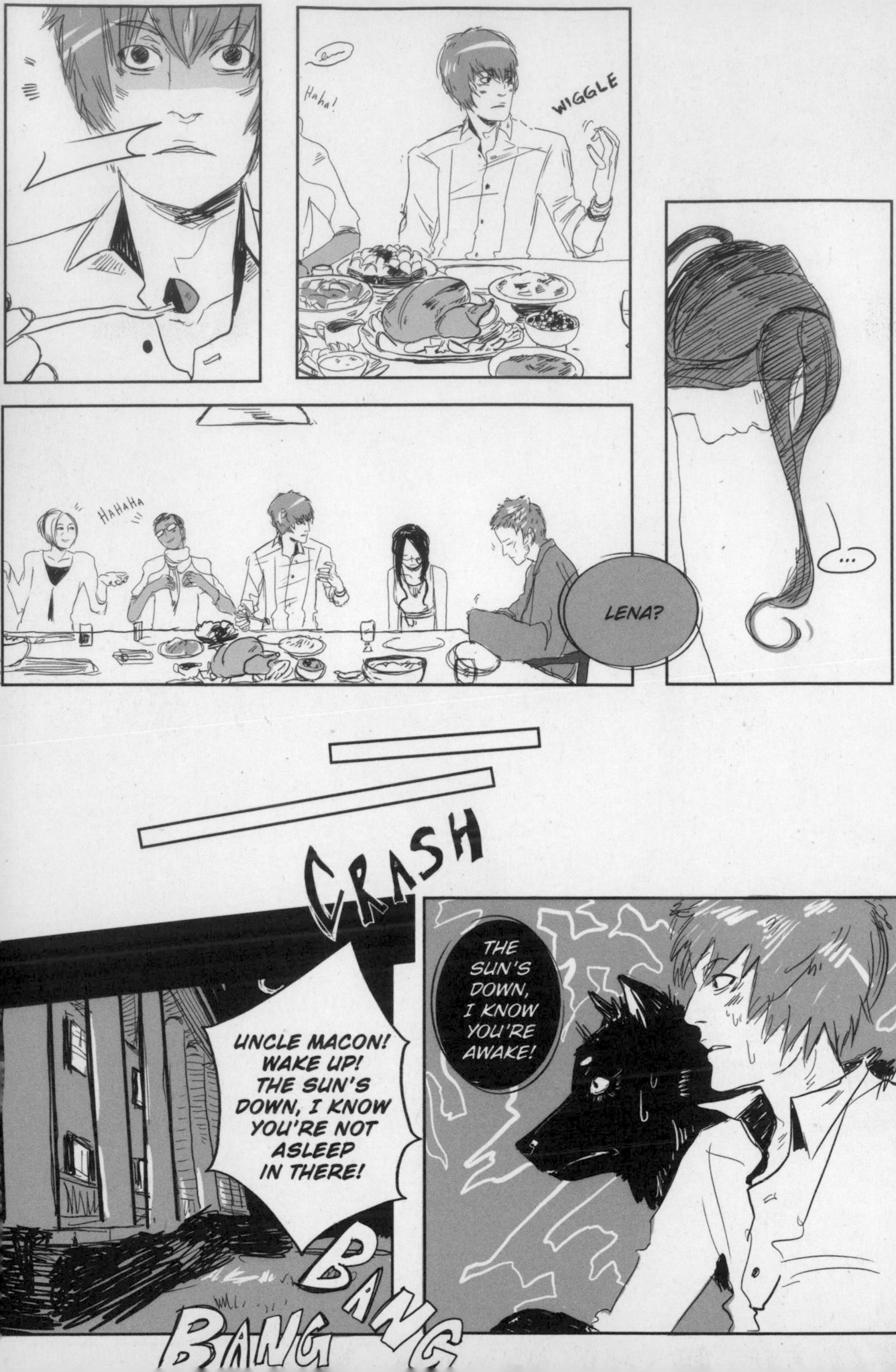
Haha!
WIGGLE
HAHAHA
LENA?
...
CRASH
UNCLE MACON! WAKE UP! THE SUN'S DOWN, I KNOW YOU'RE NOT ASLEEP IN THERE!
BANG
BANG
THE SUN'S DOWN, I KNOW YOU'RE AWAKE!

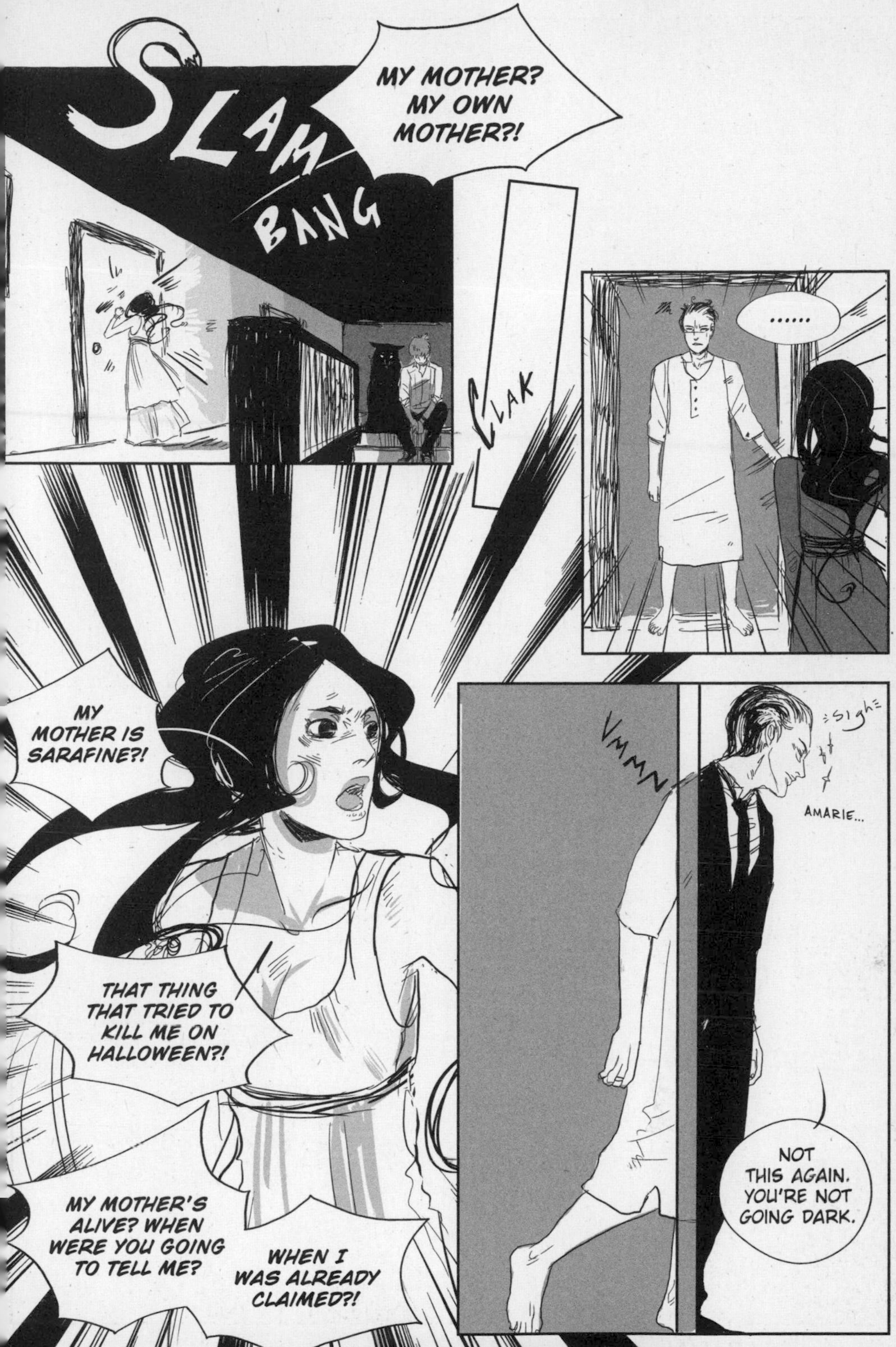
SLAM
BANG
MY MOTHER? MY OWN MOTHER?!
CLAK
....
MY MOTHER IS SARAFINE?!
THAT THING THAT TRIED TO KILL ME ON HALLOWEEN?!
MY MOTHER'S ALIVE? WHEN WERE YOU GOING TO TELL ME?
WHEN I WAS ALREADY CLAIMED?!
VMMMN
SIGH
AMARIE...
NOT THIS AGAIN. YOU'RE NOT GOING DARK.

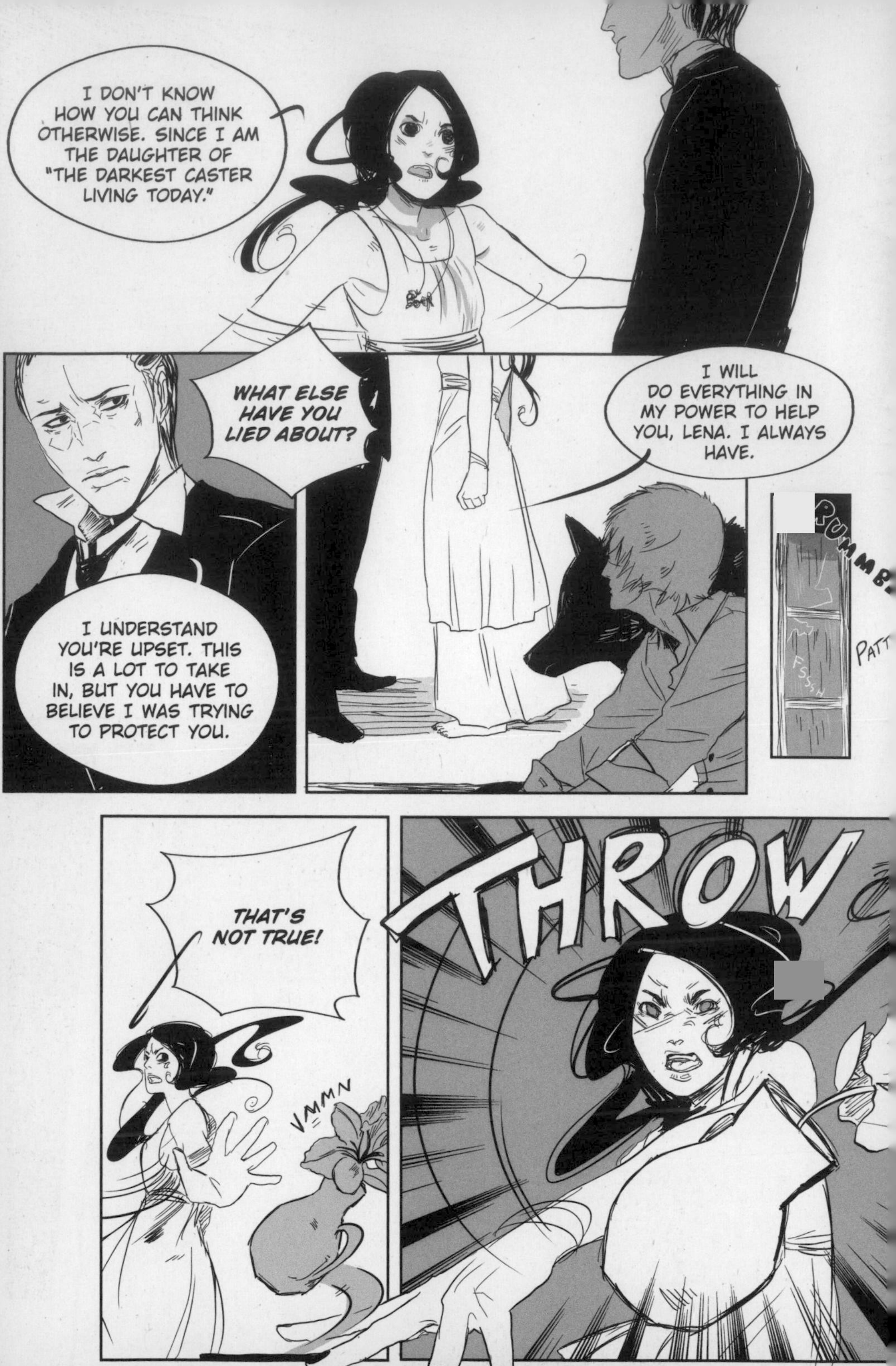
I DON'T KNOW HOW YOU CAN THINK OTHERWISE. SINCE I AM THE DAUGHTER OF "THE DARKEST CASTER LIVING TODAY."
WHAT ELSE HAVE YOU LIED ABOUT?
I UNDERSTAND YOU'RE UPSET. THIS IS A LOT TO TAKE IN, BUT YOU HAVE TO BELIEVE I WAS TRYING TO PROTECT YOU.
I WILL DO EVERYTHING IN MY POWER TO HELP YOU, LENA. I ALWAYS HAVE.
RUMMB
FSSSH
PATT
THAT'S NOT TRUE!
VMMN
THROW

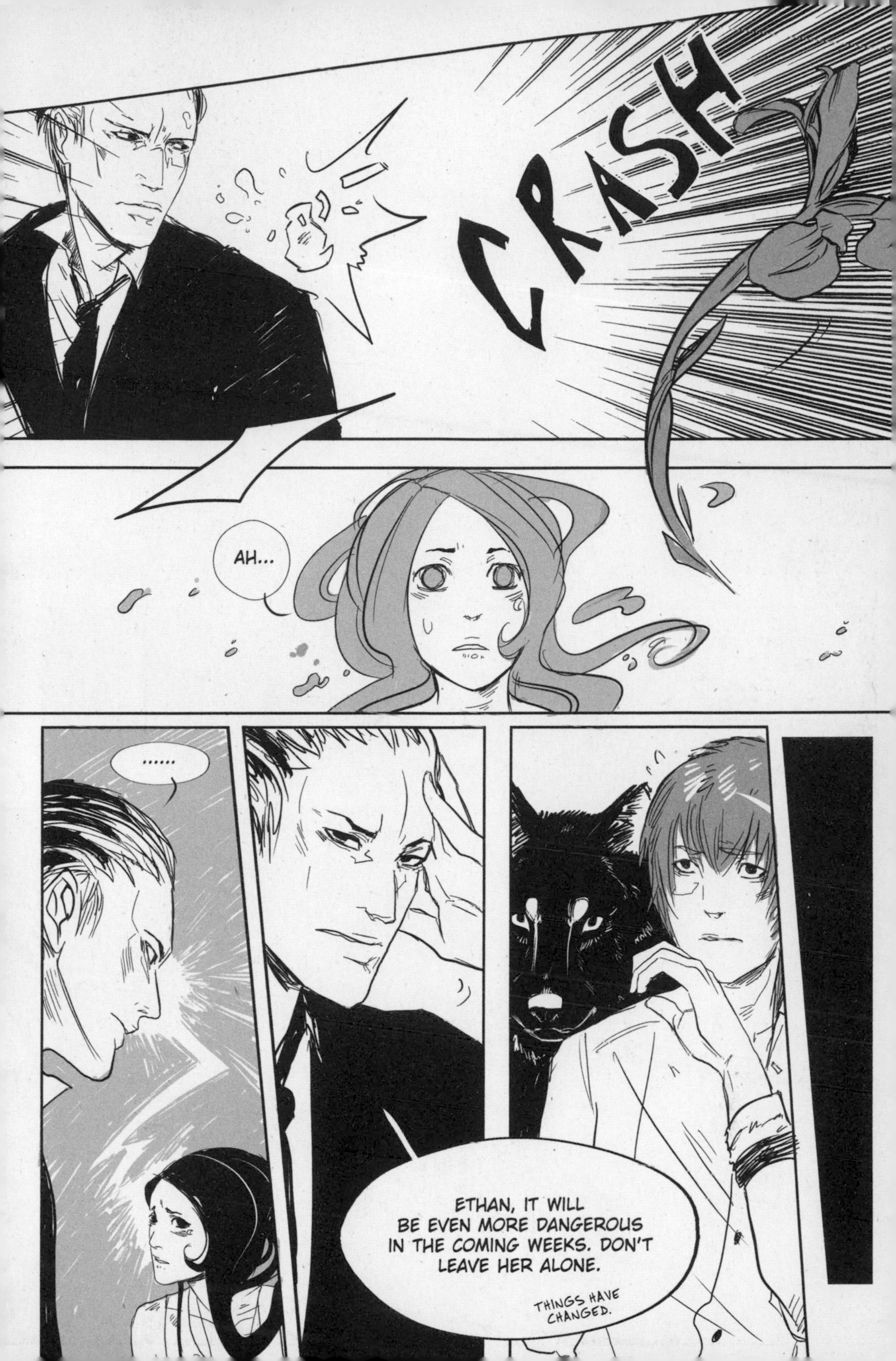
CRASH
AH...
......
ETHAN, IT WILL BE EVEN MORE DANGEROUS IN THE COMING WEEKS. DON'T LEAVE HER ALONE.
THINGS HAVE CHANGED.

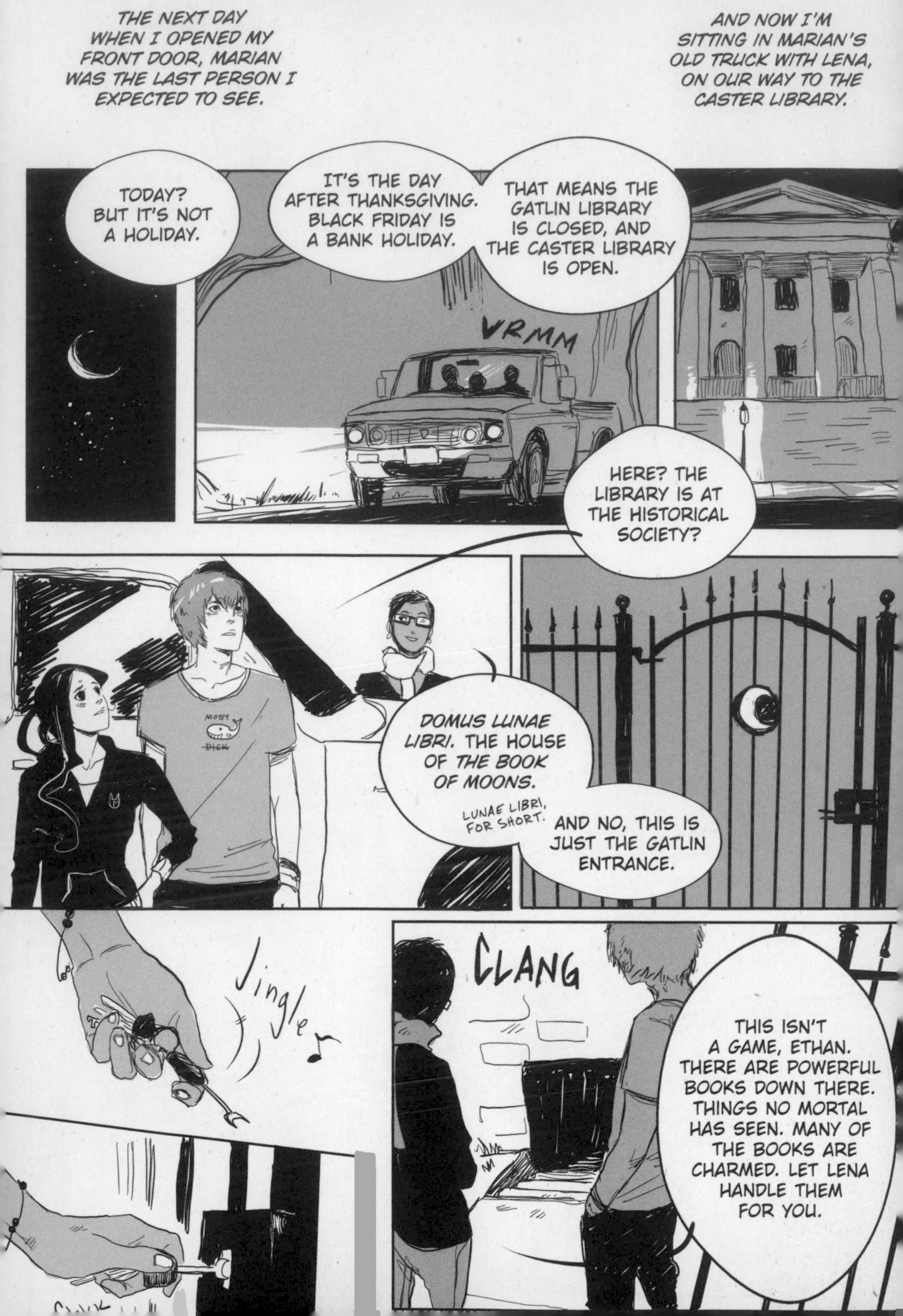
THE NEXT DAY WHEN I OPENED MY FRONT DOOR, MARIAN WAS THE LAST PERSON I EXPECTED TO SEE.
AND NOW I'M SITTING IN MARIAN'S OLD TRUCK WITH LENA, ON OUR WAY TO THE CASTER LIBRARY.
TODAY? BUT IT'S NOT A HOLIDAY.
IT'S THE DAY AFTER THANKSGIVING. BLACK FRIDAY IS A BANK HOLIDAY.
THAT MEANS THE GATLIN LIBRARY IS CLOSED, AND THE CASTER LIBRARY IS OPEN.
VRMM
HERE? THE LIBRARY IS AT THE HISTORICAL SOCIETY?
MOBY DICK
DOMUS LUNAE LIBRI. THE HOUSE OF THE BOOK OF MOONS.
LUNAE LIBRI, FOR SHORT.
AND NO, THIS IS JUST THE GATLIN ENTRANCE.
Jingle
CLANG
THIS ISN'T A GAME, ETHAN. THERE ARE POWERFUL BOOKS DOWN THERE. THINGS NO MORTAL HAS SEEN. MANY OF THE BOOKS ARE CHARMED. LET LENA HANDLE THEM FOR YOU.

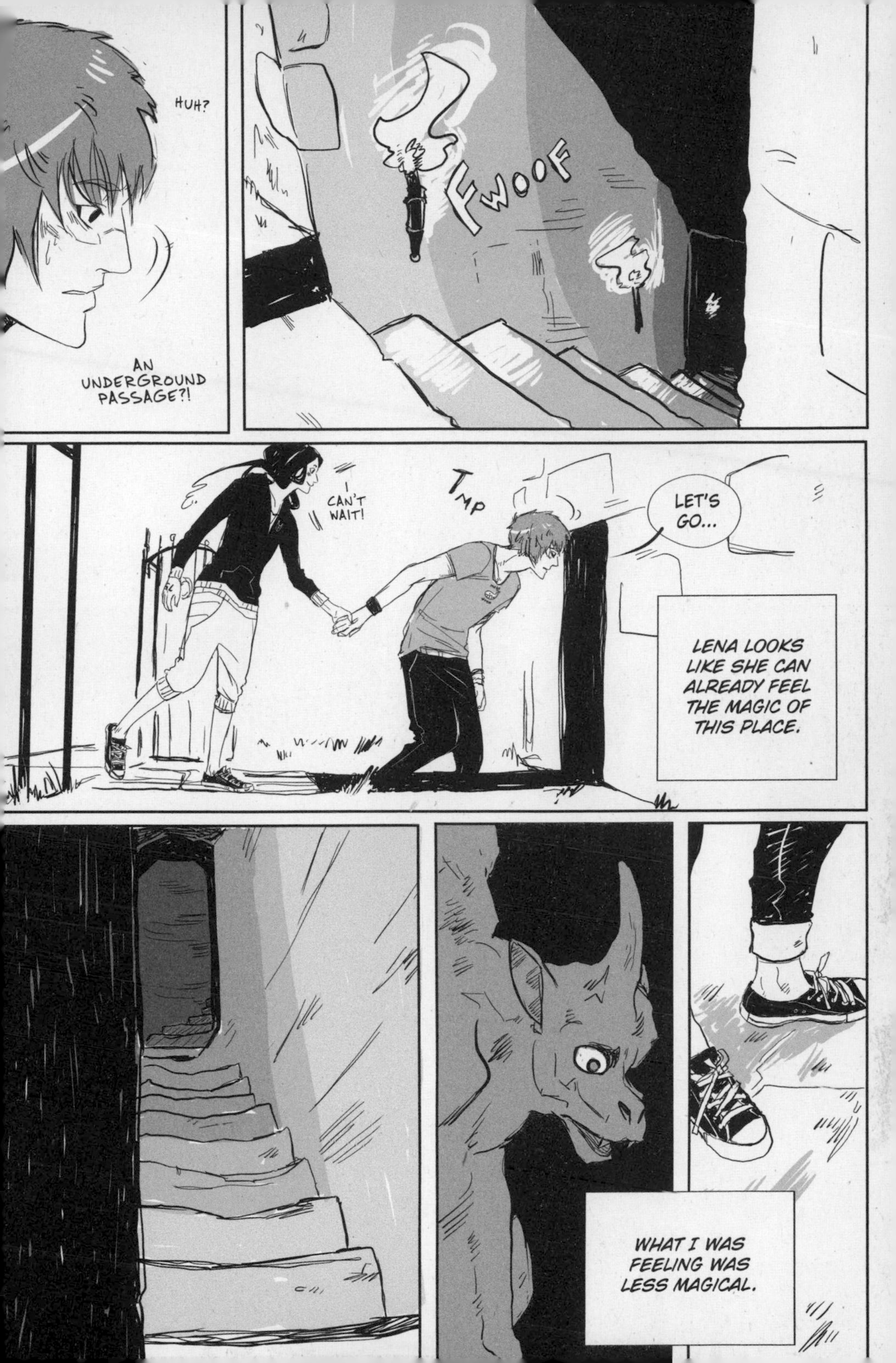
HUH?
AN UNDERGROUND PASSAGE?!
FWOOF
I CAN'T WAIT!
TMP
LET'S GO...
LENA LOOKS LIKE SHE CAN ALREADY FEEL THE MAGIC OF THIS PLACE.
WHAT I WAS FEELING WAS LESS MAGICAL.

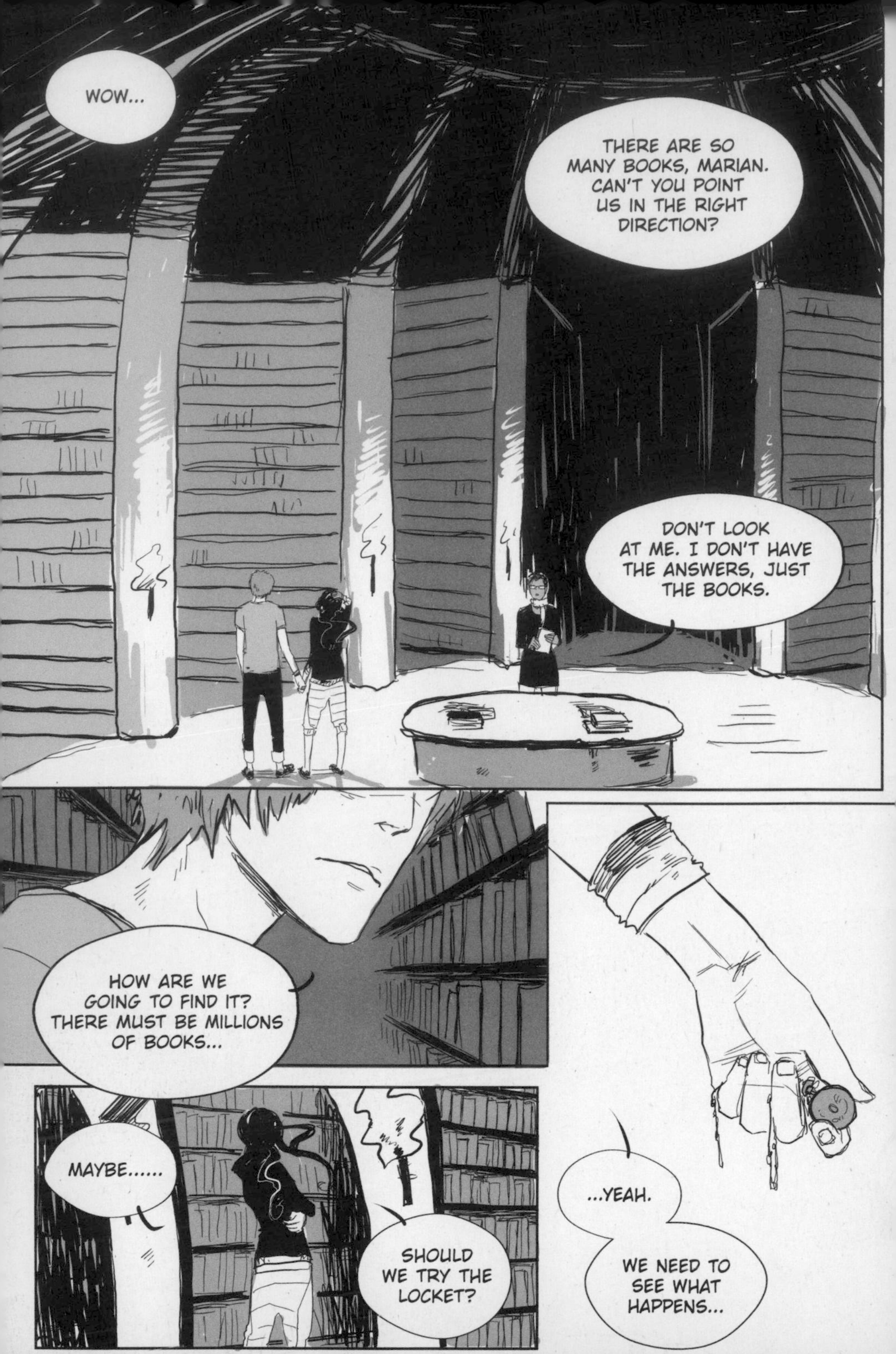
WOW...
THERE ARE SO MANY BOOKS, MARIAN. CAN'T YOU POINT US IN THE RIGHT DIRECTION?
DON'T LOOK AT ME. I DON'T HAVE THE ANSWERS, JUST THE BOOKS.
HOW ARE WE GOING TO FIND IT? THERE MUST BE MILLIONS OF BOOKS...
MAYBE......
SHOULD WE TRY THE LOCKET?
...YEAH.
WE NEED TO SEE WHAT HAPPENS...

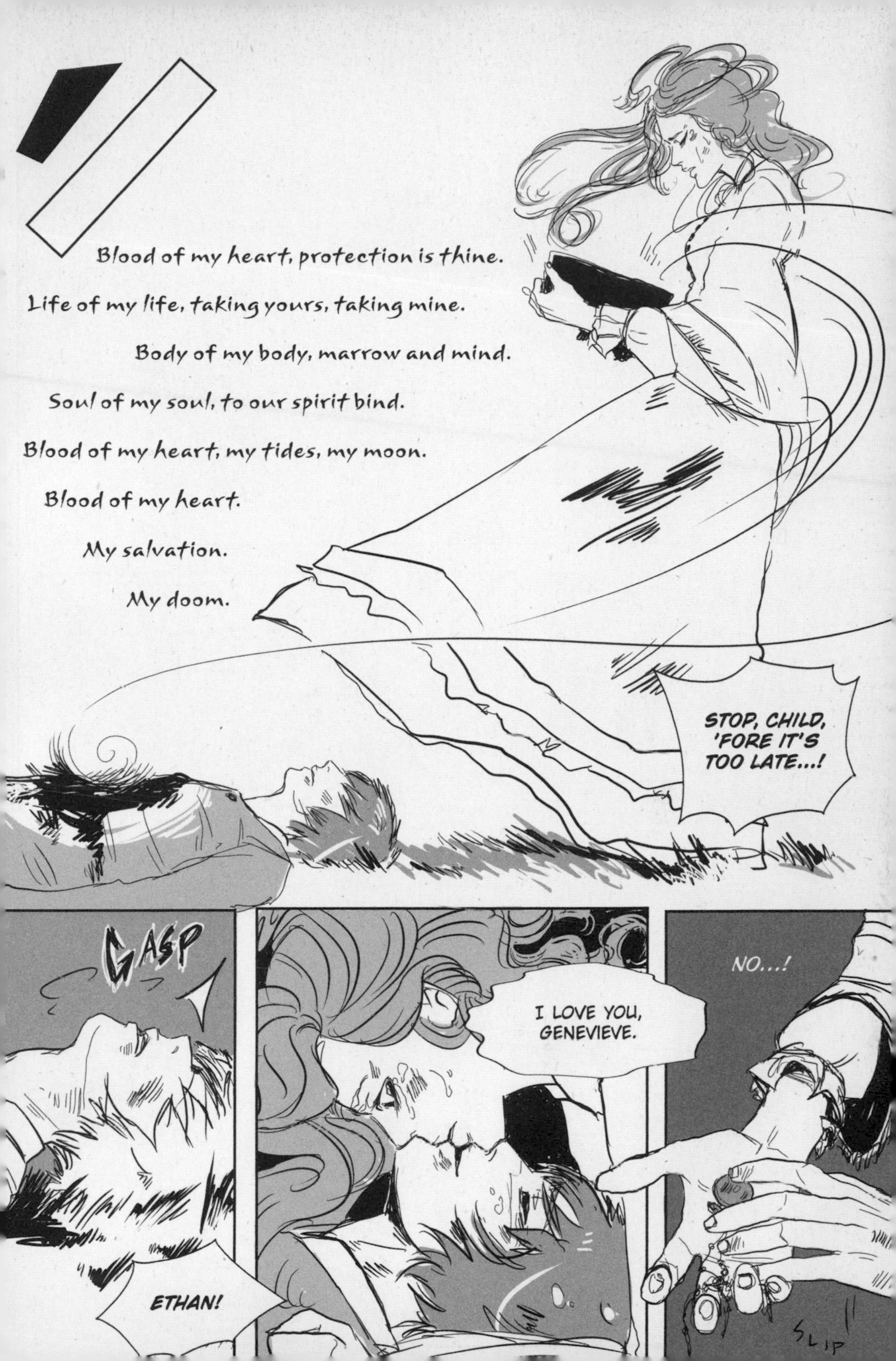
Blood of my heart, protection is thine.
Life of my life, taking yours, taking mine.
Body of my body, marrow and mind.
Soul of my soul, to our spirit bind.
Blood of my heart, my tides, my moon.
Blood of my heart.
My salvation.
My doom.
STOP, CHILD, 'FORE IT'S TOO LATE...!
GASP
ETHAN!
I LOVE YOU, GENEVIEVE.
NO...!
SLIP

ETHAN...

I'M SORRY, CHILD. HE'S GONE.

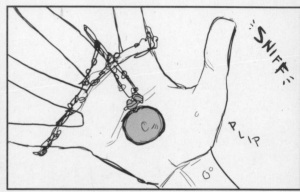

SNIFF

PLIP

?!!

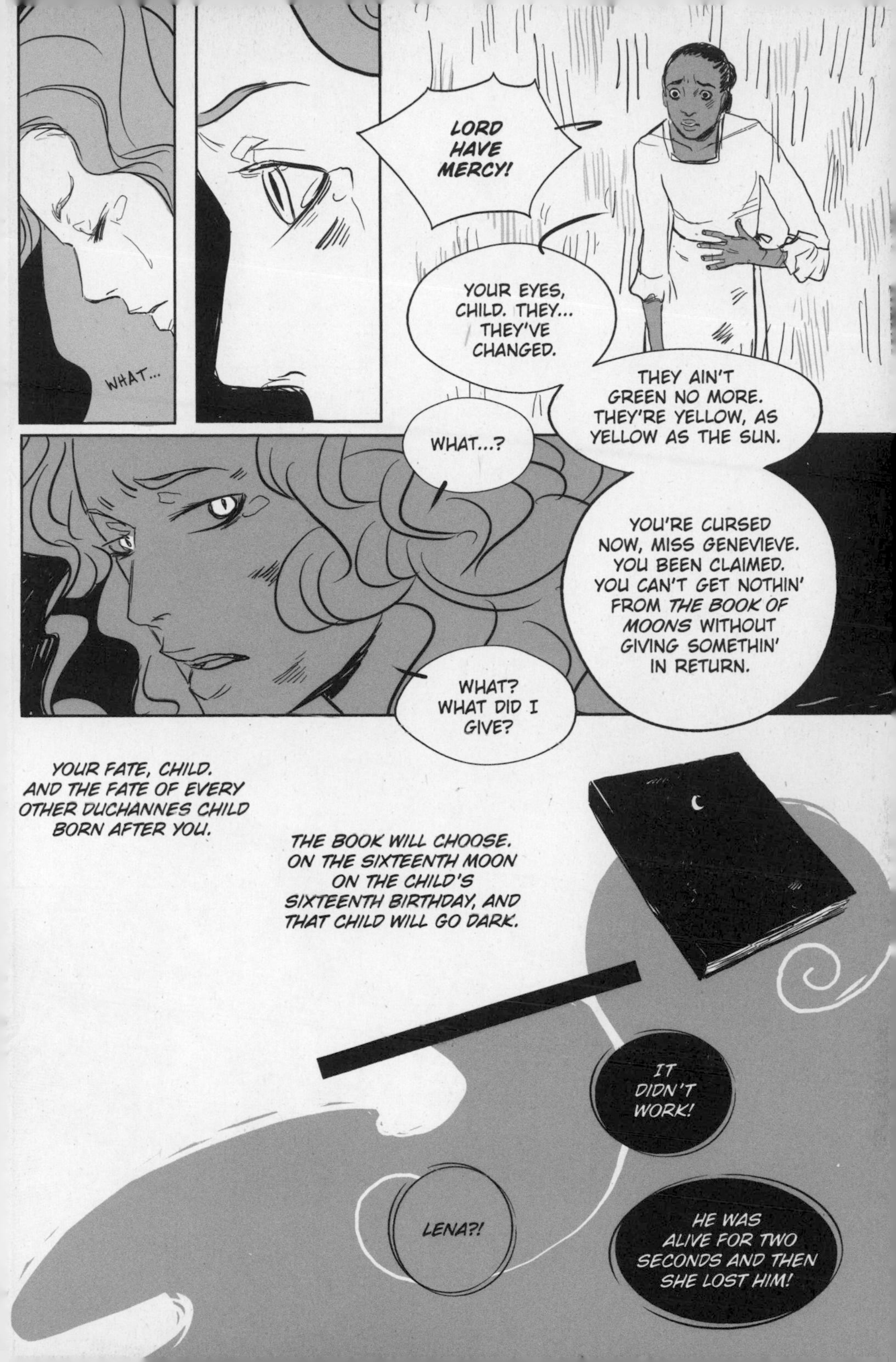
WHAT...
LORD HAVE MERCY!
YOUR EYES, CHILD. THEY... THEY'VE CHANGED.
THEY AIN'T GREEN NO MORE. THEY'RE YELLOW, AS YELLOW AS THE SUN.
WHAT...?
YOU'RE CURSED NOW, MISS GENEVIEVE. YOU BEEN CLAIMED. YOU CAN'T GET NOTHIN' FROM *THE BOOK OF MOONS* WITHOUT GIVING SOMETHIN' IN RETURN.
WHAT? WHAT DID I GIVE?
YOUR FATE, CHILD. AND THE FATE OF EVERY OTHER DUCHANNES CHILD BORN AFTER YOU.
THE BOOK WILL CHOOSE. ON THE SIXTEENTH MOON ON THE CHILD'S SIXTEENTH BIRTHDAY, AND THAT CHILD WILL GO DARK.
IT DIDN'T WORK!
LENA?!
HE WAS ALIVE FOR TWO SECONDS AND THEN SHE LOST HIM!

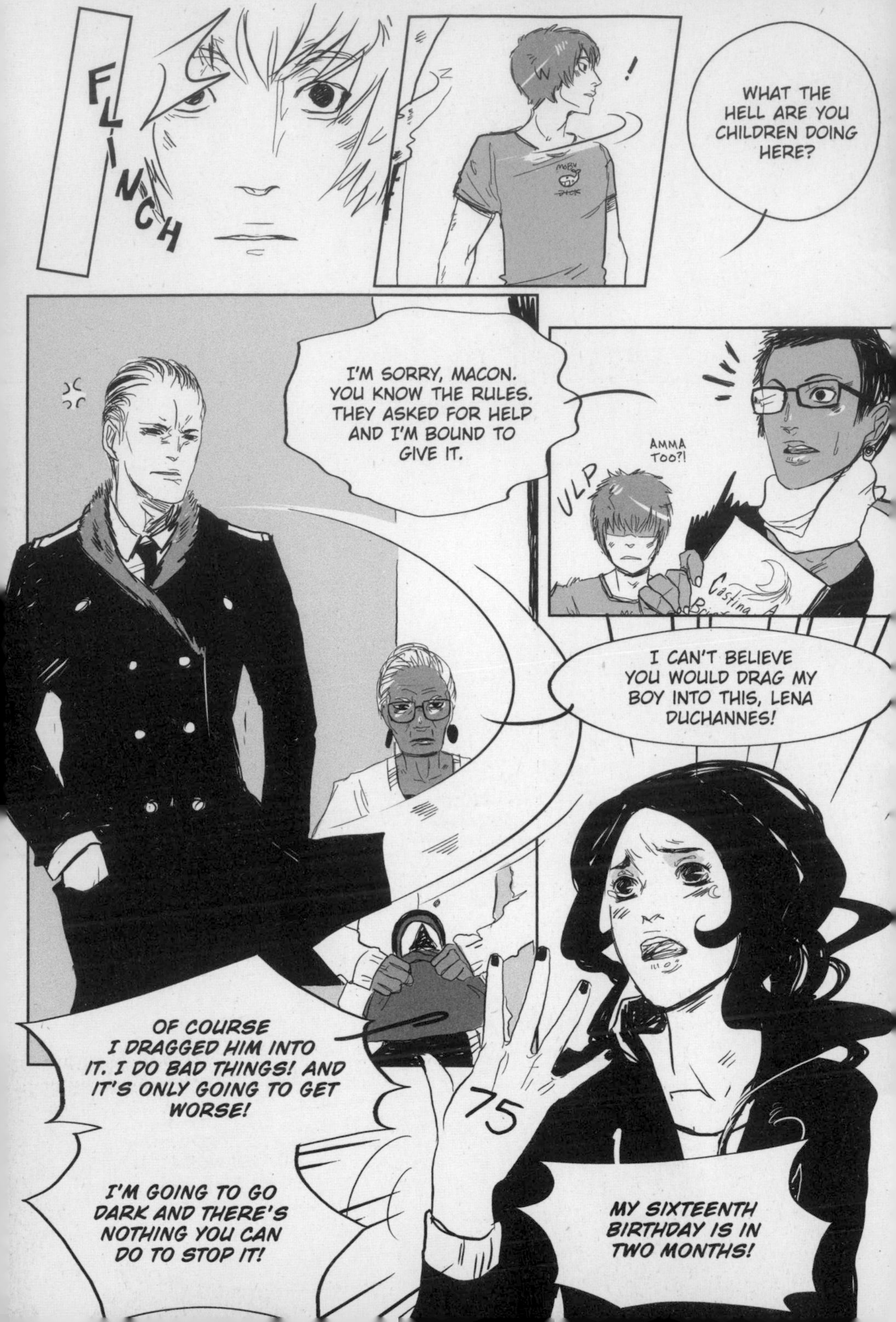
FLINCH
!
WHAT THE HELL ARE YOU CHILDREN DOING HERE?
I'M SORRY, MACON. YOU KNOW THE RULES. THEY ASKED FOR HELP AND I'M BOUND TO GIVE IT.
ULP
AMMA TOO?!
I CAN'T BELIEVE YOU WOULD DRAG MY BOY INTO THIS, LENA DUCHANNES!
OF COURSE I DRAGGED HIM INTO IT. I DO BAD THINGS! AND IT'S ONLY GOING TO GET WORSE!
I'M GOING TO GO DARK AND THERE'S NOTHING YOU CAN DO TO STOP IT!
75
MY SIXTEENTH BIRTHDAY IS IN TWO MONTHS!

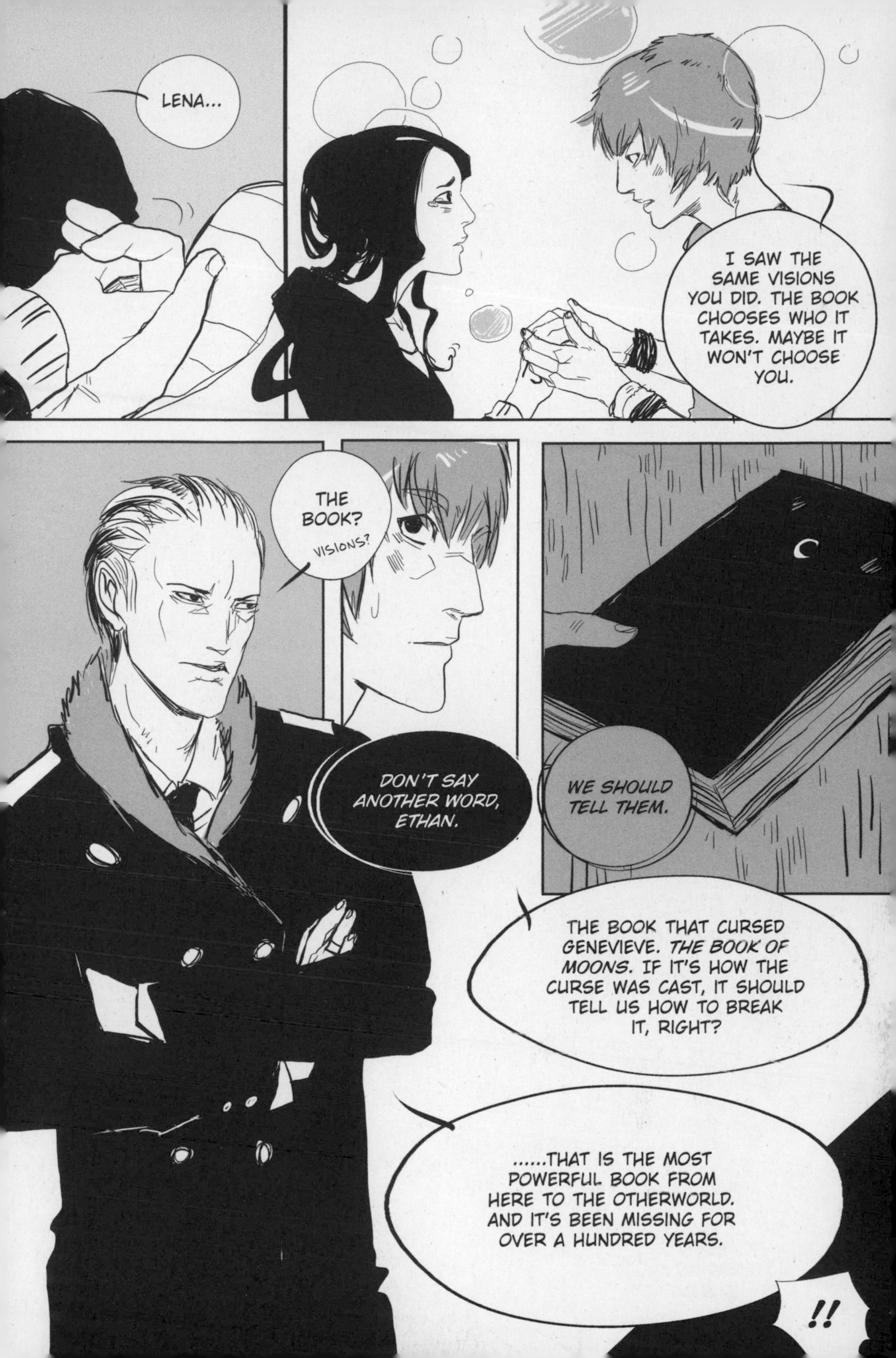
LENA...
I SAW THE SAME VISIONS YOU DID. THE BOOK CHOOSES WHO IT TAKES. MAYBE IT WON'T CHOOSE YOU.
THE BOOK?
VISIONS?
DON'T SAY ANOTHER WORD, ETHAN.
WE SHOULD TELL THEM.
THE BOOK THAT CURSED GENEVIEVE. *THE BOOK OF MOONS*. IF IT'S HOW THE CURSE WAS CAST, IT SHOULD TELL US HOW TO BREAK IT, RIGHT?
......THAT IS THE MOST POWERFUL BOOK FROM HERE TO THE OTHERWORLD. AND IT'S BEEN MISSING FOR OVER A HUNDRED YEARS.
!!

THE BOOK OF MOONS HAS BEEN MISSING FOR OVER A HUNDRED YEARS...

ON MONDAY, LINK AND I PICKED LENA UP AT THE FORK IN THE ROAD. LINK LIKED LENA, BUT THERE'S NO WAY THAT HE'S GOING TO DRIVE RIGHT UP TO RAVENWOOD MANOR. IT'S STILL A HAUNTED MANSION TO HIM.

IF HE ONLY KNEW.

BUT ACCORDING TO LINK, THERE WAS TROUBLE OF ANOTHER KIND BREWING. HIS MOM HAD BEEN WHISPERING ON THE PHONE FOR THE PAST TWENTY-FOUR HOURS. WHEN LINK LISTENED IN, HE DIDN'T CATCH MUCH, BUT IT WAS ENOUGH TO FIGURE OUT HIS MOM'S END GAME.

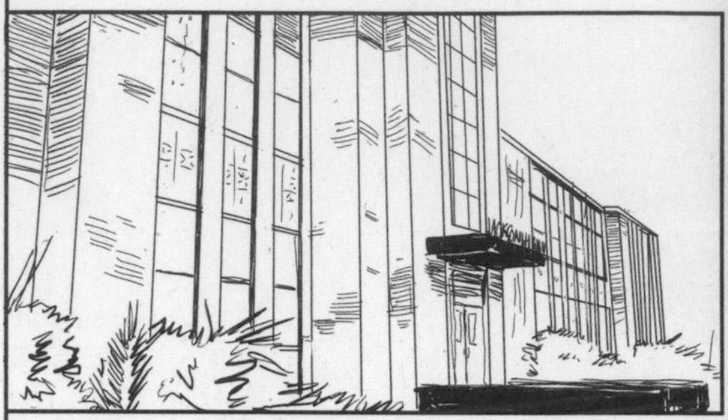

"WE'LL GET HER OUTTA OUR SCHOOL, ONE WAY OR ANOTHER."

AND HER LITTLE DOG TOO.

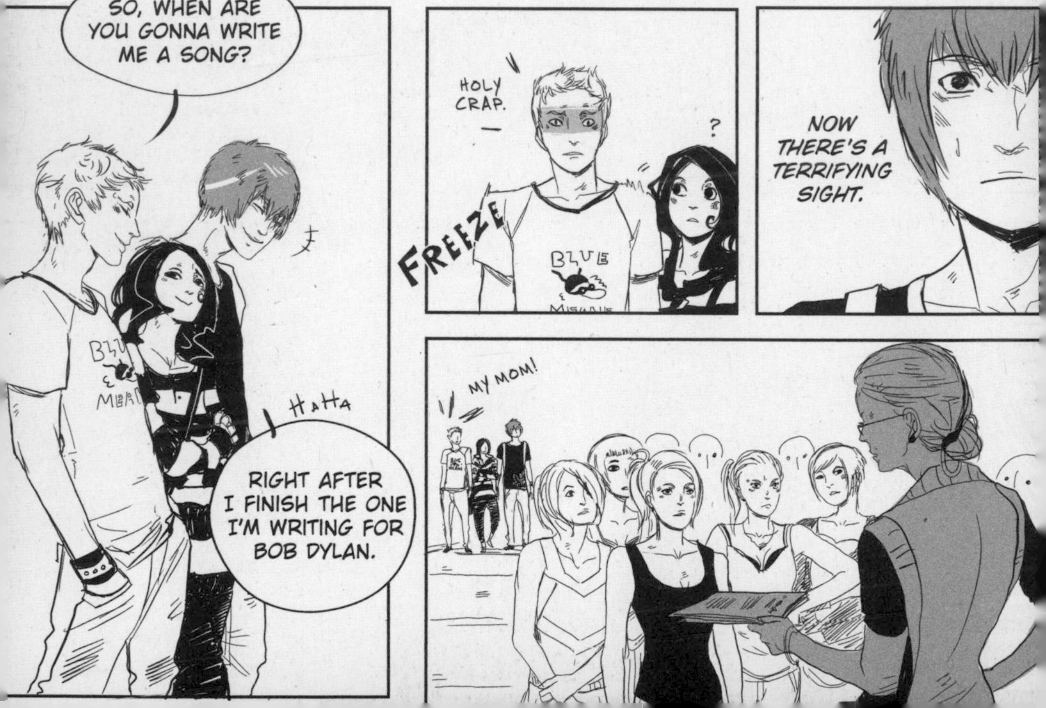
SO, WHEN ARE YOU GONNA WRITE ME A SONG?
HaHa
RIGHT AFTER I FINISH THE ONE I'M WRITING FOR BOB DYLAN.
HOLY CRAP.
?
FREEZE
NOW THERE'S A TERRIFYING SIGHT.
MY MOM!

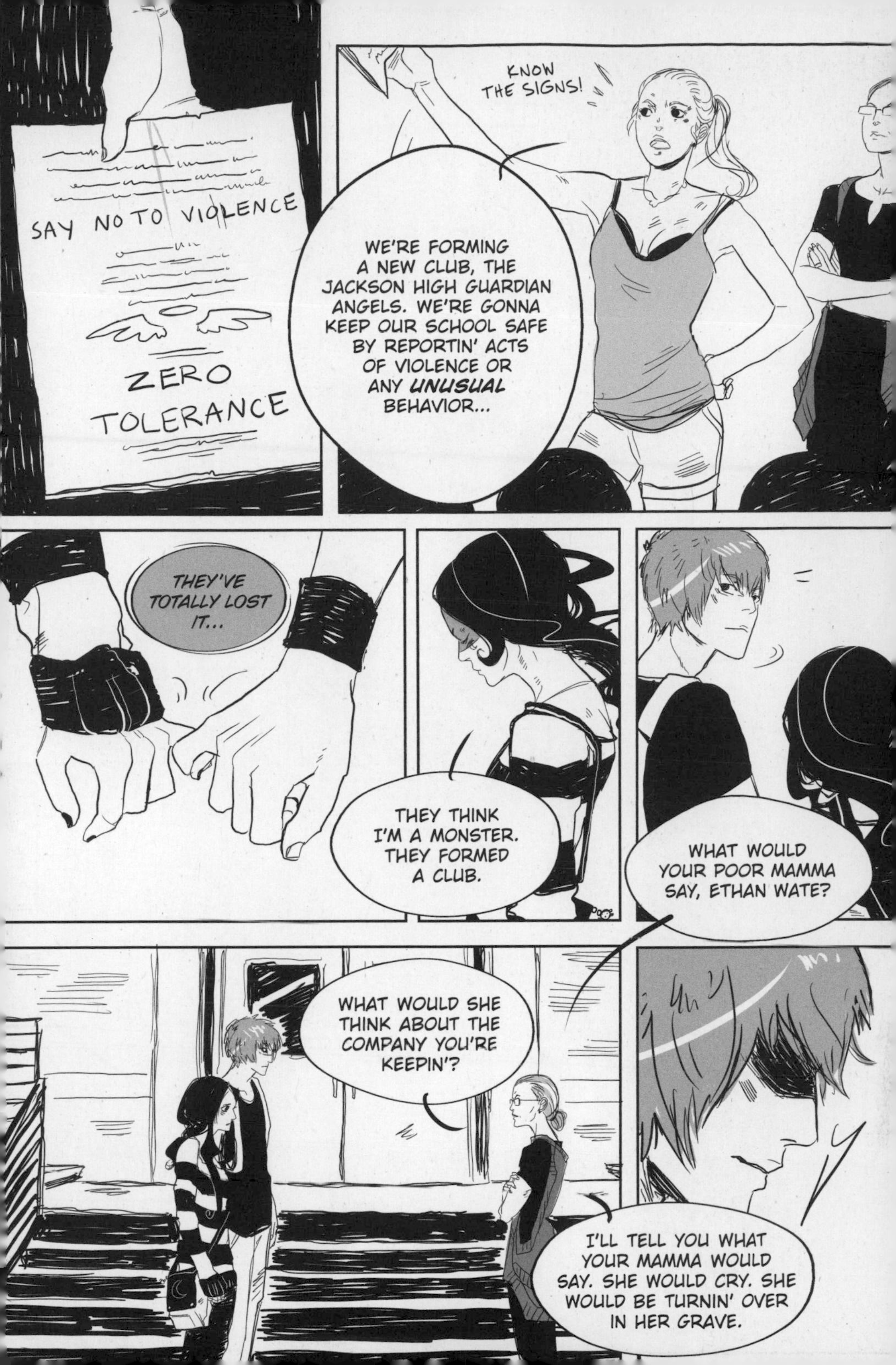
SAY NO TO VIOLENCE
ZERO TOLERANCE
KNOW THE SIGNS!
WE'RE FORMING A NEW CLUB, THE JACKSON HIGH GUARDIAN ANGELS. WE'RE GONNA KEEP OUR SCHOOL SAFE BY REPORTIN' ACTS OF VIOLENCE OR ANY UNUSUAL BEHAVIOR...
THEY'VE TOTALLY LOST IT...
THEY THINK I'M A MONSTER. THEY FORMED A CLUB.
WHAT WOULD YOUR POOR MAMMA SAY, ETHAN WATE?
WHAT WOULD SHE THINK ABOUT THE COMPANY YOU'RE KEEPIN'?
I'LL TELL YOU WHAT YOUR MAMMA WOULD SAY. SHE WOULD CRY. SHE WOULD BE TURNIN' OVER IN HER GRAVE.

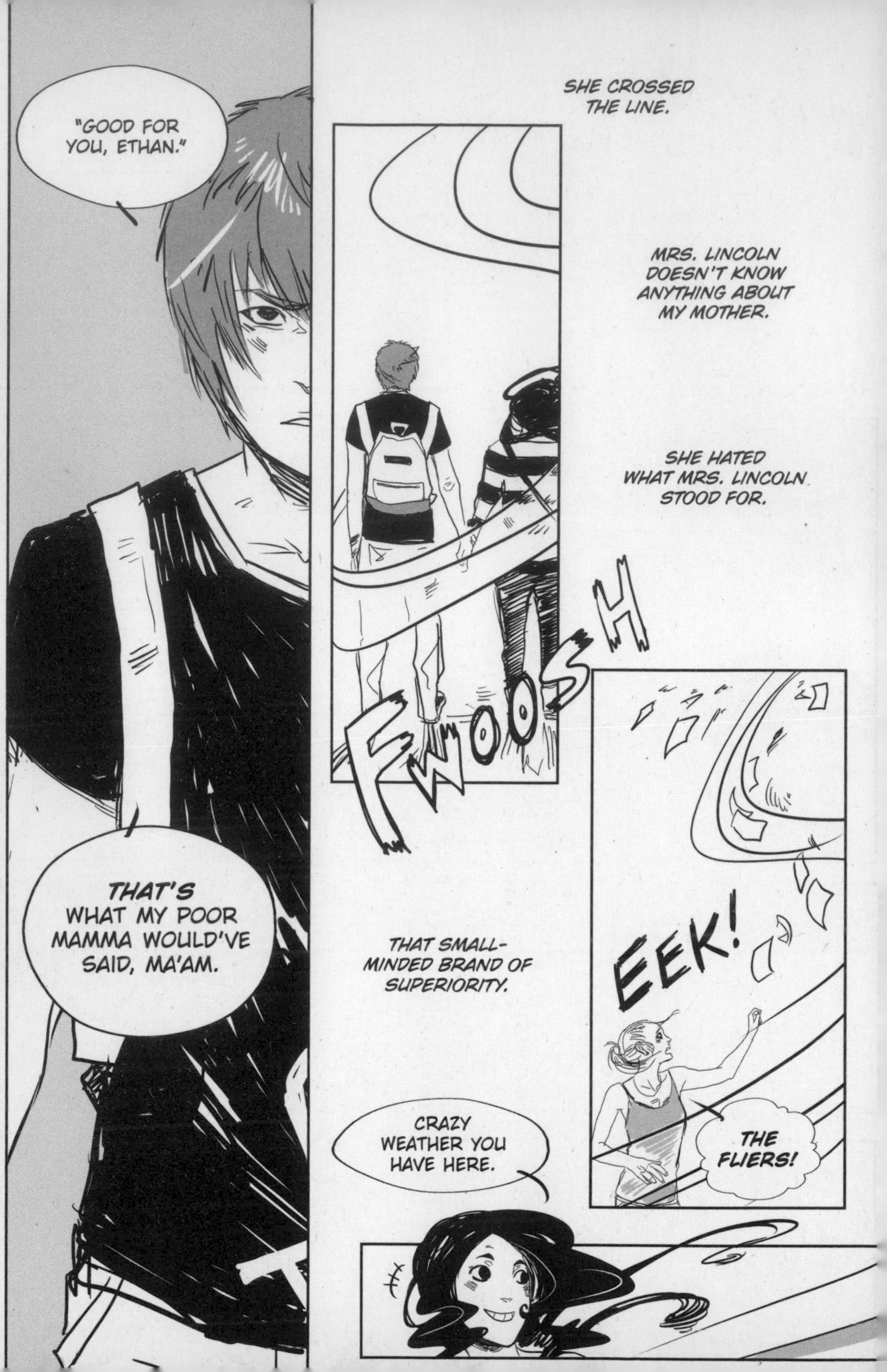
"GOOD FOR YOU, ETHAN."
THAT'S WHAT MY POOR MAMMA WOULD'VE SAID, MA'AM.
SHE CROSSED THE LINE.
MRS. LINCOLN DOESN'T KNOW ANYTHING ABOUT MY MOTHER.
SHE HATED WHAT MRS. LINCOLN STOOD FOR.
FWOOSH
THAT SMALL-MINDED BRAND OF SUPERIORITY.
EEK!
THE FLIERS!
CRAZY WEATHER YOU HAVE HERE.

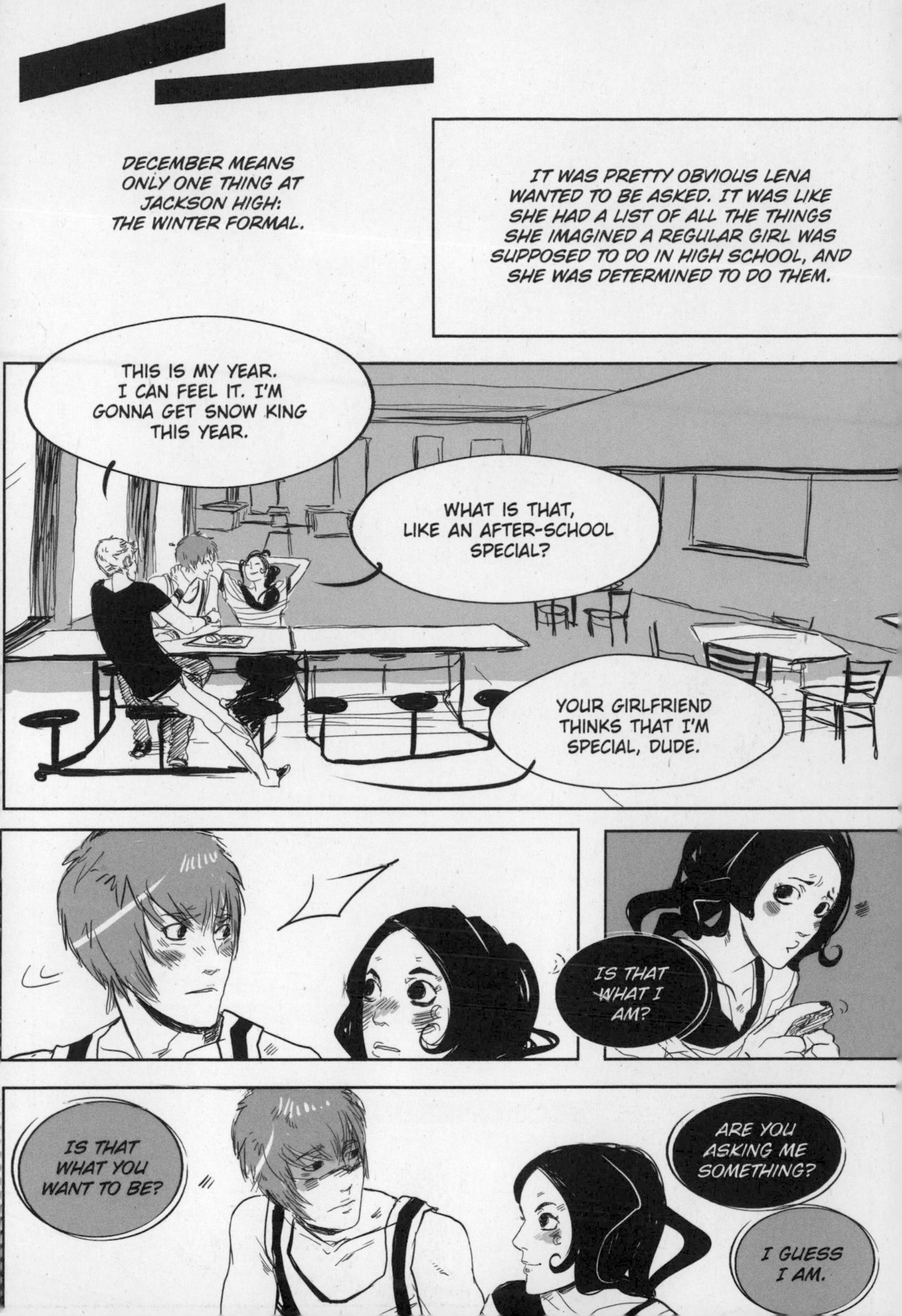

DECEMBER MEANS ONLY ONE THING AT JACKSON HIGH: THE WINTER FORMAL.
IT WAS PRETTY OBVIOUS LENA WANTED TO BE ASKED. IT WAS LIKE SHE HAD A LIST OF ALL THE THINGS SHE IMAGINED A REGULAR GIRL WAS SUPPOSED TO DO IN HIGH SCHOOL, AND SHE WAS DETERMINED TO DO THEM.
THIS IS MY YEAR. I CAN FEEL IT. I'M GONNA GET SNOW KING THIS YEAR.
WHAT IS THAT, LIKE AN AFTER-SCHOOL SPECIAL?
YOUR GIRLFRIEND THINKS THAT I'M SPECIAL, DUDE.
IS THAT WHAT I AM?
IS THAT WHAT YOU WANT TO BE?
ARE YOU ASKING ME SOMETHING?
I GUESS I AM.

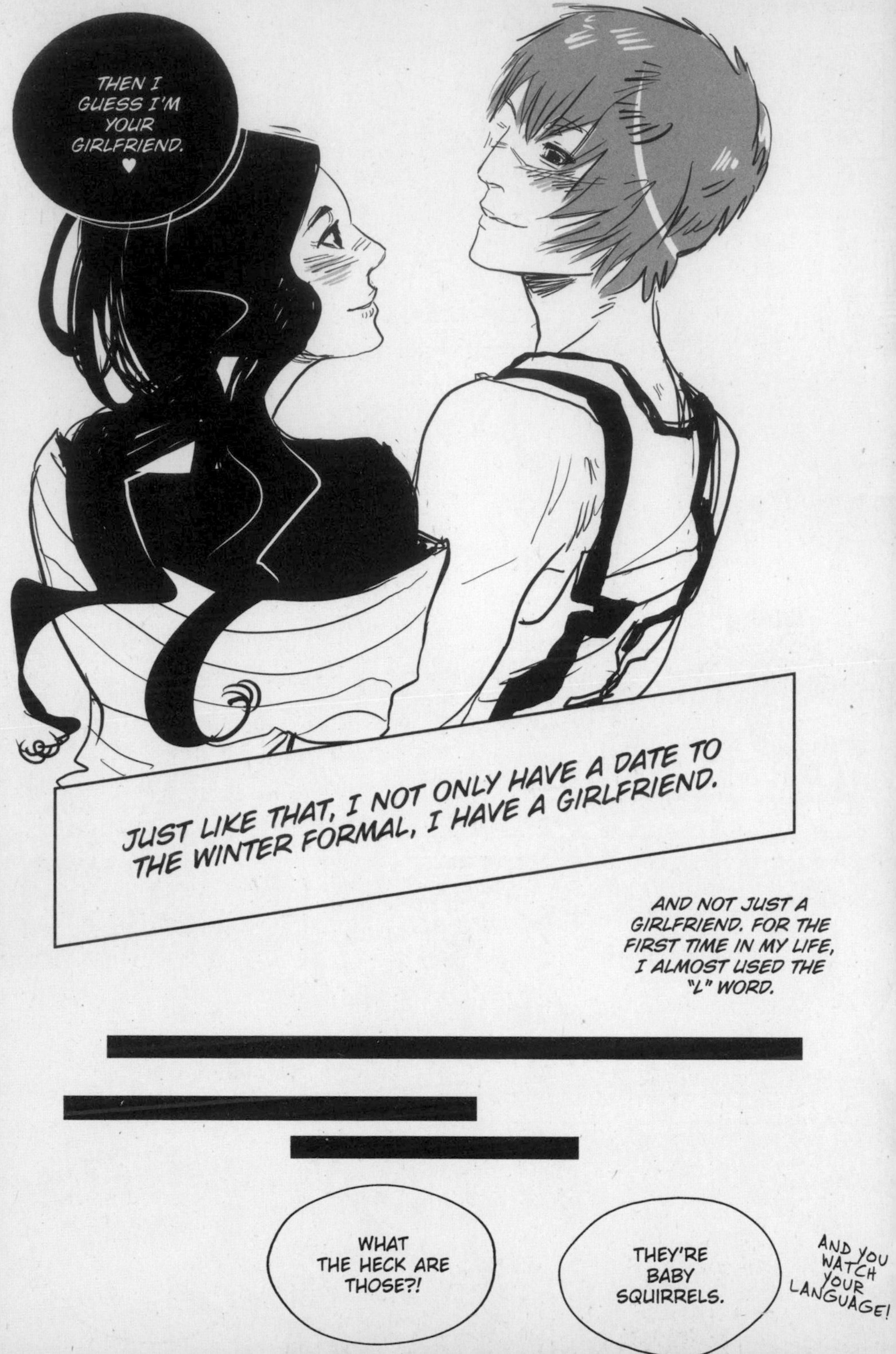
THEN I GUESS I'M YOUR GIRLFRIEND. ♥
JUST LIKE THAT, I NOT ONLY HAVE A DATE TO THE WINTER FORMAL, I HAVE A GIRLFRIEND.
AND NOT JUST A GIRLFRIEND. FOR THE FIRST TIME IN MY LIFE, I ALMOST USED THE "L" WORD.
WHAT THE HECK ARE THOSE?!
THEY'RE BABY SQUIRRELS.
AND YOU WATCH YOUR LANGUAGE!

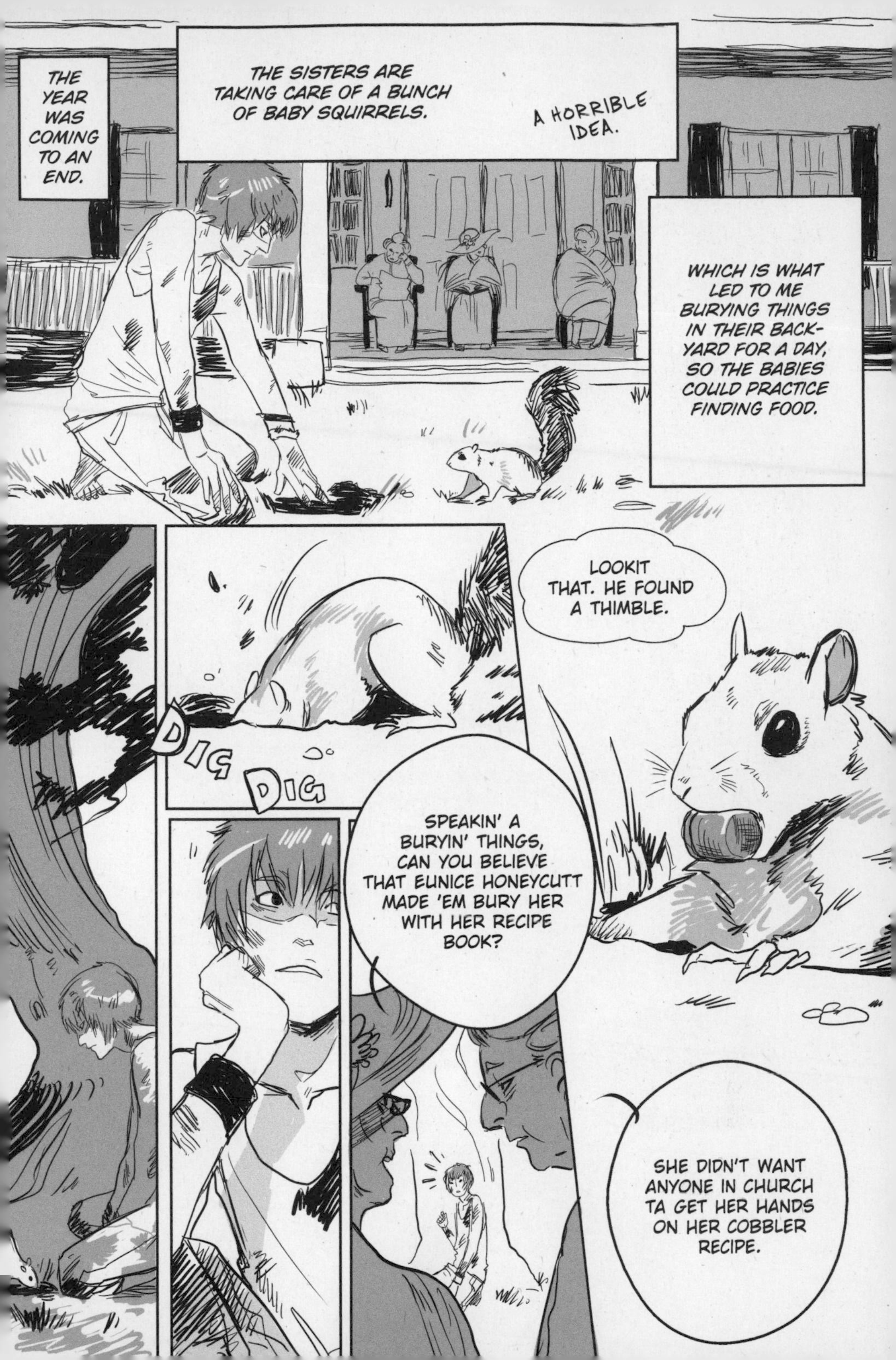
THE YEAR WAS COMING TO AN END.
THE SISTERS ARE TAKING CARE OF A BUNCH OF BABY SQUIRRELS.
A HORRIBLE IDEA.
WHICH IS WHAT LED TO ME BURYING THINGS IN THEIR BACK-YARD FOR A DAY, SO THE BABIES COULD PRACTICE FINDING FOOD.
DIG DIG
LOOKIT THAT. HE FOUND A THIMBLE.
SPEAKIN' A BURYIN' THINGS, CAN YOU BELIEVE THAT EUNICE HONEYCUTT MADE 'EM BURY HER WITH HER RECIPE BOOK?
SHE DIDN'T WANT ANYONE IN CHURCH TA GET HER HANDS ON HER COBBLER RECIPE.

WHAT IF
THE BOOK
OF MOONS
IS BURIED
SOMEWHERE?

MAYBE WITH THE PERSON WHO UNDERSTOOD ITS POWER
BETTER THAN ANYONE.

LENA! I THINK
I KNOW WHERE
THE BOOK IS!

I THINK IT'S
WITH GENEVIEVE.

GENEVIEVE
IS DEAD.

I
KNOW.

WHAT ARE
YOU SAYING,
ETHAN?

I THINK
YOU KNOW
WHAT I'M
SAYING.

BEAUTIFUL CREATURES

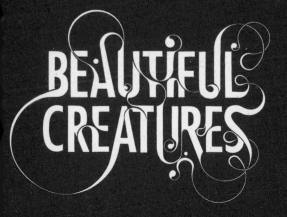

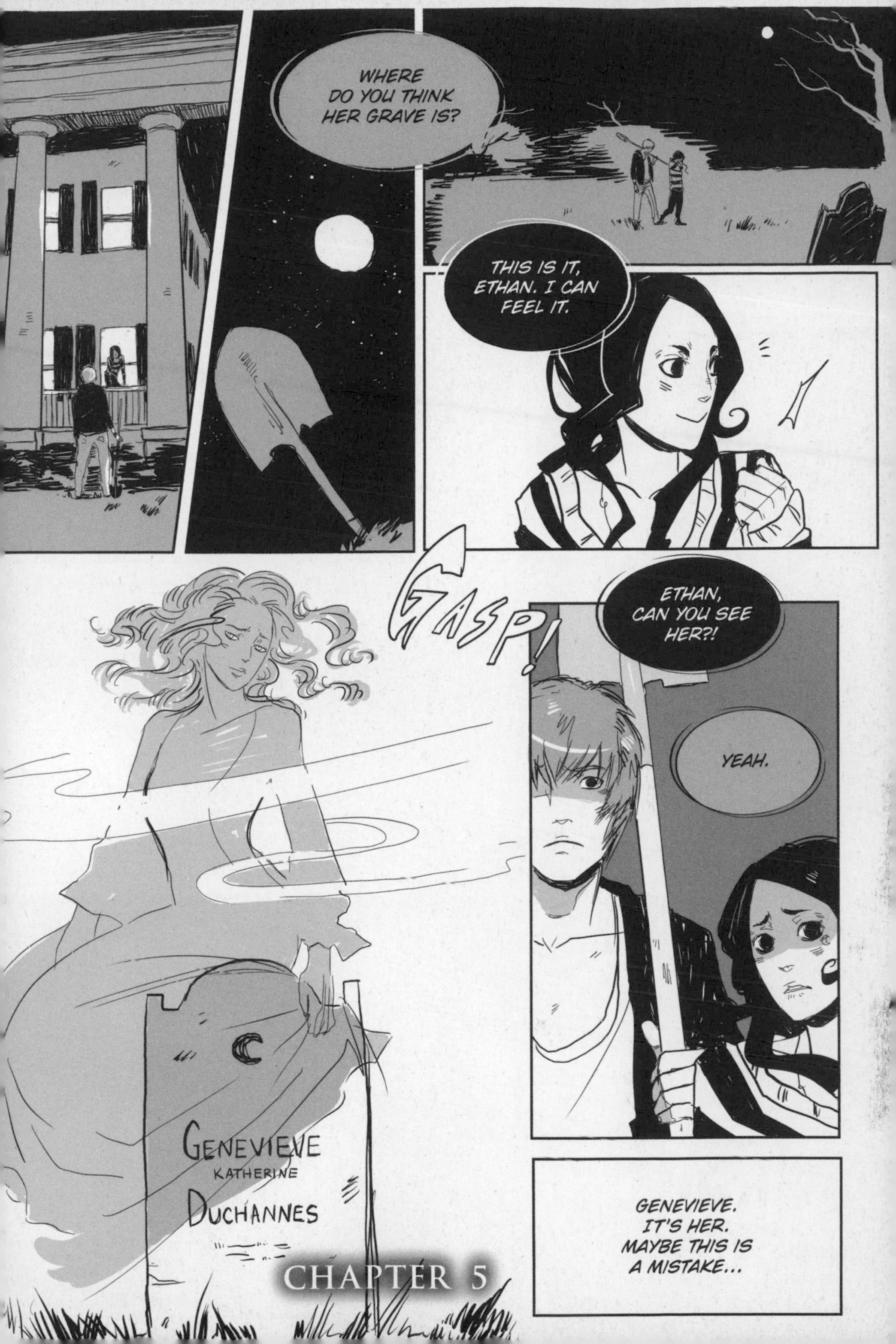
WHERE DO YOU THINK HER GRAVE IS?
THIS IS IT, ETHAN. I CAN FEEL IT.
GASP!
ETHAN, CAN YOU SEE HER?!
YEAH.
GENEVIEVE KATHERINE DUCHANNES
GENEVIEVE. IT'S HER. MAYBE THIS IS A MISTAKE...
CHAPTER 5

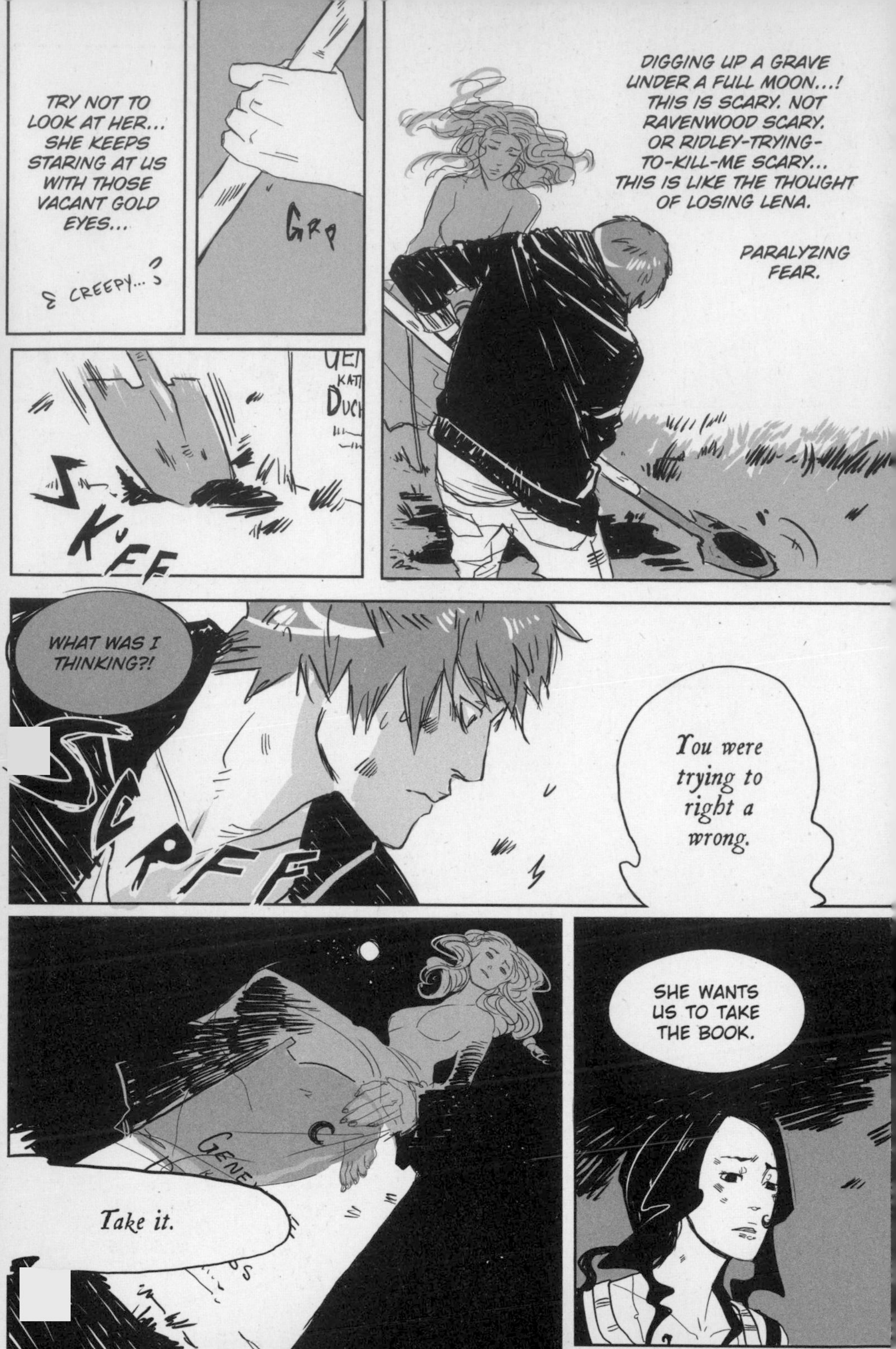

TRY NOT TO LOOK AT HER... SHE KEEPS STARING AT US WITH THOSE VACANT GOLD EYES...
CREEPY...
GRP
SKUFF
DIGGING UP A GRAVE UNDER A FULL MOON...! THIS IS SCARY. NOT RAVENWOOD SCARY. OR RIDLEY-TRYING-TO-KILL-ME SCARY... THIS IS LIKE THE THOUGHT OF LOSING LENA.
PARALYZING FEAR.
WHAT WAS I THINKING?!
SCRFF
You were trying to right a wrong.
Take it.
SHE WANTS US TO TAKE THE BOOK.

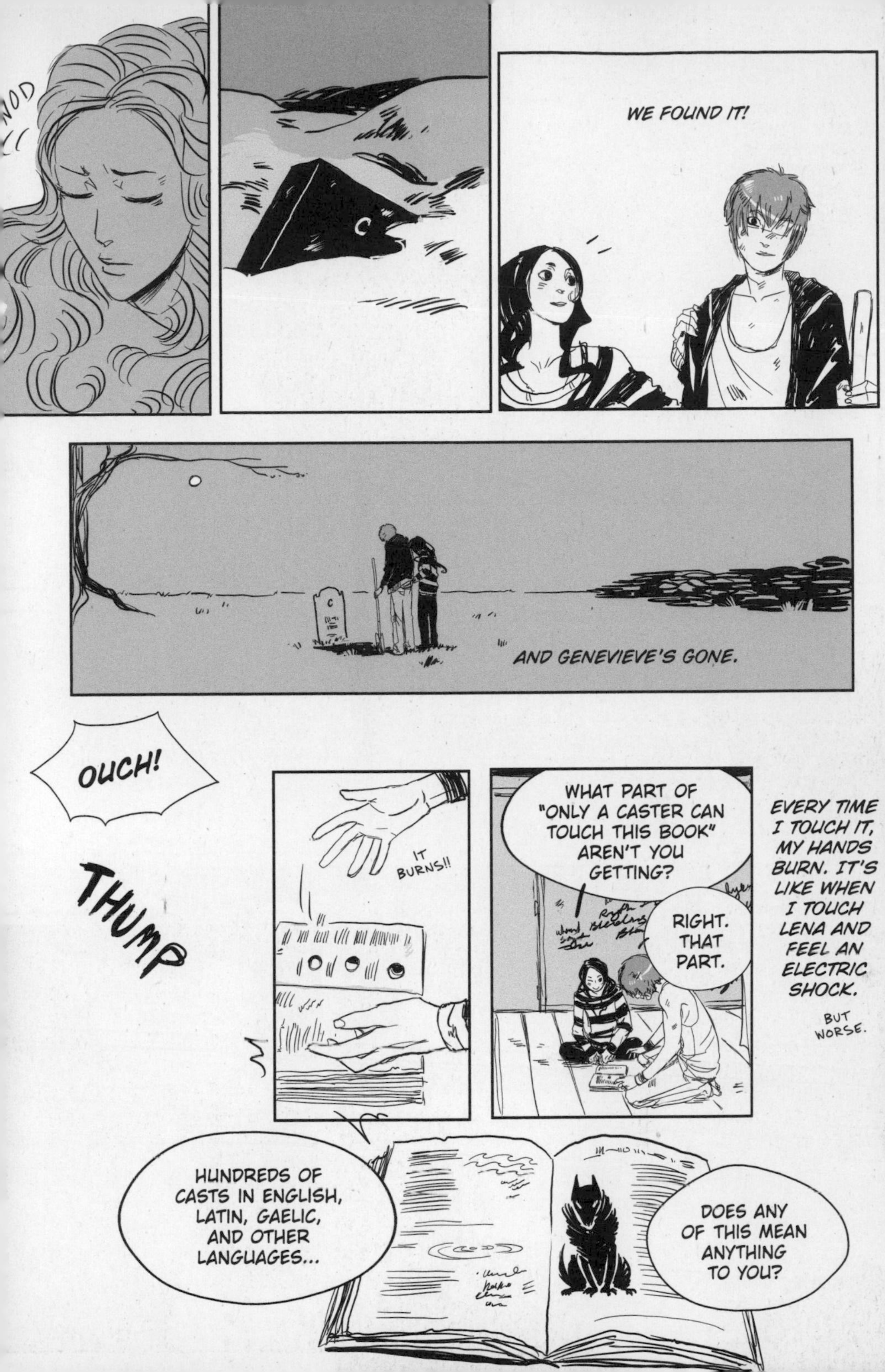
NOD
WE FOUND IT!
AND GENEVIEVE'S GONE.
OUCH!
THUMP
IT BURNS!!
WHAT PART OF "ONLY A CASTER CAN TOUCH THIS BOOK" AREN'T YOU GETTING?
RIGHT. THAT PART.
EVERY TIME I TOUCH IT, MY HANDS BURN. IT'S LIKE WHEN I TOUCH LENA AND FEEL AN ELECTRIC SHOCK.
BUT WORSE.
HUNDREDS OF CASTS IN ENGLISH, LATIN, GAELIC, AND OTHER LANGUAGES...
DOES ANY OF THIS MEAN ANYTHING TO YOU?

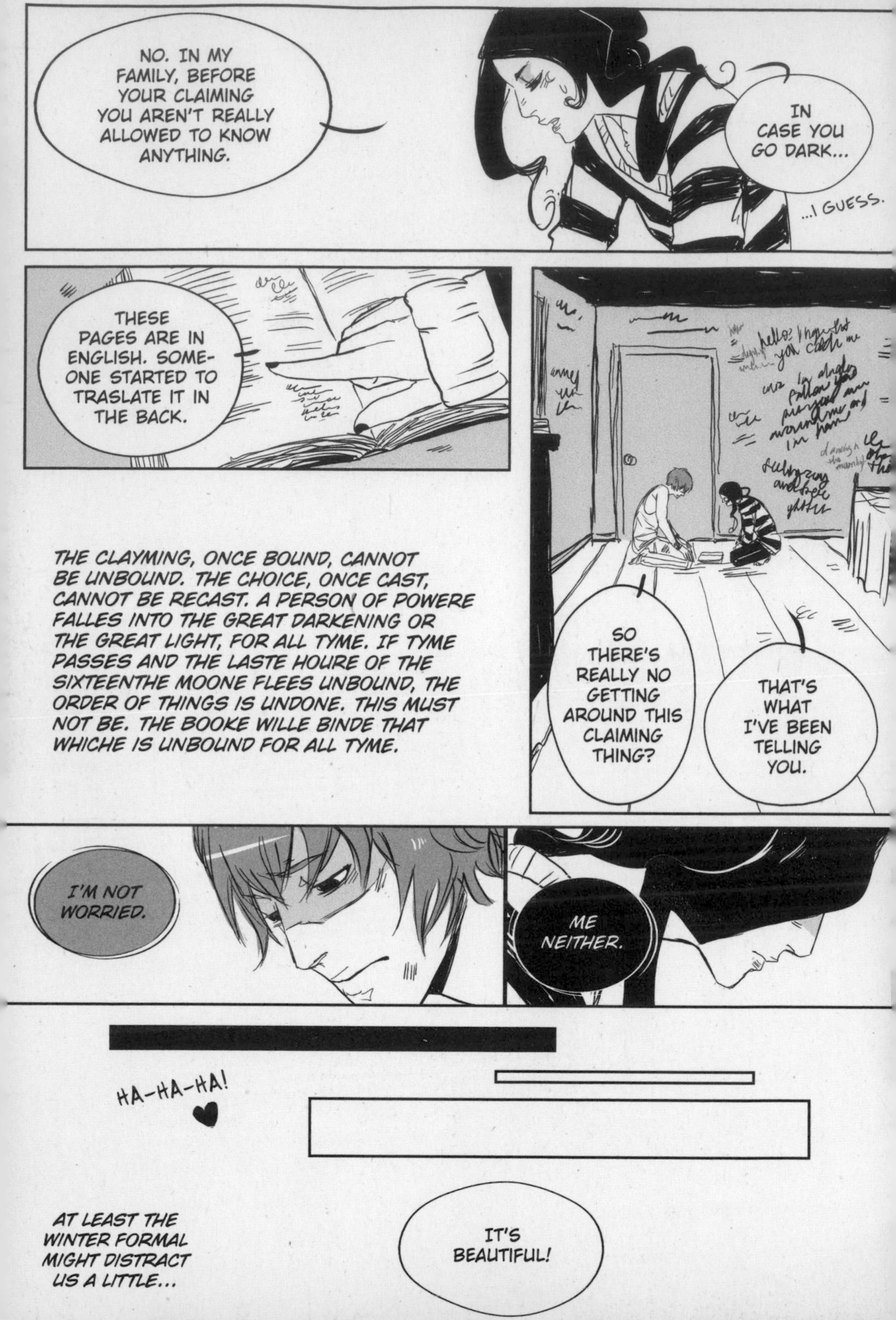
NO. IN MY FAMILY, BEFORE YOUR CLAIMING YOU AREN'T REALLY ALLOWED TO KNOW ANYTHING.
IN CASE YOU GO DARK...
...I GUESS.
THESE PAGES ARE IN ENGLISH. SOME-ONE STARTED TO TRASLATE IT IN THE BACK.
THE CLAYMING, ONCE BOUND, CANNOT BE UNBOUND. THE CHOICE, ONCE CAST, CANNOT BE RECAST. A PERSON OF POWERE FALLES INTO THE GREAT DARKENING OR THE GREAT LIGHT, FOR ALL TYME. IF TYME PASSES AND THE LASTE HOURE OF THE SIXTEENTHE MOONE FLEES UNBOUND, THE ORDER OF THINGS IS UNDONE. THIS MUST NOT BE. THE BOOKE WILLE BINDE THAT WHICHE IS UNBOUND FOR ALL TYME.
SO THERE'S REALLY NO GETTING AROUND THIS CLAIMING THING?
THAT'S WHAT I'VE BEEN TELLING YOU.
I'M NOT WORRIED.
ME NEITHER.
HA-HA-HA!
AT LEAST THE WINTER FORMAL MIGHT DISTRACT US A LITTLE...
IT'S BEAUTIFUL!

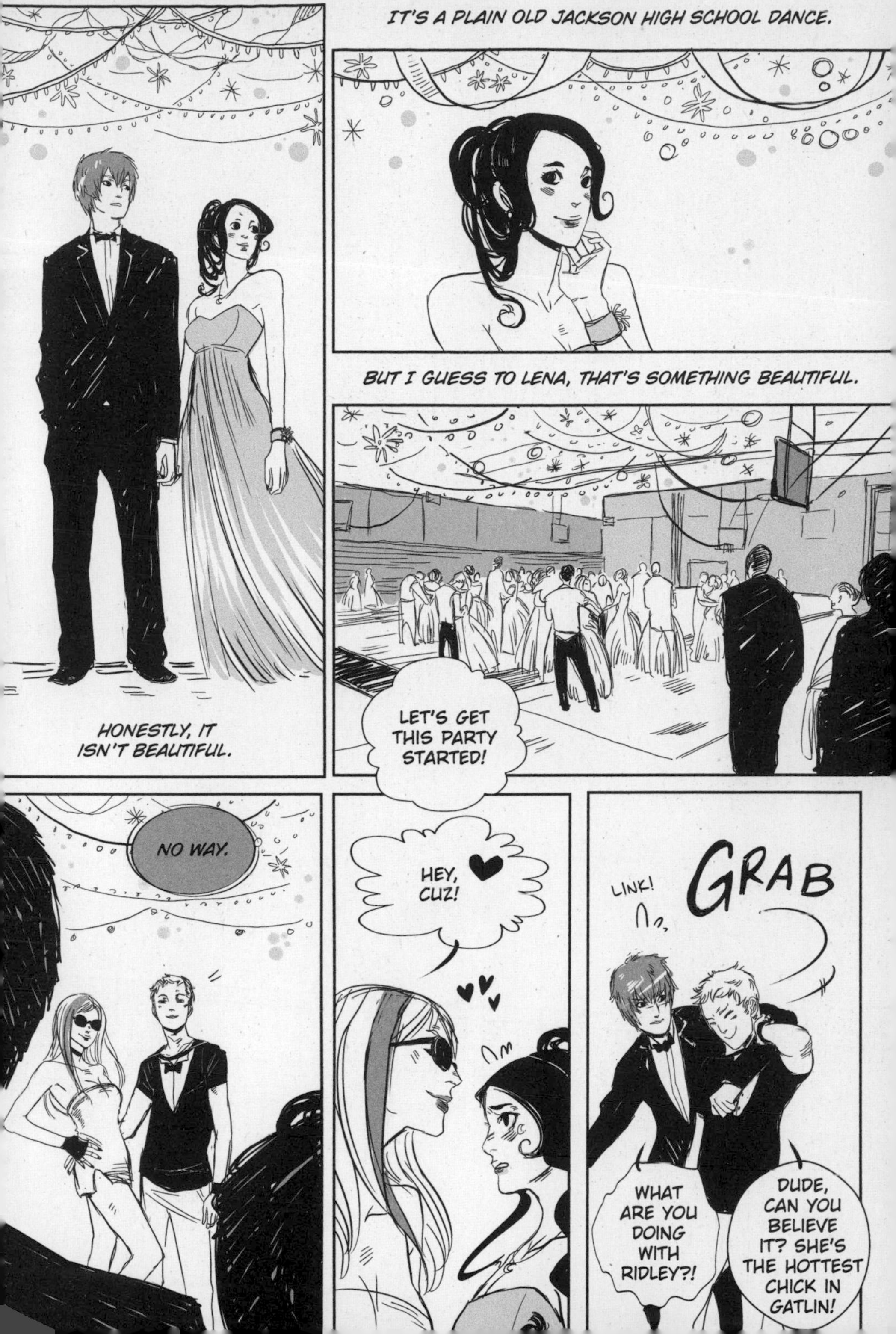
HONESTLY, IT ISN'T BEAUTIFUL.
IT'S A PLAIN OLD JACKSON HIGH SCHOOL DANCE.
BUT I GUESS TO LENA, THAT'S SOMETHING BEAUTIFUL.
LET'S GET THIS PARTY STARTED!
NO WAY.
HEY, CUZ!
LINK!
GRAB
WHAT ARE YOU DOING WITH RIDLEY?!
DUDE, CAN YOU BELIEVE IT? SHE'S THE HOTTEST CHICK IN GATLIN!

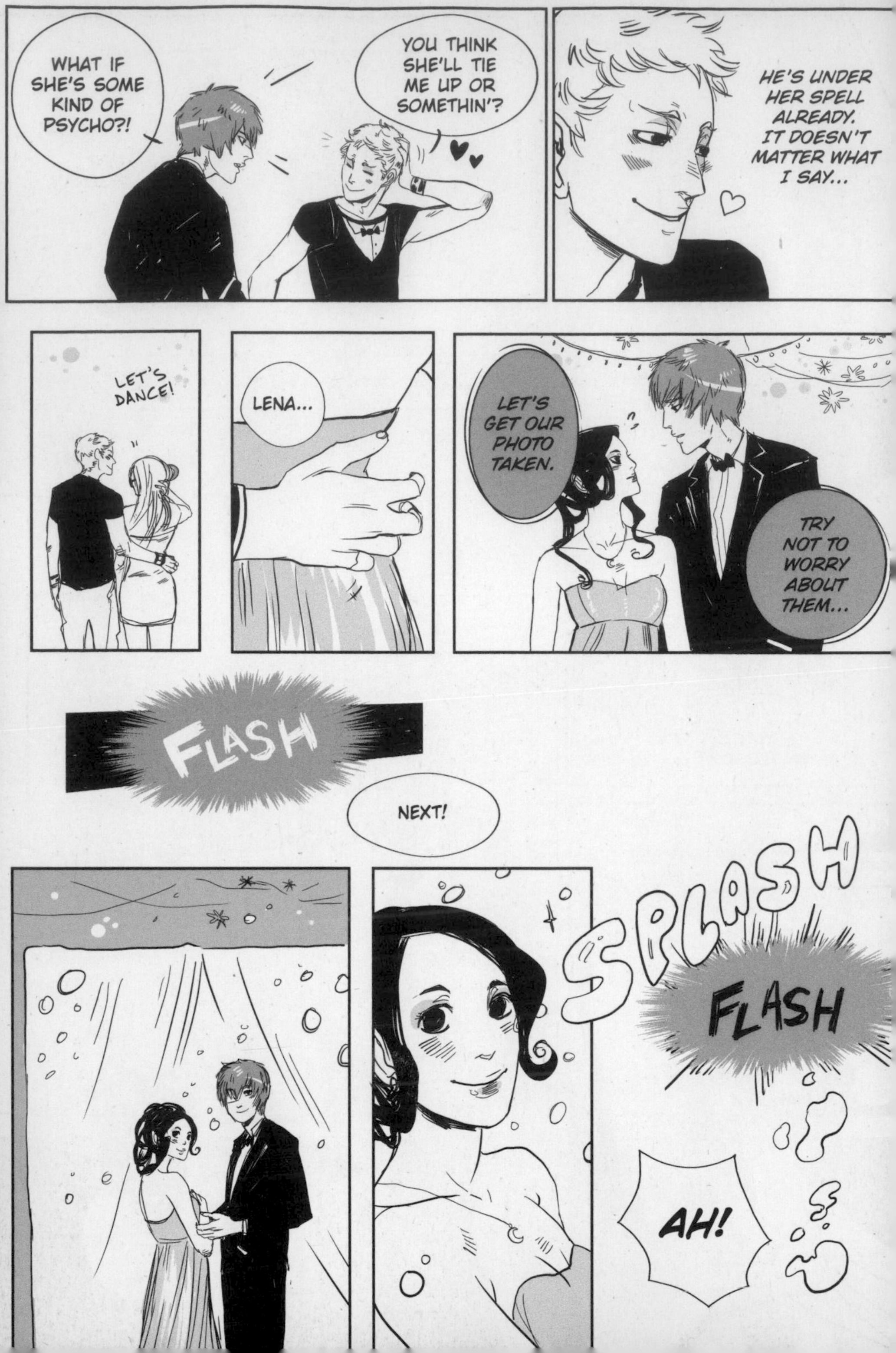
WHAT IF SHE'S SOME KIND OF PSYCHO?!
YOU THINK SHE'LL TIE ME UP OR SOMETHIN'?
HE'S UNDER HER SPELL ALREADY. IT DOESN'T MATTER WHAT I SAY...
LET'S DANCE!
LENA...
LET'S GET OUR PHOTO TAKEN.
TRY NOT TO WORRY ABOUT THEM...
FLASH
NEXT!
SPLASH
FLASH
AH!

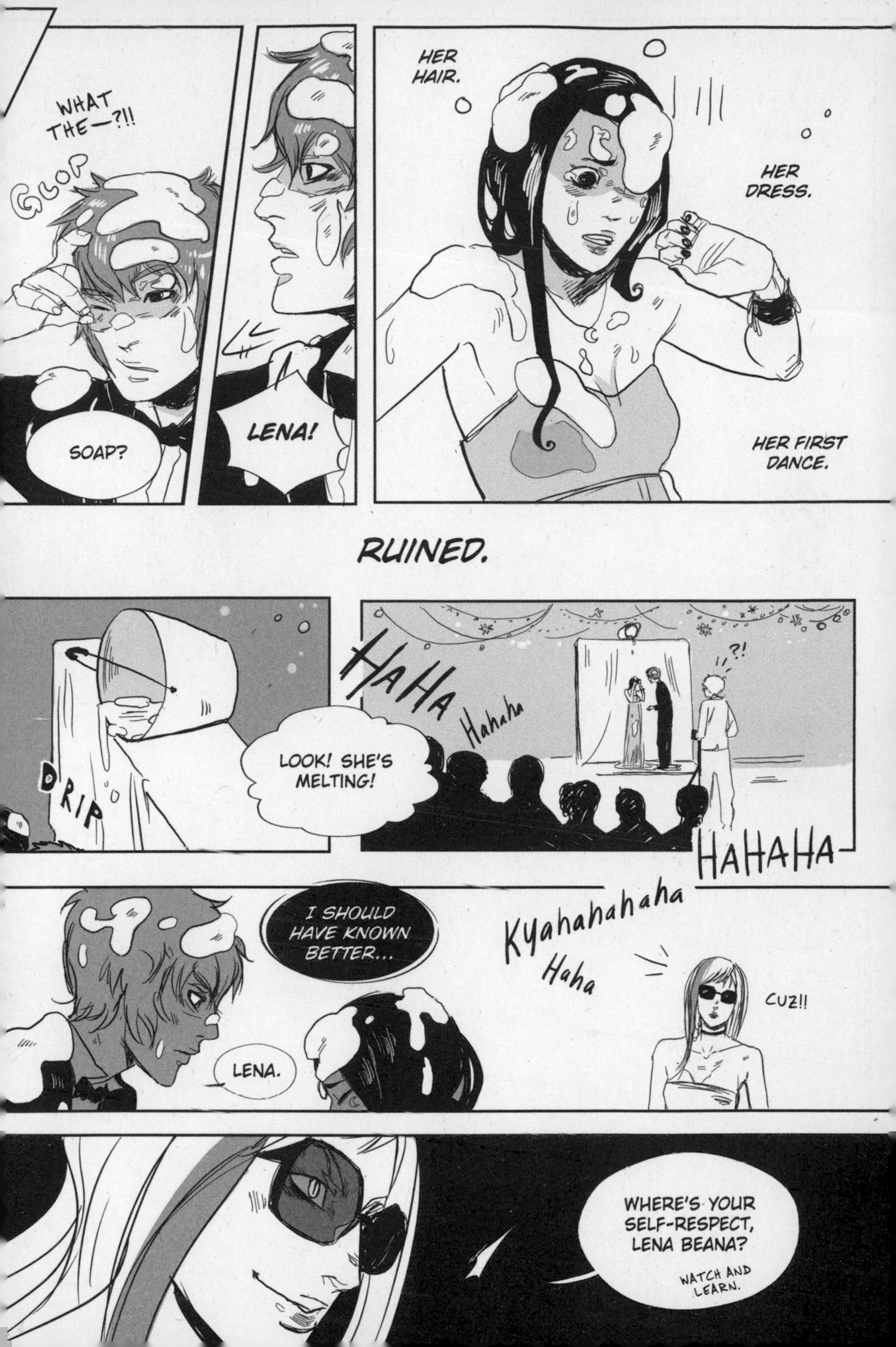
WHAT THE—?!!
GLOP
SOAP?
LENA!
HER HAIR.
HER DRESS.
HER FIRST DANCE.
RUINED.
DRIP
HaHa
Hahaha
LOOK! SHE'S MELTING!
?!
HAHAHA-
I SHOULD HAVE KNOWN BETTER...
LENA.
Kyahahahaha
Haha
CUZ!!
WHERE'S YOUR SELF-RESPECT, LENA BEANA?
WATCH AND LEARN.

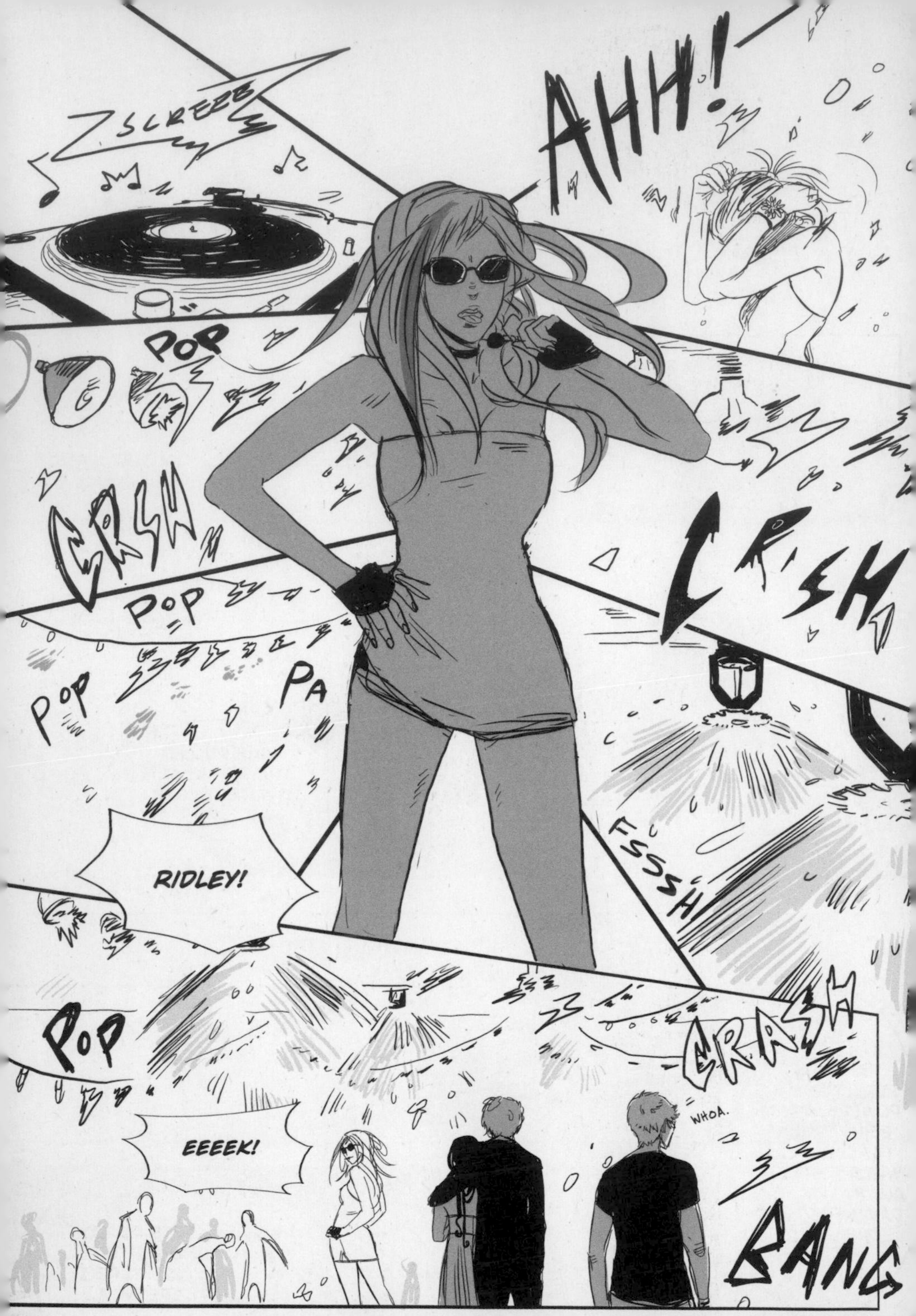
ZSCREEE
POP
AHH!
CRSH
CRSH
POP
POP
PA
RIDLEY!
FSSSH
POP
CRASH
EEEEK!
WHOA.
BANG
EVERYTHING RUINED.

I FELT SORRY FOR WHOEVER THEY WOULD BLAME FOR THIS MESS...

BUT OF COURSE—

AFTERWARD, I HEARD...

...MRS. LINCOLN FOUND SOMEONE TO BLAME.

HOW COULD MRS. LINCOLN BLAME LENA?!

WHY DOES SHE HAVE IT IN FOR HER?!

THAT RAVENWOOD GIRL!

SHE PULLED THE FIRE ALARM AND DESTROYED EVERYTHING!

IT'S...INSANE.

54 DAYS LEFT.

"AMONGST PERSONNES OF POWERE, THERE BEING TWINNE FORCES FROM WHYCHE SPRING ALL MAGICK, THE DARKNESSE AND THE LIGHT."

YOU THINK WE CAN SKIP TO THE GOOD PART? LIKE, LOOPHOLES FOR YOUR CLAIMING DAY?

IT GETS REALLY COMPLICATED. I'M NOT SURE I UNDERSTAND...

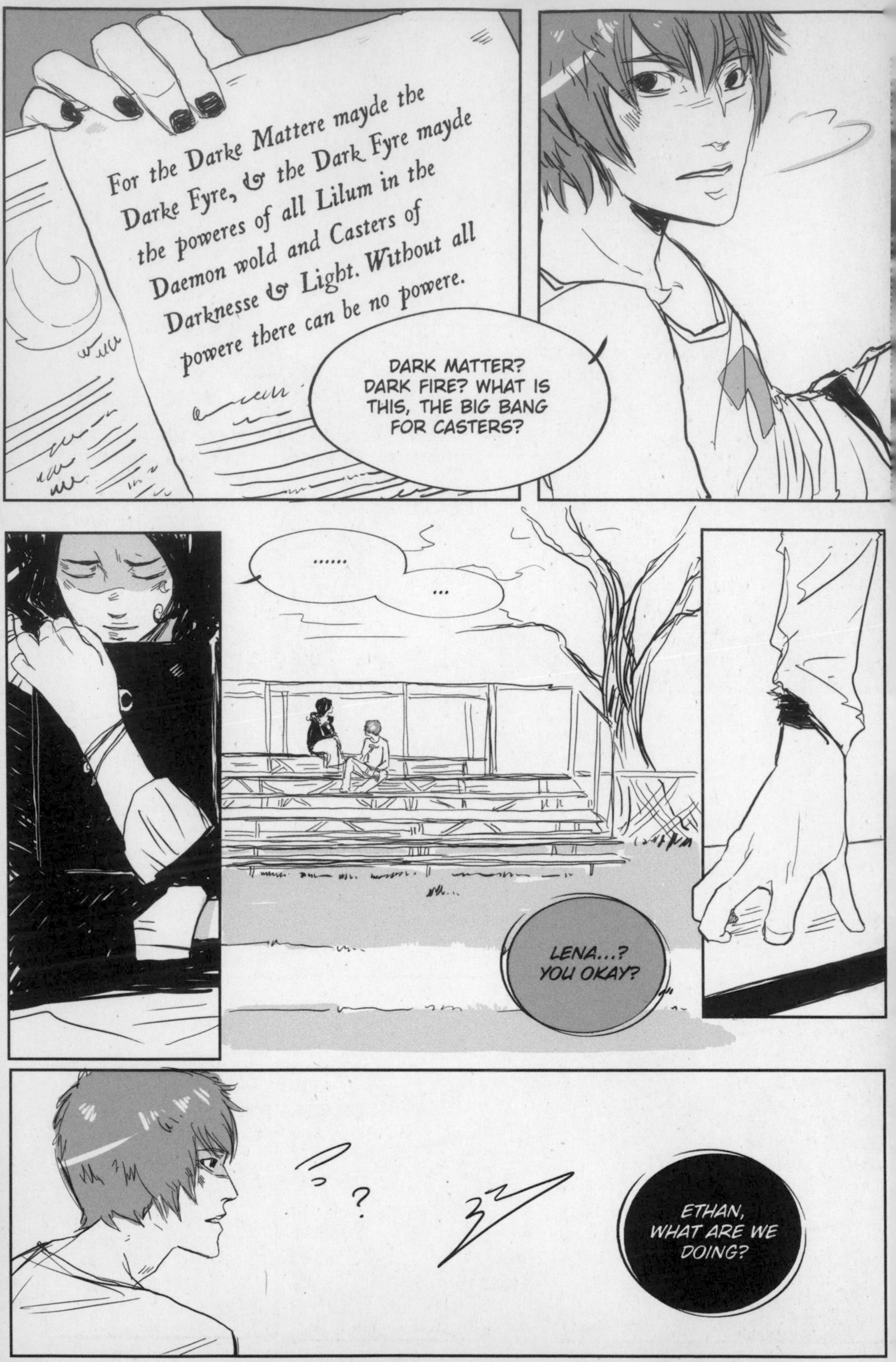
For the Darke Mattere mayde the Darke Fyre, & the Dark Fyre mayde the poweres of all Lilum in the Daemon wold and Casters of Darknesse & Light. Without all powere there can be no powere.
DARK MATTER? DARK FIRE? WHAT IS THIS, THE BIG BANG FOR CASTERS?
......
...
LENA...? YOU OKAY?
?
ETHAN, WHAT ARE WE DOING?

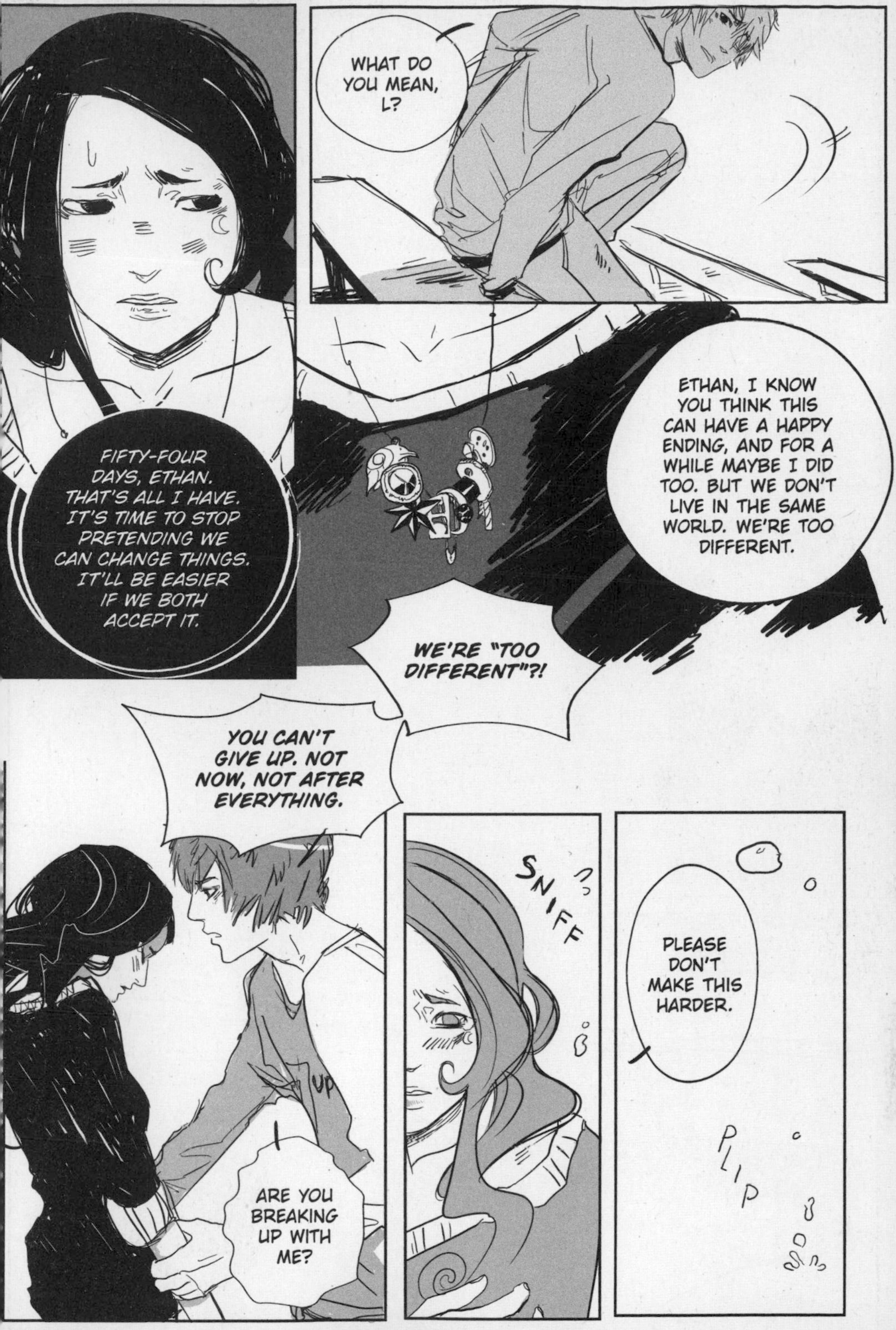

WHAT DO YOU MEAN, L?
FIFTY-FOUR DAYS, ETHAN. THAT'S ALL I HAVE. IT'S TIME TO STOP PRETENDING WE CAN CHANGE THINGS. IT'LL BE EASIER IF WE BOTH ACCEPT IT.
ETHAN, I KNOW YOU THINK THIS CAN HAVE A HAPPY ENDING, AND FOR A WHILE MAYBE I DID TOO. BUT WE DON'T LIVE IN THE SAME WORLD. WE'RE TOO DIFFERENT.
WE'RE "TOO DIFFERENT"?!
YOU CAN'T GIVE UP. NOT NOW, NOT AFTER EVERYTHING.
ARE YOU BREAKING UP WITH ME?
SNIFF
PLEASE DON'T MAKE THIS HARDER.
PLIP

LENA...

SHE SHUT ME OUT.
I CAN'T HEAR HER
THOUGHTS OR TALK
TO HER...

HEY,
MAN.

I GOT A
FAVOR TO
ASK YOU.

SURE.

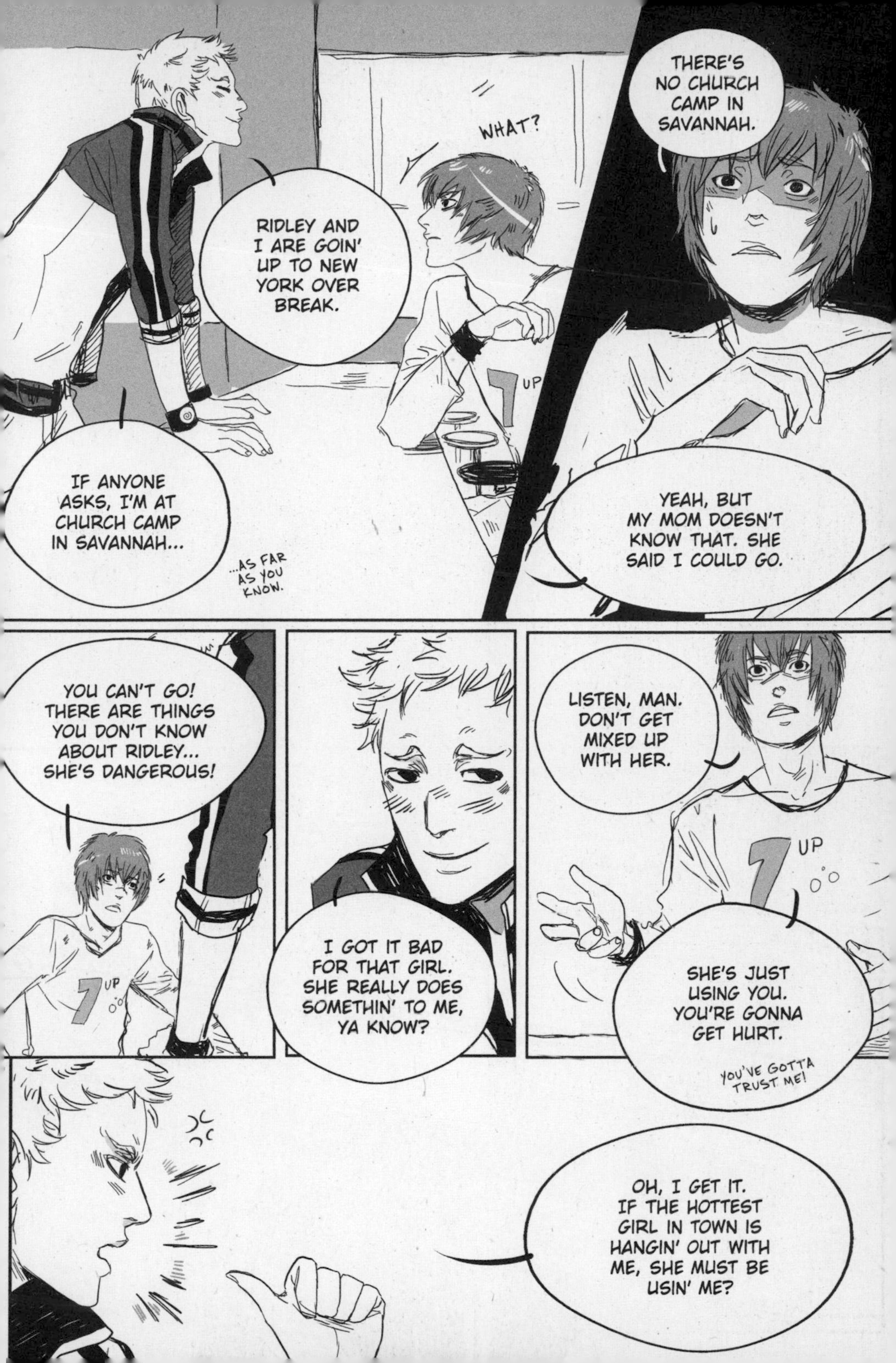
RIDLEY AND I ARE GOIN' UP TO NEW YORK OVER BREAK.
WHAT?
IF ANYONE ASKS, I'M AT CHURCH CAMP IN SAVANNAH...
...AS FAR AS YOU KNOW.
THERE'S NO CHURCH CAMP IN SAVANNAH.
YEAH, BUT MY MOM DOESN'T KNOW THAT. SHE SAID I COULD GO.
YOU CAN'T GO! THERE ARE THINGS YOU DON'T KNOW ABOUT RIDLEY... SHE'S DANGEROUS!
I GOT IT BAD FOR THAT GIRL. SHE REALLY DOES SOMETHIN' TO ME, YA KNOW?
LISTEN, MAN. DON'T GET MIXED UP WITH HER.
SHE'S JUST USING YOU. YOU'RE GONNA GET HURT.
YOU'VE GOTTA TRUST ME!
OH, I GET IT. IF THE HOTTEST GIRL IN TOWN IS HANGIN' OUT WITH ME, SHE MUST BE USIN' ME?

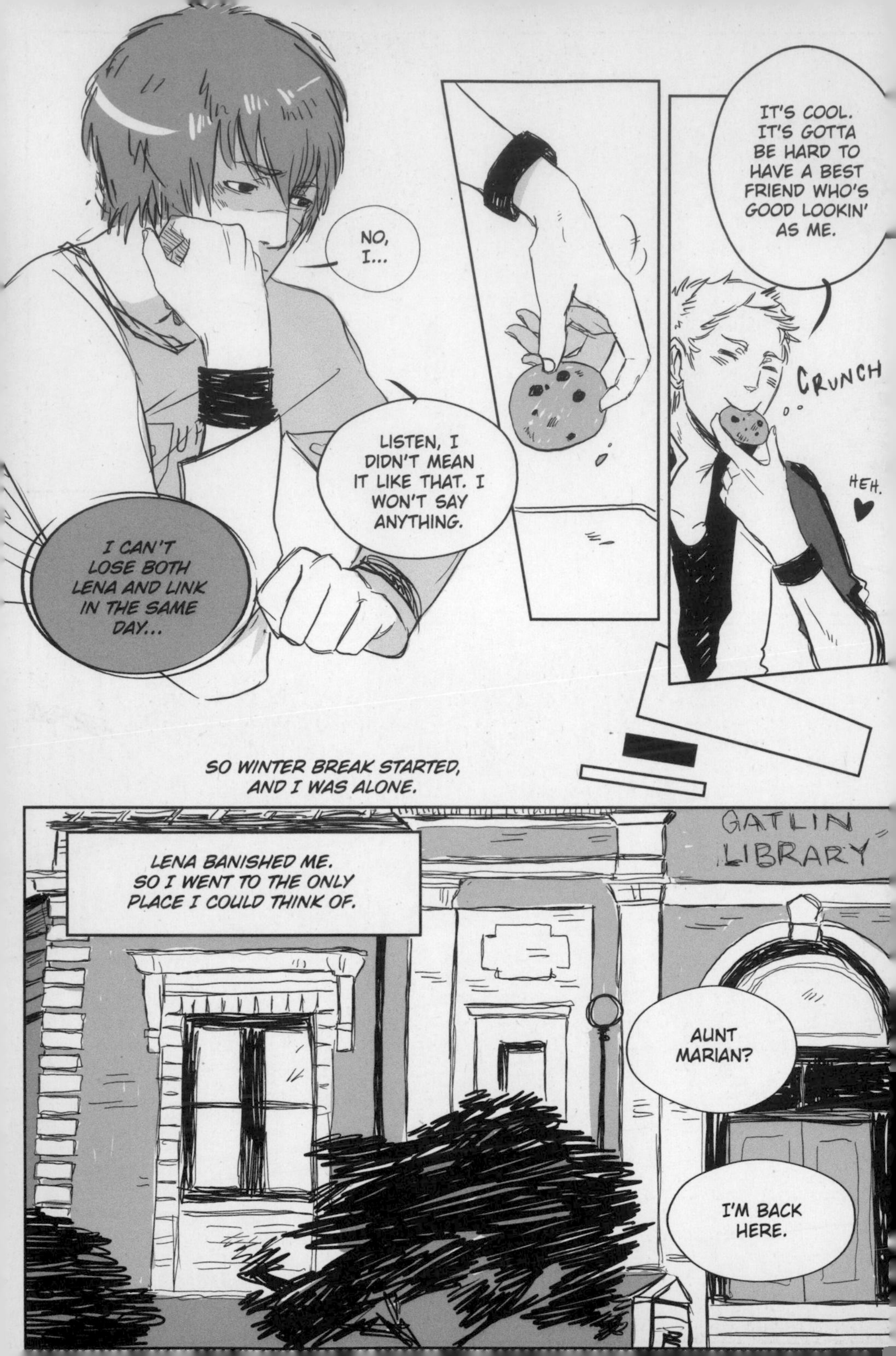
NO, I...
LISTEN, I DIDN'T MEAN IT LIKE THAT. I WON'T SAY ANYTHING.
I CAN'T LOSE BOTH LENA AND LINK IN THE SAME DAY...
IT'S COOL. IT'S GOTTA BE HARD TO HAVE A BEST FRIEND WHO'S GOOD LOOKIN' AS ME.
CRUNCH
HEH.
SO WINTER BREAK STARTED, AND I WAS ALONE.
LENA BANISHED ME. SO I WENT TO THE ONLY PLACE I COULD THINK OF.
GATLIN LIBRARY
AUNT MARIAN?
I'M BACK HERE.

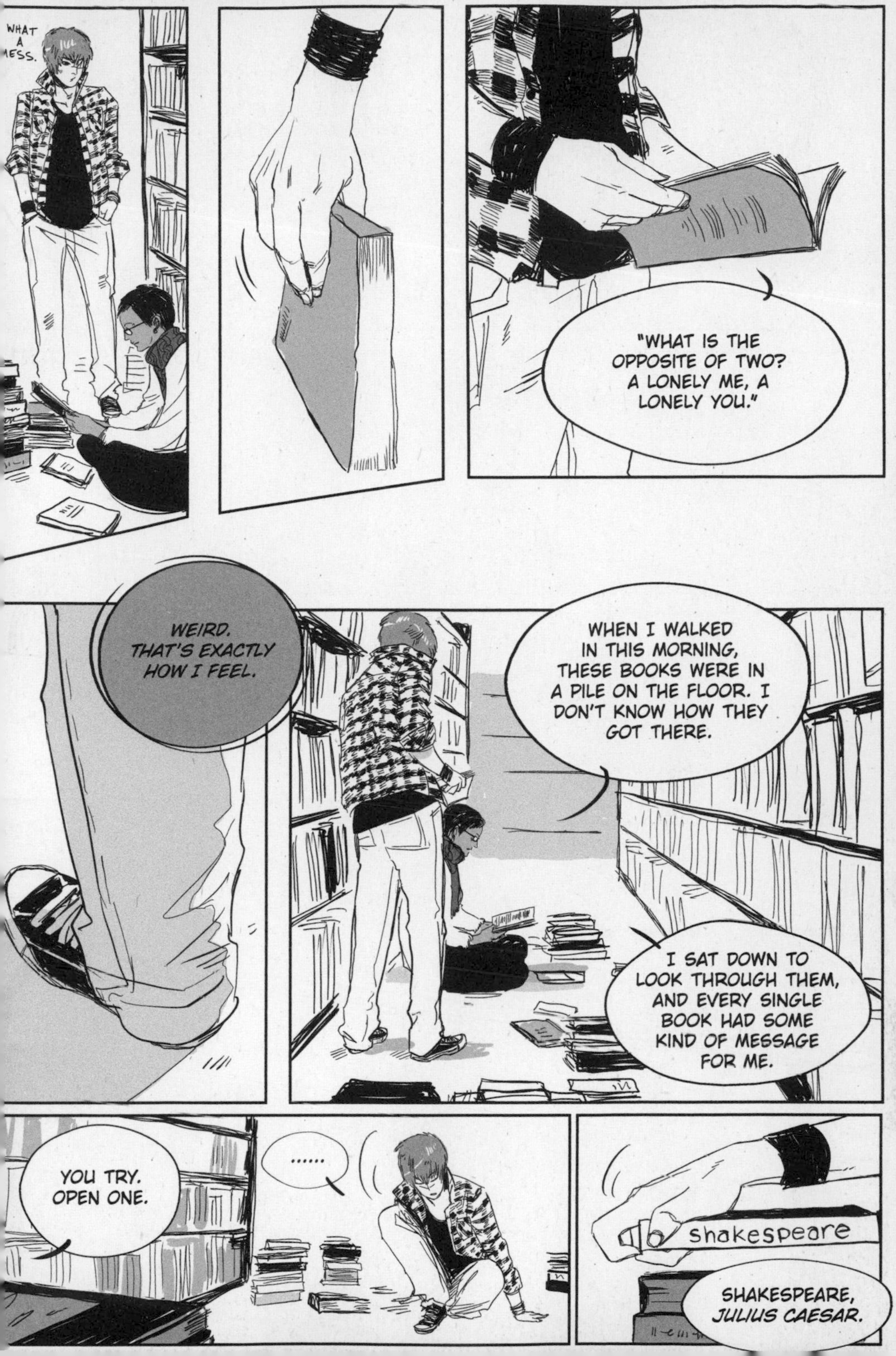
WHAT A MESS.
"WHAT IS THE OPPOSITE OF TWO? A LONELY ME, A LONELY YOU."
WEIRD. THAT'S EXACTLY HOW I FEEL.
WHEN I WALKED IN THIS MORNING, THESE BOOKS WERE IN A PILE ON THE FLOOR. I DON'T KNOW HOW THEY GOT THERE.
I SAT DOWN TO LOOK THROUGH THEM, AND EVERY SINGLE BOOK HAD SOME KIND OF MESSAGE FOR ME.
YOU TRY. OPEN ONE.
......
shakespeare
SHAKESPEARE, JULIUS CAESAR.

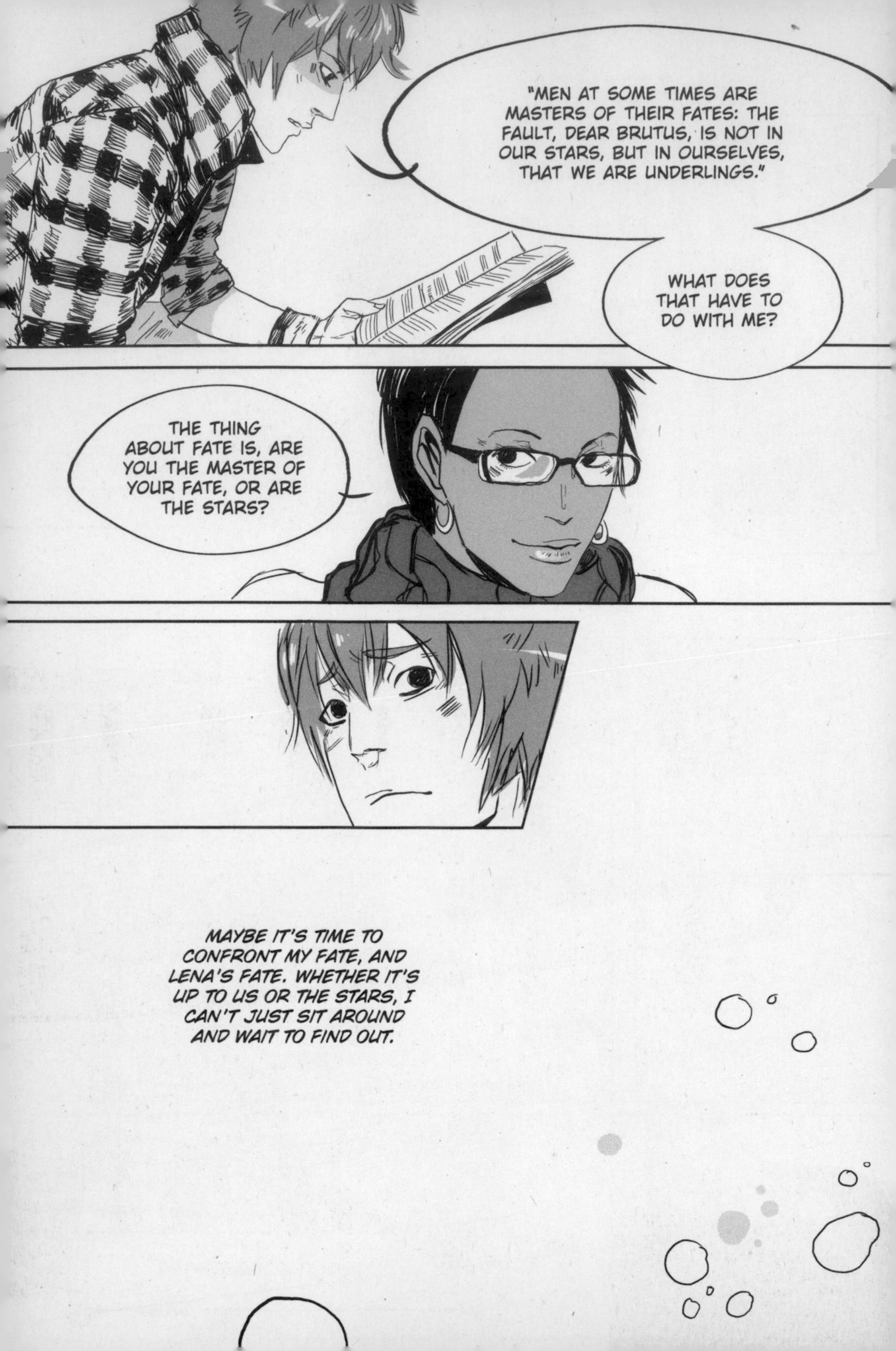
"MEN AT SOME TIMES ARE MASTERS OF THEIR FATES: THE FAULT, DEAR BRUTUS, IS NOT IN OUR STARS, BUT IN OURSELVES, THAT WE ARE UNDERLINGS."
WHAT DOES THAT HAVE TO DO WITH ME?
THE THING ABOUT FATE IS, ARE YOU THE MASTER OF YOUR FATE, OR ARE THE STARS?
MAYBE IT'S TIME TO CONFRONT MY FATE, AND LENA'S FATE. WHETHER IT'S UP TO US OR THE STARS, I CAN'T JUST SIT AROUND AND WAIT TO FIND OUT.

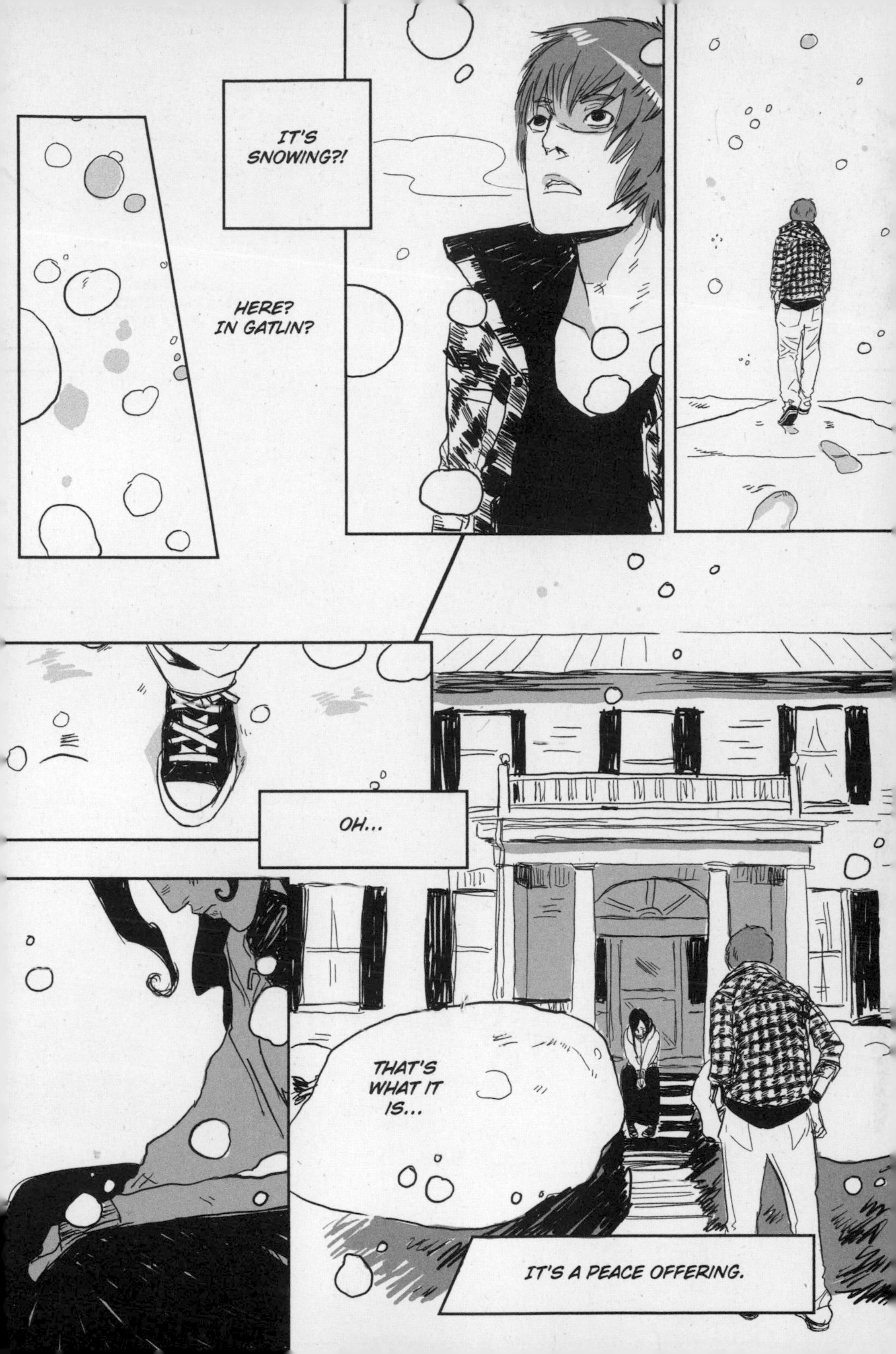
IT'S SNOWING?!
HERE? IN GATLIN?
OH...
THAT'S WHAT IT IS...
IT'S A PEACE OFFERING.

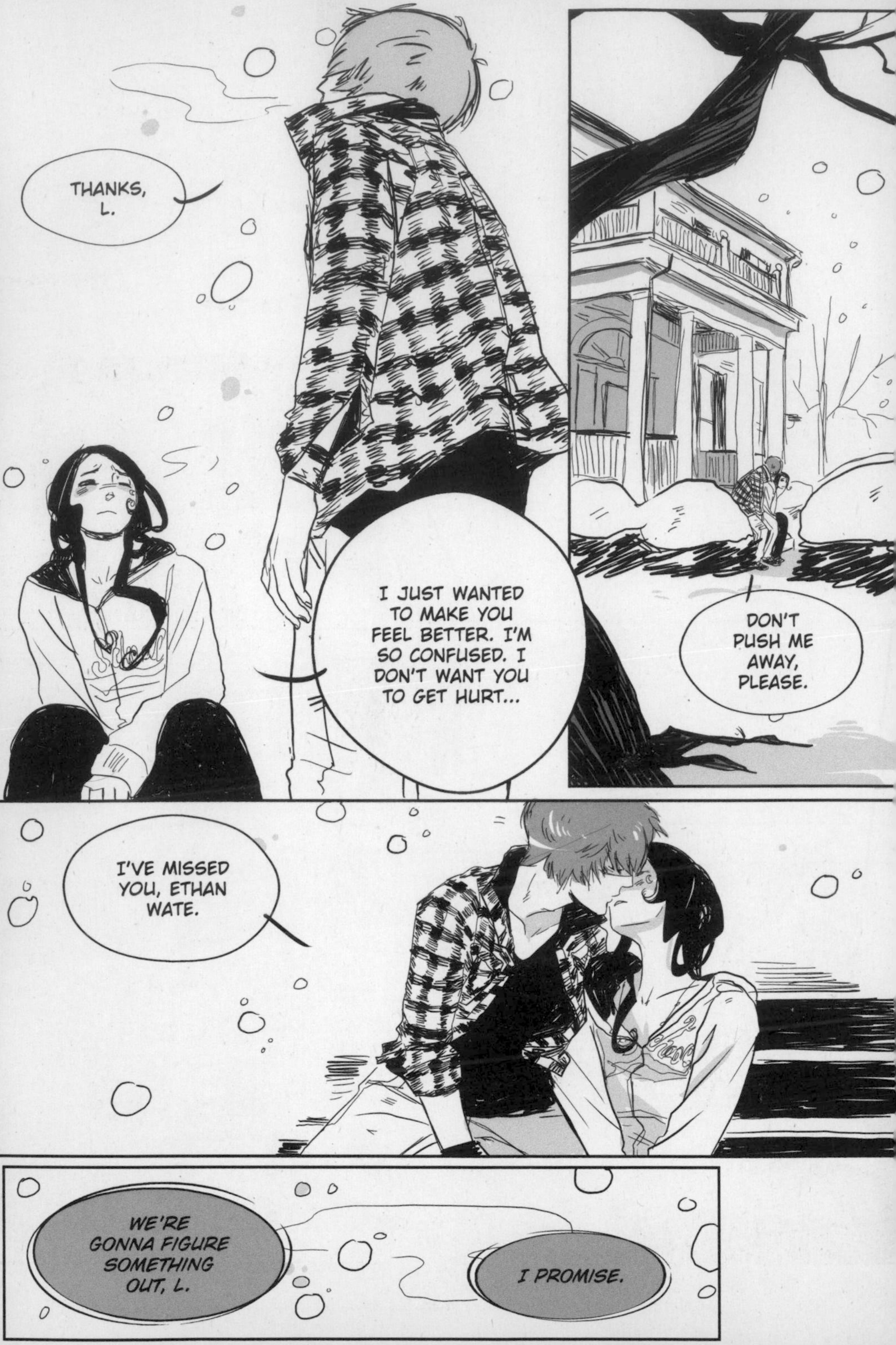
THANKS, L.
I JUST WANTED TO MAKE YOU FEEL BETTER. I'M SO CONFUSED. I DON'T WANT YOU TO GET HURT...
DON'T PUSH ME AWAY, PLEASE.
I'VE MISSED YOU, ETHAN WATE.
WE'RE GONNA FIGURE SOMETHING OUT, L.
I PROMISE.

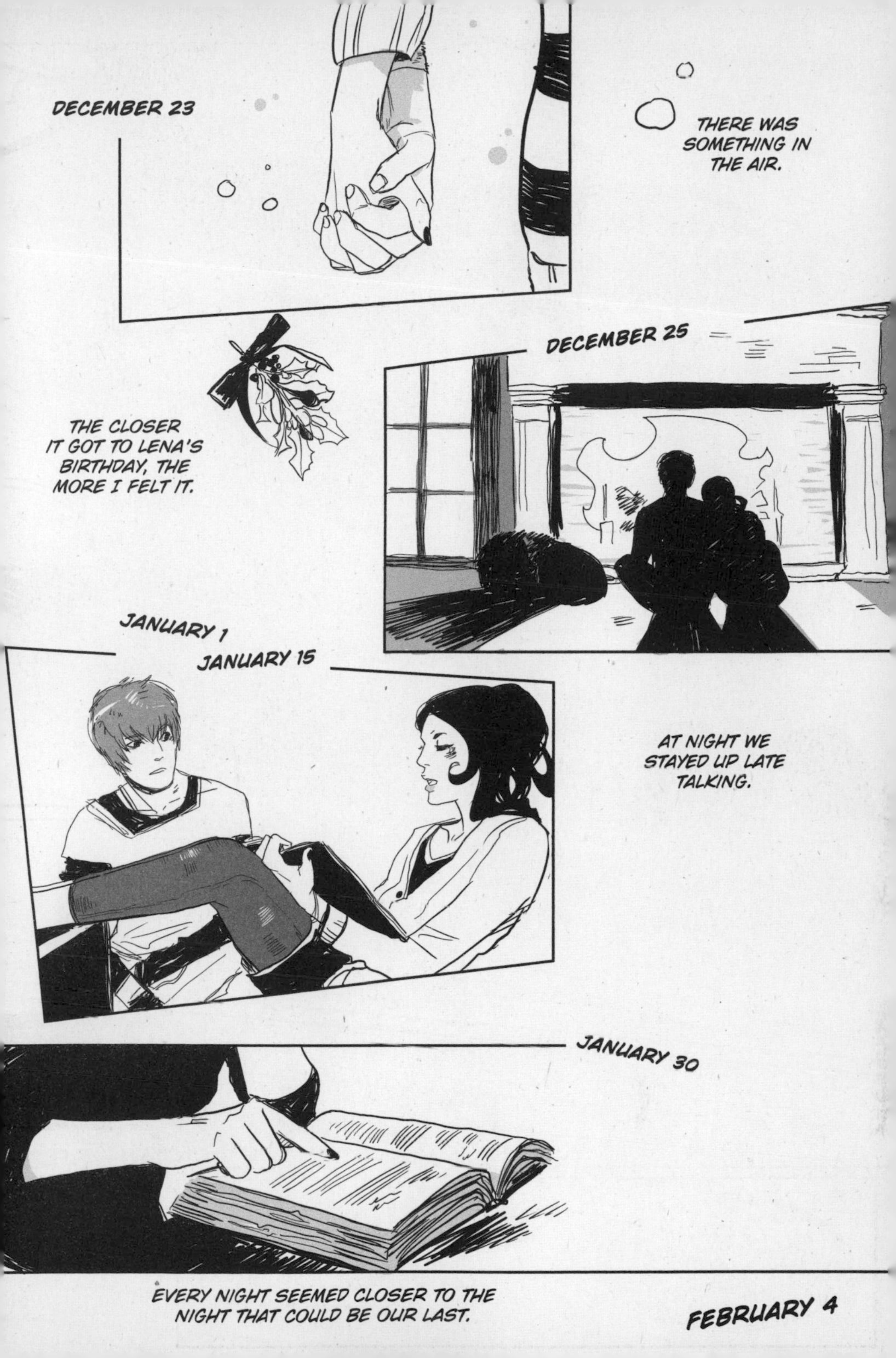
DECEMBER 23
THERE WAS SOMETHING IN THE AIR.
THE CLOSER IT GOT TO LENA'S BIRTHDAY, THE MORE I FELT IT.
DECEMBER 25
JANUARY 1
JANUARY 15
AT NIGHT WE STAYED UP LATE TALKING.
JANUARY 30
EVERY NIGHT SEEMED CLOSER TO THE NIGHT THAT COULD BE OUR LAST.
FEBRUARY 4

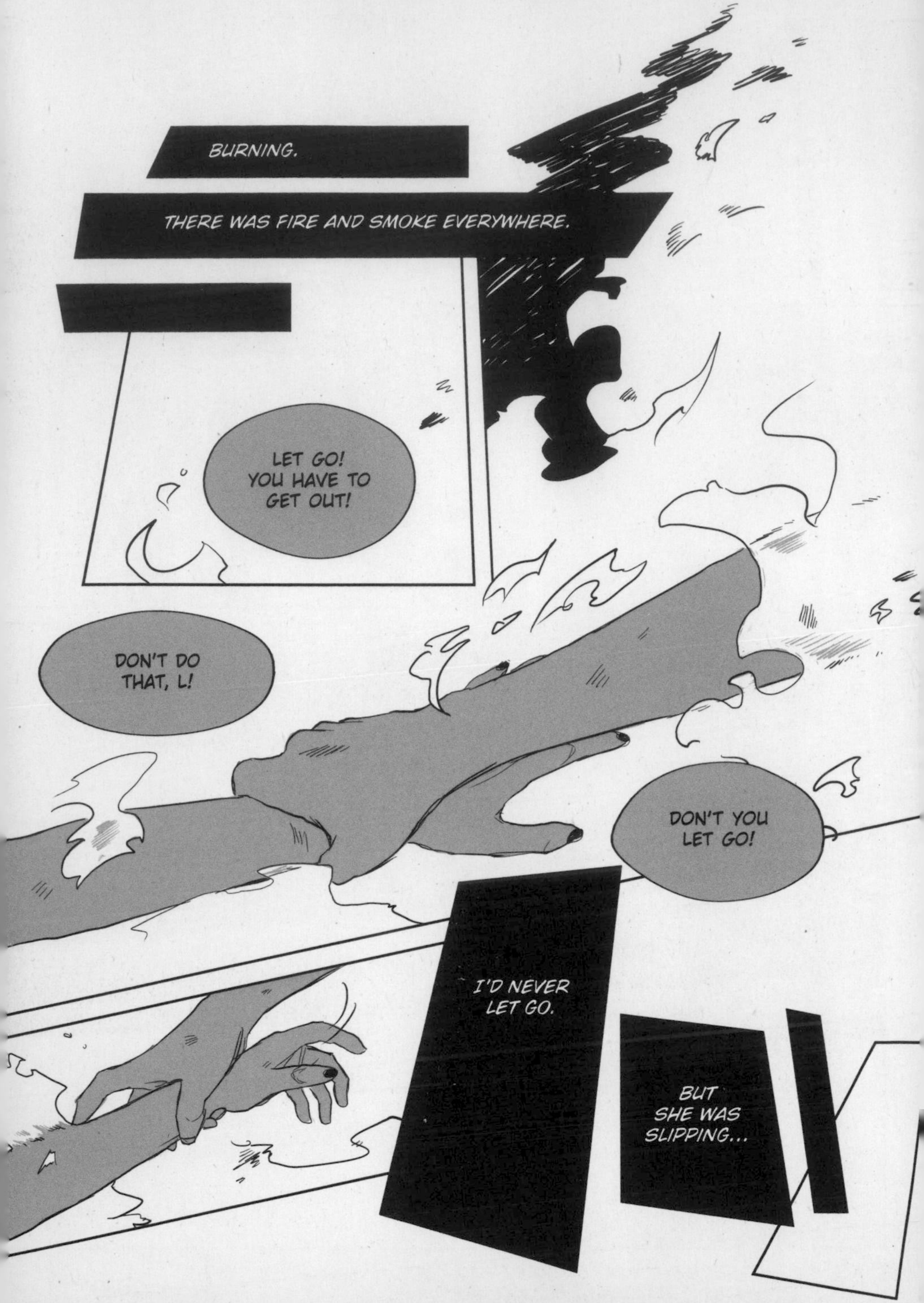
BURNING.
THERE WAS FIRE AND SMOKE EVERYWHERE.
LET GO! YOU HAVE TO GET OUT!
DON'T DO THAT, L!
DON'T YOU LET GO!
I'D NEVER LET GO.
BUT SHE WAS SLIPPING...

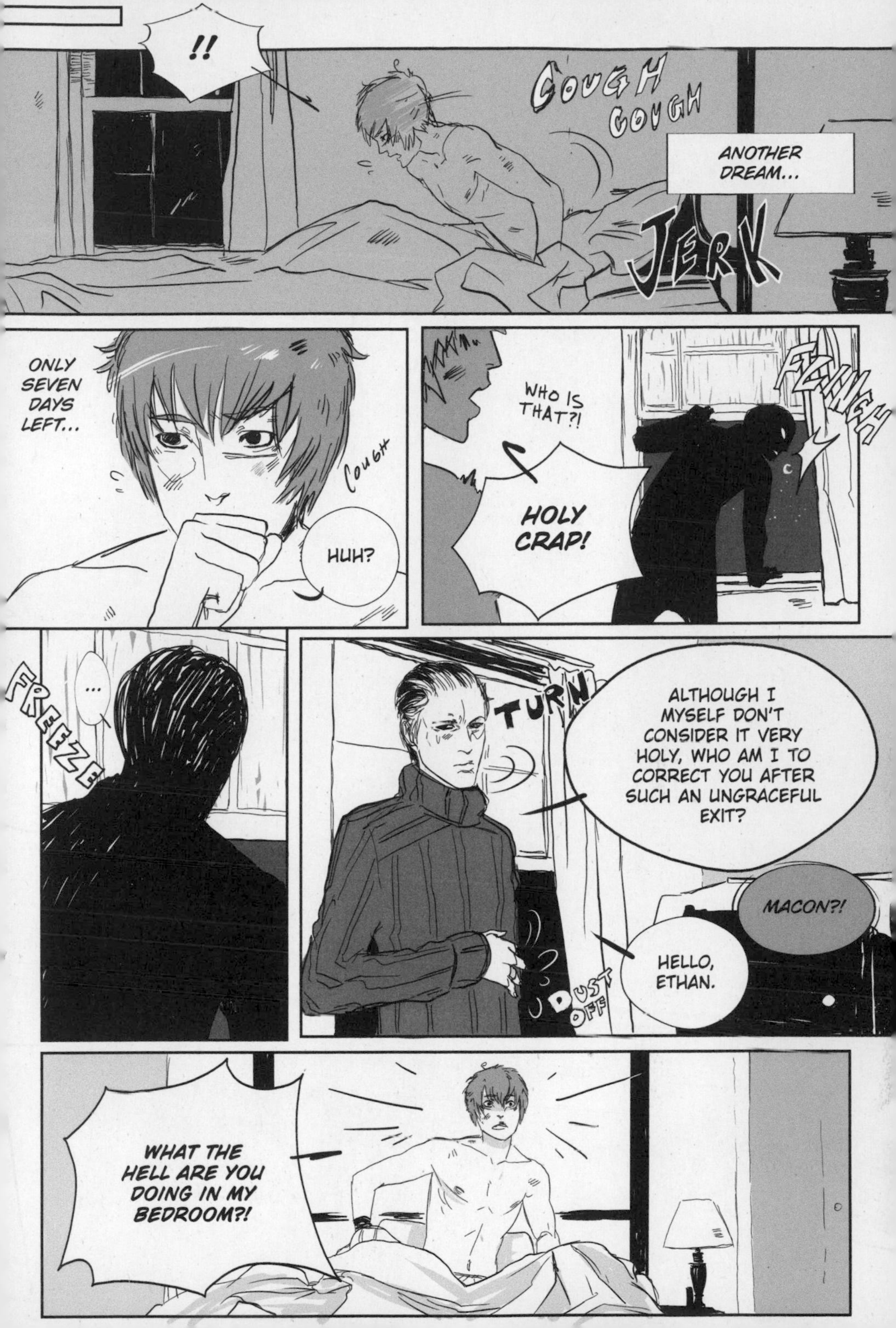
!!
COUGH COUGH
ANOTHER DREAM...
JERK
ONLY SEVEN DAYS LEFT...
COUGH
HUH?
WHO IS THAT?!
HOLY CRAP!
FLINCH
FREEZE
...
TURN
ALTHOUGH I MYSELF DON'T CONSIDER IT VERY HOLY, WHO AM I TO CORRECT YOU AFTER SUCH AN UNGRACEFUL EXIT?
DUST OFF
HELLO, ETHAN.
MACON?!
WHAT THE HELL ARE YOU DOING IN MY BEDROOM?!

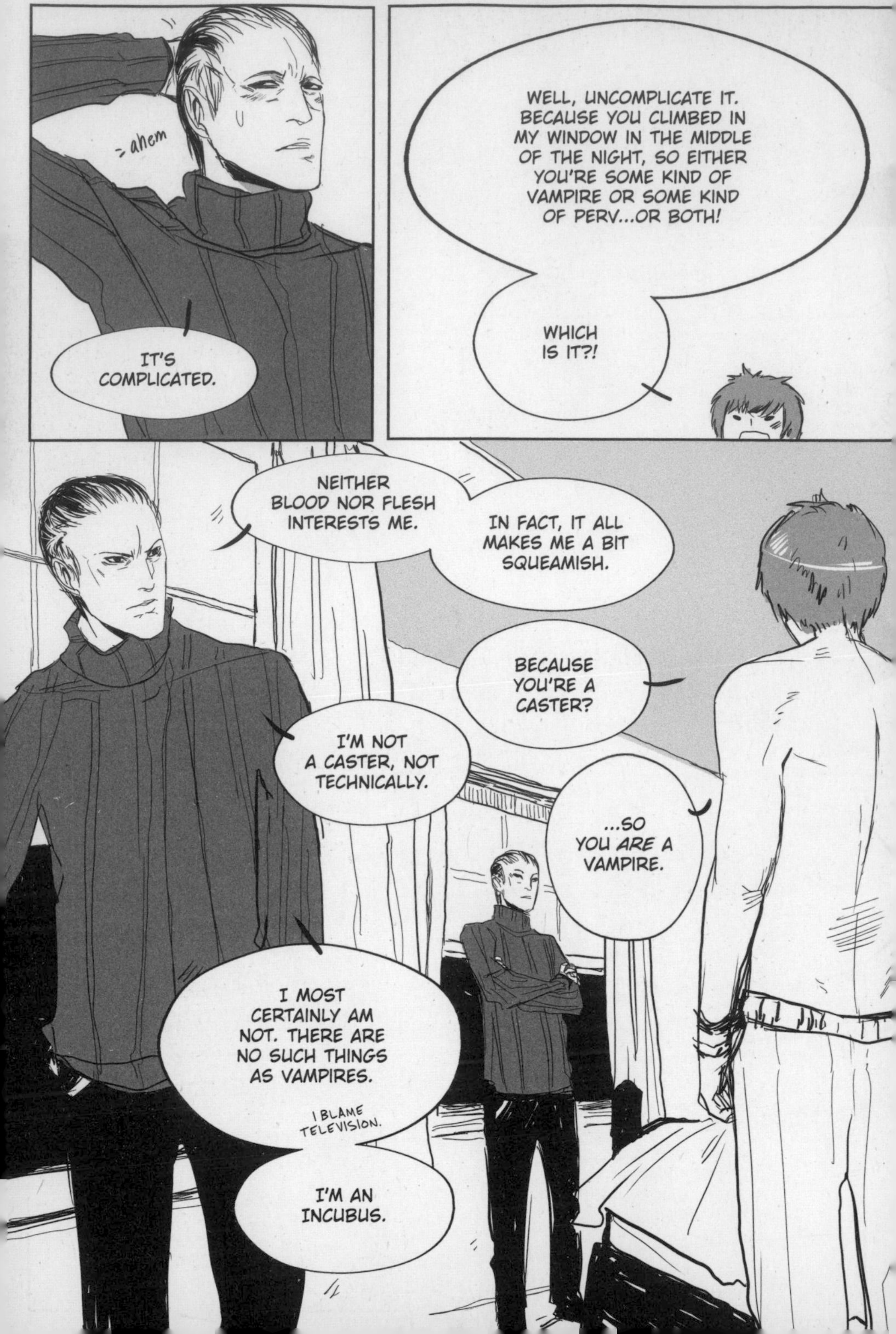

=ahem
IT'S COMPLICATED.
WELL, UNCOMPLICATE IT. BECAUSE YOU CLIMBED IN MY WINDOW IN THE MIDDLE OF THE NIGHT, SO EITHER YOU'RE SOME KIND OF VAMPIRE OR SOME KIND OF PERV...OR BOTH!
WHICH IS IT?!
NEITHER BLOOD NOR FLESH INTERESTS ME.
IN FACT, IT ALL MAKES ME A BIT SQUEAMISH.
BECAUSE YOU'RE A CASTER?
I'M NOT A CASTER, NOT TECHNICALLY.
...SO YOU *ARE* A VAMPIRE.
I MOST CERTAINLY AM NOT. THERE ARE NO SUCH THINGS AS VAMPIRES.
I BLAME TELEVISION.
I'M AN INCUBUS.

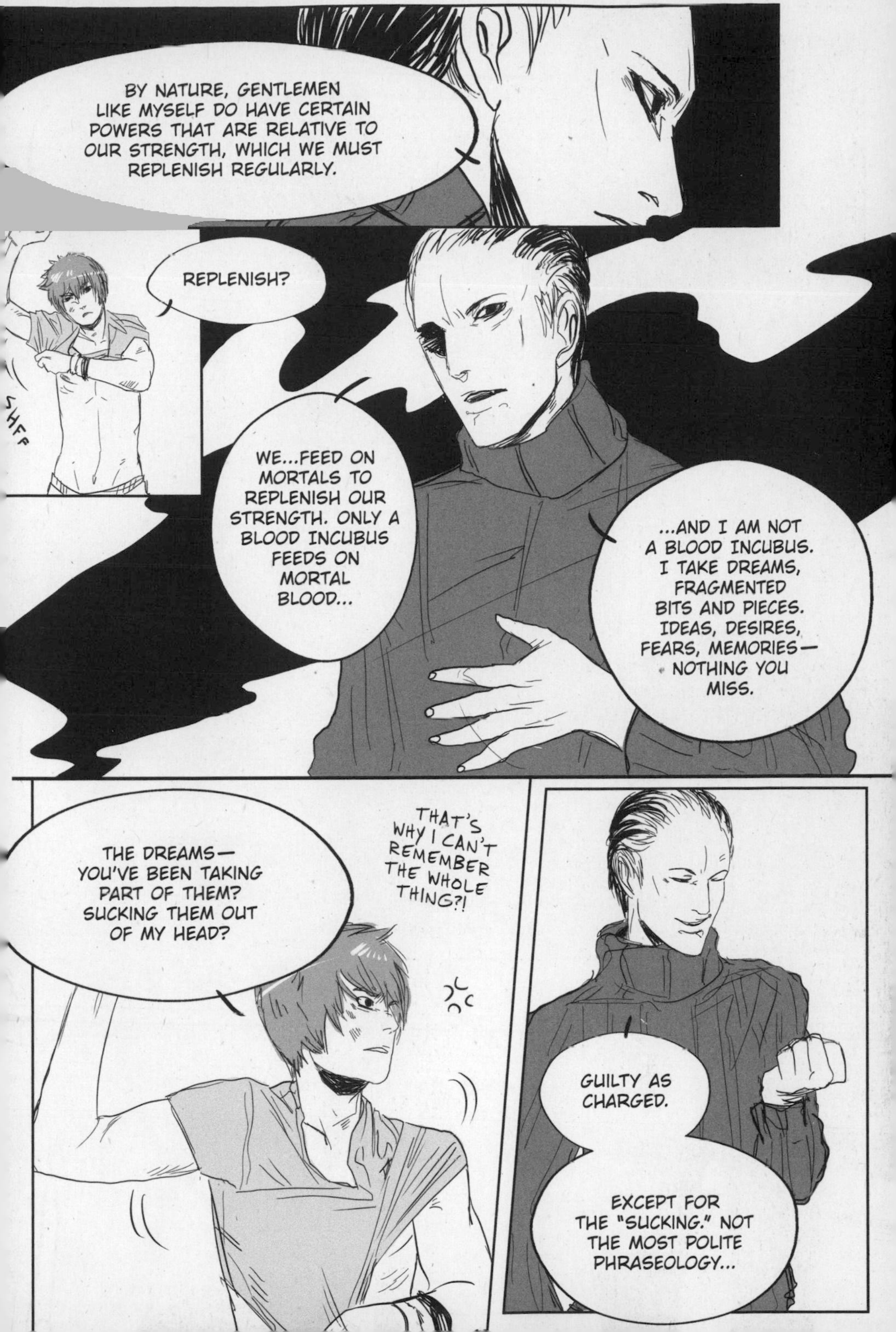
BY NATURE, GENTLEMEN LIKE MYSELF DO HAVE CERTAIN POWERS THAT ARE RELATIVE TO OUR STRENGTH, WHICH WE MUST REPLENISH REGULARLY.
REPLENISH?
SHFF
WE...FEED ON MORTALS TO REPLENISH OUR STRENGTH. ONLY A BLOOD INCUBUS FEEDS ON MORTAL BLOOD...
...AND I AM NOT A BLOOD INCUBUS. I TAKE DREAMS, FRAGMENTED BITS AND PIECES. IDEAS, DESIRES, FEARS, MEMORIES—NOTHING YOU MISS.
THE DREAMS—YOU'VE BEEN TAKING PART OF THEM? SUCKING THEM OUT OF MY HEAD?
THAT'S WHY I CAN'T REMEMBER THE WHOLE THING?!
GUILTY AS CHARGED.
EXCEPT FOR THE "SUCKING." NOT THE MOST POLITE PHRASEOLOGY...

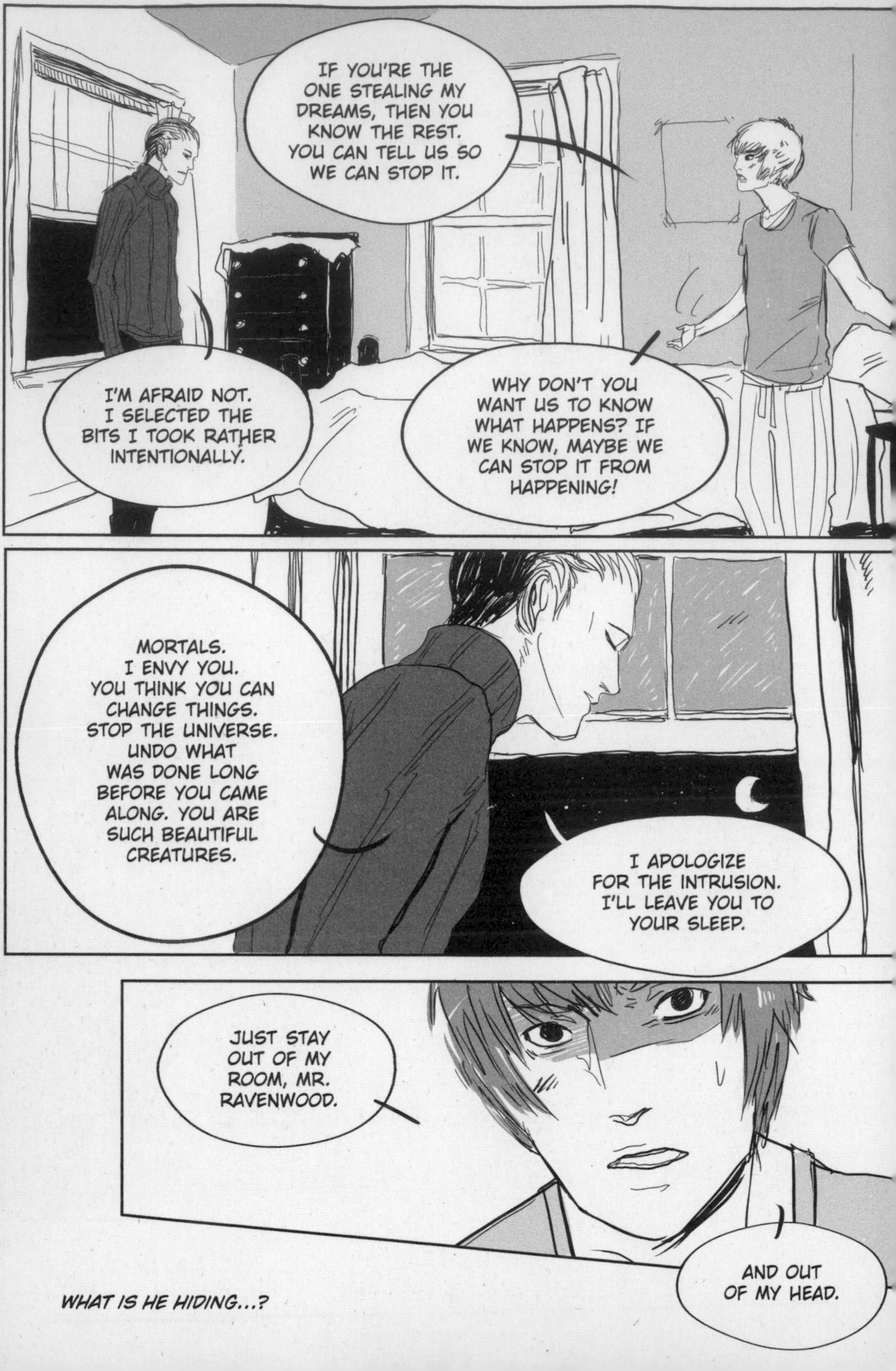
IF YOU'RE THE ONE STEALING MY DREAMS, THEN YOU KNOW THE REST. YOU CAN TELL US SO WE CAN STOP IT.
I'M AFRAID NOT. I SELECTED THE BITS I TOOK RATHER INTENTIONALLY.
WHY DON'T YOU WANT US TO KNOW WHAT HAPPENS? IF WE KNOW, MAYBE WE CAN STOP IT FROM HAPPENING!
MORTALS. I ENVY YOU. YOU THINK YOU CAN CHANGE THINGS. STOP THE UNIVERSE. UNDO WHAT WAS DONE LONG BEFORE YOU CAME ALONG. YOU ARE SUCH BEAUTIFUL CREATURES.
I APOLOGIZE FOR THE INTRUSION. I'LL LEAVE YOU TO YOUR SLEEP.
JUST STAY OUT OF MY ROOM, MR. RAVENWOOD.
AND OUT OF MY HEAD.
WHAT IS HE HIDING...?

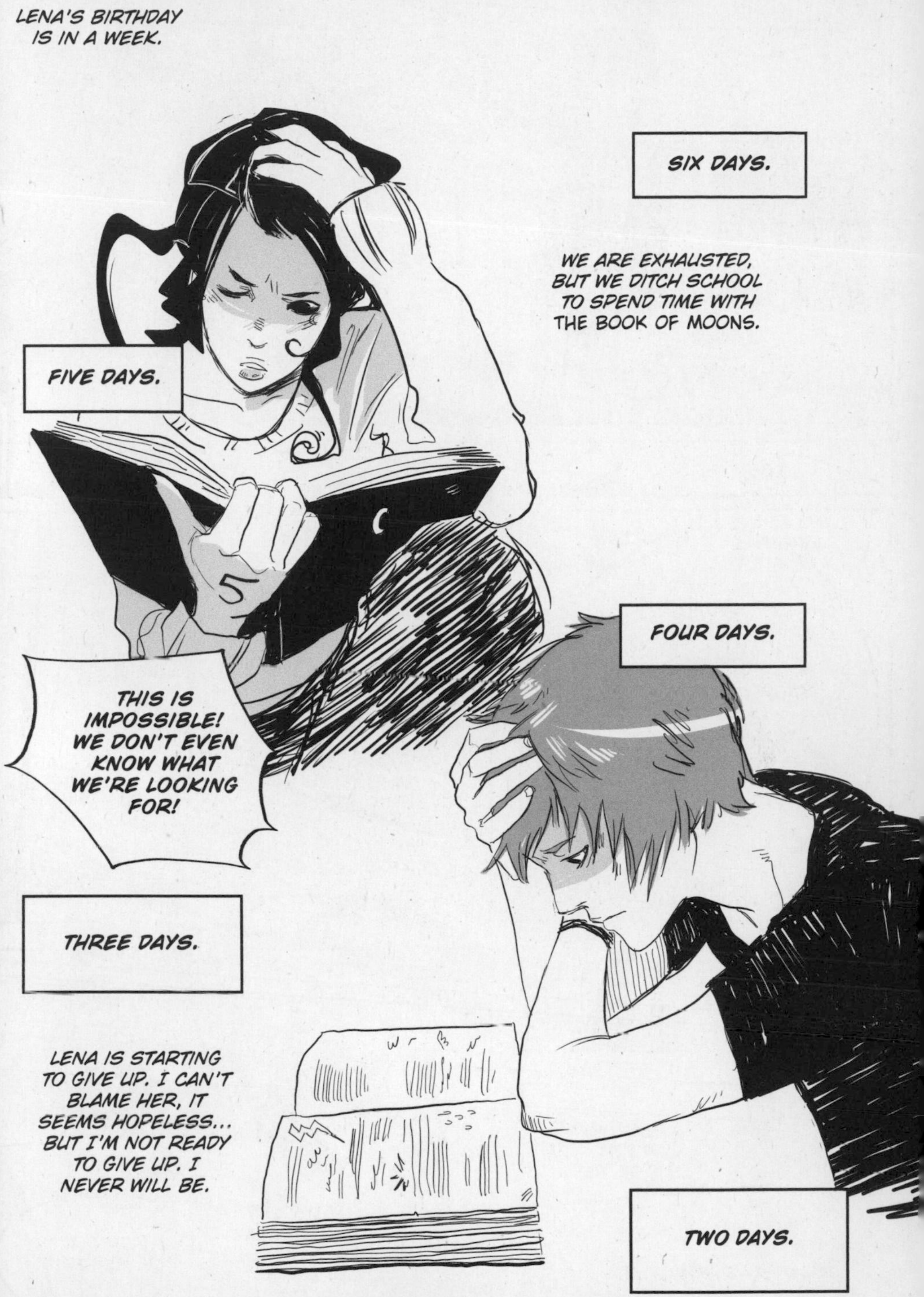

LENA'S BIRTHDAY IS IN A WEEK.
SIX DAYS.
WE ARE EXHAUSTED, BUT WE DITCH SCHOOL TO SPEND TIME WITH THE BOOK OF MOONS.
FIVE DAYS.
FOUR DAYS.
THIS IS IMPOSSIBLE! WE DON'T EVEN KNOW WHAT WE'RE LOOKING FOR!
THREE DAYS.
LENA IS STARTING TO GIVE UP. I CAN'T BLAME HER, IT SEEMS HOPELESS... BUT I'M NOT READY TO GIVE UP. I NEVER WILL BE.
TWO DAYS.

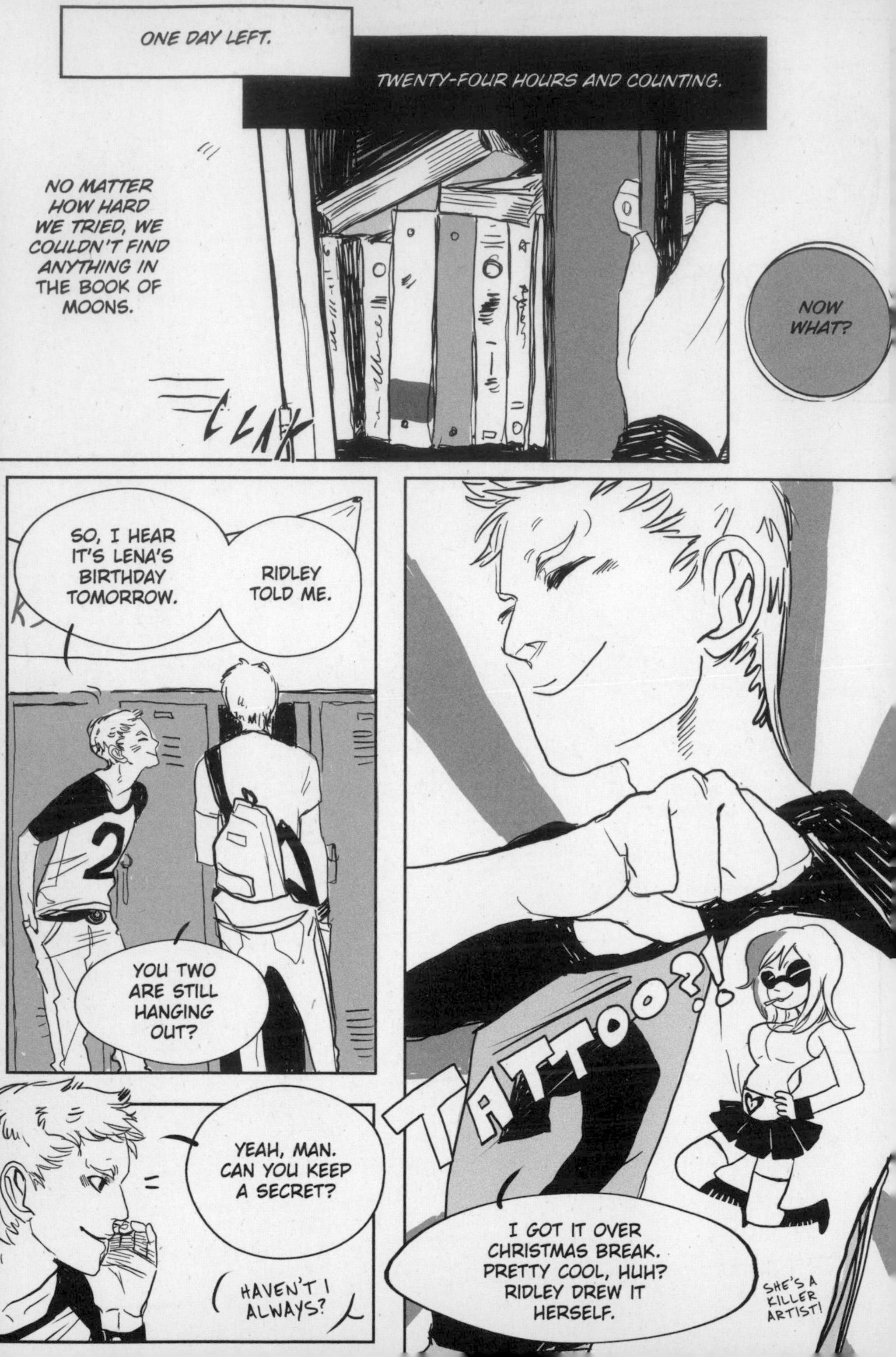
ONE DAY LEFT.
TWENTY-FOUR HOURS AND COUNTING.
NO MATTER HOW HARD WE TRIED, WE COULDN'T FIND ANYTHING IN THE BOOK OF MOONS.
CLAK
NOW WHAT?
SO, I HEAR IT'S LENA'S BIRTHDAY TOMORROW.
RIDLEY TOLD ME.
YOU TWO ARE STILL HANGING OUT?
YEAH, MAN. CAN YOU KEEP A SECRET?
HAVEN'T I ALWAYS?
TATTOO?!
I GOT IT OVER CHRISTMAS BREAK. PRETTY COOL, HUH? RIDLEY DREW IT HERSELF.
SHE'S A KILLER ARTIST!

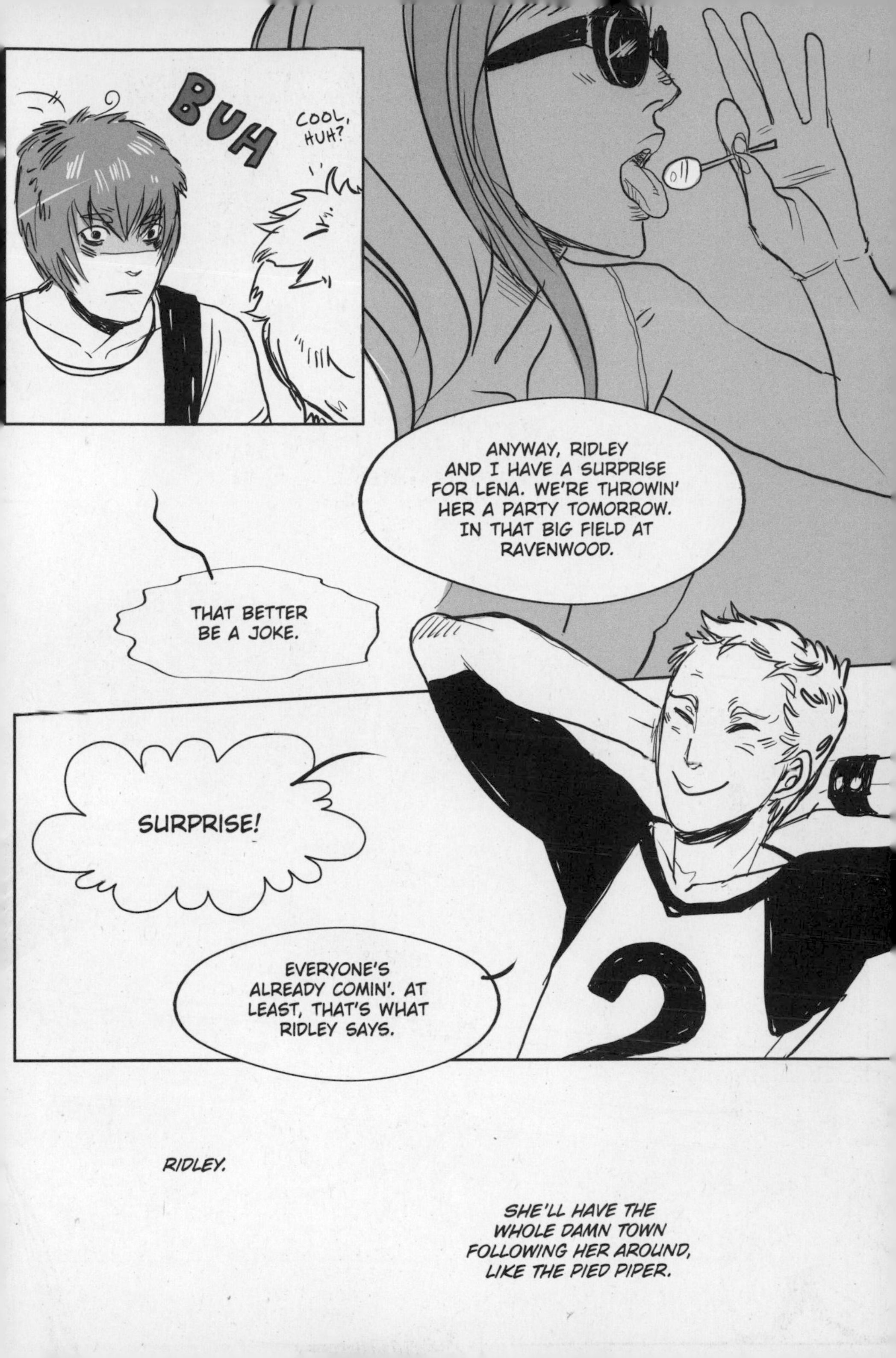
BUH
COOL, HUH?
ANYWAY, RIDLEY AND I HAVE A SURPRISE FOR LENA. WE'RE THROWIN' HER A PARTY TOMORROW. IN THAT BIG FIELD AT RAVENWOOD.
THAT BETTER BE A JOKE.
SURPRISE!
EVERYONE'S ALREADY COMIN'. AT LEAST, THAT'S WHAT RIDLEY SAYS.
RIDLEY.
SHE'LL HAVE THE WHOLE DAMN TOWN FOLLOWING HER AROUND, LIKE THE PIED PIPER.

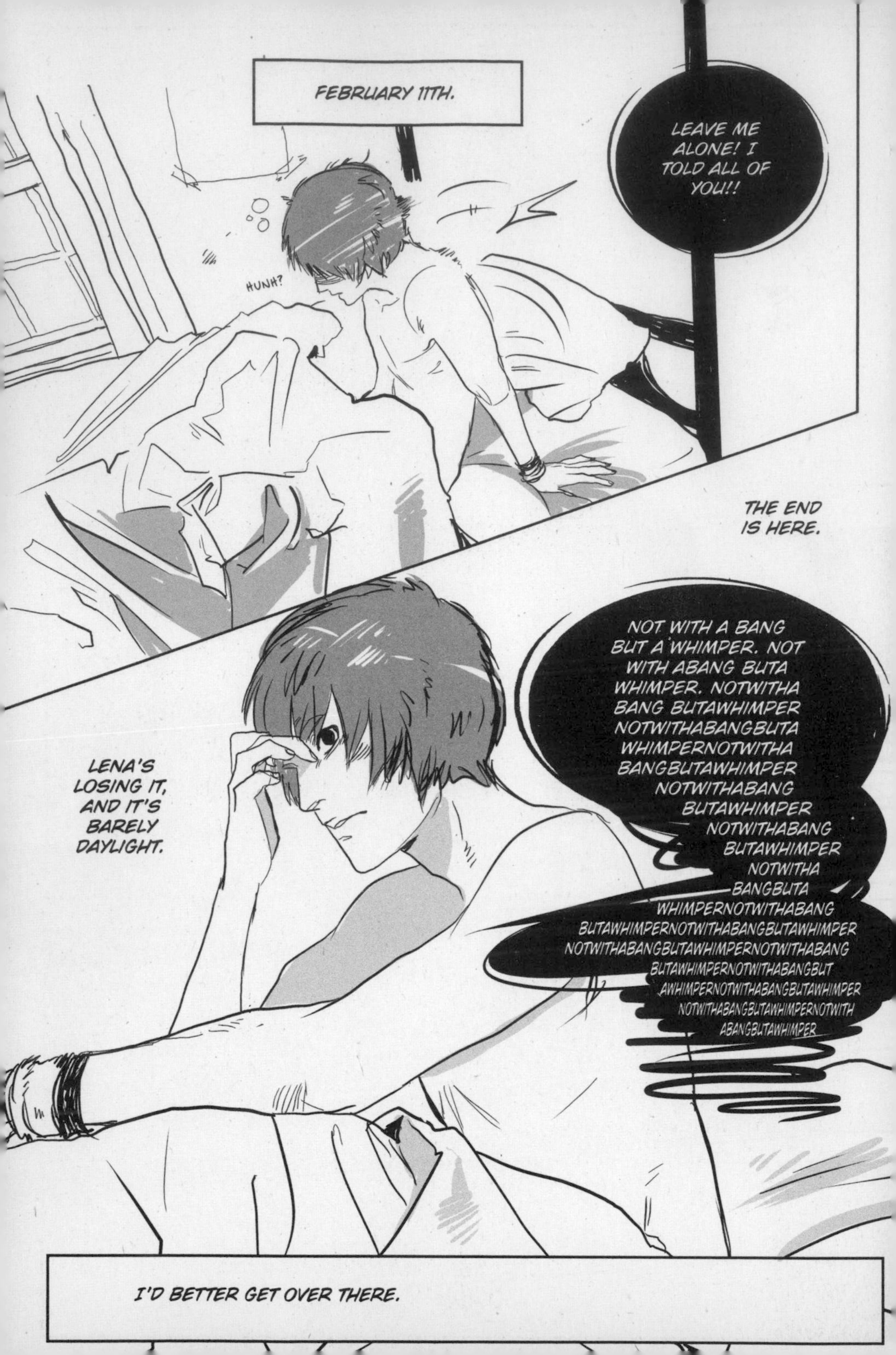
FEBRUARY 11TH.
HUNH?
LEAVE ME ALONE! I TOLD ALL OF YOU!!
THE END IS HERE.
LENA'S LOSING IT, AND IT'S BARELY DAYLIGHT.
NOT WITH A BANG BUT A WHIMPER. NOT WITH ABANG BUTA WHIMPER. NOTWITHA BANG BUTAWHIMPER NOTWITHABANGBUTA WHIMPERNOTWITHA BANGBUTAWHIMPER NOTWITHABANG BUTAWHIMPER NOTWITHABANG BUTAWHIMPER NOTWITHA BANGBUTA WHIMPERNOTWITHABANG BUTAWHIMPERNOTWITHABANGBUTAWHIMPER NOTWITHABANGBUTAWHIMPERNOTWITHABANG BUTAWHIMPERNOTWITHABANGBUT AWHIMPERNOTWITHABANGBUTAWHIMPER NOTWITHABANGBUTAWHIMPERNOTWITH ABANGBUTAWHIMPER
I'D BETTER GET OVER THERE.

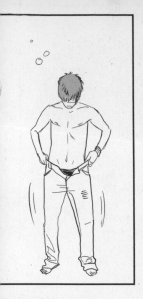

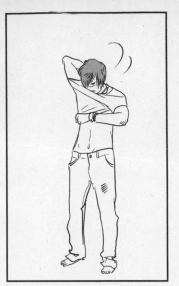

EVEN THOUGH WE NEVER FOUND ANYTHING, I BETTER BRING THE BOOK.

SHFF

WHAT?

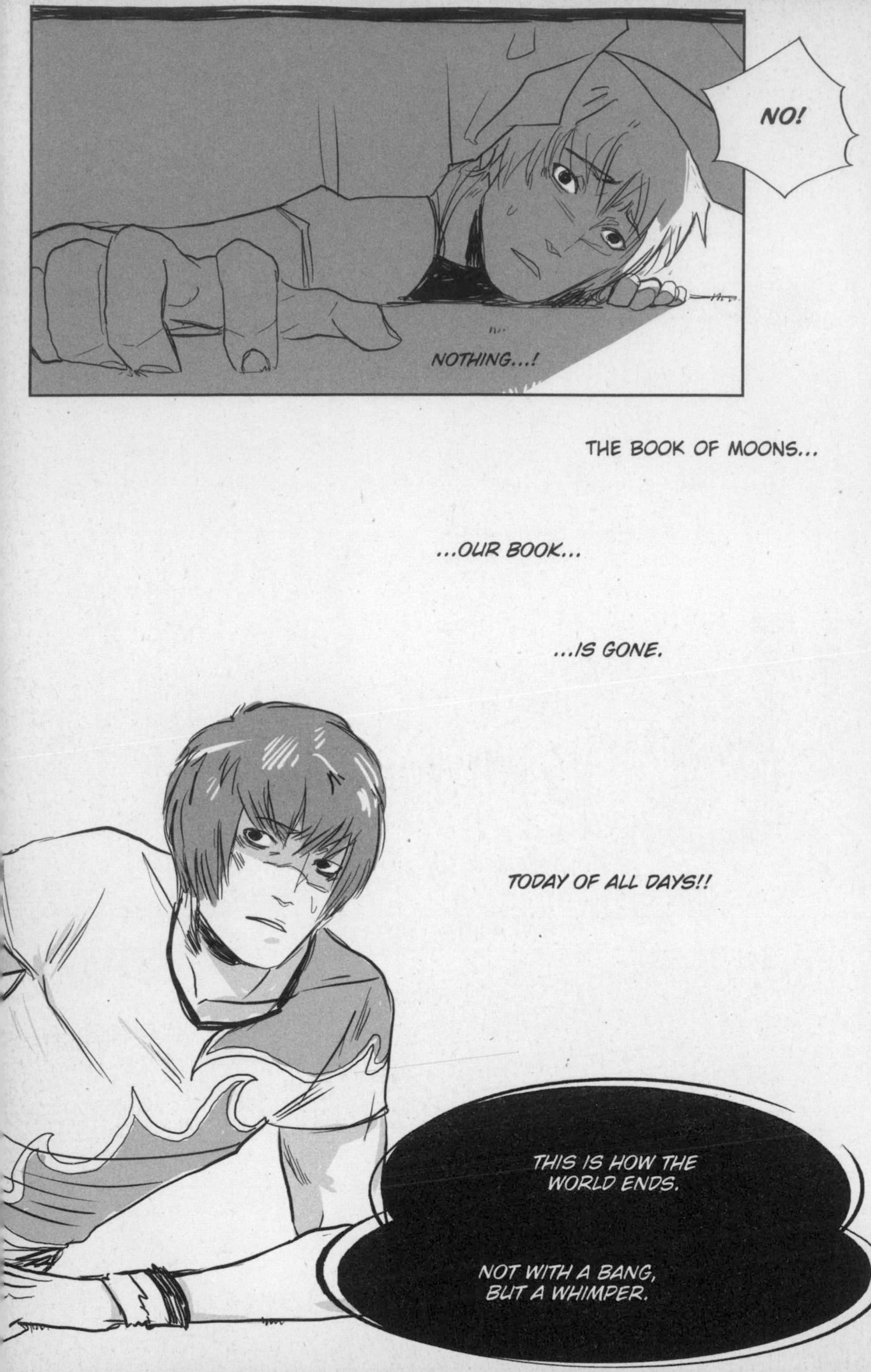
NO!
NOTHING...!
THE BOOK OF MOONS...
...OUR BOOK...
...IS GONE.
TODAY OF ALL DAYS!!
THIS IS HOW THE WORLD ENDS.
NOT WITH A BANG, BUT A WHIMPER.

BEAUTIFUL CREATURES

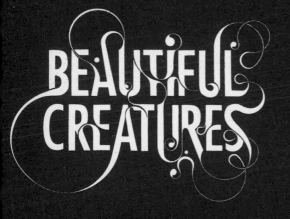

CHAPTER 6

Sixteen moons, sixteen years
Sixteen of your deepest fears
Sixteen times you dreamed my tears
Falling, falling through the years...

Sixteen moons, sixteen years
Sound of thunder in your ears
Sixteen miles before she nears
Sixteen seeks what sixteen fears...

Sixteen moons, sixteen years
Sixteen times you dreamed my fears,
Sixteen will try to Bind the spheres,
Sixteen screams but just one hears...

Sixteen moons, sixteen years
The Claiming moon, the hour nears,
In these pages Darkness clears,
Powers Bind what fire sears...

Sixteenth Moon, Sixteenth Year
Now has come the day you tear,
Claim or be Claimed,
Shed blood, shed tear,
Moon or Sun—destroy, revere...

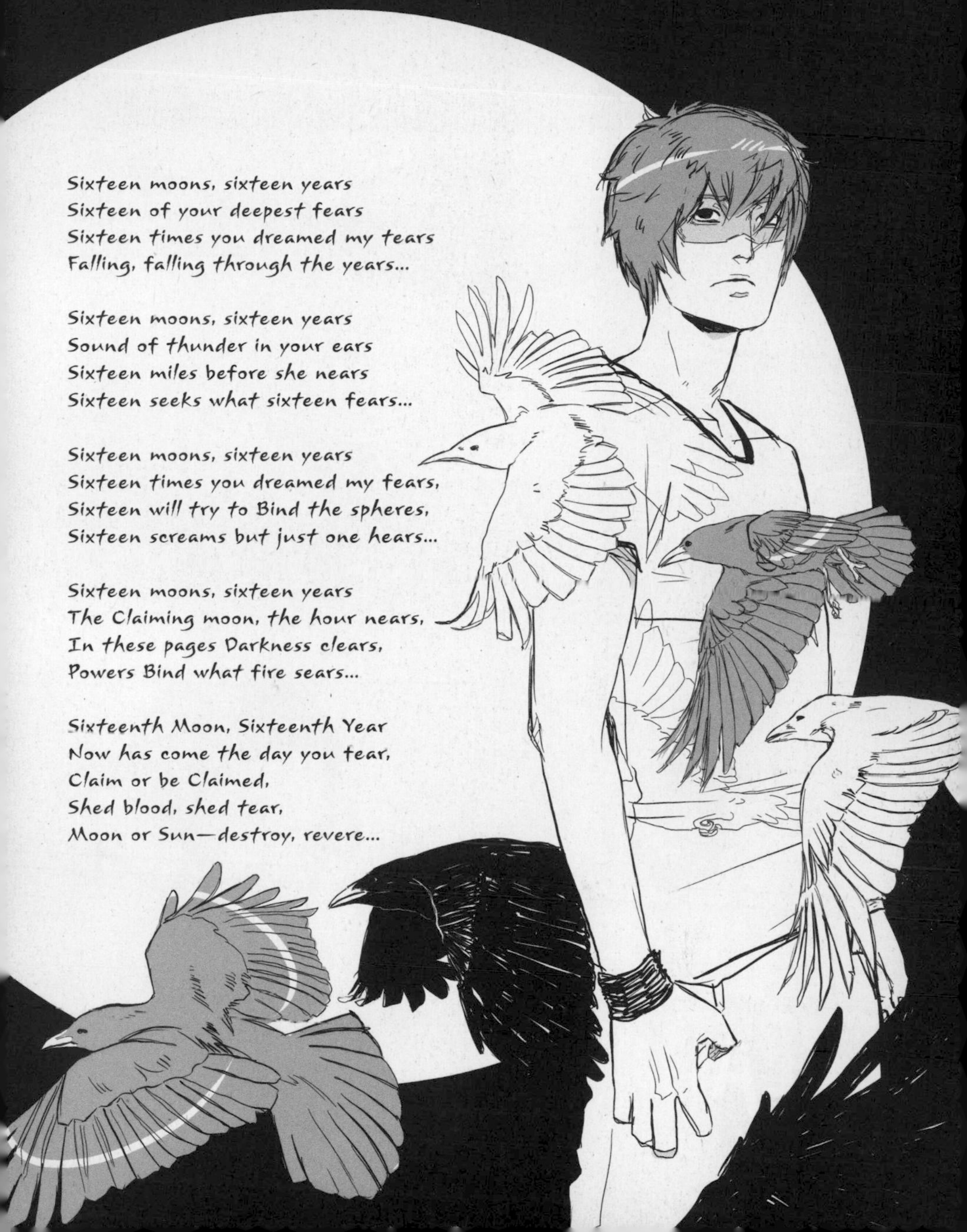

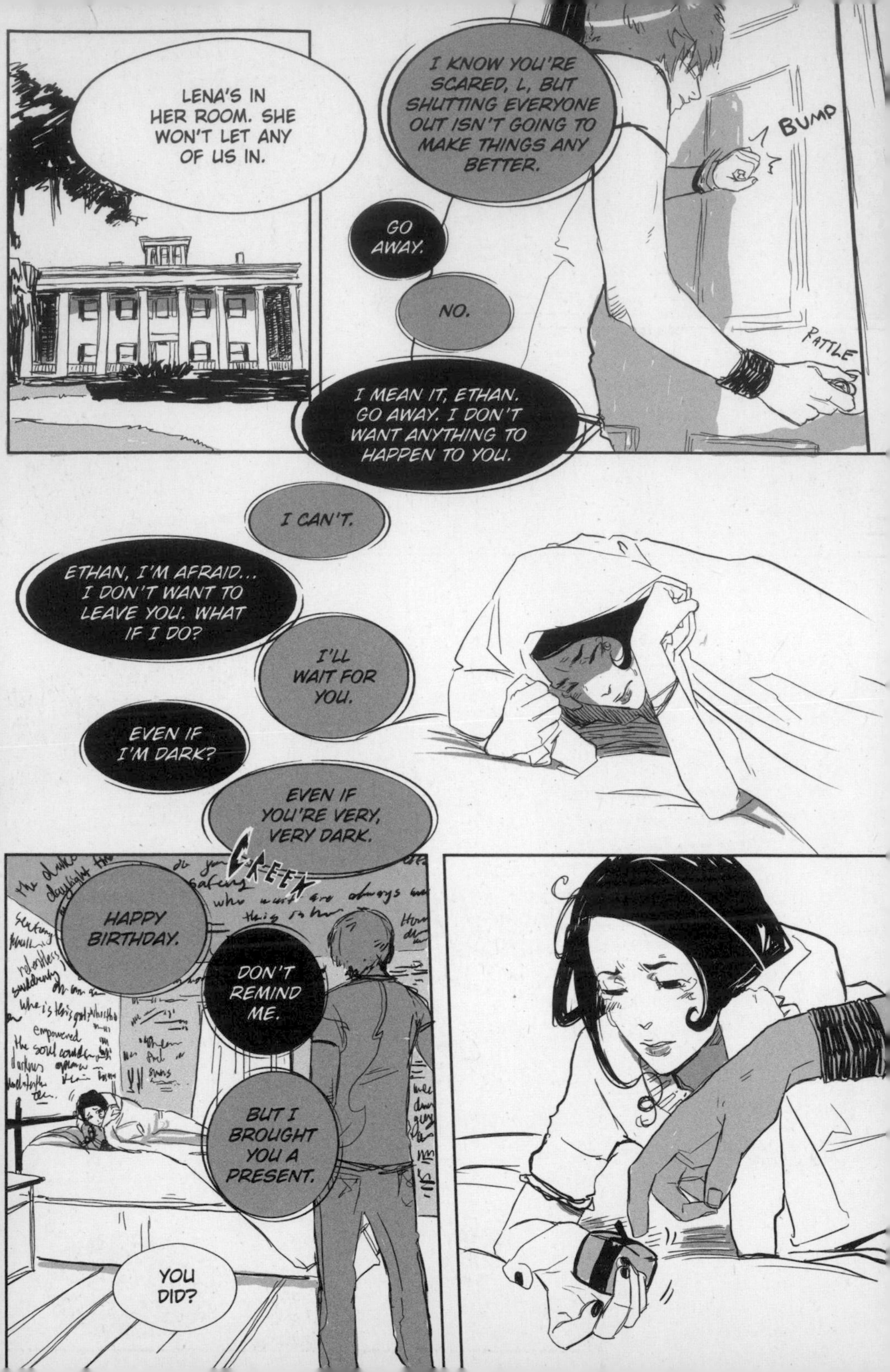
LENA'S IN HER ROOM. SHE WON'T LET ANY OF US IN.
I KNOW YOU'RE SCARED, L, BUT SHUTTING EVERYONE OUT ISN'T GOING TO MAKE THINGS ANY BETTER.
BUMP
GO AWAY.
NO.
RATTLE
I MEAN IT, ETHAN. GO AWAY. I DON'T WANT ANYTHING TO HAPPEN TO YOU.
I CAN'T.
ETHAN, I'M AFRAID... I DON'T WANT TO LEAVE YOU. WHAT IF I DO?
I'LL WAIT FOR YOU.
EVEN IF I'M DARK?
EVEN IF YOU'RE VERY, VERY DARK.
CREEK
HAPPY BIRTHDAY.
DON'T REMIND ME.
BUT I BROUGHT YOU A PRESENT.
YOU DID?

RUSTLE

OH...

OH YEAH, THIS IS POSSIBLY THE ONLY PRESENT LENA IS GETTING TODAY.

GRAB

ETHAN, I LOVE IT!

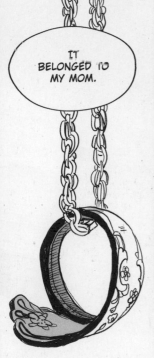

IT BELONGED TO MY MOM.

ARE YOU SURE ABOUT THIS?

LENA KNOWS HOW I FEEL ABOUT MY MOM.

THIS IS A BIG DEAL.

I'M SURE... BECAUSE YOU'RE REALLY SPECIAL TO ME.

HOW SPECIAL?

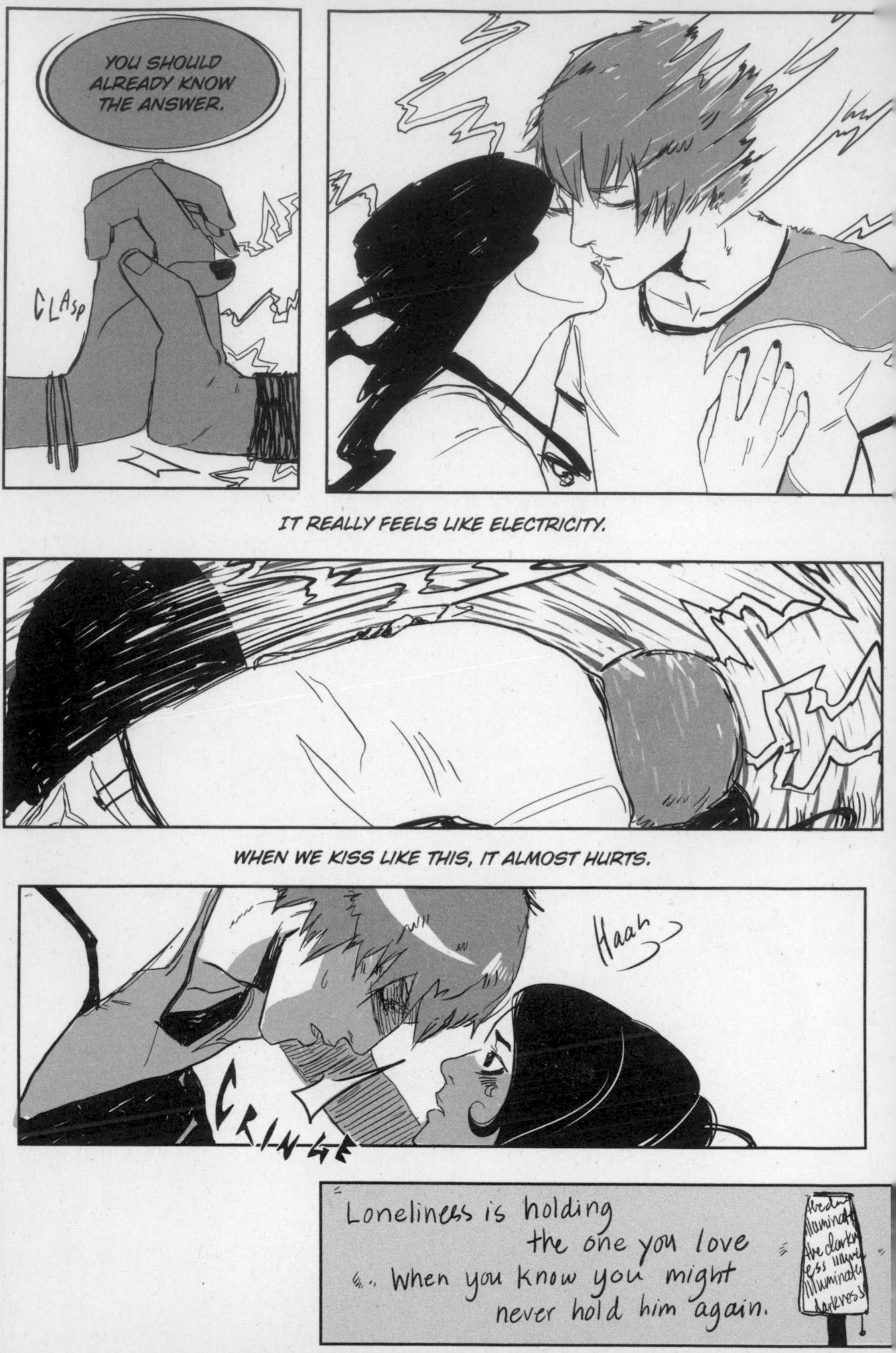
YOU SHOULD ALREADY KNOW THE ANSWER.
CLASP
IT REALLY FEELS LIKE ELECTRICITY.
WHEN WE KISS LIKE THIS, IT ALMOST HURTS.
Haah
CRINGE
Loneliness is holding the one you love when you know you might never hold him again.

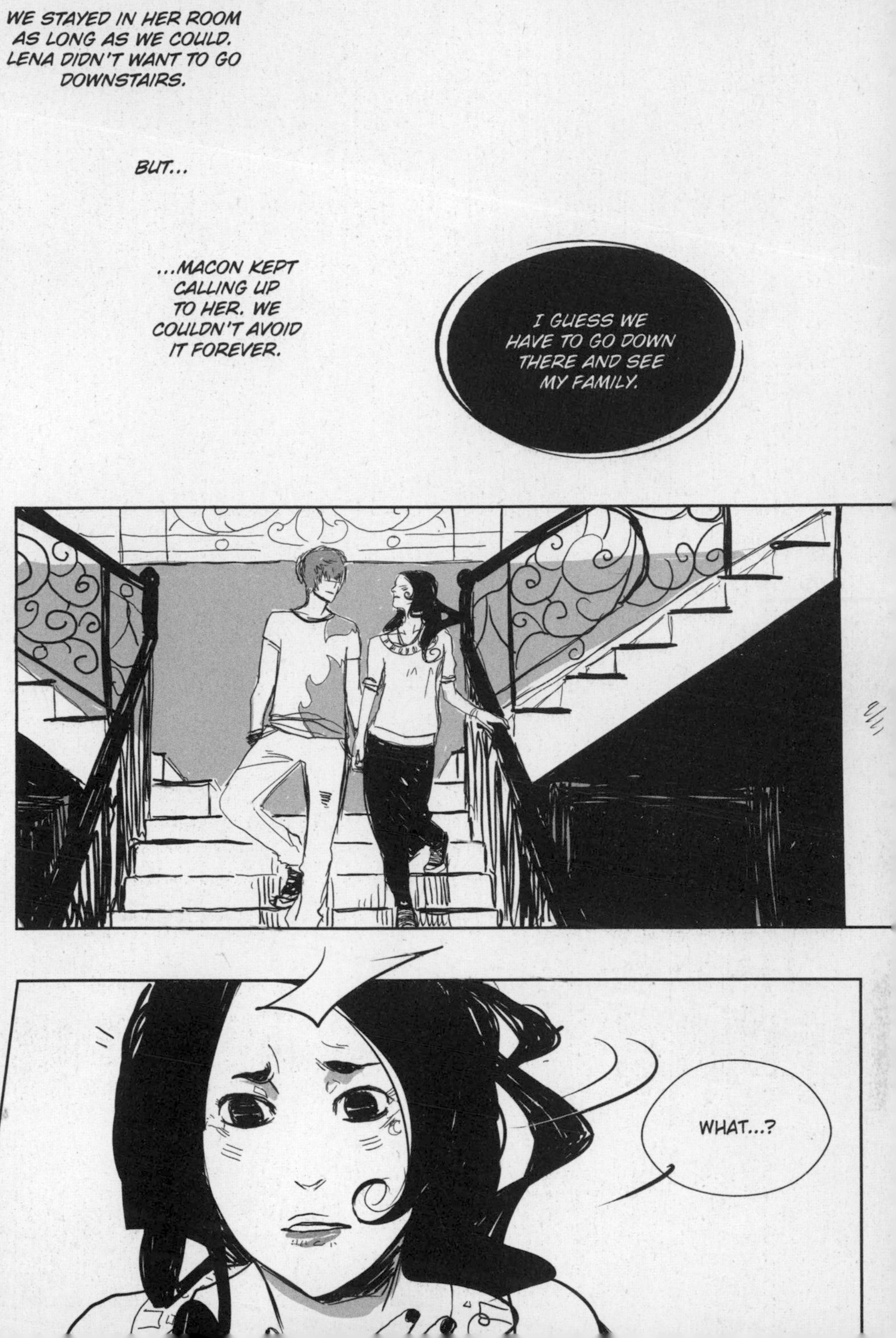
WE STAYED IN HER ROOM AS LONG AS WE COULD. LENA DIDN'T WANT TO GO DOWNSTAIRS.
BUT...
...MACON KEPT CALLING UP TO HER. WE COULDN'T AVOID IT FOREVER.
I GUESS WE HAVE TO GO DOWN THERE AND SEE MY FAMILY.
WHAT...?

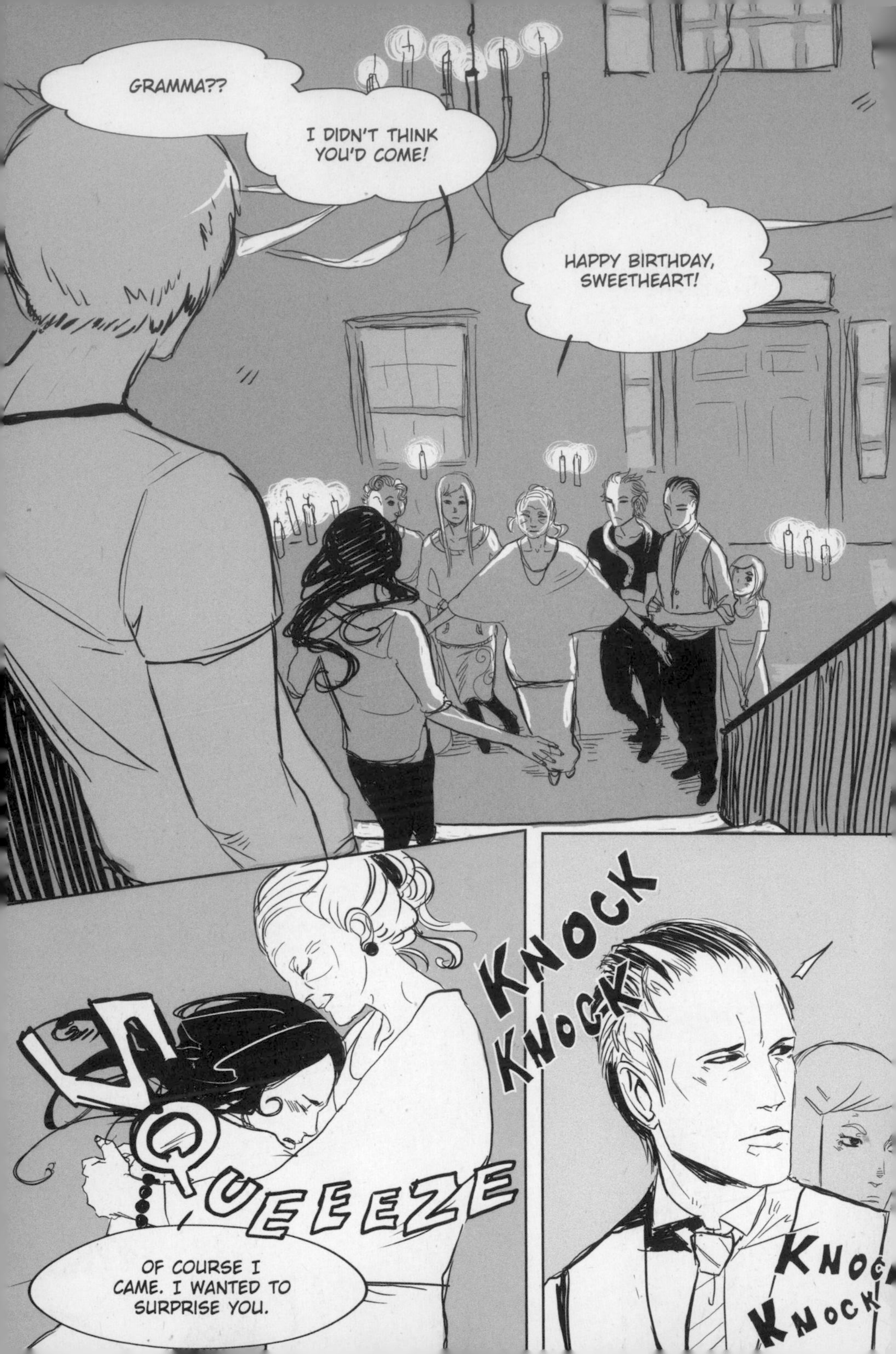
GRAMMA??
I DIDN'T THINK YOU'D COME!
HAPPY BIRTHDAY, SWEETHEART!
SQUEEEZE
OF COURSE I CAME. I WANTED TO SURPRISE YOU.
KNOCK KNOCK
KNOC
KNOCK

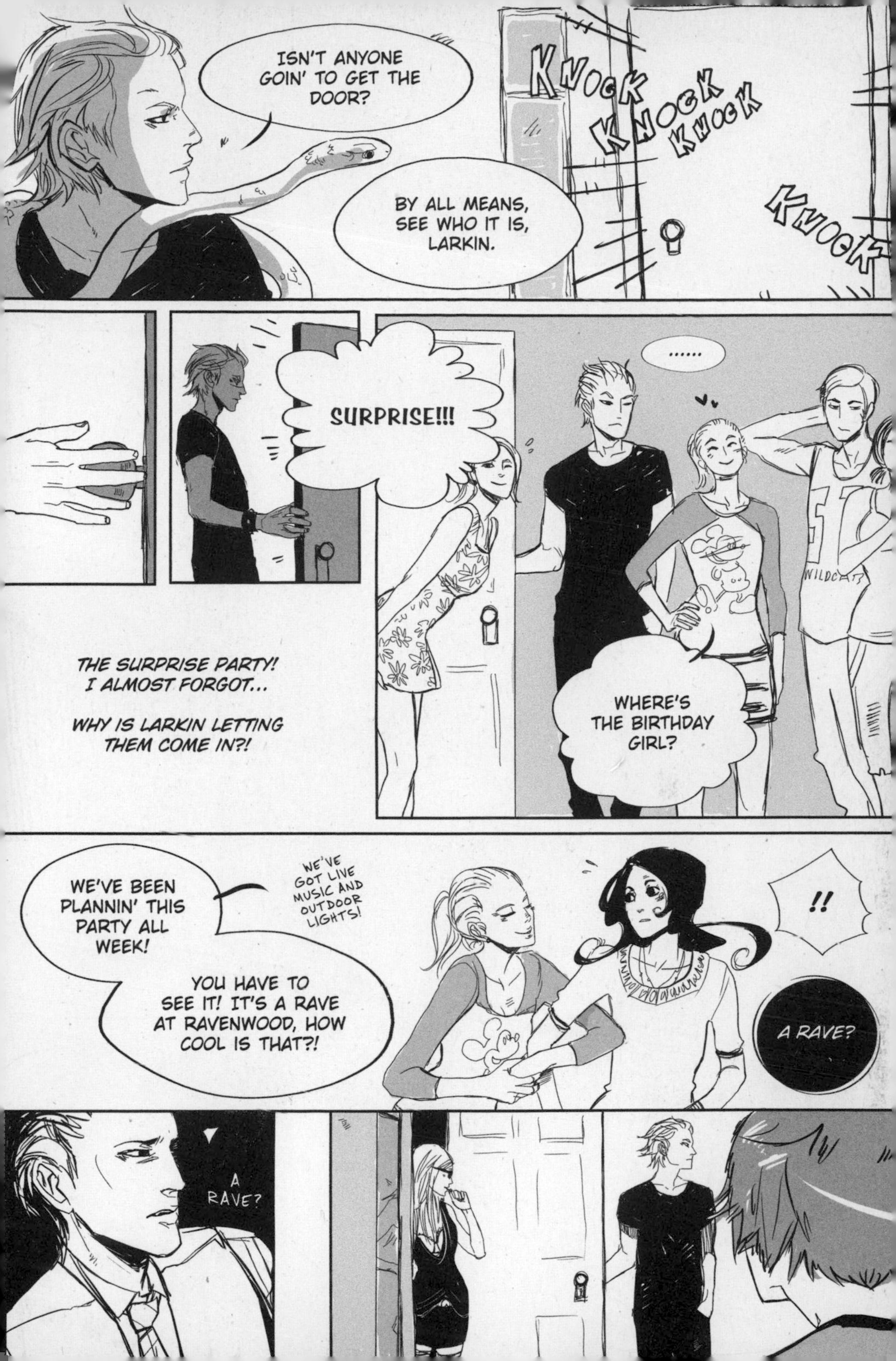
ISN'T ANYONE GOIN' TO GET THE DOOR?
KNOCK KNOCK KNOCK
BY ALL MEANS, SEE WHO IT IS, LARKIN.
KNOCK
SURPRISE!!!
......
THE SURPRISE PARTY! I ALMOST FORGOT...
WHY IS LARKIN LETTING THEM COME IN?!
WHERE'S THE BIRTHDAY GIRL?
WE'VE BEEN PLANNIN' THIS PARTY ALL WEEK!
YOU HAVE TO SEE IT! IT'S A RAVE AT RAVENWOOD, HOW COOL IS THAT?!
WE'VE GOT LIVE MUSIC AND OUTDOOR LIGHTS!
!!
A RAVE?
A RAVE?

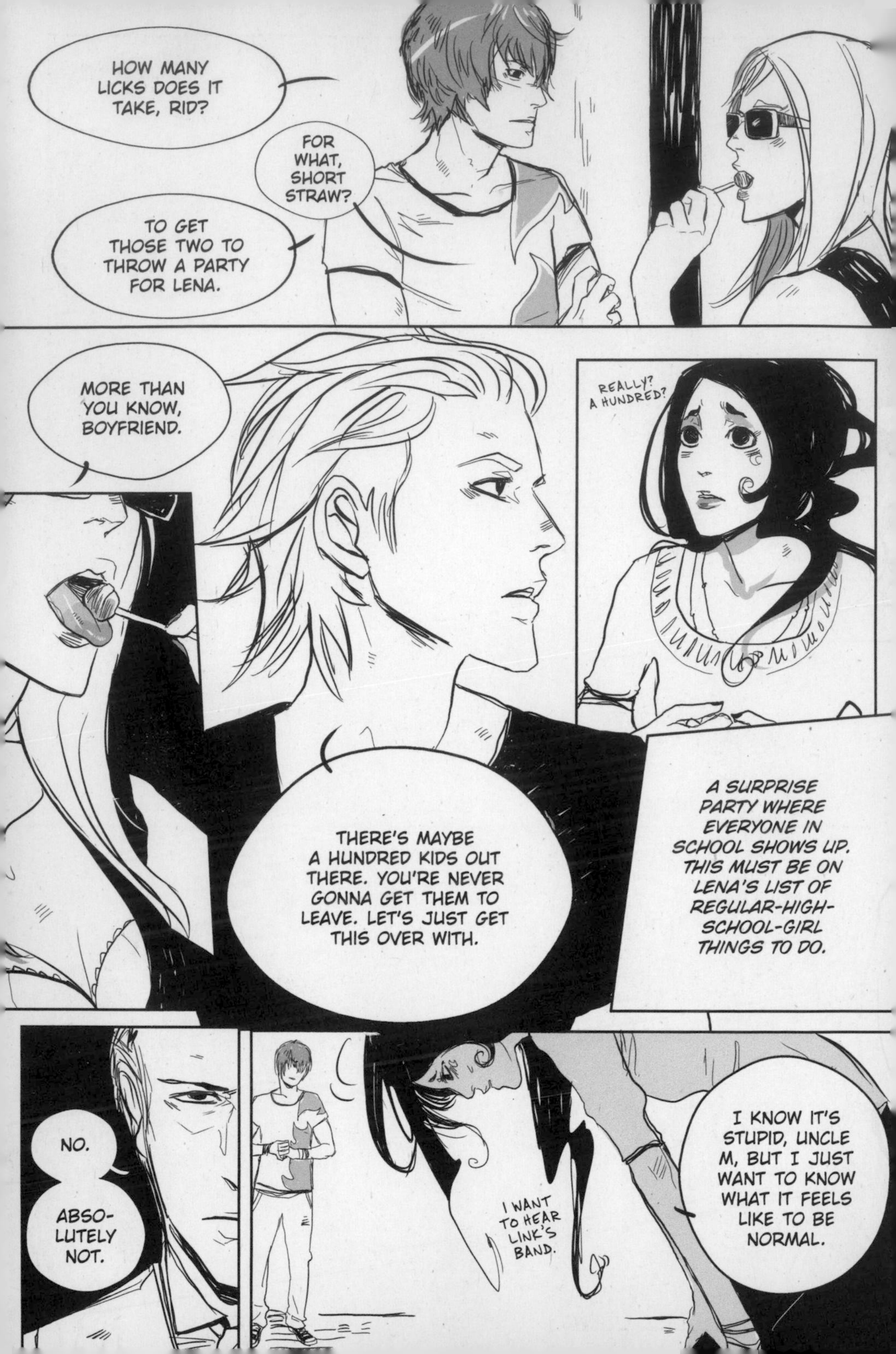
HOW MANY LICKS DOES IT TAKE, RID?
FOR WHAT, SHORT STRAW?
TO GET THOSE TWO TO THROW A PARTY FOR LENA.
MORE THAN YOU KNOW, BOYFRIEND.
REALLY? A HUNDRED?
THERE'S MAYBE A HUNDRED KIDS OUT THERE. YOU'RE NEVER GONNA GET THEM TO LEAVE. LET'S JUST GET THIS OVER WITH.
A SURPRISE PARTY WHERE EVERYONE IN SCHOOL SHOWS UP. THIS MUST BE ON LENA'S LIST OF REGULAR-HIGH-SCHOOL-GIRL THINGS TO DO.
NO.
ABSO-LUTELY NOT.
I WANT TO HEAR LINK'S BAND.
I KNOW IT'S STUPID, UNCLE M, BUT I JUST WANT TO KNOW WHAT IT FEELS LIKE TO BE NORMAL.

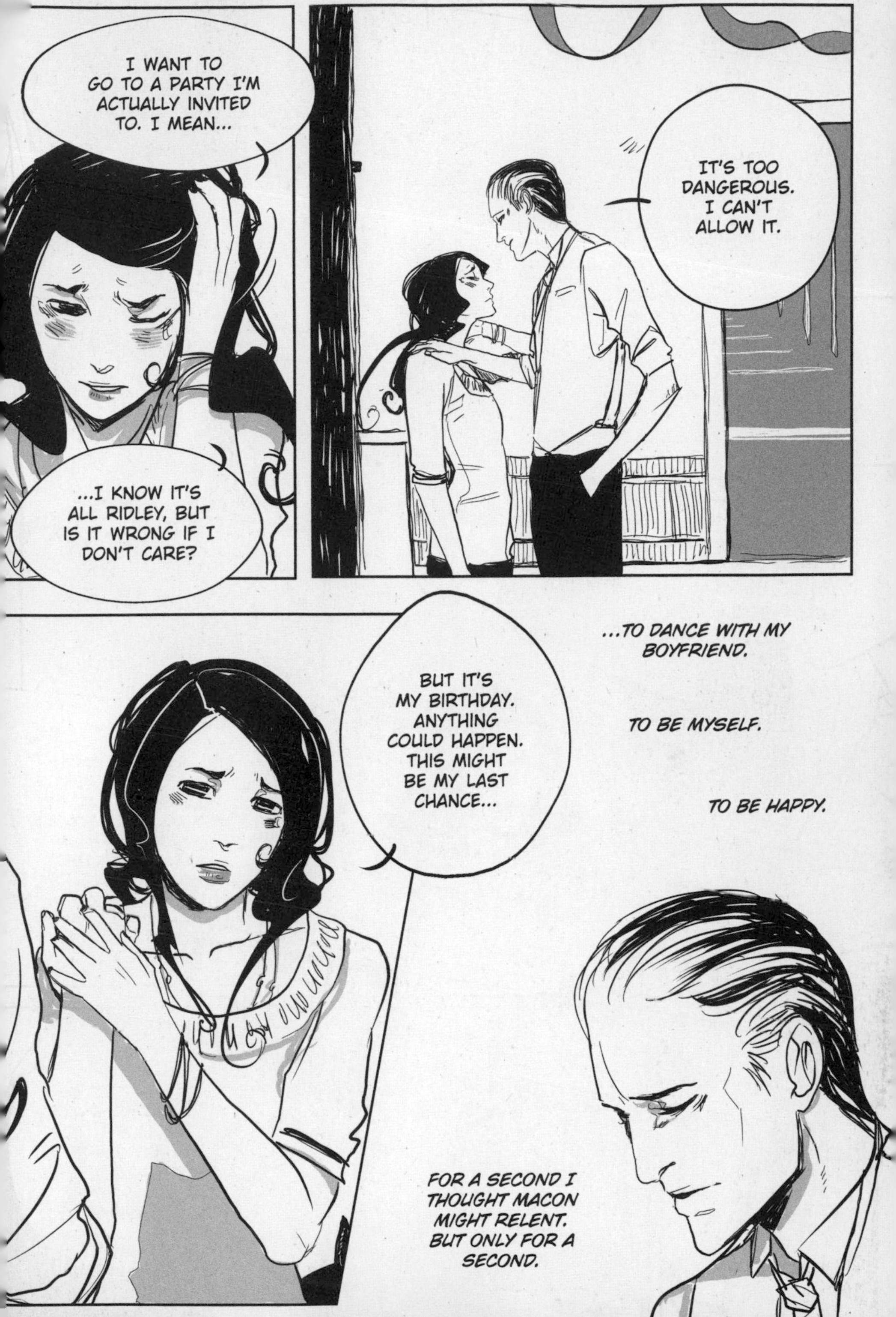
I WANT TO GO TO A PARTY I'M ACTUALLY INVITED TO. I MEAN...
...I KNOW IT'S ALL RIDLEY, BUT IS IT WRONG IF I DON'T CARE?
IT'S TOO DANGEROUS. I CAN'T ALLOW IT.
BUT IT'S MY BIRTHDAY. ANYTHING COULD HAPPEN. THIS MIGHT BE MY LAST CHANCE...
...TO DANCE WITH MY BOYFRIEND.
TO BE MYSELF.
TO BE HAPPY.
FOR A SECOND I THOUGHT MACON MIGHT RELENT. BUT ONLY FOR A SECOND.

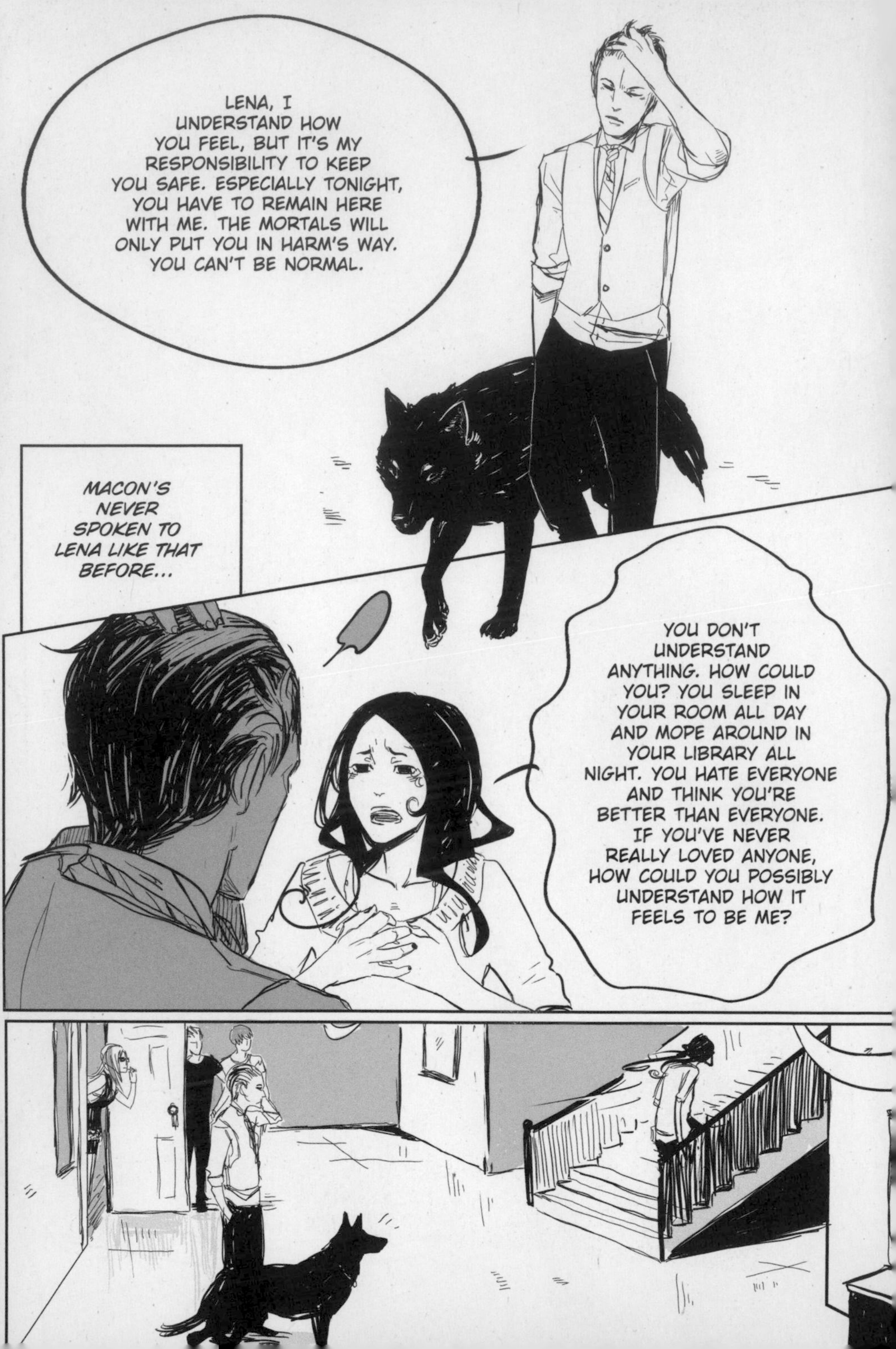
LENA, I UNDERSTAND HOW YOU FEEL, BUT IT'S MY RESPONSIBILITY TO KEEP YOU SAFE. ESPECIALLY TONIGHT, YOU HAVE TO REMAIN HERE WITH ME. THE MORTALS WILL ONLY PUT YOU IN HARM'S WAY. YOU CAN'T BE NORMAL.
MACON'S NEVER SPOKEN TO LENA LIKE THAT BEFORE...
YOU DON'T UNDERSTAND ANYTHING. HOW COULD YOU? YOU SLEEP IN YOUR ROOM ALL DAY AND MOPE AROUND IN YOUR LIBRARY ALL NIGHT. YOU HATE EVERYONE AND THINK YOU'RE BETTER THAN EVERYONE. IF YOU'VE NEVER REALLY LOVED ANYONE, HOW COULD YOU POSSIBLY UNDERSTAND HOW IT FEELS TO BE ME?

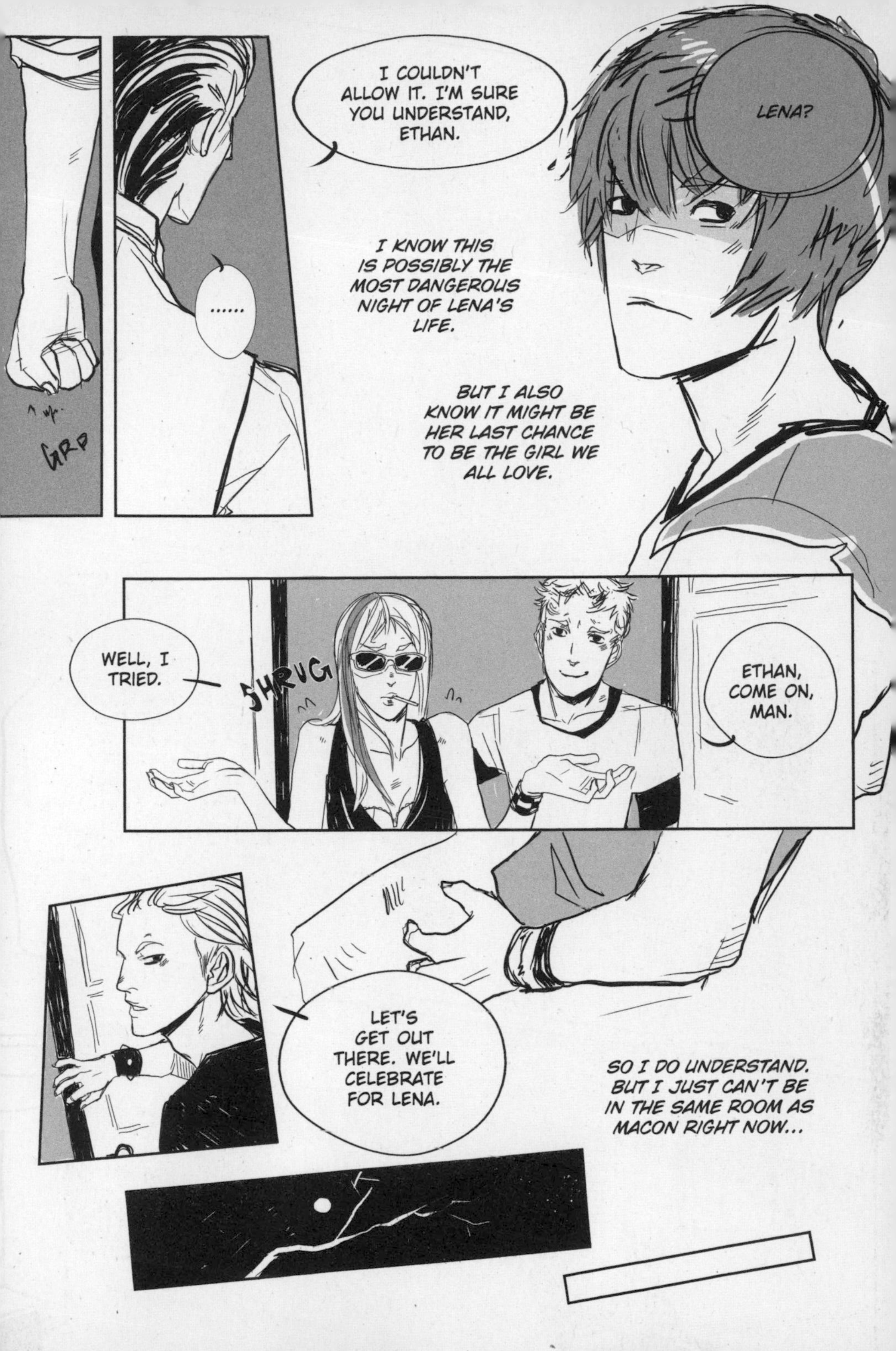
GRP
......
I COULDN'T ALLOW IT. I'M SURE YOU UNDERSTAND, ETHAN.
LENA?
I KNOW THIS IS POSSIBLY THE MOST DANGEROUS NIGHT OF LENA'S LIFE.
BUT I ALSO KNOW IT MIGHT BE HER LAST CHANCE TO BE THE GIRL WE ALL LOVE.
WELL, I TRIED.
SHRUG
ETHAN, COME ON, MAN.
LET'S GET OUT THERE. WE'LL CELEBRATE FOR LENA.
SO I DO UNDERSTAND. BUT I JUST CAN'T BE IN THE SAME ROOM AS MACON RIGHT NOW...

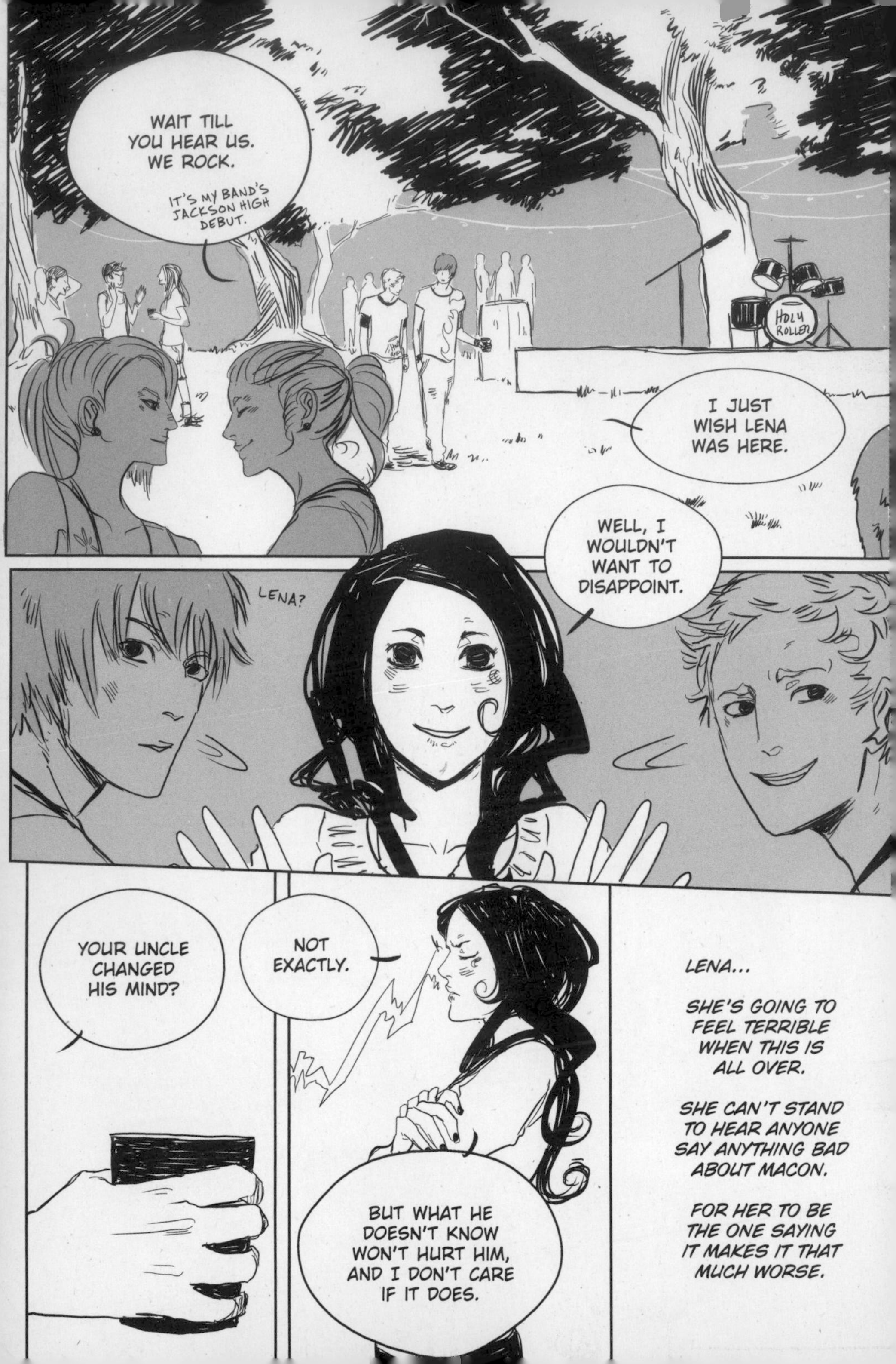

WAIT TILL YOU HEAR US. WE ROCK.
IT'S MY BAND'S JACKSON HIGH DEBUT.
HOLY ROLLER
I JUST WISH LENA WAS HERE.
WELL, I WOULDN'T WANT TO DISAPPOINT.
LENA?
YOUR UNCLE CHANGED HIS MIND?
NOT EXACTLY.
BUT WHAT HE DOESN'T KNOW WON'T HURT HIM, AND I DON'T CARE IF IT DOES.
LENA...
SHE'S GOING TO FEEL TERRIBLE WHEN THIS IS ALL OVER.
SHE CAN'T STAND TO HEAR ANYONE SAY ANYTHING BAD ABOUT MACON.
FOR HER TO BE THE ONE SAYING IT MAKES IT THAT MUCH WORSE.

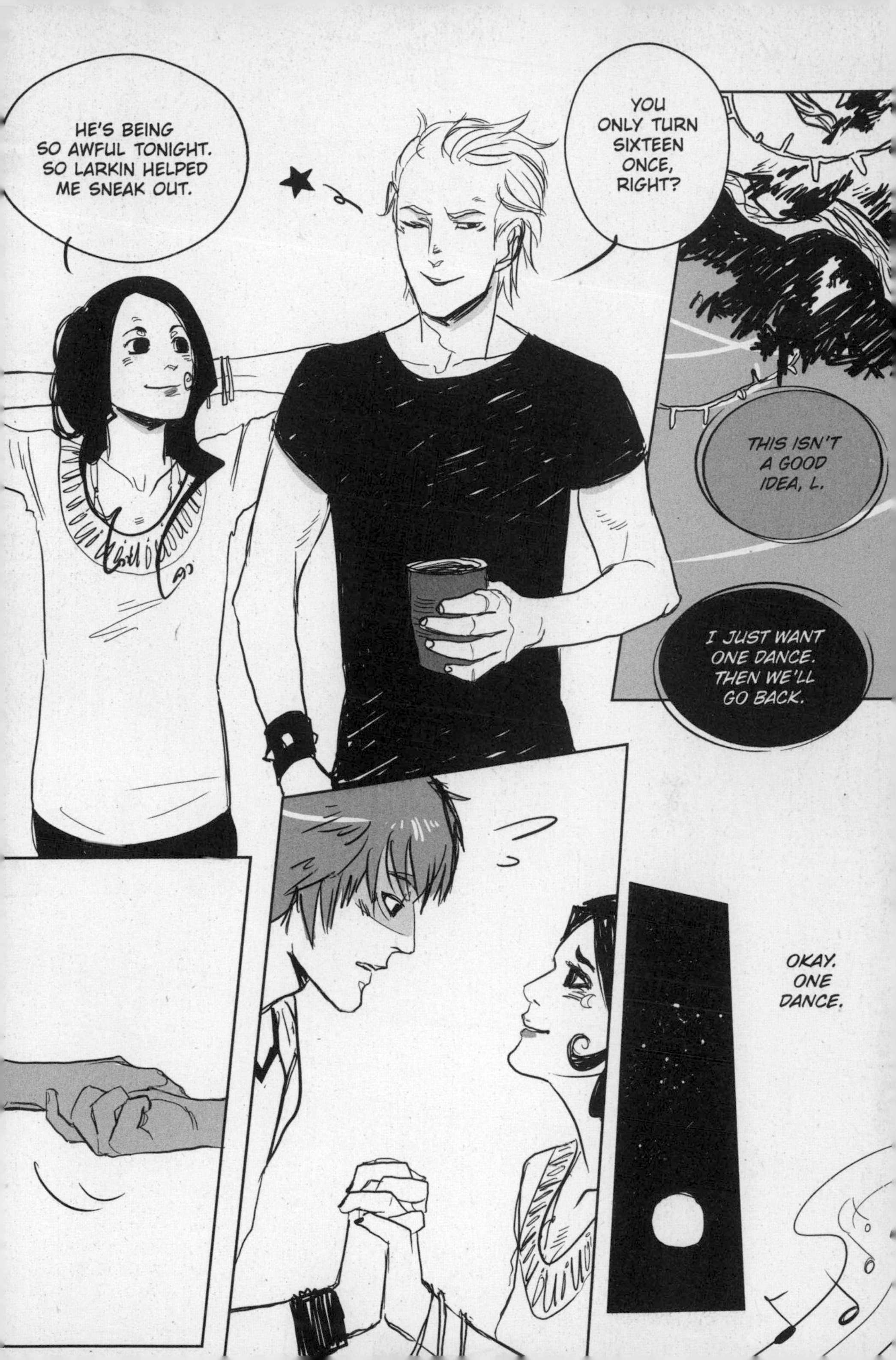
HE'S BEING SO AWFUL TONIGHT. SO LARKIN HELPED ME SNEAK OUT.
YOU ONLY TURN SIXTEEN ONCE, RIGHT?
THIS ISN'T A GOOD IDEA, L.
I JUST WANT ONE DANCE. THEN WE'LL GO BACK.
OKAY. ONE DANCE.

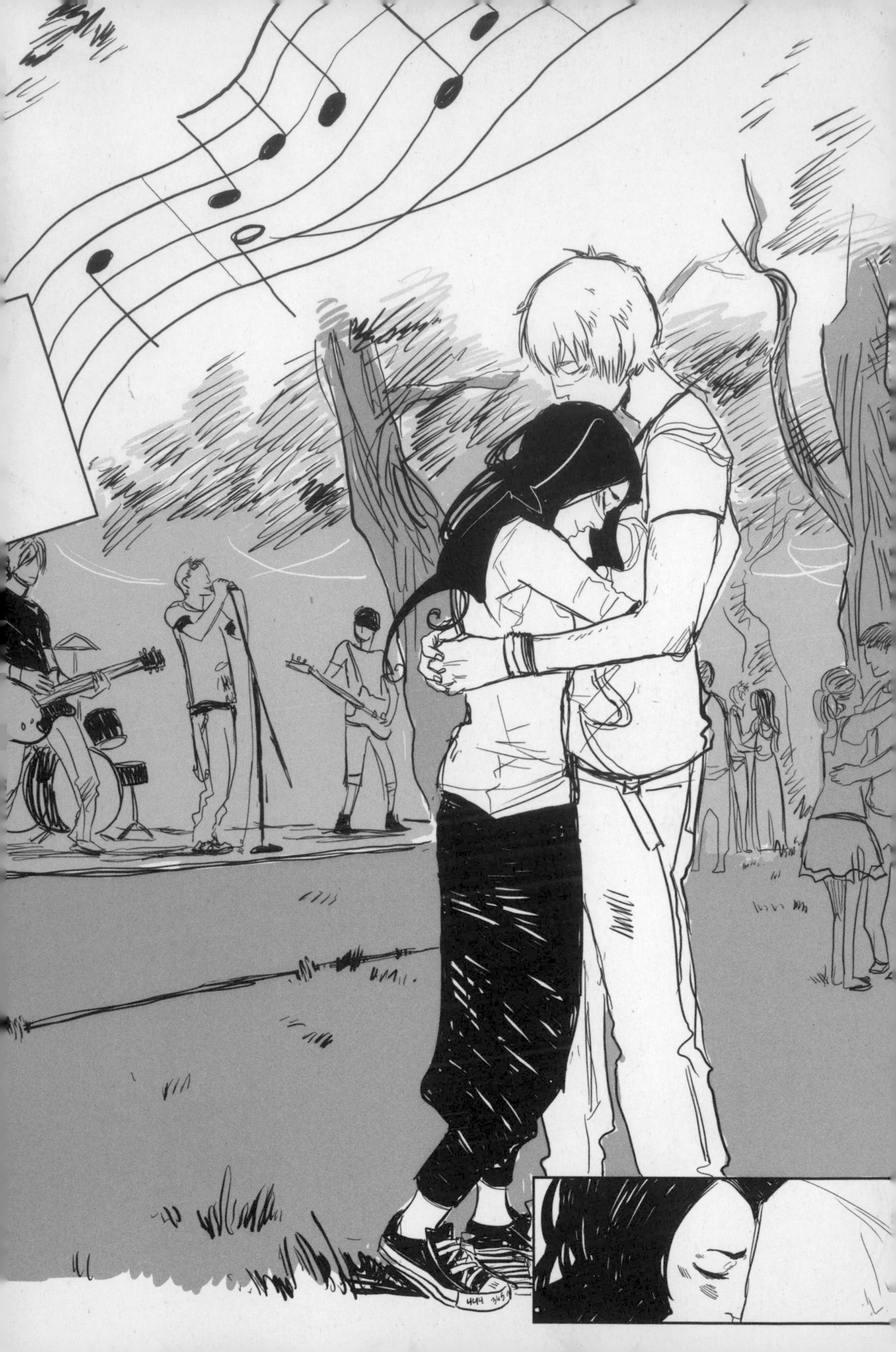

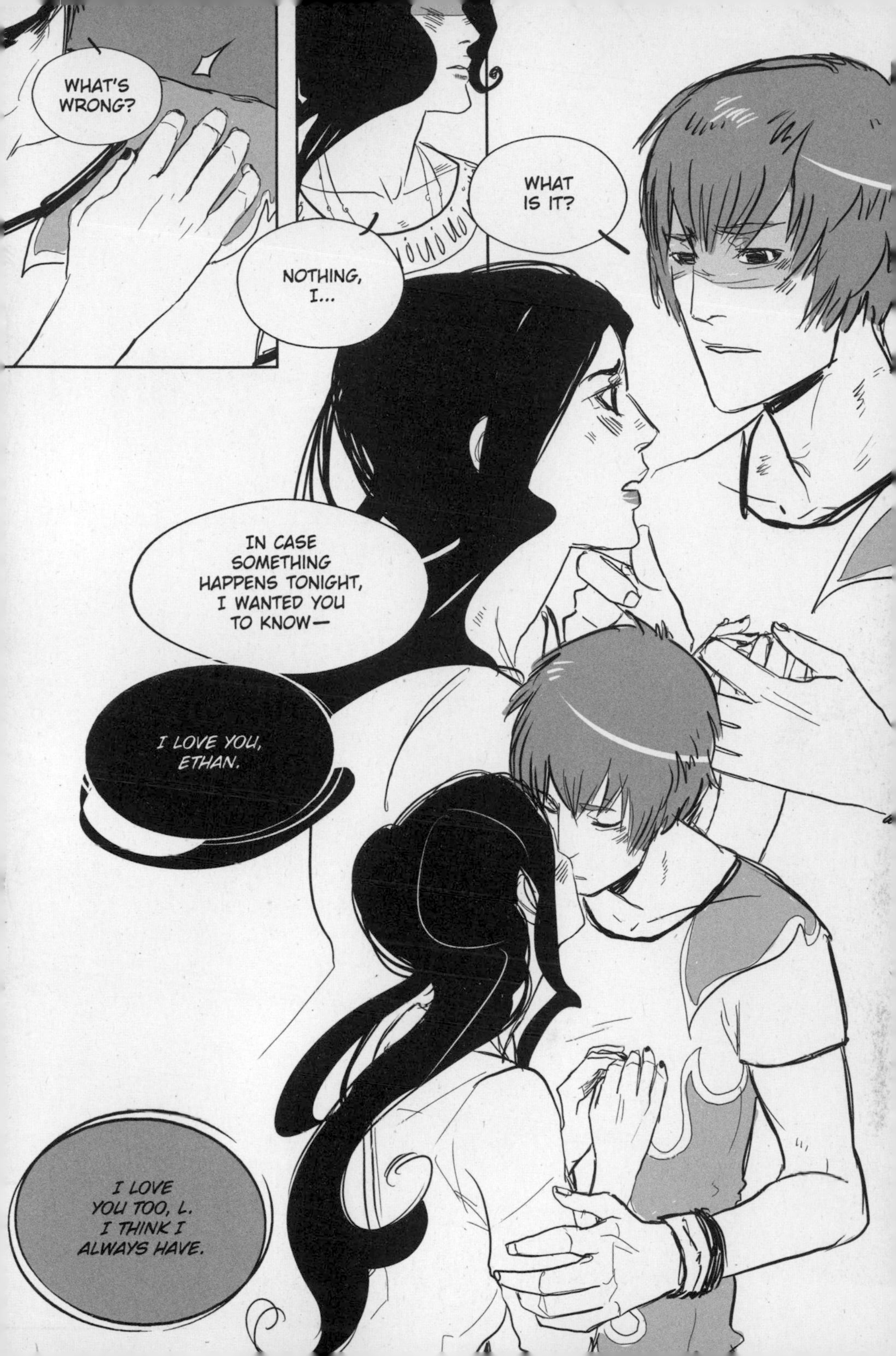
WHAT'S WRONG?
WHAT IS IT?
NOTHING, I...
IN CASE SOMETHING HAPPENS TONIGHT, I WANTED YOU TO KNOW—
I LOVE YOU, ETHAN.
I LOVE YOU TOO, L. I THINK I ALWAYS HAVE.

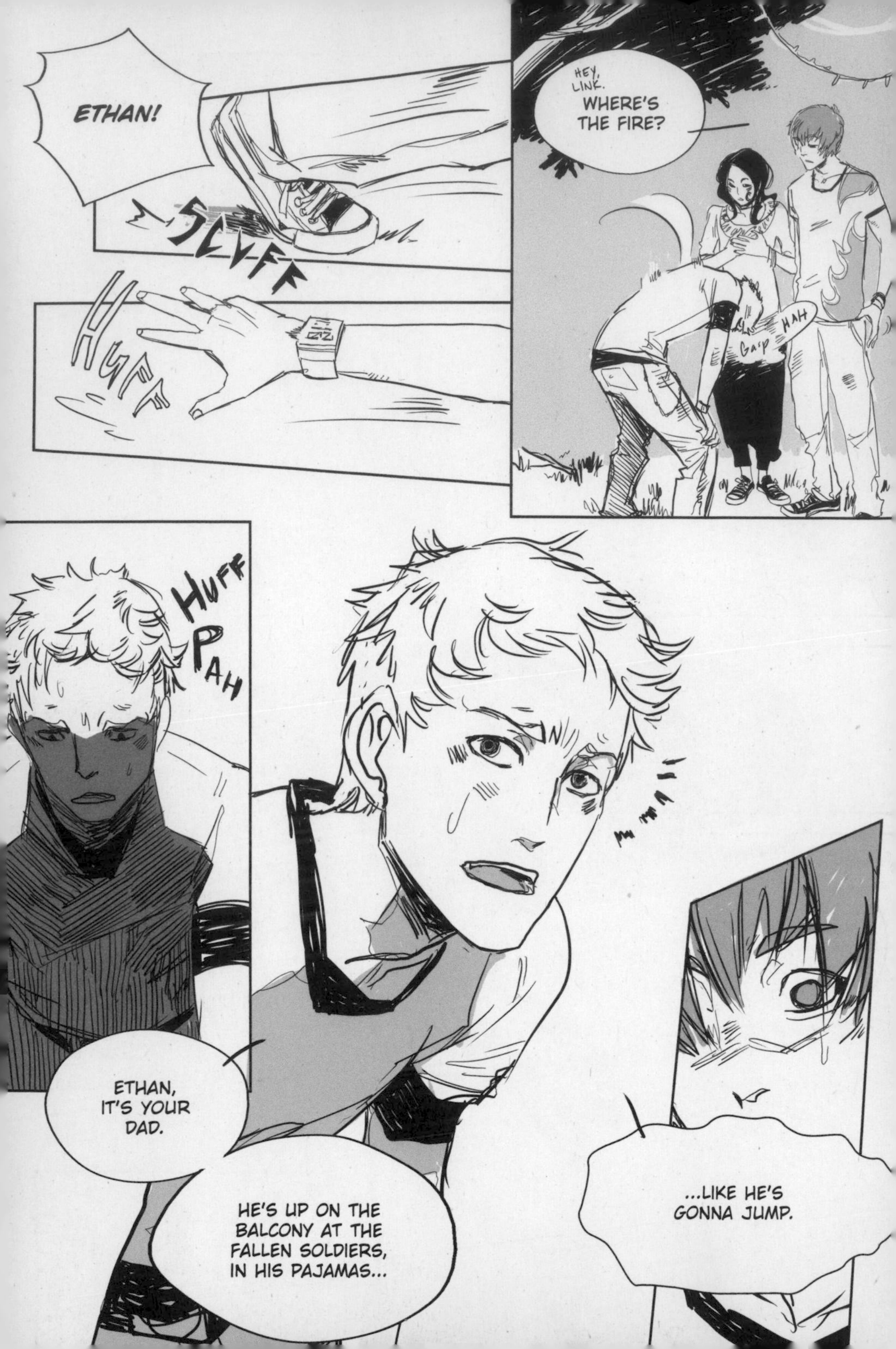
ETHAN!
SCUFF
HUFF
HEY, LINK. WHERE'S THE FIRE?
GASP HAH
HUFF PAH
ETHAN, IT'S YOUR DAD.
HE'S UP ON THE BALCONY AT THE FALLEN SOLDIERS, IN HIS PAJAMAS...
...LIKE HE'S GONNA JUMP.

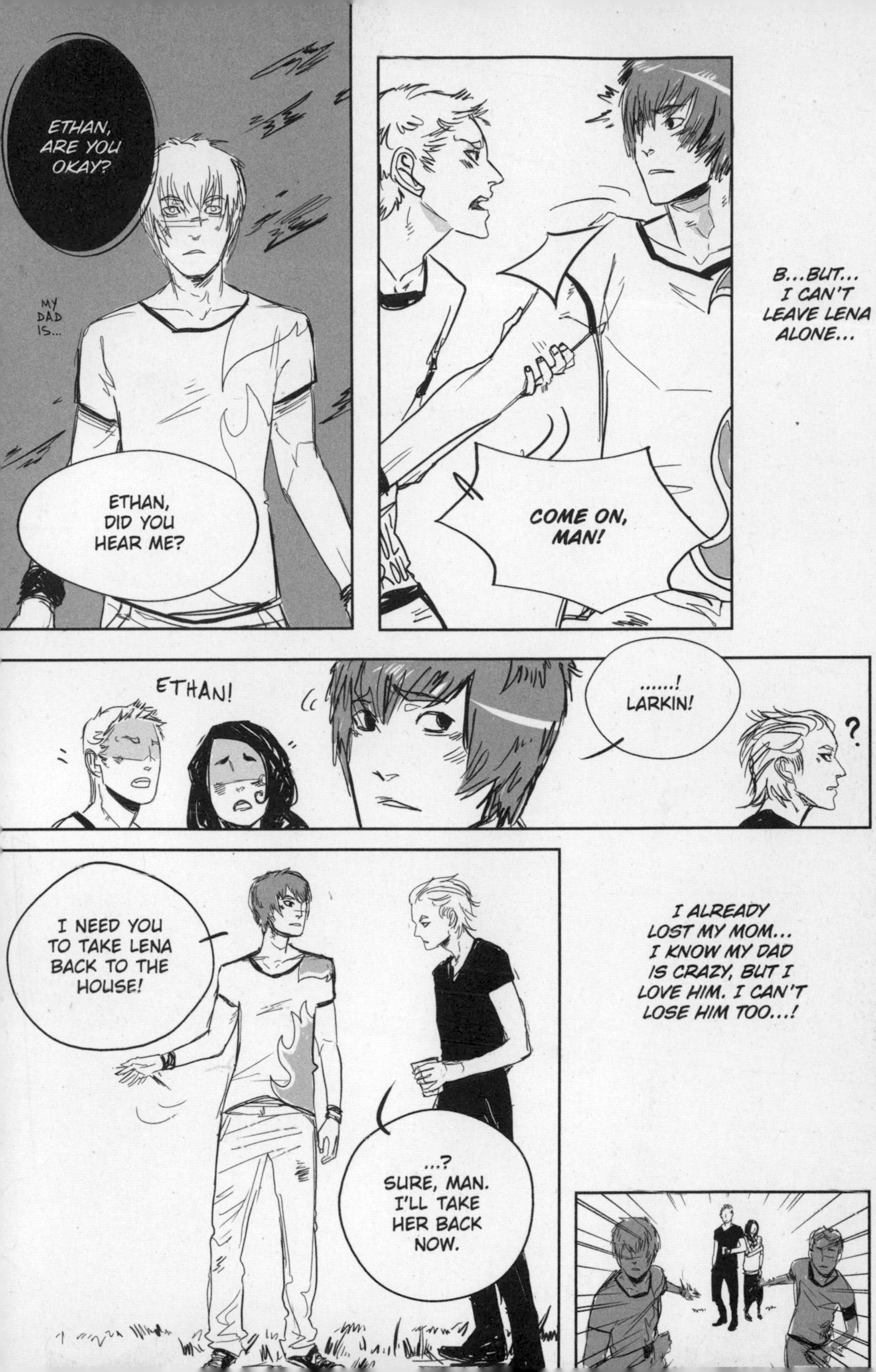
ETHAN, ARE YOU OKAY?
MY DAD IS...
ETHAN, DID YOU HEAR ME?
COME ON, MAN!
B...BUT... I CAN'T LEAVE LENA ALONE...
ETHAN!
......! LARKIN!
?
I NEED YOU TO TAKE LENA BACK TO THE HOUSE!
...? SURE, MAN. I'LL TAKE HER BACK NOW.
I ALREADY LOST MY MOM... I KNOW MY DAD IS CRAZY, BUT I LOVE HIM. I CAN'T LOSE HIM TOO...!

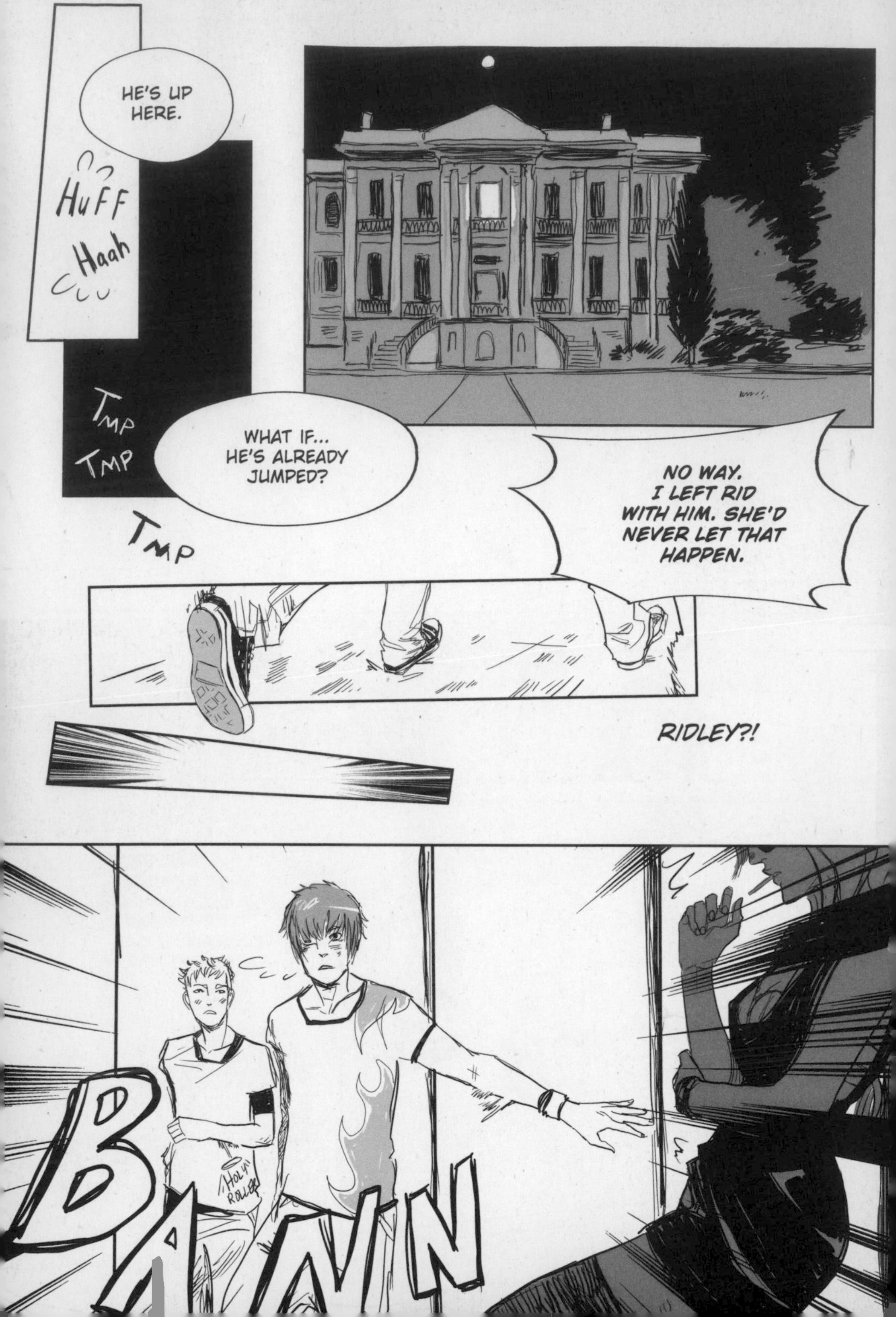
HE'S UP HERE.
HUFF
Haah
TMP
TMP
WHAT IF... HE'S ALREADY JUMPED?
NO WAY. I LEFT RID WITH HIM. SHE'D NEVER LET THAT HAPPEN.
TMP
RIDLEY?!
BAMN

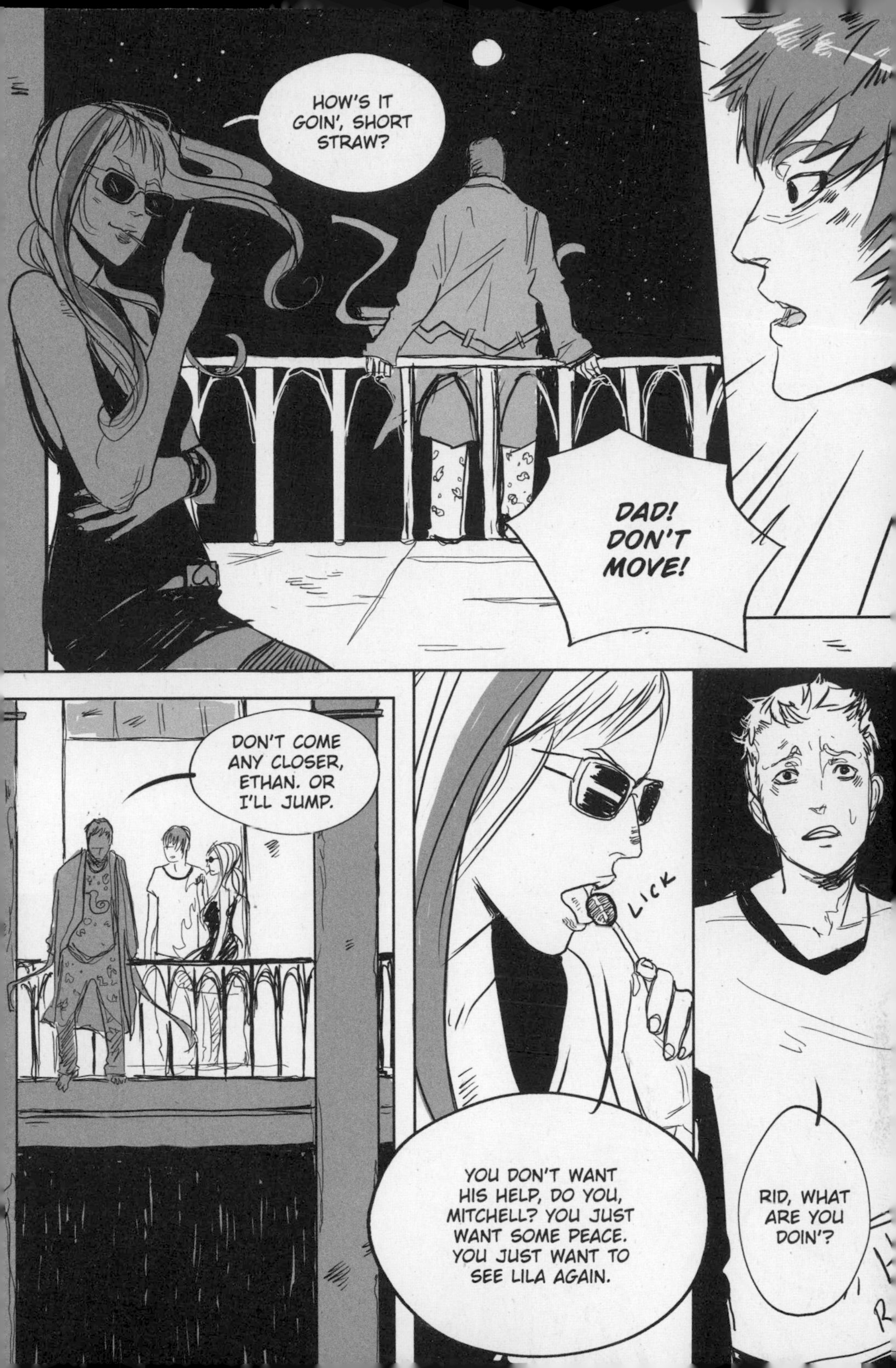
HOW'S IT GOIN', SHORT STRAW?
DAD! DON'T MOVE!
DON'T COME ANY CLOSER, ETHAN. OR I'LL JUMP.
LICK
YOU DON'T WANT HIS HELP, DO YOU, MITCHELL? YOU JUST WANT SOME PEACE. YOU JUST WANT TO SEE LILA AGAIN.
RID, WHAT ARE YOU DOIN'?

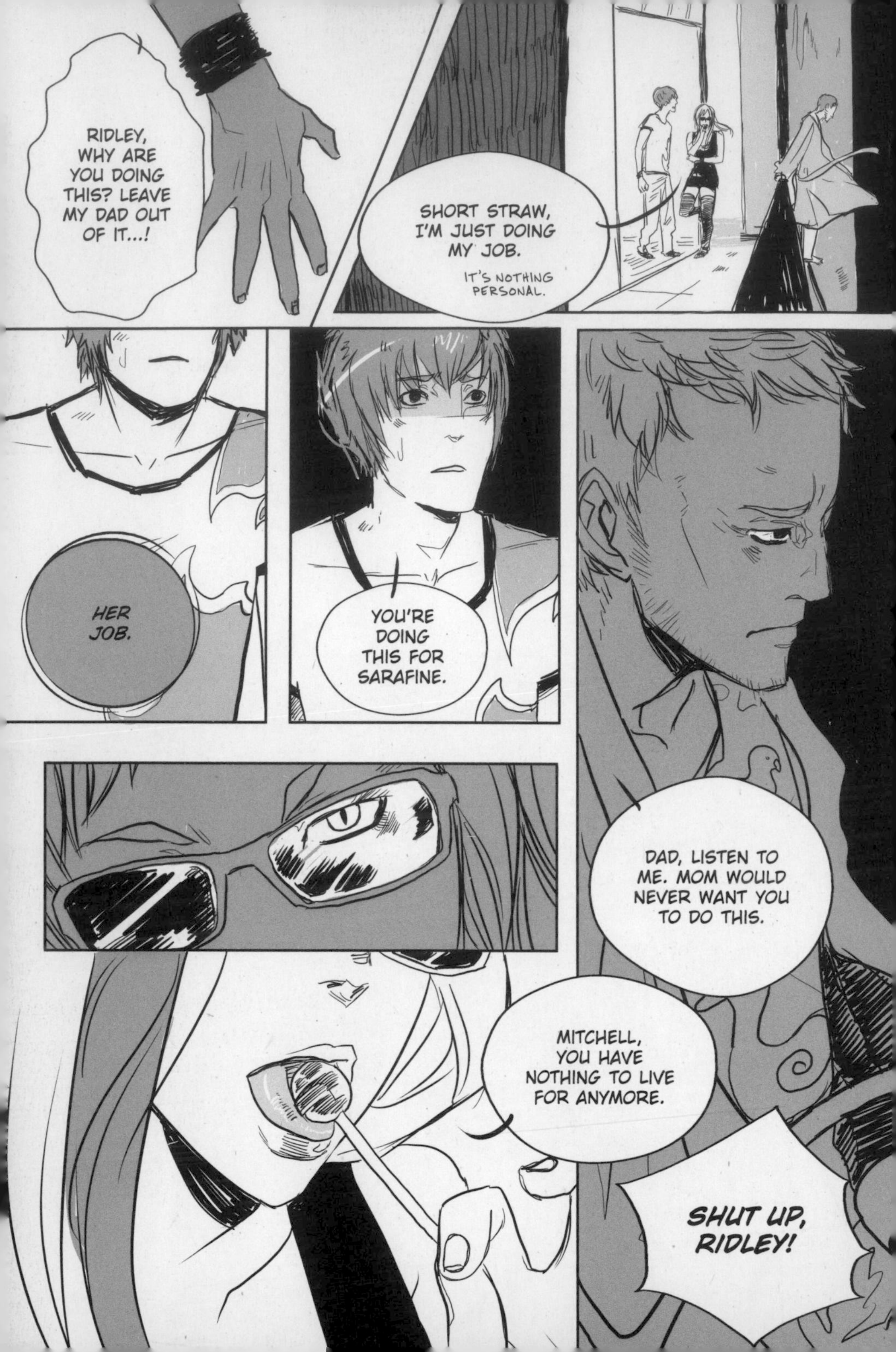

RIDLEY, WHY ARE YOU DOING THIS? LEAVE MY DAD OUT OF IT...!
SHORT STRAW, I'M JUST DOING MY JOB.
IT'S NOTHING PERSONAL.
HER JOB.
YOU'RE DOING THIS FOR SARAFINE.
DAD, LISTEN TO ME. MOM WOULD NEVER WANT YOU TO DO THIS.
MITCHELL, YOU HAVE NOTHING TO LIVE FOR ANYMORE.
SHUT UP, RIDLEY!

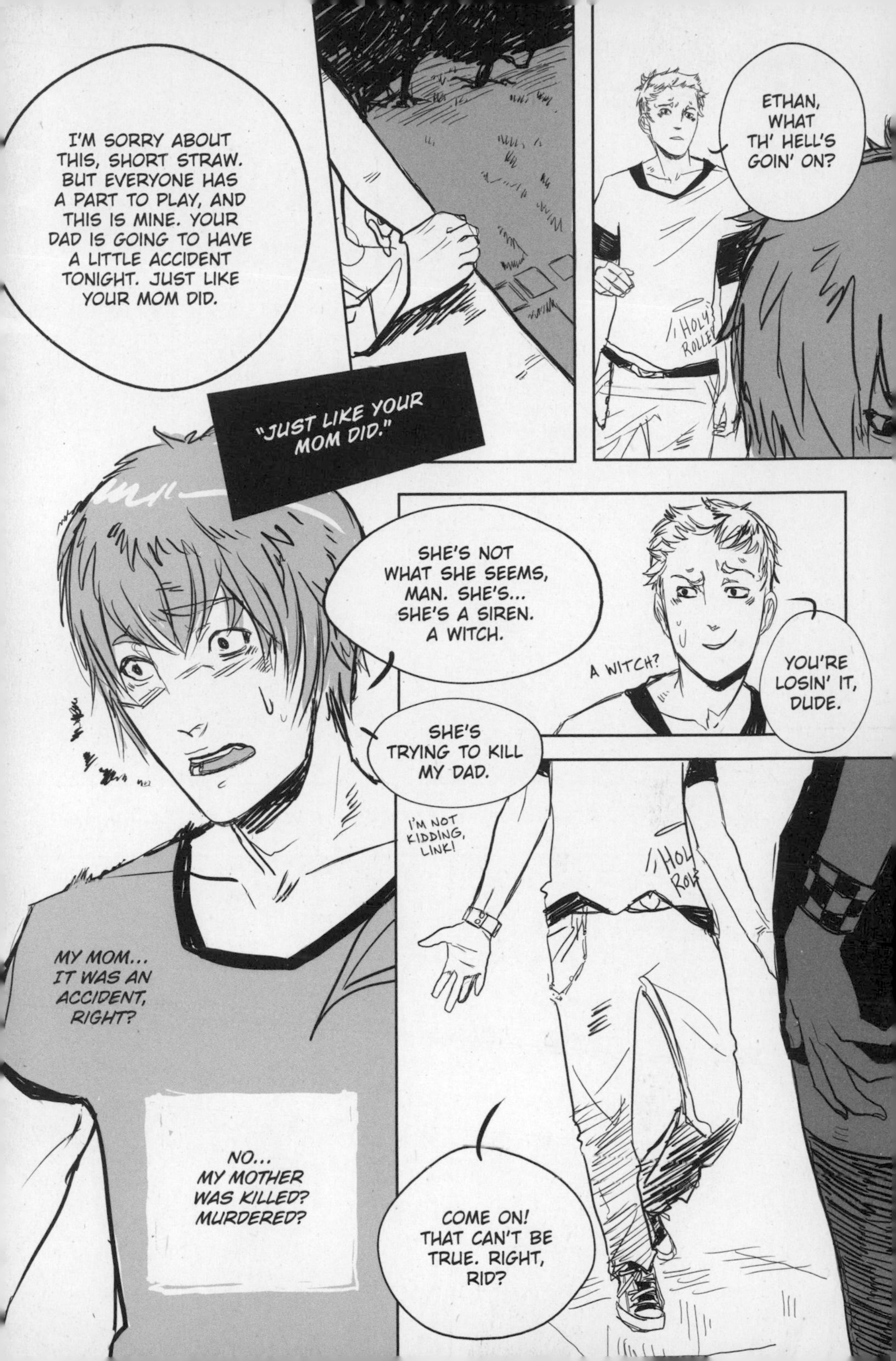
I'M SORRY ABOUT THIS, SHORT STRAW. BUT EVERYONE HAS A PART TO PLAY, AND THIS IS MINE. YOUR DAD IS GOING TO HAVE A LITTLE ACCIDENT TONIGHT. JUST LIKE YOUR MOM DID.
ETHAN, WHAT TH' HELL'S GOIN' ON?
"JUST LIKE YOUR MOM DID."
MY MOM... IT WAS AN ACCIDENT, RIGHT?
NO... MY MOTHER WAS KILLED? MURDERED?
SHE'S NOT WHAT SHE SEEMS, MAN. SHE'S... SHE'S A SIREN. A WITCH.
A WITCH?
YOU'RE LOSIN' IT, DUDE.
SHE'S TRYING TO KILL MY DAD.
I'M NOT KIDDING, LINK!
COME ON! THAT CAN'T BE TRUE. RIGHT, RID?

DIDN'T YOU HEAR WHAT YOUR FRIEND SAID? I'M A WITCH. A BAD ONE.

THAT LOOK ON HIS FACE. THIS IS PROBABLY THE FIRST TIME LINK IS REALLY SEEING HER.

BUT YOU AREN'T ALL BAD. I KNOW THAT. WE'VE SHARED THINGS.

GASP

THAT WAS THE PLAN, HOT ROD. I NEEDED AN IN.

SO I COULD STAY CLOSE TO LENA.

I DON'T BELIEVE YOU...

LINK...WHATEVER SPELL RIDLEY CAST, HIS FEELINGS FOR HER ARE BIGGER THAN THAT.

WHAT ABOUT EVERYTHING YOU TOLD ME ABOUT YOU AND LENA GROWIN' UP TOGETHER?

WHY WOULD YOU WANT TO HURT HER?

LIKE I SAID, THIS IS MY JOB. GET ETHAN AWAY FROM LENA. THIS OLD GUY WAS JUST AN EASY TARGET.

HIS MIND IS WEAK.

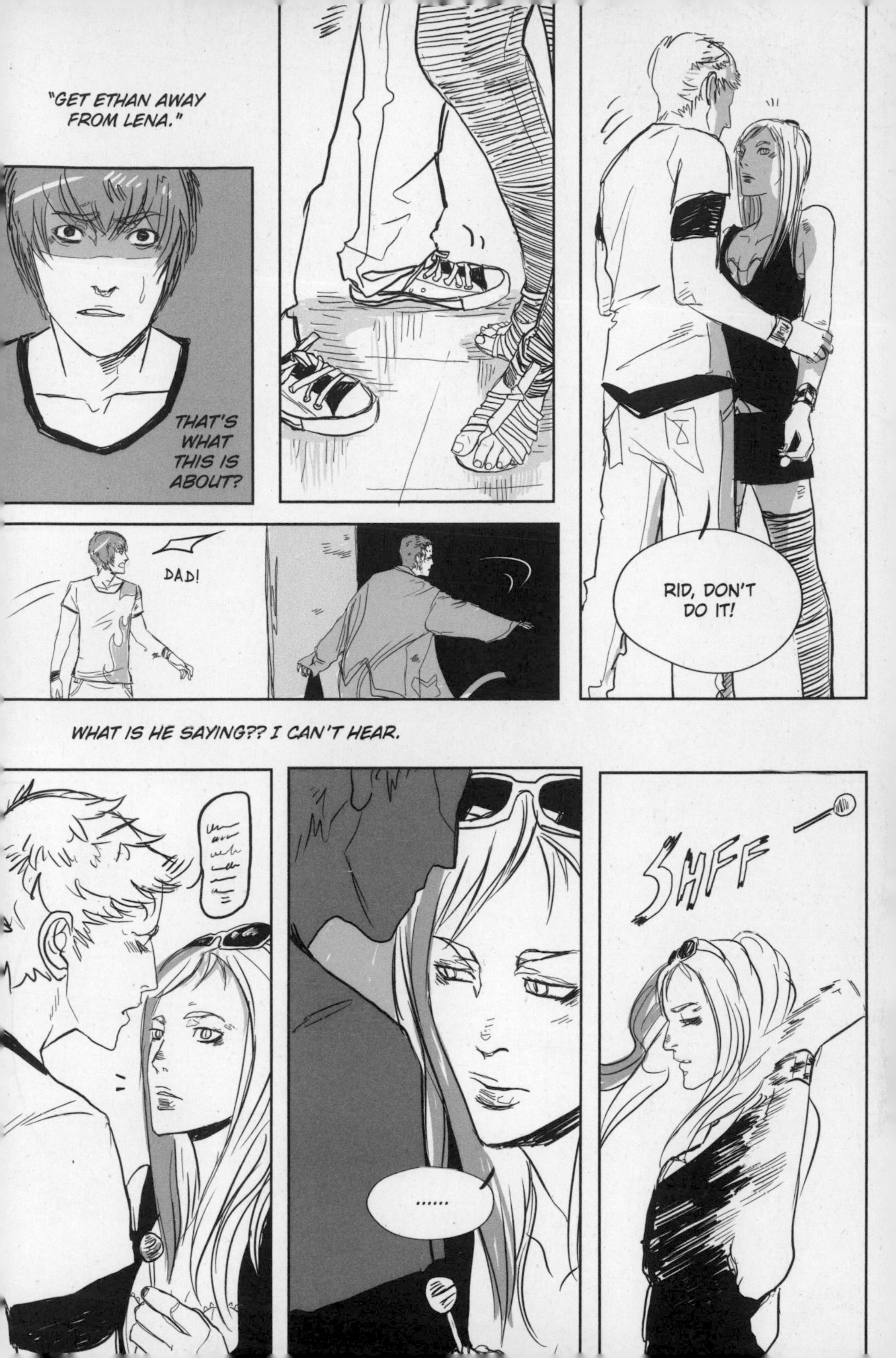
"GET ETHAN AWAY FROM LENA."
THAT'S WHAT THIS IS ABOUT?
DAD!
RID, DON'T DO IT!
WHAT IS HE SAYING?? I CAN'T HEAR.
......
SHFF

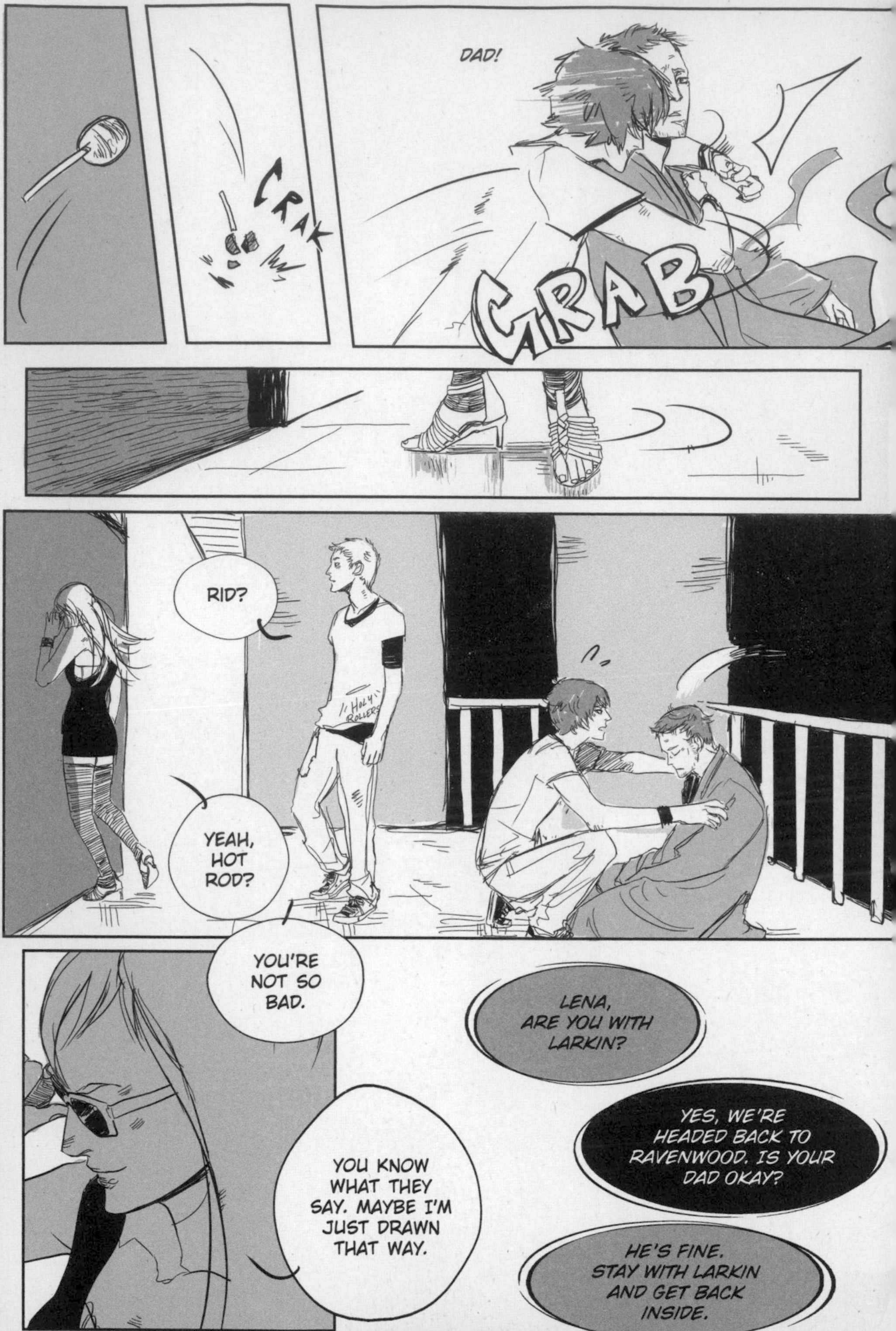
CRAK
DAD!
GRAB
RID?
YEAH, HOT ROD?
HOLY ROLLERS
YOU'RE NOT SO BAD.
YOU KNOW WHAT THEY SAY. MAYBE I'M JUST DRAWN THAT WAY.
LENA, ARE YOU WITH LARKIN?
YES, WE'RE HEADED BACK TO RAVENWOOD. IS YOUR DAD OKAY?
HE'S FINE. STAY WITH LARKIN AND GET BACK INSIDE.

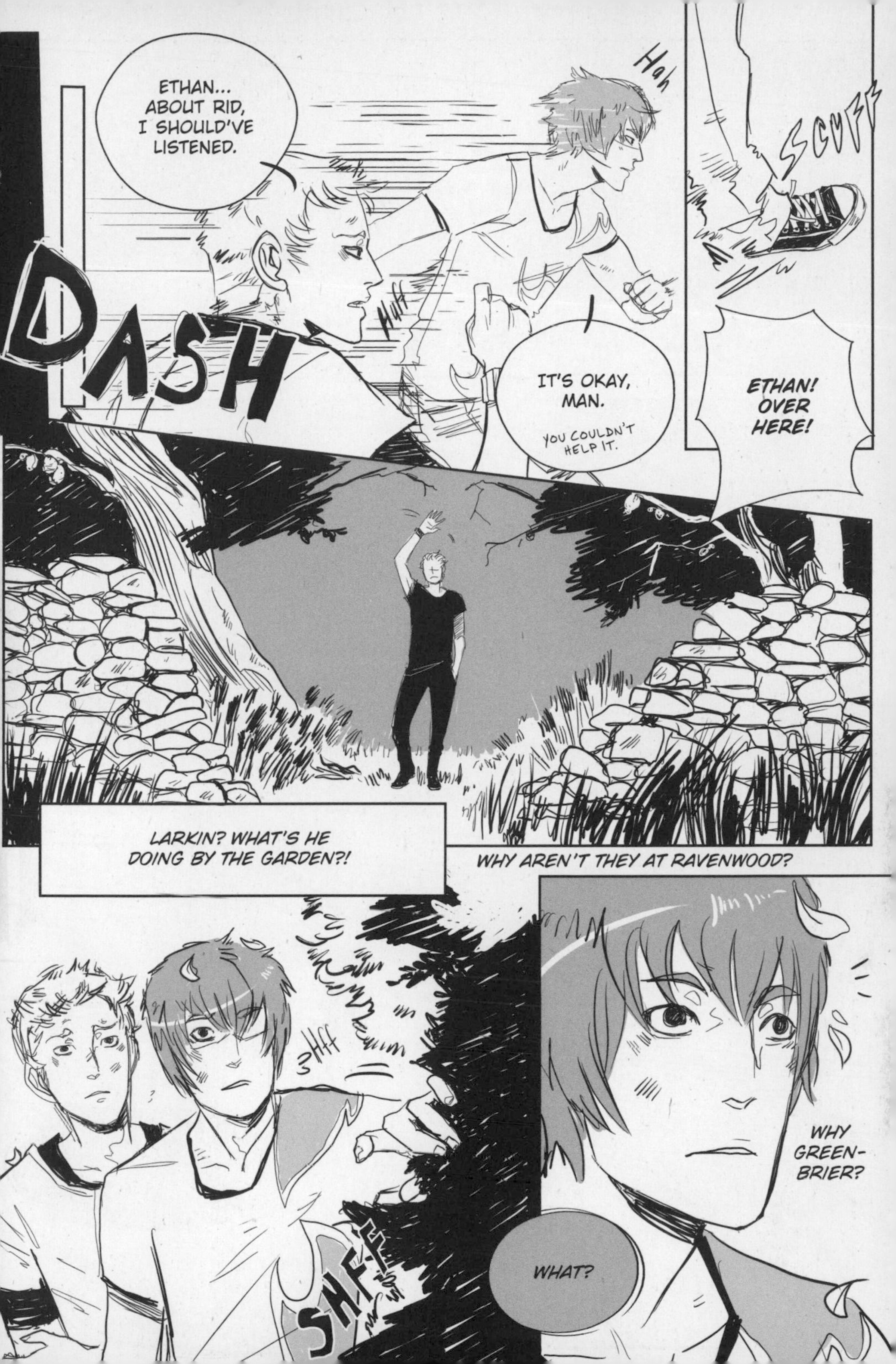
ETHAN... ABOUT RID, I SHOULD'VE LISTENED.
DASH
Hah
Huff
IT'S OKAY, MAN.
YOU COULDN'T HELP IT.
SCUFF
ETHAN! OVER HERE!
LARKIN? WHAT'S HE DOING BY THE GARDEN?!
WHY AREN'T THEY AT RAVENWOOD?
SHff
SHFF
WHY GREEN-BRIER?
WHAT?

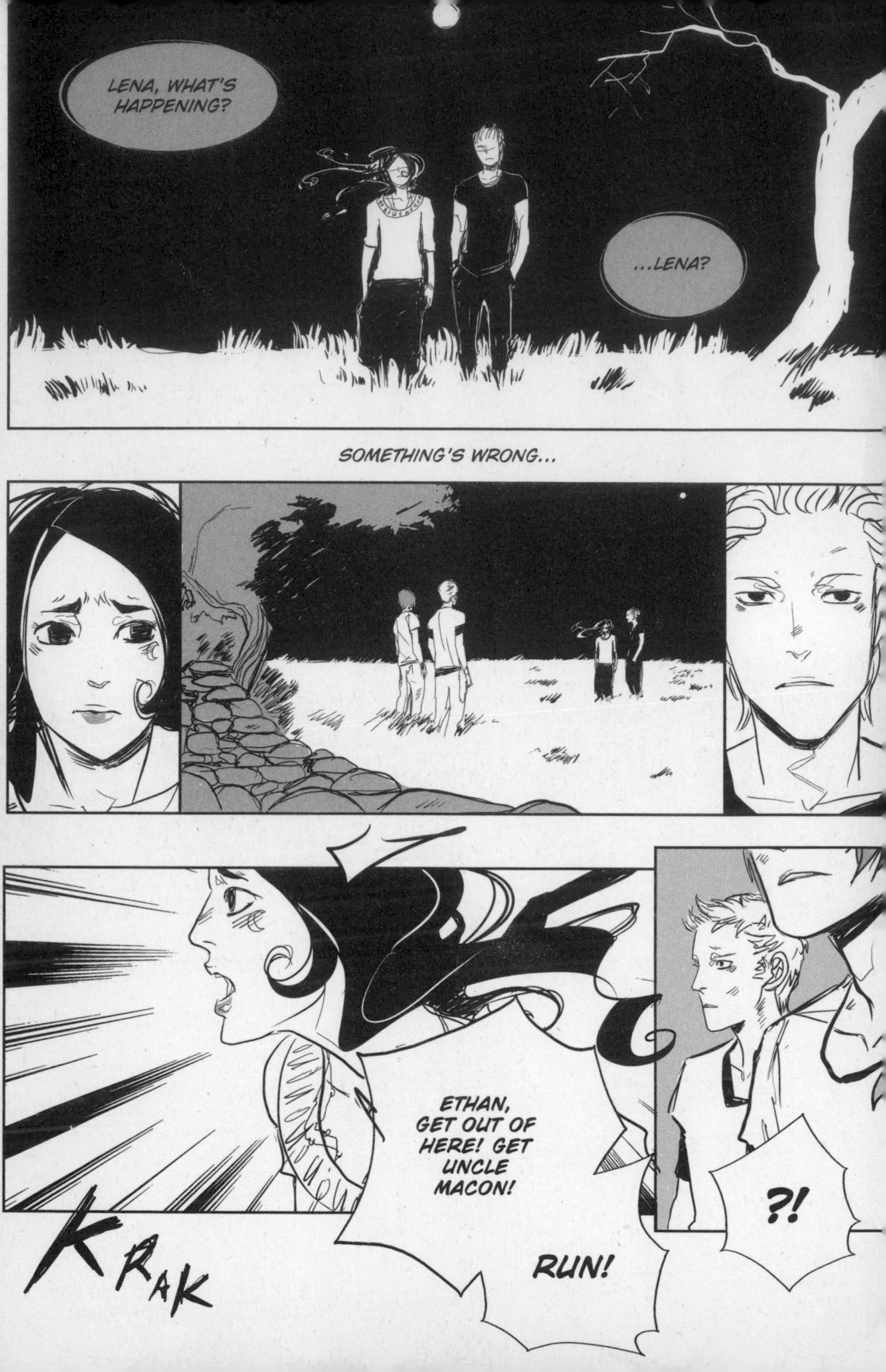
LENA, WHAT'S HAPPENING?
...LENA?
SOMETHING'S WRONG...
ETHAN, GET OUT OF HERE! GET UNCLE MACON!
?!
KRAK
RUN!

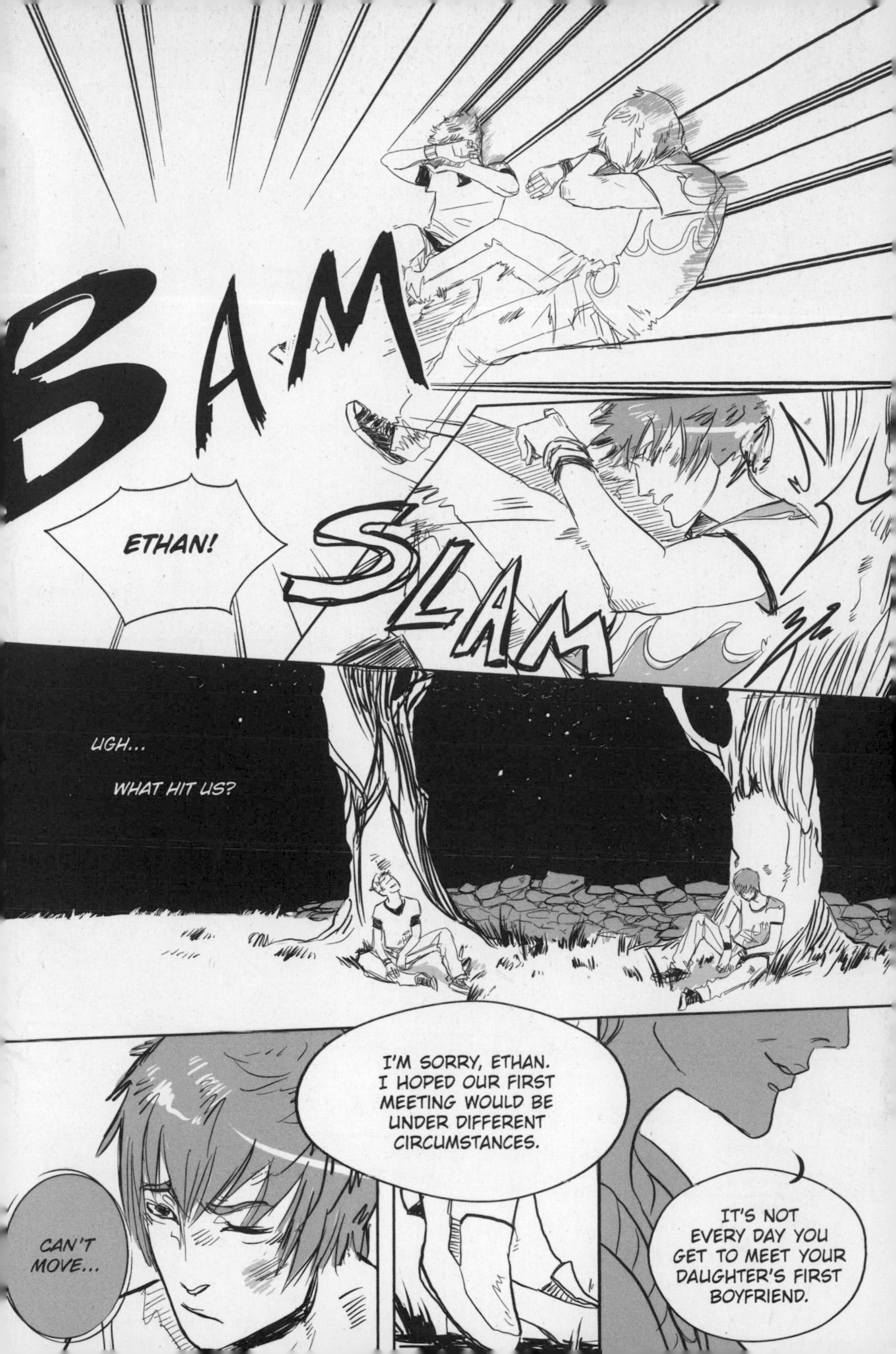
BAM
ETHAN!
SLAM
UGH...
WHAT HIT US?
I'M SORRY, ETHAN. I HOPED OUR FIRST MEETING WOULD BE UNDER DIFFERENT CIRCUMSTANCES.
CAN'T MOVE...
IT'S NOT EVERY DAY YOU GET TO MEET YOUR DAUGHTER'S FIRST BOYFRIEND.

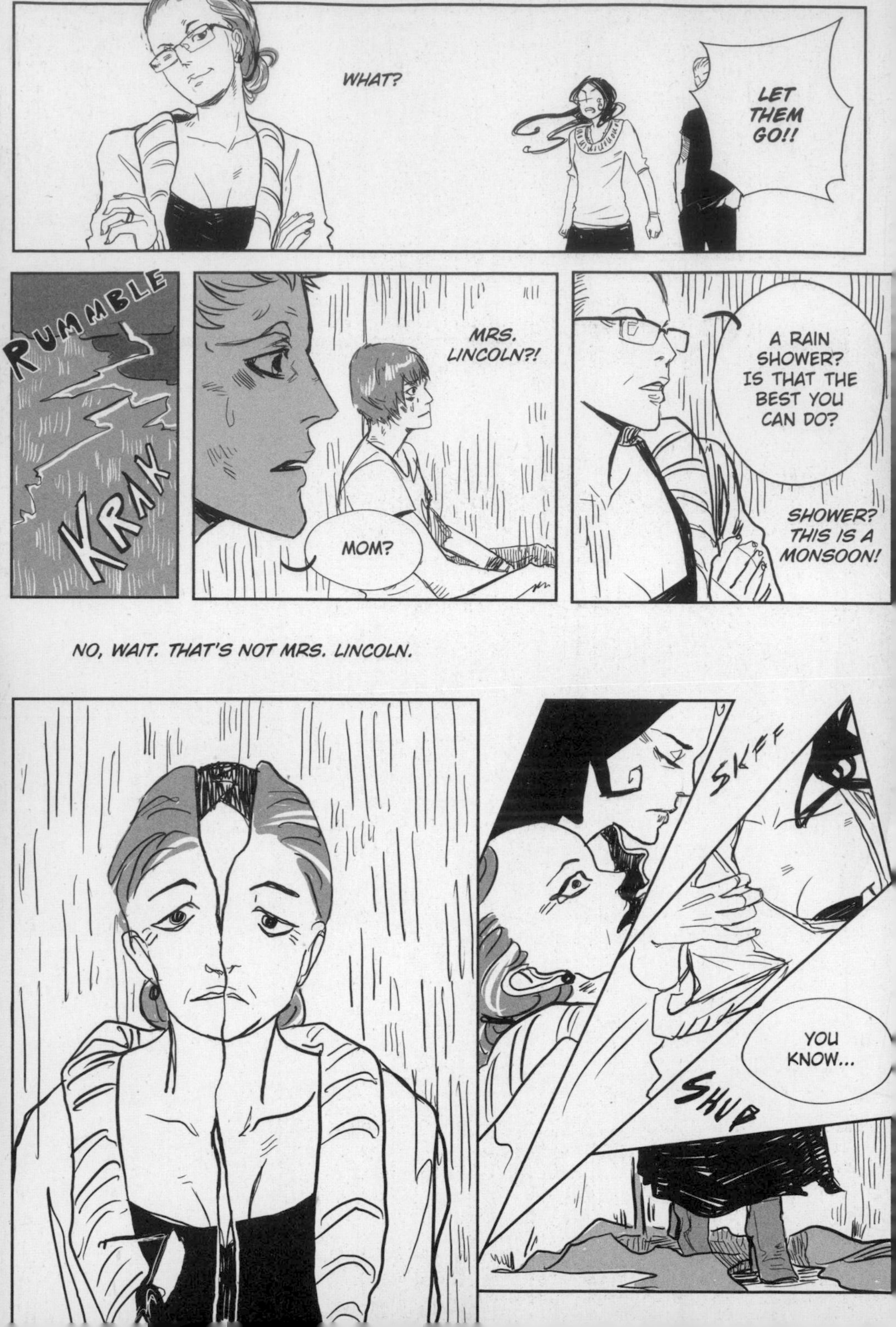
WHAT?
LET THEM GO!!
RUMMBLE
KRAK
MRS. LINCOLN?!
MOM?
A RAIN SHOWER? IS THAT THE BEST YOU CAN DO?
SHOWER? THIS IS A MONSOON!
NO, WAIT. THAT'S NOT MRS. LINCOLN.
SKFF
YOU KNOW...
SHUB

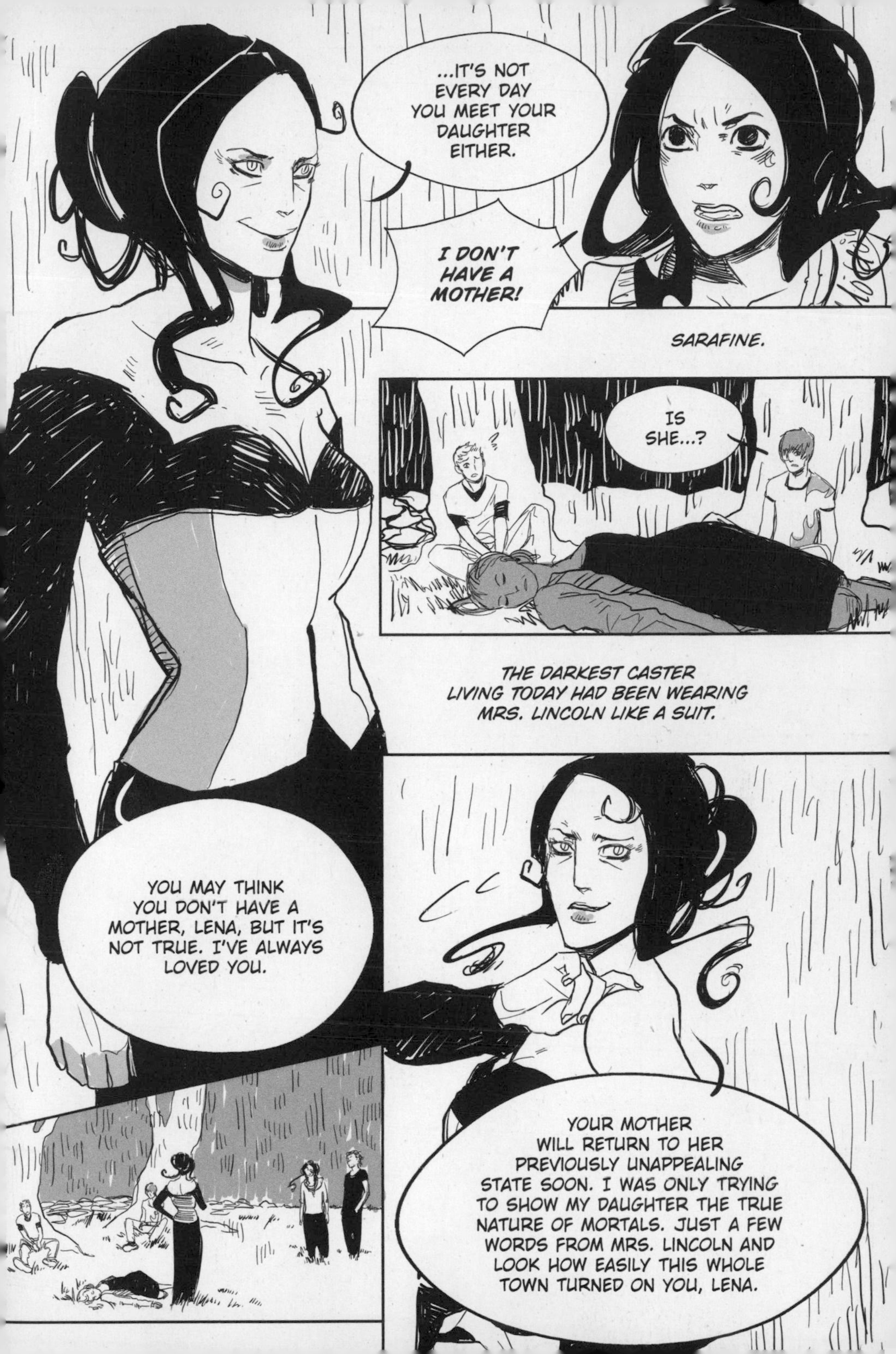

...IT'S NOT EVERY DAY YOU MEET YOUR DAUGHTER EITHER.
I DON'T HAVE A MOTHER!
SARAFINE.
IS SHE...?
THE DARKEST CASTER LIVING TODAY HAD BEEN WEARING MRS. LINCOLN LIKE A SUIT.
YOU MAY THINK YOU DON'T HAVE A MOTHER, LENA, BUT IT'S NOT TRUE. I'VE ALWAYS LOVED YOU.
YOUR MOTHER WILL RETURN TO HER PREVIOUSLY UNAPPEALING STATE SOON. I WAS ONLY TRYING TO SHOW MY DAUGHTER THE TRUE NATURE OF MORTALS. JUST A FEW WORDS FROM MRS. LINCOLN AND LOOK HOW EASILY THIS WHOLE TOWN TURNED ON YOU, LENA.

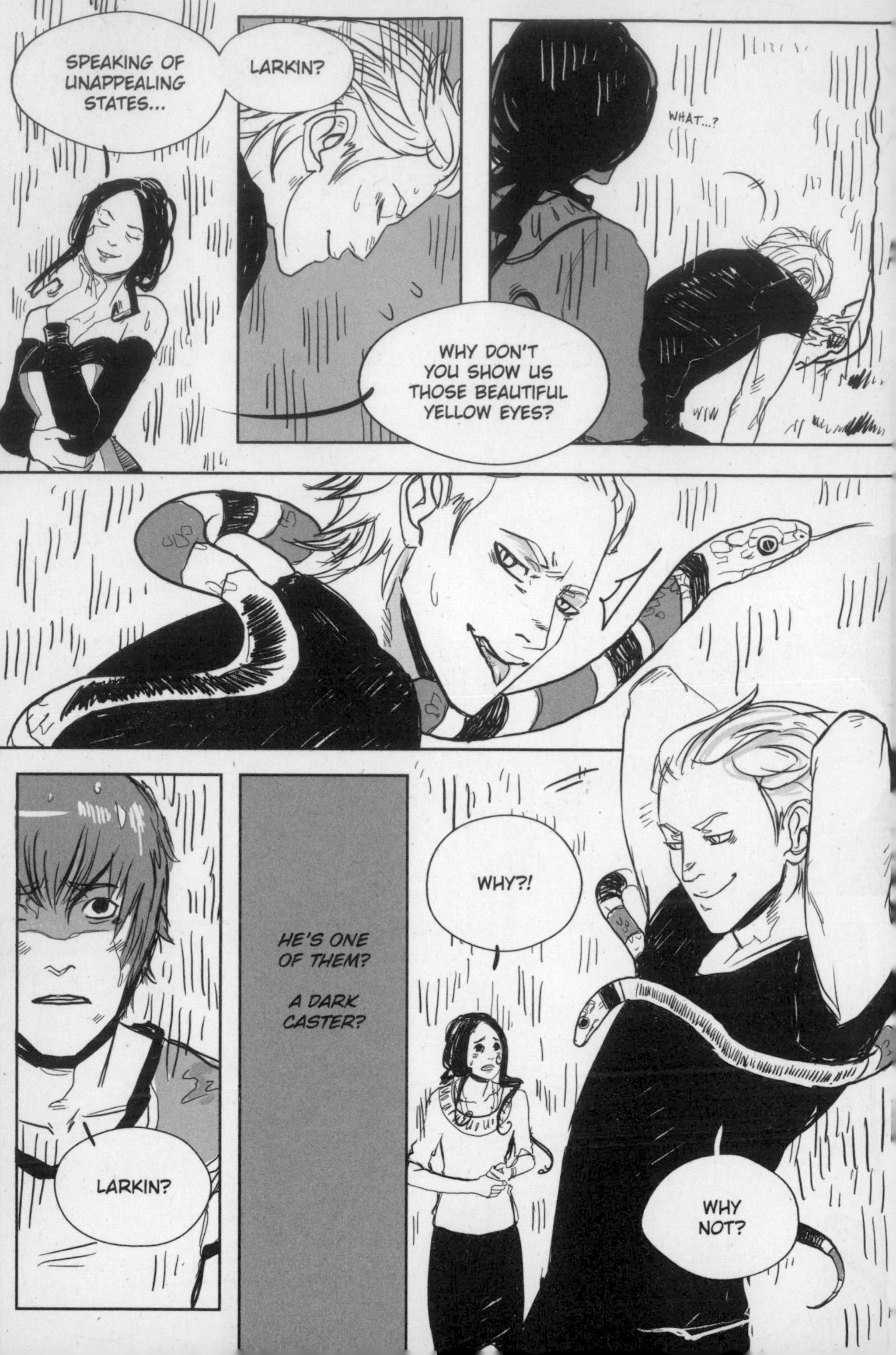
SPEAKING OF UNAPPEALING STATES...
LARKIN?
WHAT...?
WHY DON'T YOU SHOW US THOSE BEAUTIFUL YELLOW EYES?
HE'S ONE OF THEM?
A DARK CASTER?
LARKIN?
WHY?!
WHY NOT?

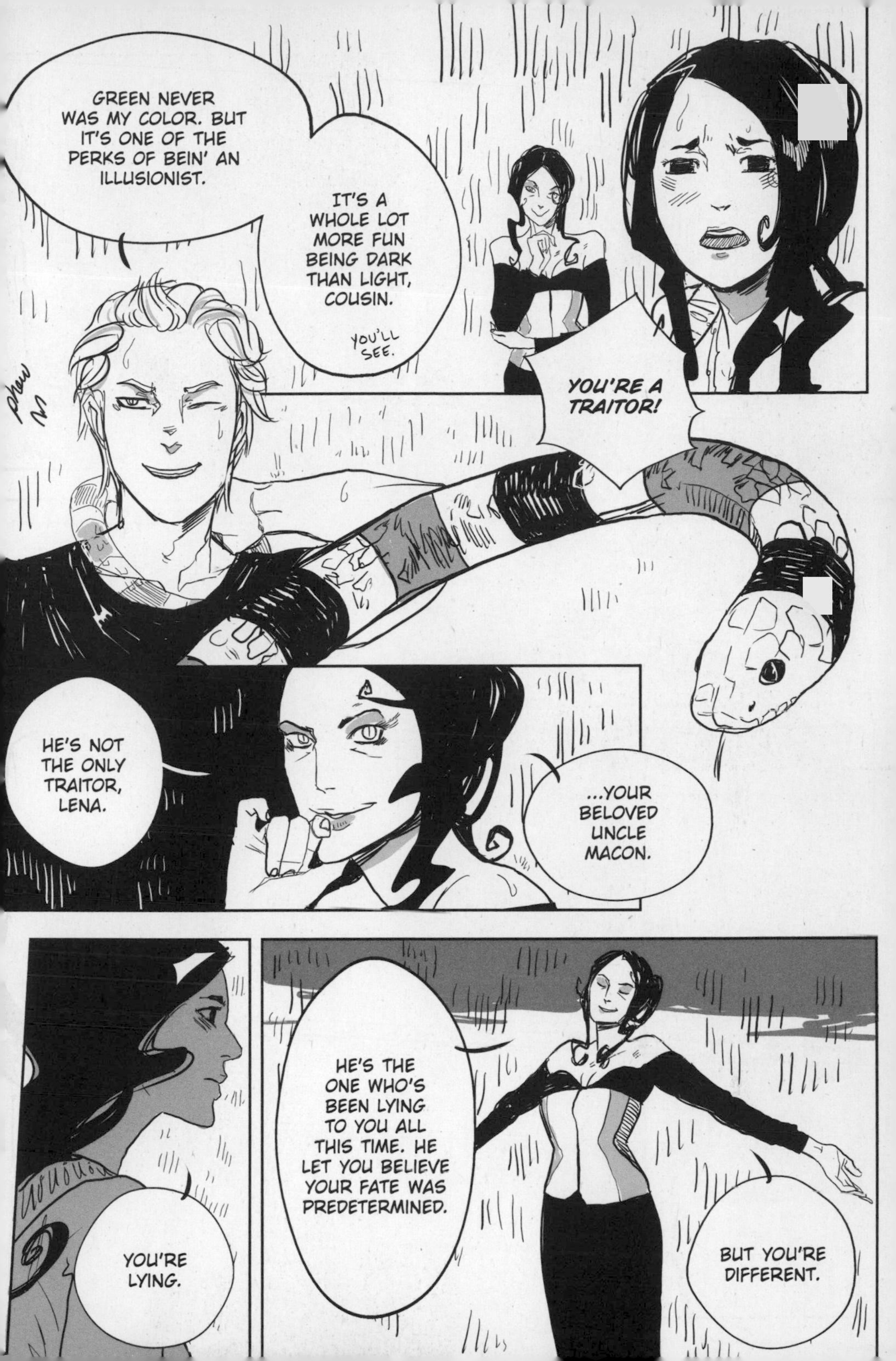

GREEN NEVER WAS MY COLOR. BUT IT'S ONE OF THE PERKS OF BEIN' AN ILLUSIONIST.
IT'S A WHOLE LOT MORE FUN BEING DARK THAN LIGHT, COUSIN.
YOU'LL SEE.
phew
YOU'RE A TRAITOR!
HE'S NOT THE ONLY TRAITOR, LENA.
...YOUR BELOVED UNCLE MACON.
YOU'RE LYING.
HE'S THE ONE WHO'S BEEN LYING TO YOU ALL THIS TIME. HE LET YOU BELIEVE YOUR FATE WAS PREDETERMINED.
BUT YOU'RE DIFFERENT.

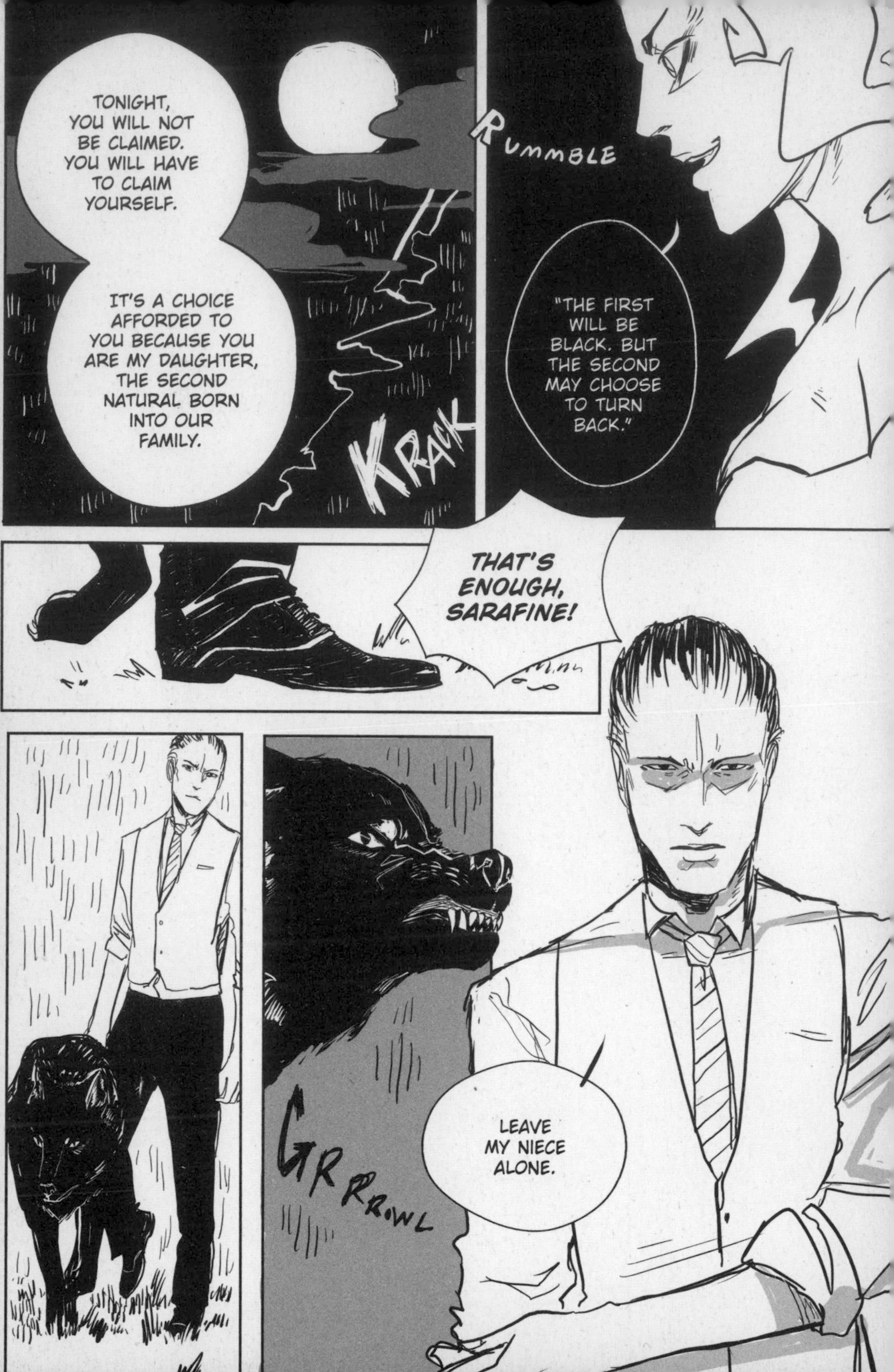
TONIGHT, YOU WILL NOT BE CLAIMED. YOU WILL HAVE TO CLAIM YOURSELF.
IT'S A CHOICE AFFORDED TO YOU BECAUSE YOU ARE MY DAUGHTER, THE SECOND NATURAL BORN INTO OUR FAMILY.
KRACK
RUMMBLE
"THE FIRST WILL BE BLACK. BUT THE SECOND MAY CHOOSE TO TURN BACK."
THAT'S ENOUGH, SARAFINE!
GRRRROWL
LEAVE MY NIECE ALONE.

BEAUTIFUL CREATURES

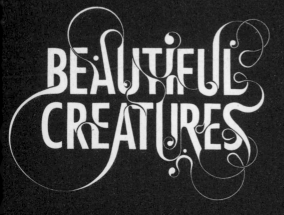

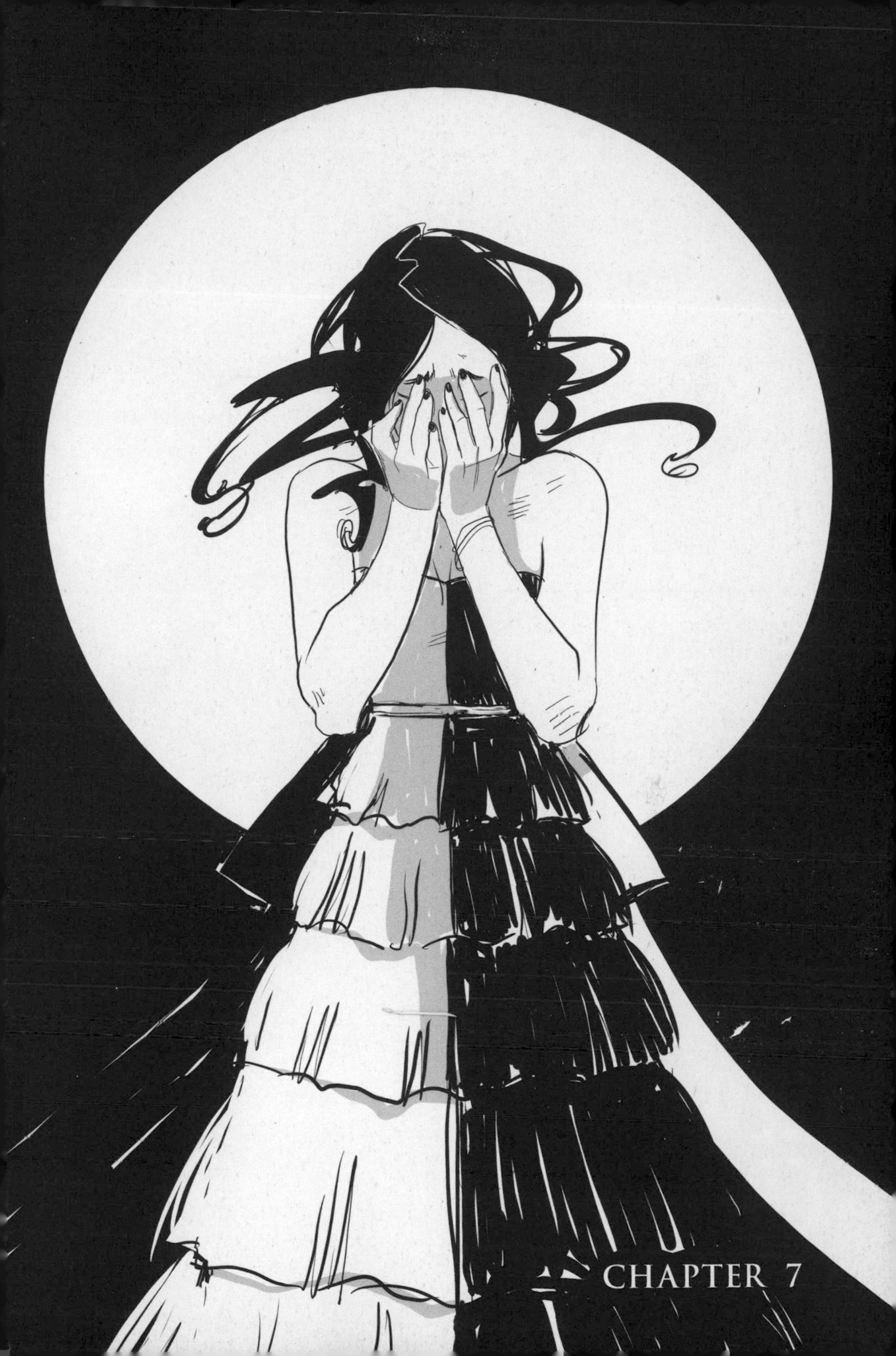

CHAPTER 7

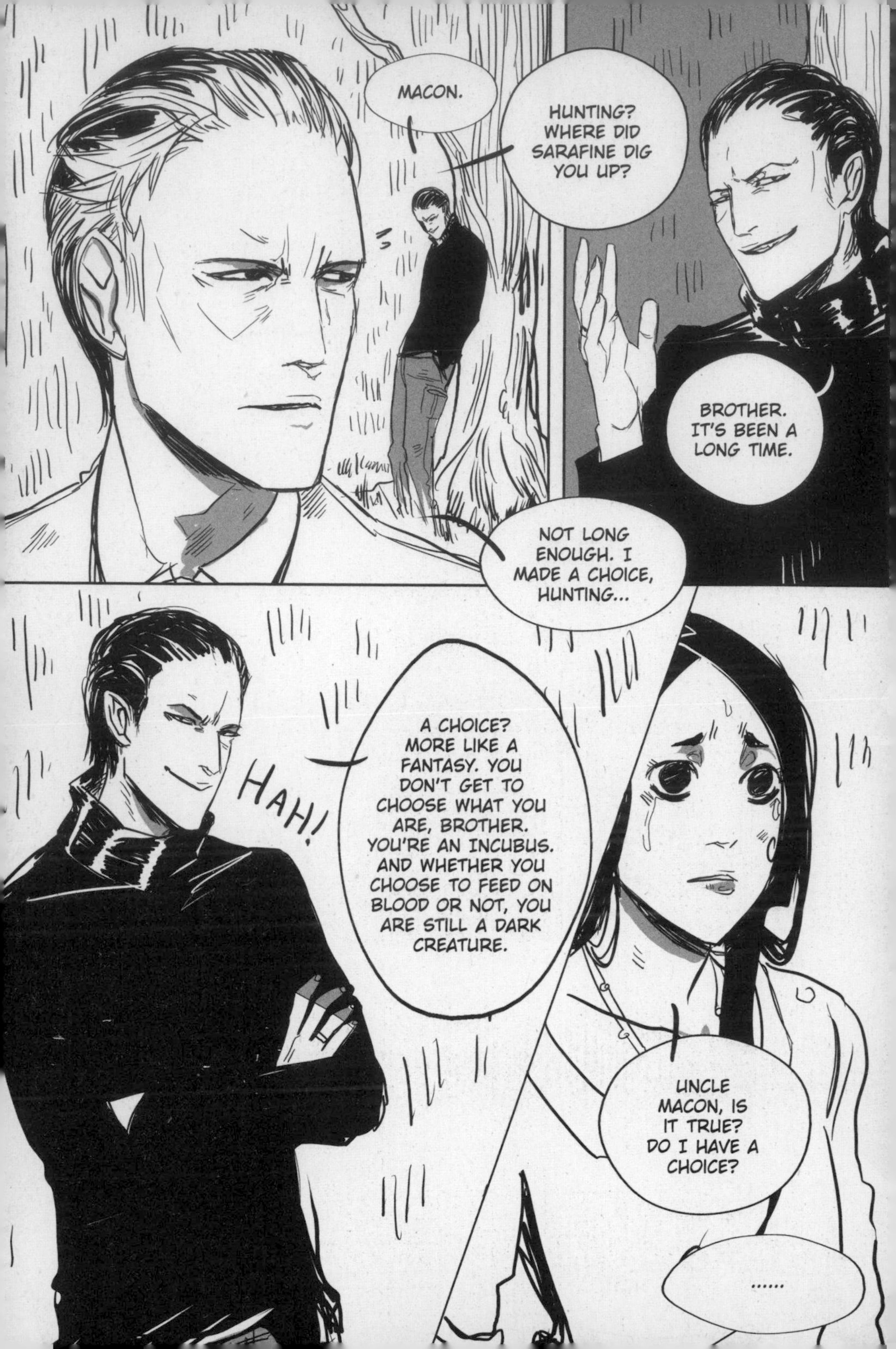
MACON.
HUNTING? WHERE DID SARAFINE DIG YOU UP?
BROTHER. IT'S BEEN A LONG TIME.
NOT LONG ENOUGH. I MADE A CHOICE, HUNTING...
HAH!
A CHOICE? MORE LIKE A FANTASY. YOU DON'T GET TO CHOOSE WHAT YOU ARE, BROTHER. YOU'RE AN INCUBUS. AND WHETHER YOU CHOOSE TO FEED ON BLOOD OR NOT, YOU ARE STILL A DARK CREATURE.
UNCLE MACON, IS IT TRUE? DO I HAVE A CHOICE?
......

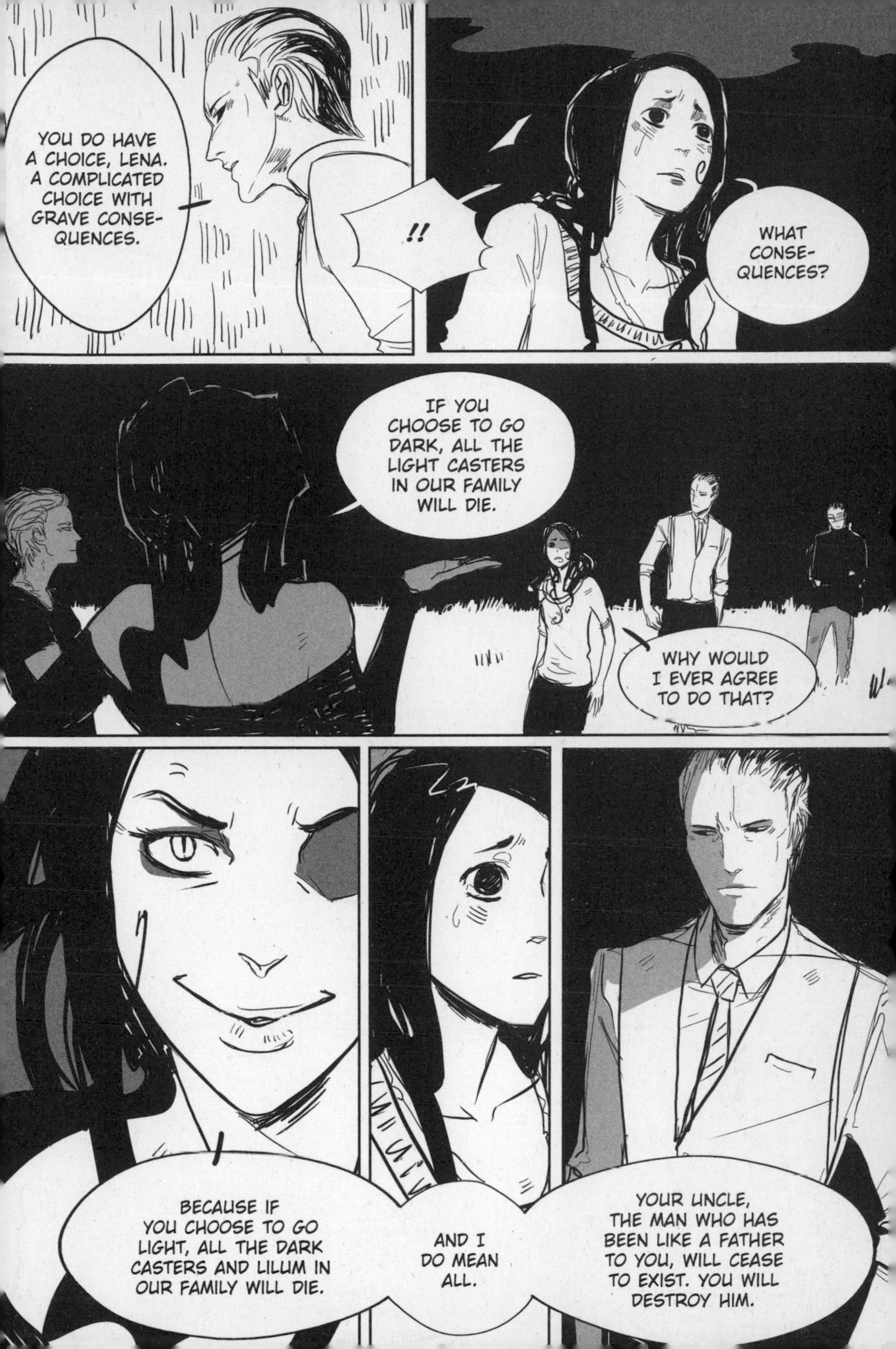
YOU DO HAVE A CHOICE, LENA. A COMPLICATED CHOICE WITH GRAVE CONSE-QUENCES.
!!
WHAT CONSE-QUENCES?
IF YOU CHOOSE TO GO DARK, ALL THE LIGHT CASTERS IN OUR FAMILY WILL DIE.
WHY WOULD I EVER AGREE TO DO THAT?
BECAUSE IF YOU CHOOSE TO GO LIGHT, ALL THE DARK CASTERS AND LILUM IN OUR FAMILY WILL DIE.
AND I DO MEAN ALL.
YOUR UNCLE, THE MAN WHO HAS BEEN LIKE A FATHER TO YOU, WILL CEASE TO EXIST. YOU WILL DESTROY HIM.

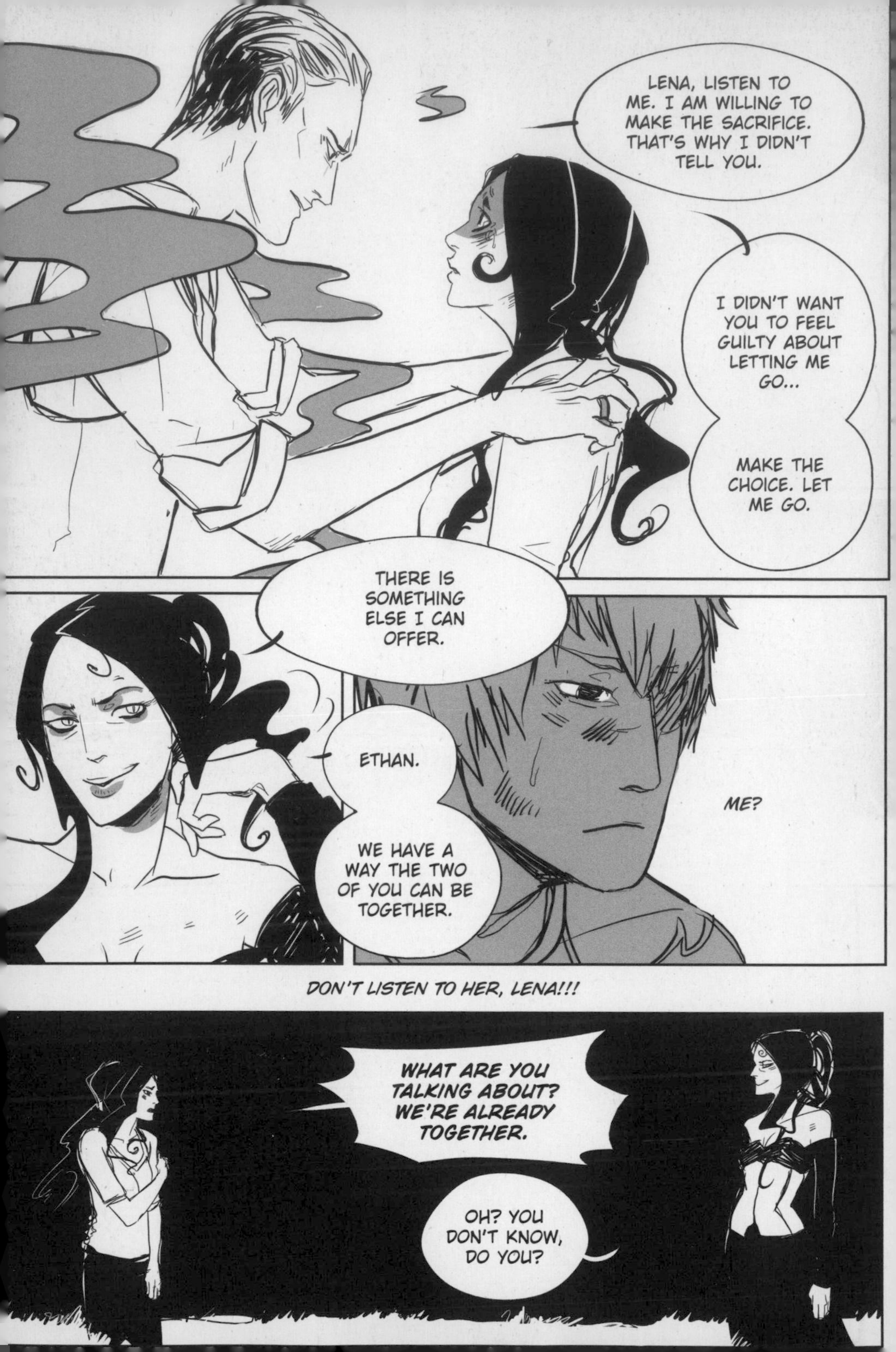
LENA, LISTEN TO ME. I AM WILLING TO MAKE THE SACRIFICE. THAT'S WHY I DIDN'T TELL YOU.
I DIDN'T WANT YOU TO FEEL GUILTY ABOUT LETTING ME GO...
MAKE THE CHOICE. LET ME GO.
THERE IS SOMETHING ELSE I CAN OFFER.
ETHAN.
WE HAVE A WAY THE TWO OF YOU CAN BE TOGETHER.
ME?
DON'T LISTEN TO HER, LENA!!!
WHAT ARE YOU TALKING ABOUT? WE'RE ALREADY TOGETHER.
OH? YOU DON'T KNOW, DO YOU?

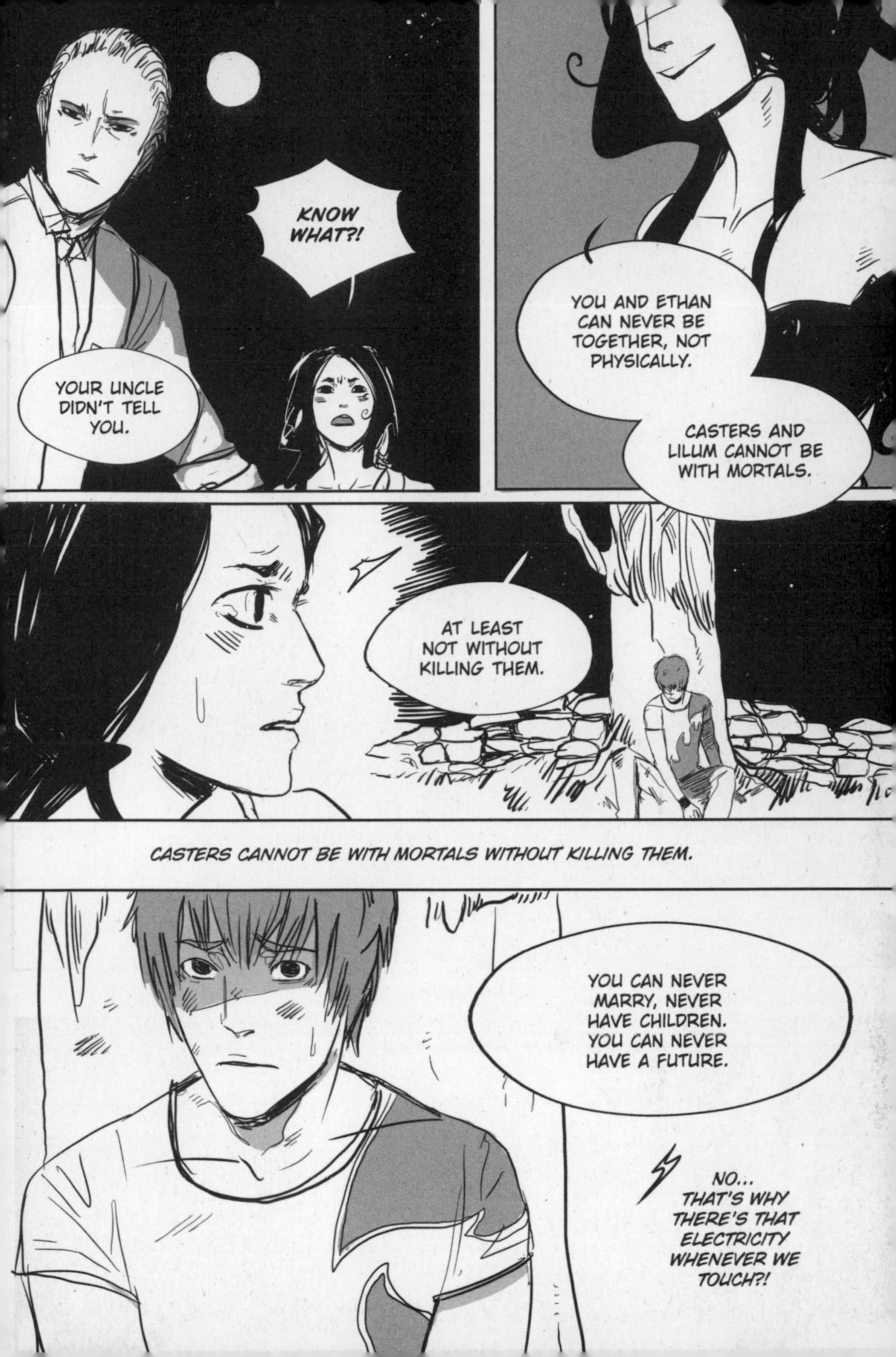
KNOW WHAT?!
YOUR UNCLE DIDN'T TELL YOU.
YOU AND ETHAN CAN NEVER BE TOGETHER, NOT PHYSICALLY.
CASTERS AND LILUM CANNOT BE WITH MORTALS.
AT LEAST NOT WITHOUT KILLING THEM.
CASTERS CANNOT BE WITH MORTALS WITHOUT KILLING THEM.
YOU CAN NEVER MARRY, NEVER HAVE CHILDREN. YOU CAN NEVER HAVE A FUTURE.
NO... THAT'S WHY THERE'S THAT ELECTRICITY WHENEVER WE TOUCH?!

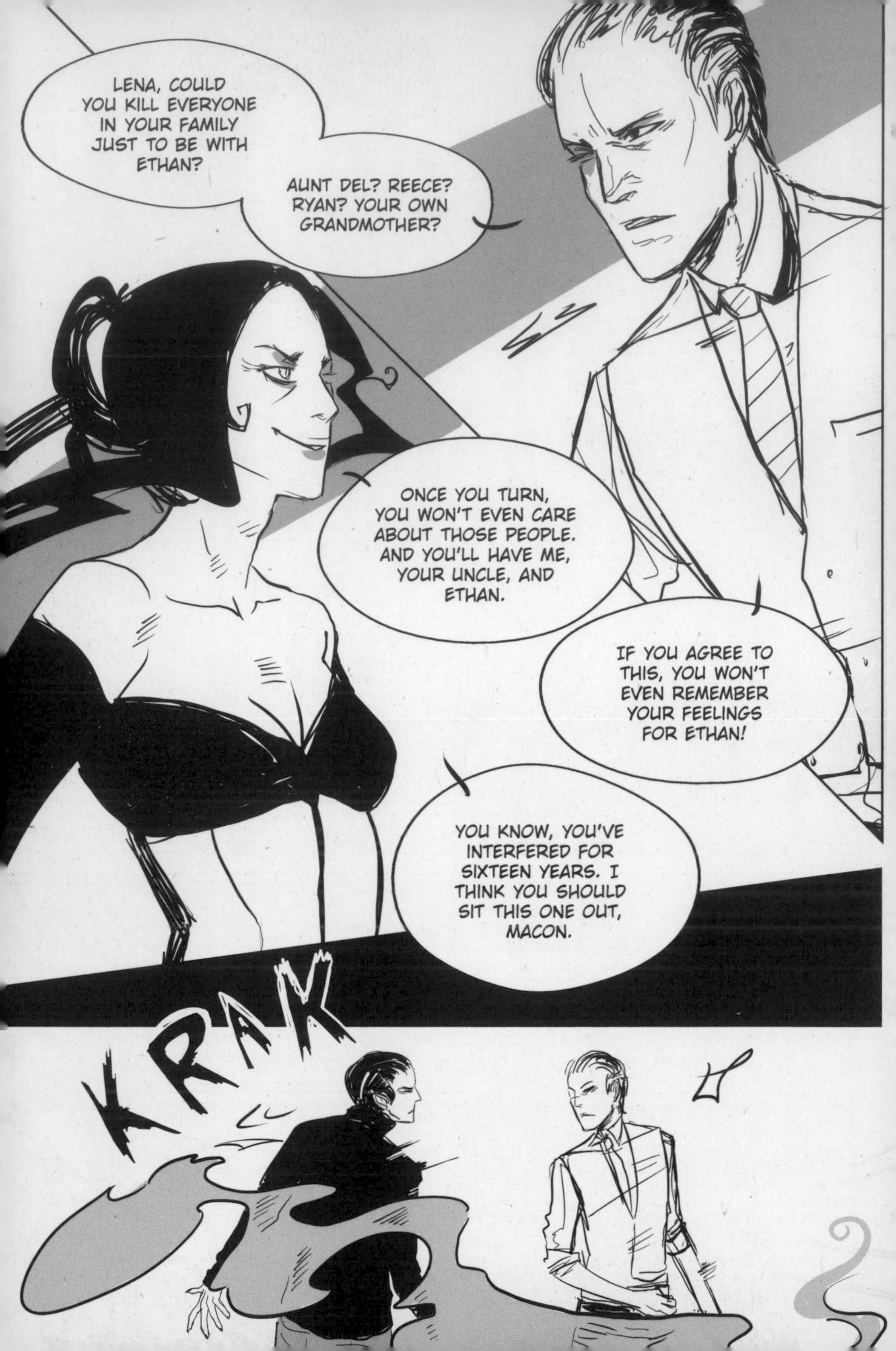

LENA, COULD YOU KILL EVERYONE IN YOUR FAMILY JUST TO BE WITH ETHAN?
AUNT DEL? REECE? RYAN? YOUR OWN GRANDMOTHER?
ONCE YOU TURN, YOU WON'T EVEN CARE ABOUT THOSE PEOPLE. AND YOU'LL HAVE ME, YOUR UNCLE, AND ETHAN.
IF YOU AGREE TO THIS, YOU WON'T EVEN REMEMBER YOUR FEELINGS FOR ETHAN!
YOU KNOW, YOU'VE INTERFERED FOR SIXTEEN YEARS. I THINK YOU SHOULD SIT THIS ONE OUT, MACON.
KRAK

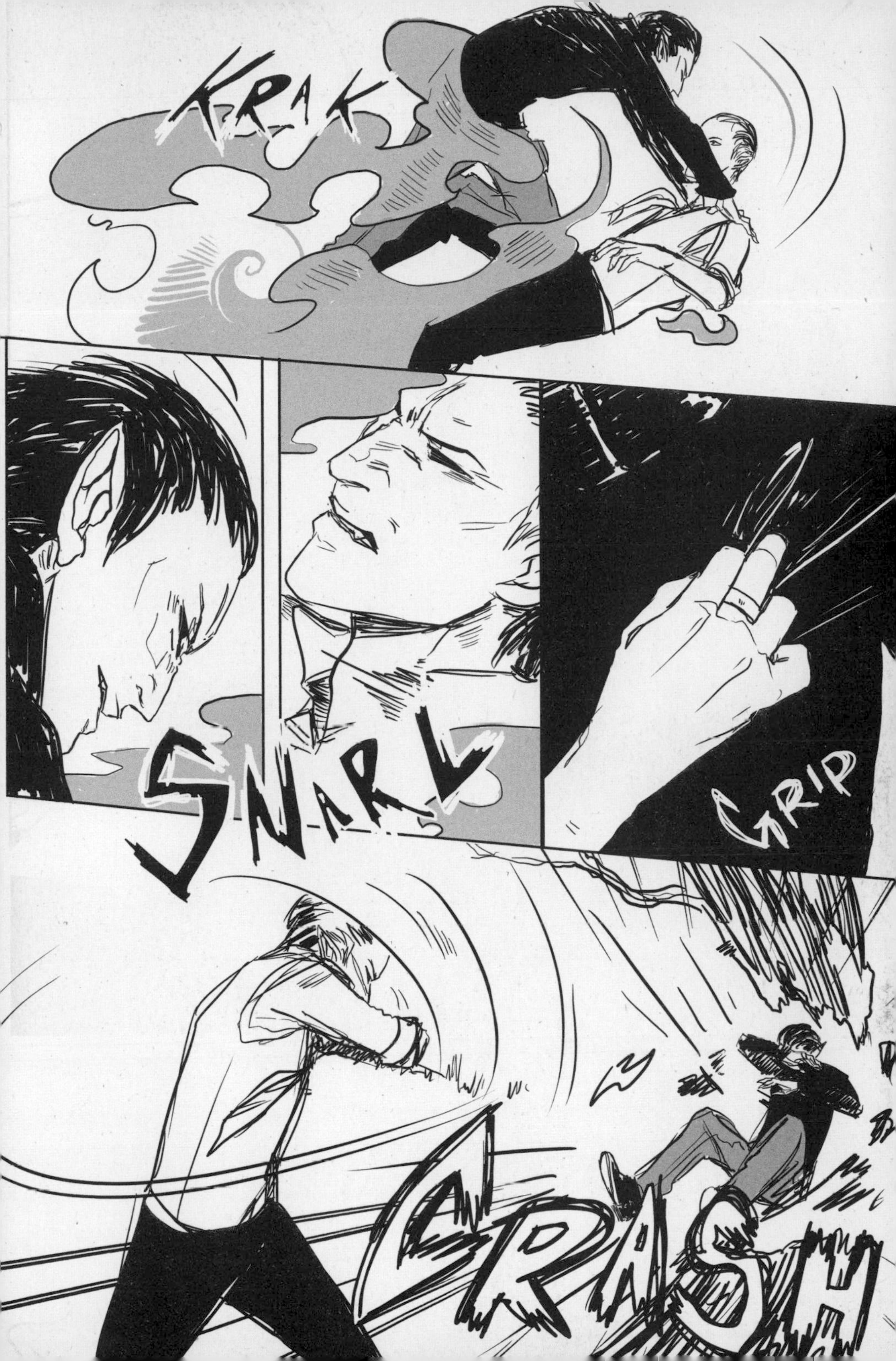
KRAK
SNARL
GRIP
CRASH

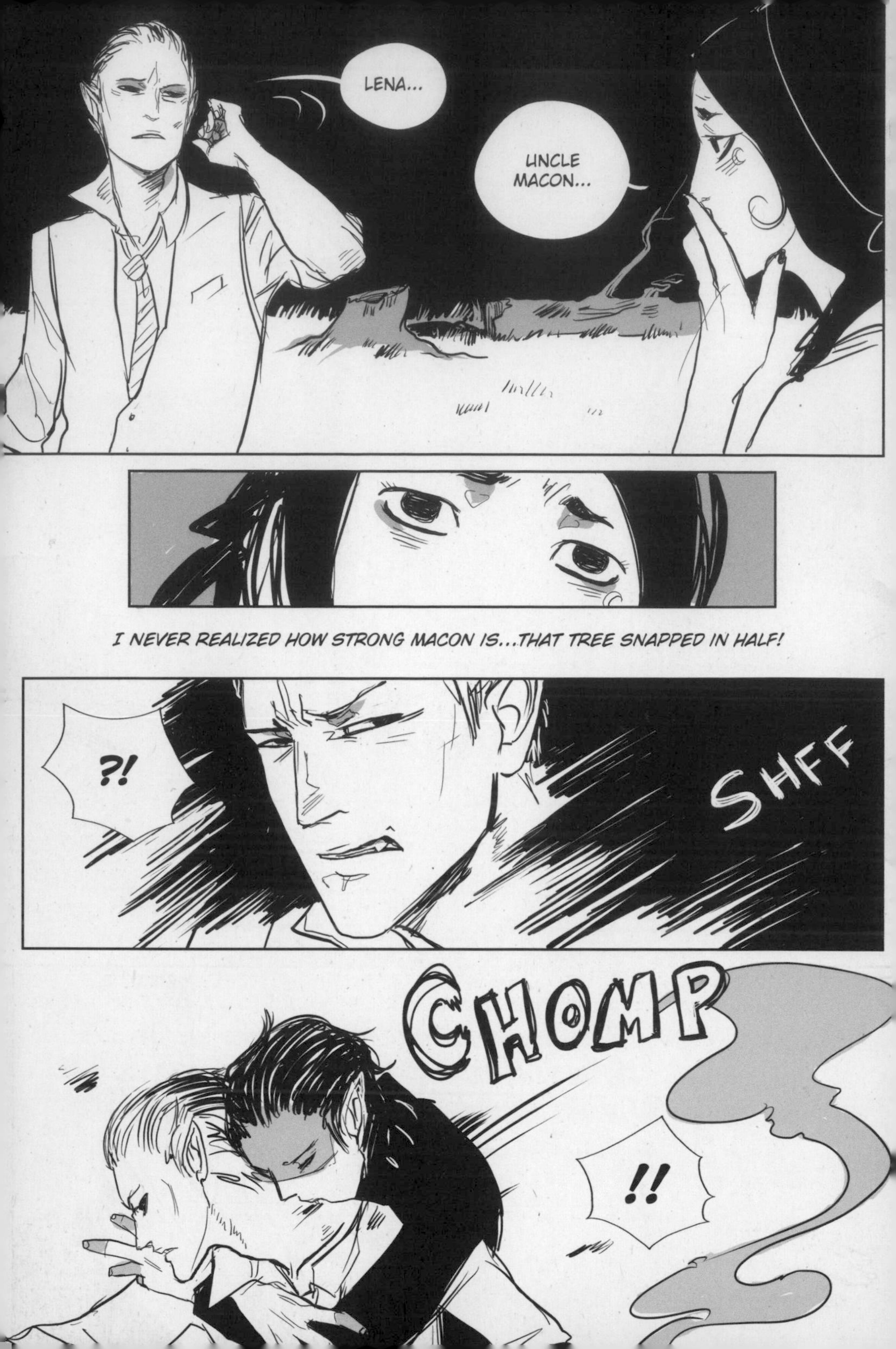
LENA...
UNCLE MACON...
I NEVER REALIZED HOW STRONG MACON IS...THAT TREE SNAPPED IN HALF!
?!
SHFF
CHOMP
!!

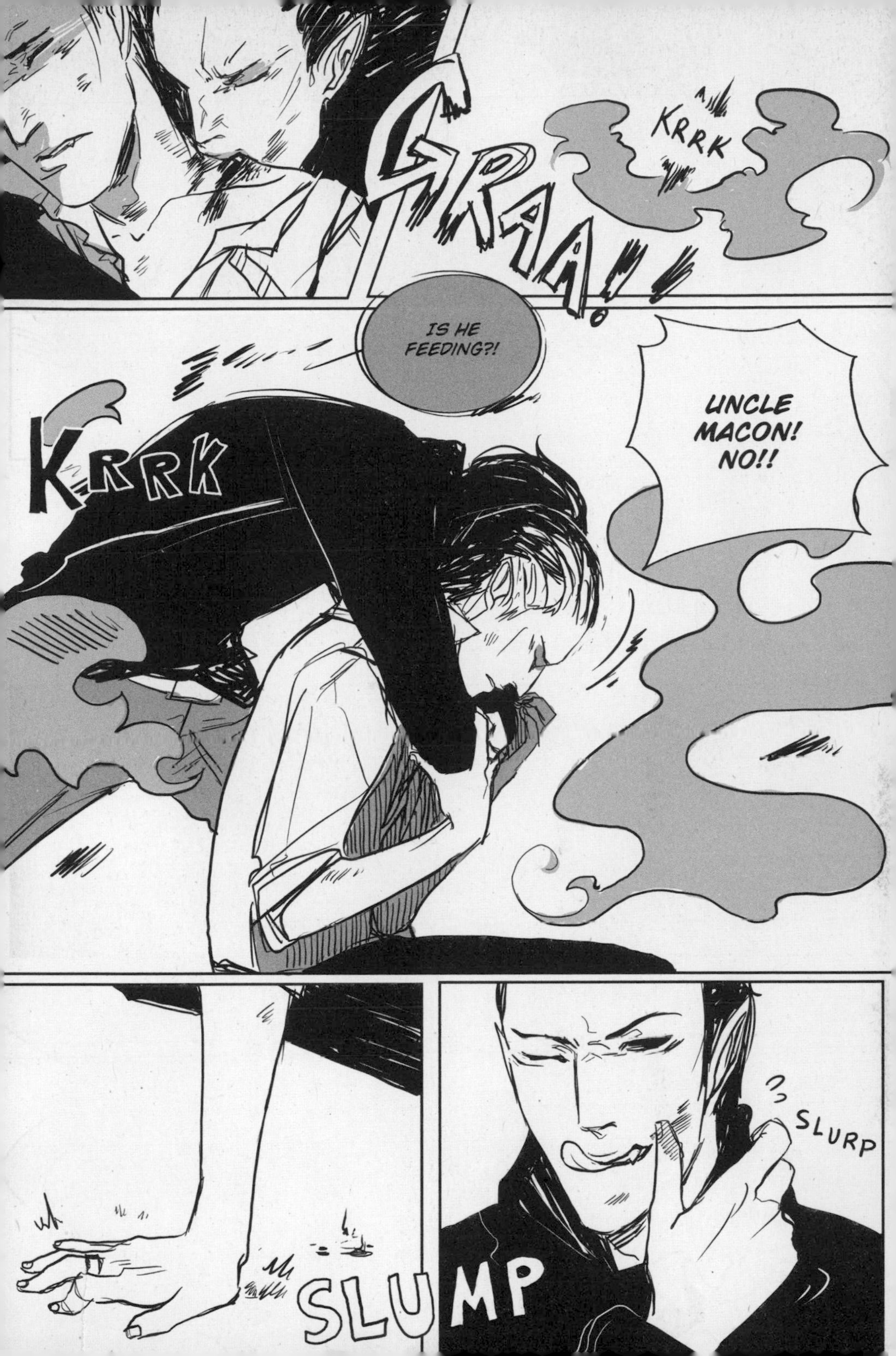
GRAA!!
KRRK
IS HE FEEDING?!
UNCLE MACON! NO!!
KRRK
SLUMP
SLURP

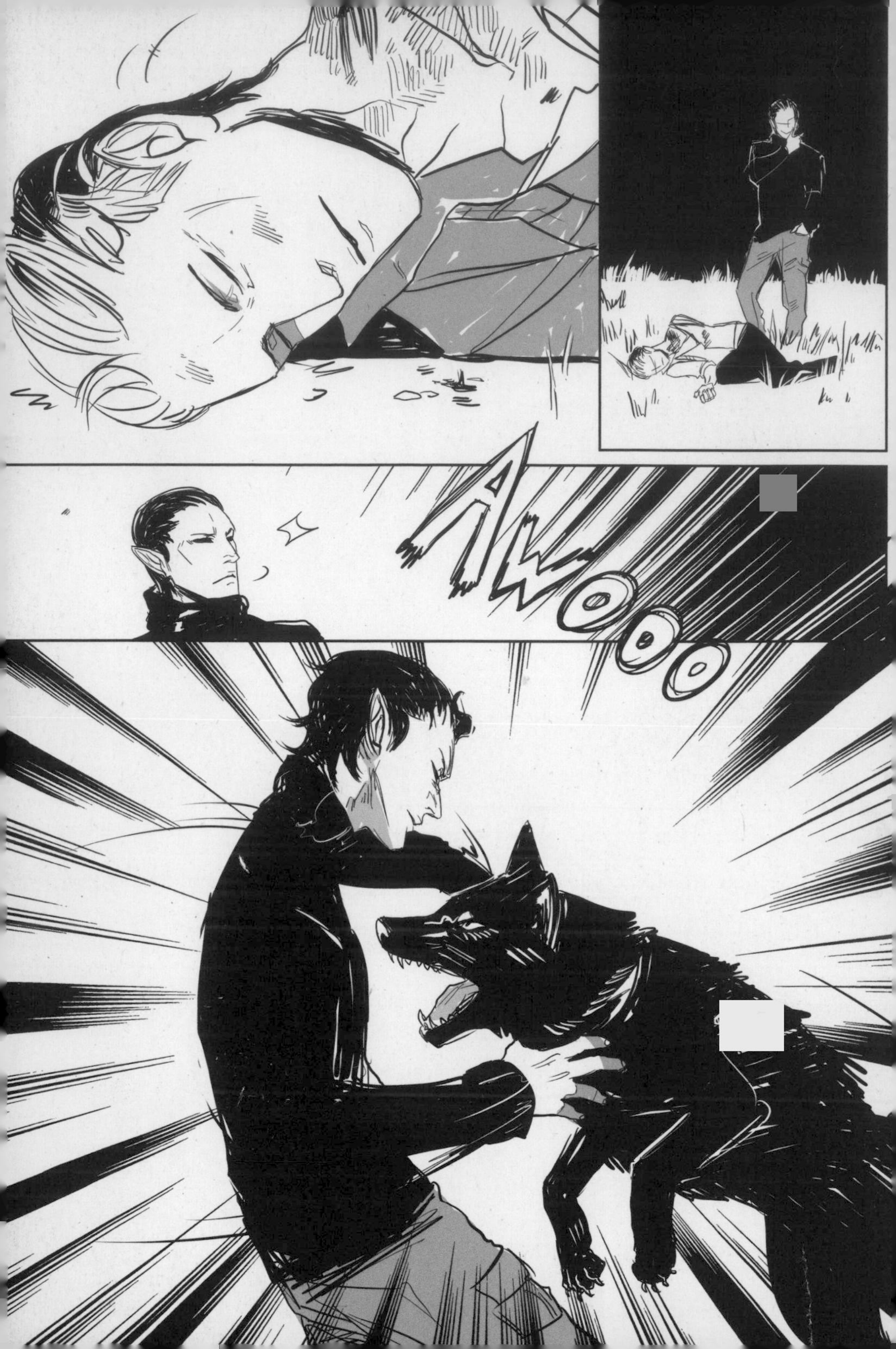
AWOOOO

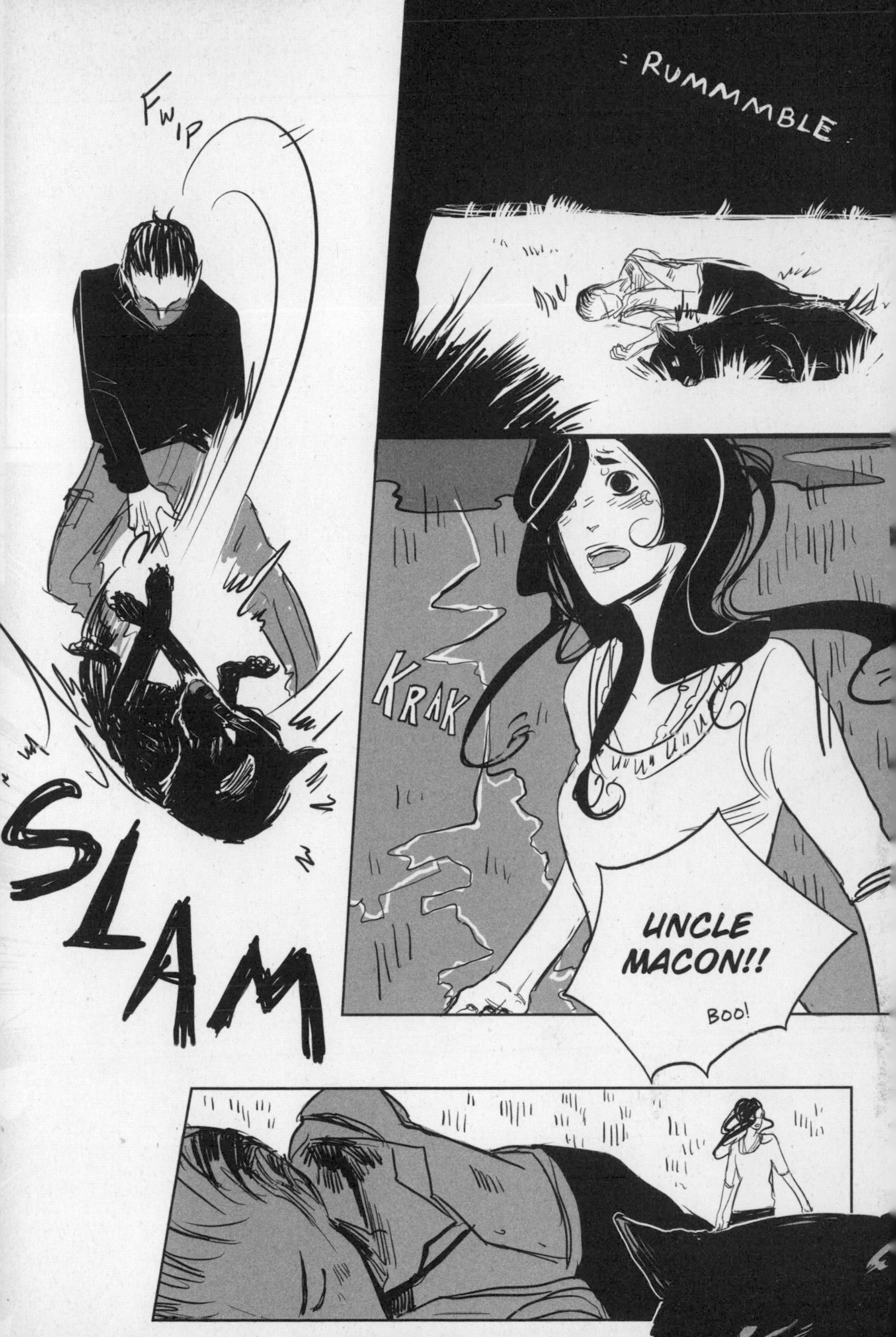
FWIP
SLAM
RUMMMMBLE
KRAK
UNCLE MACON!!
BOO!

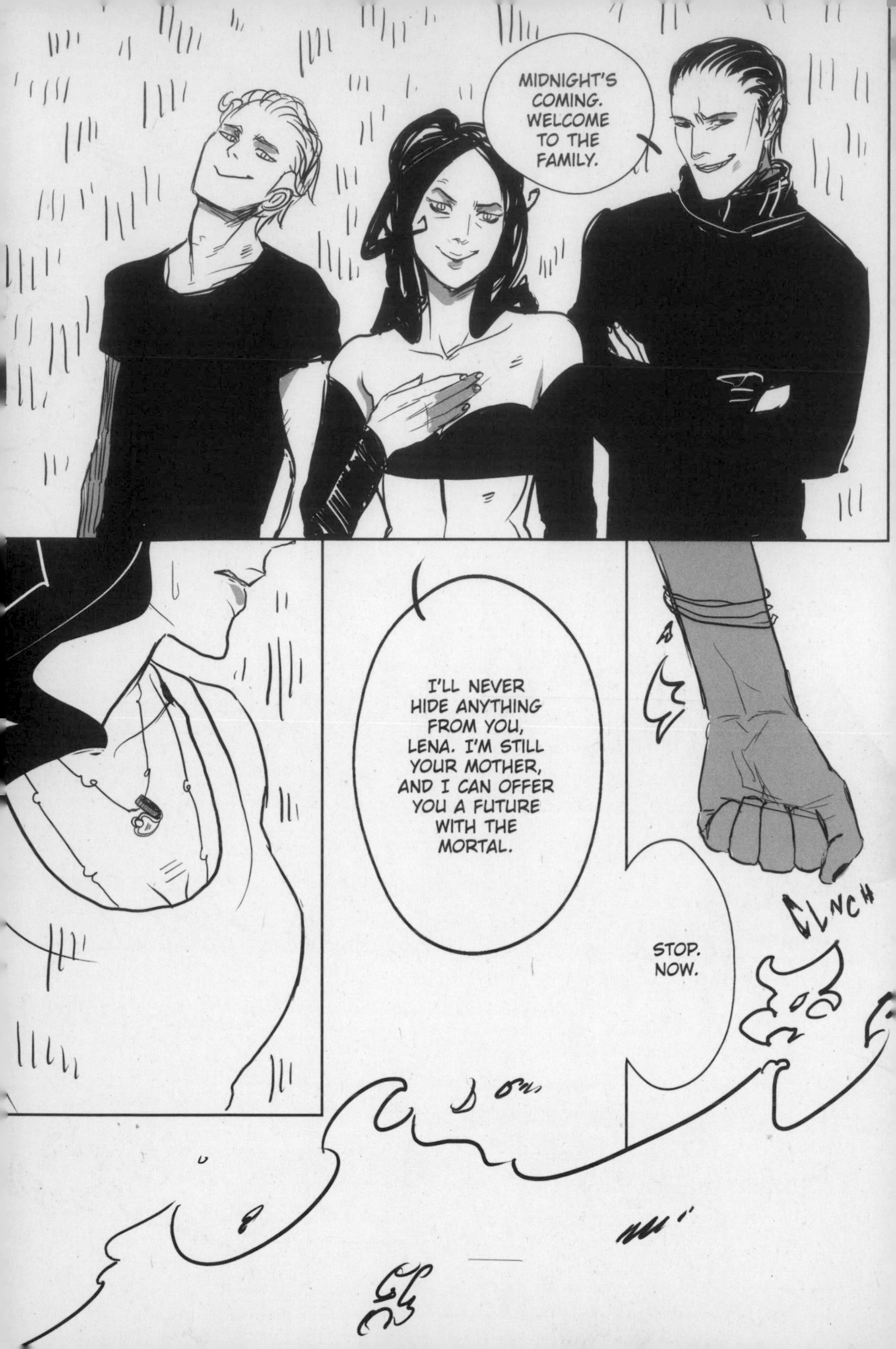
MIDNIGHT'S COMING. WELCOME TO THE FAMILY.
I'LL NEVER HIDE ANYTHING FROM YOU, LENA. I'M STILL YOUR MOTHER, AND I CAN OFFER YOU A FUTURE WITH THE MORTAL.
STOP. NOW.
CLNCH

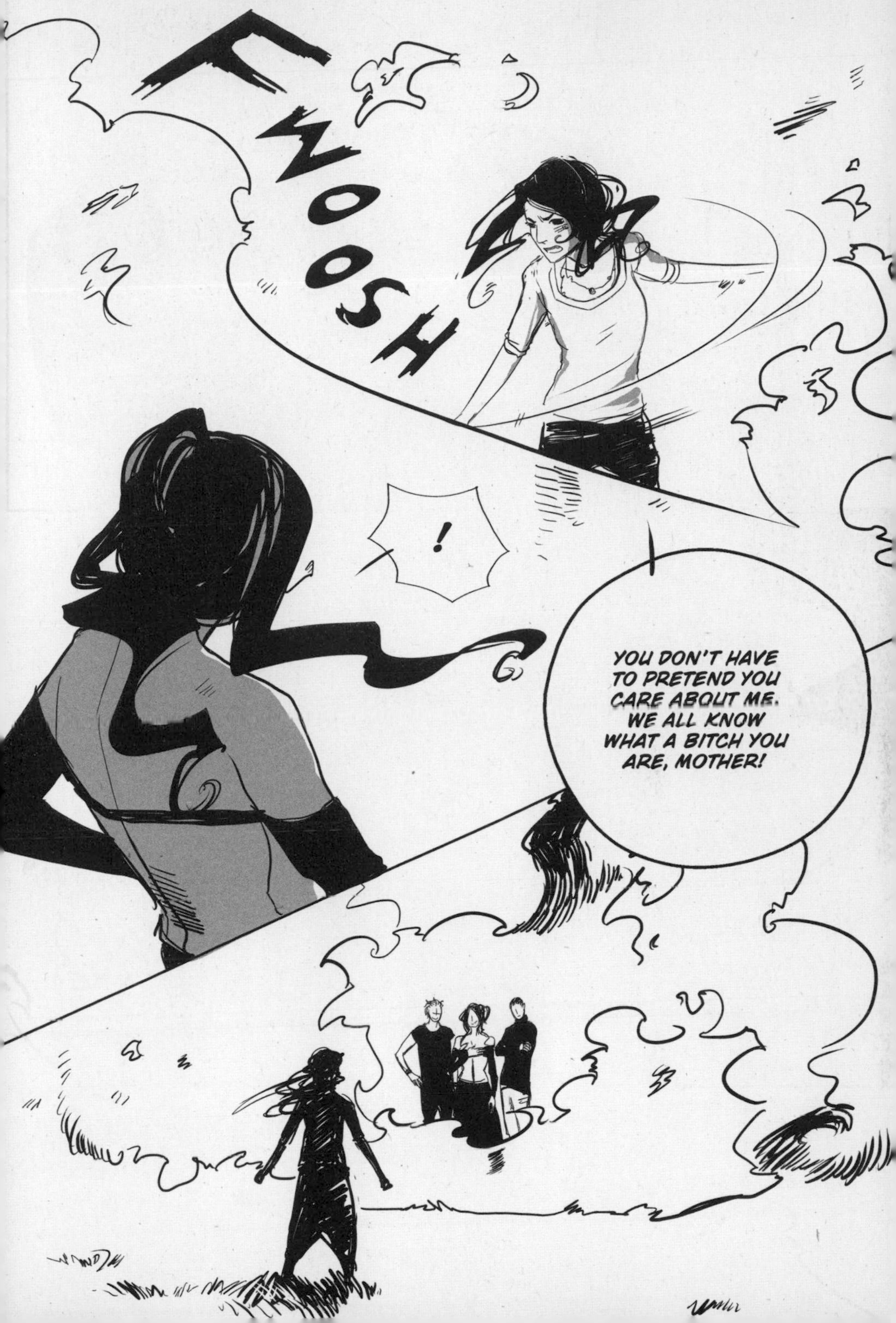
FWOSH
!
YOU DON'T HAVE TO PRETEND YOU CARE ABOUT ME. WE ALL KNOW WHAT A BITCH YOU ARE, MOTHER!

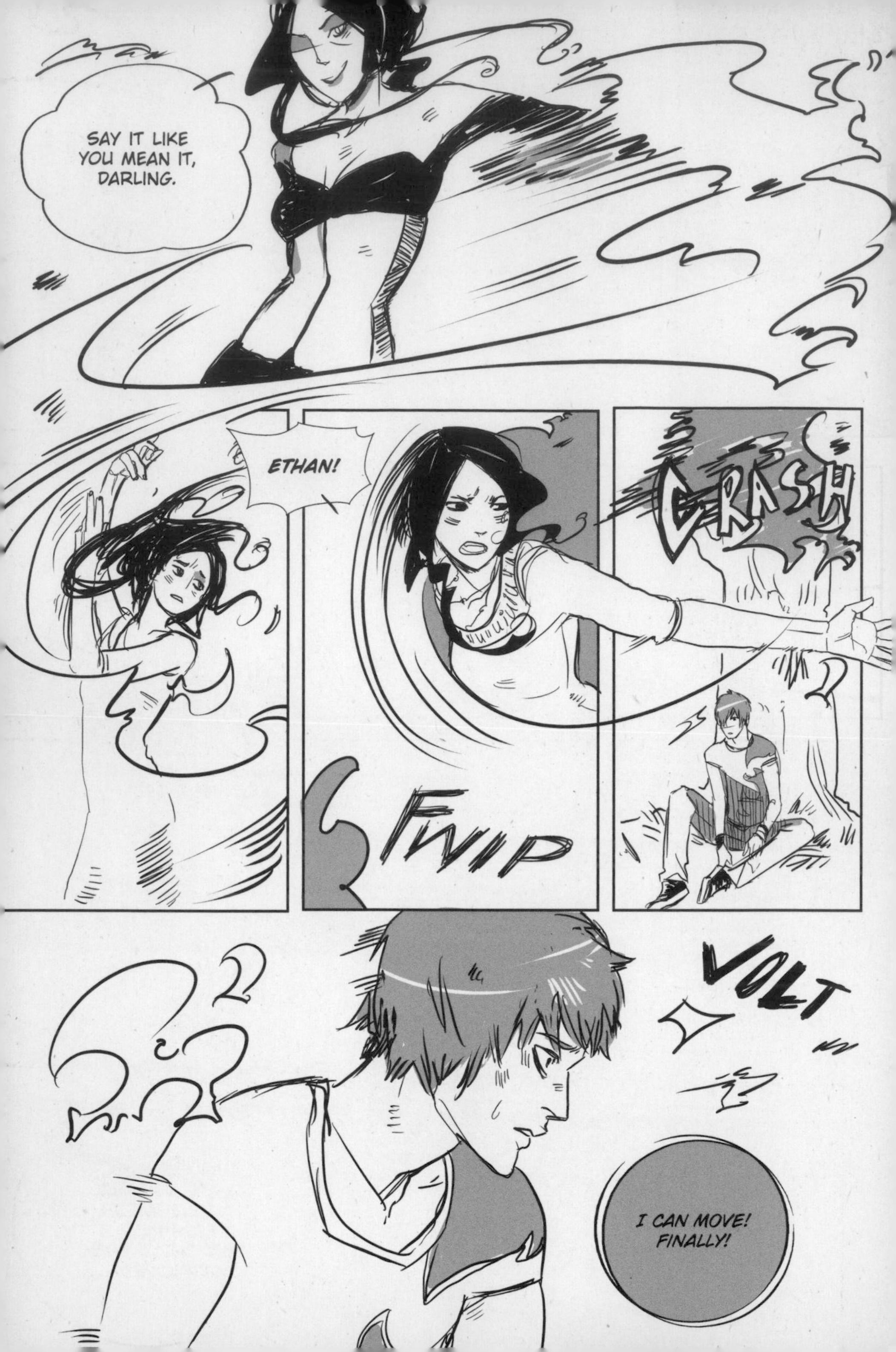
SAY IT LIKE YOU MEAN IT, DARLING.
ETHAN!
FWIP
CRASH
VOLT
I CAN MOVE! FINALLY!

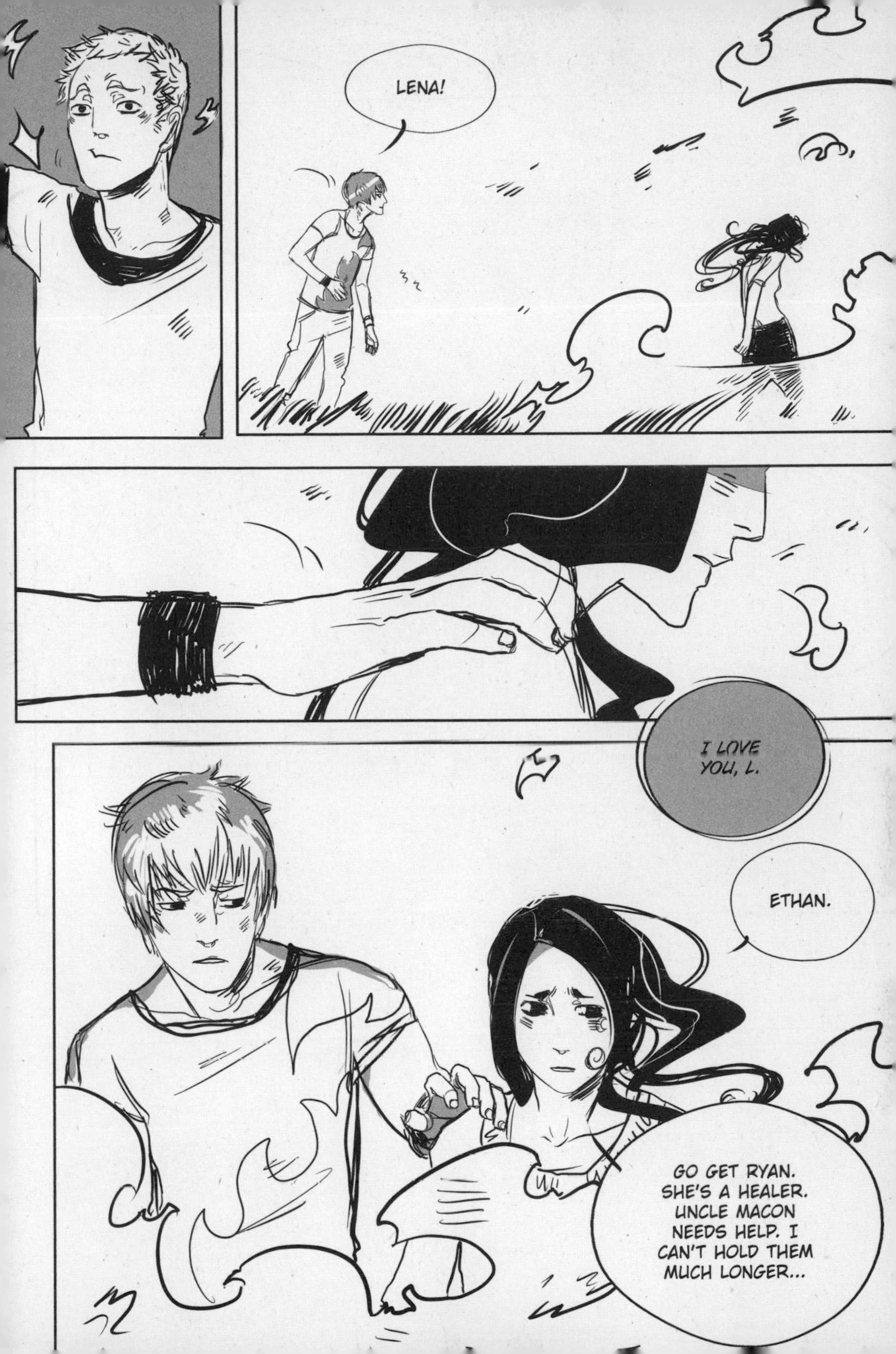
LENA!
I LOVE YOU, L.
ETHAN.
GO GET RYAN. SHE'S A HEALER. UNCLE MACON NEEDS HELP. I CAN'T HOLD THEM MUCH LONGER...

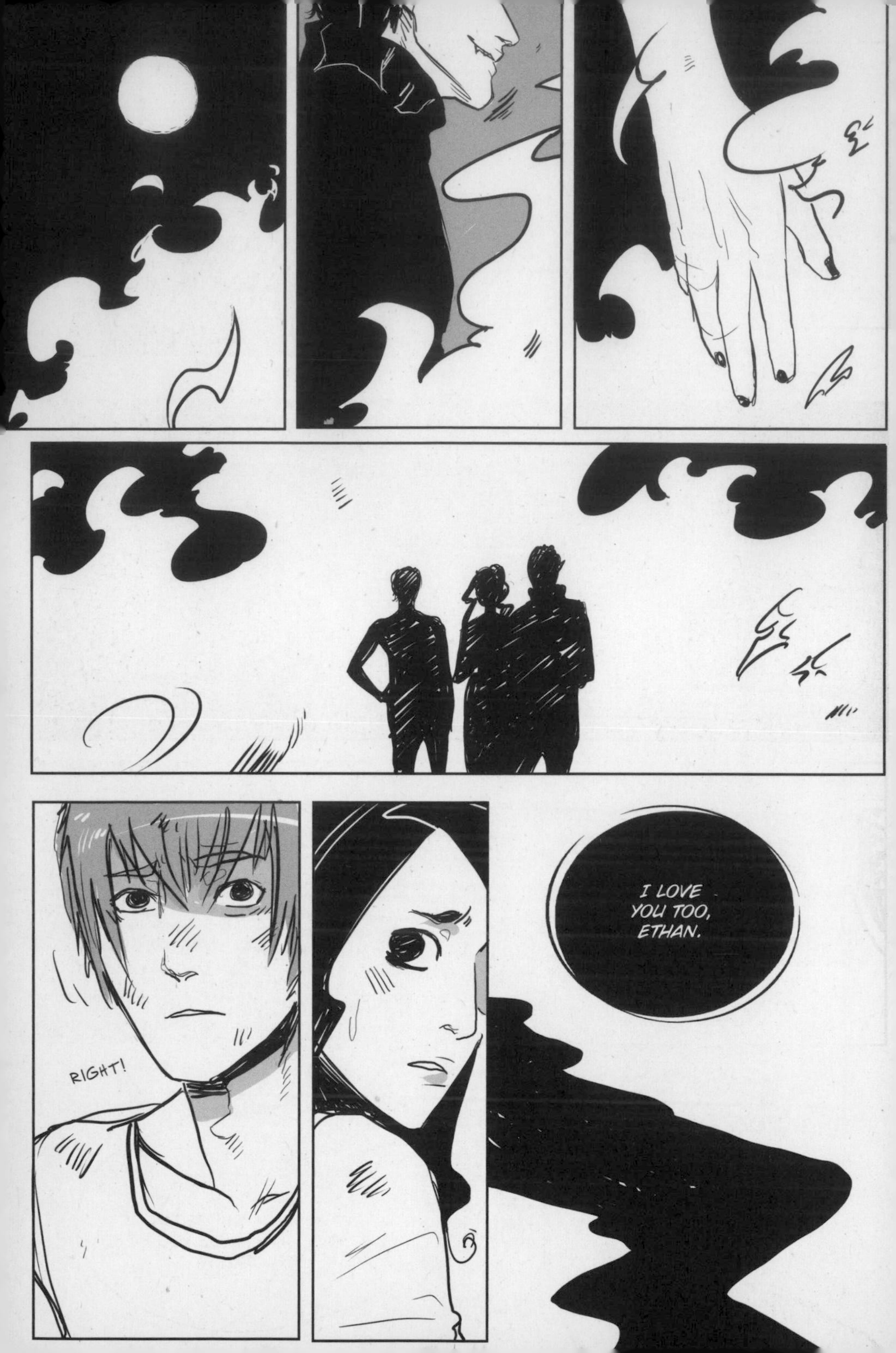
I LOVE YOU TOO, ETHAN.
RIGHT!

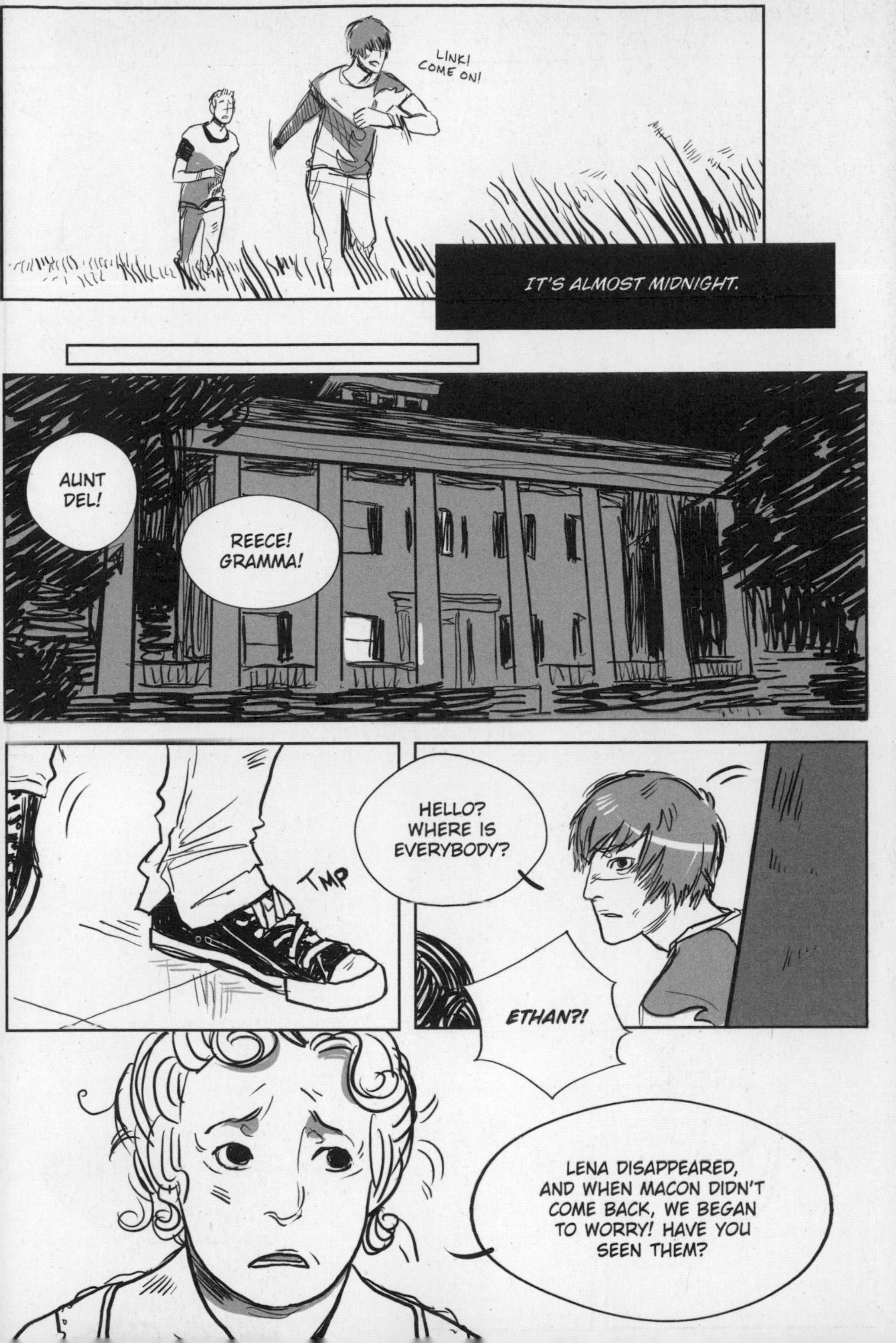
LINK! COME ON!
IT'S ALMOST MIDNIGHT.
AUNT DEL!
REECE! GRAMMA!
TMP
HELLO? WHERE IS EVERYBODY?
ETHAN?!
LENA DISAPPEARED, AND WHEN MACON DIDN'T COME BACK, WE BEGAN TO WORRY! HAVE YOU SEEN THEM?

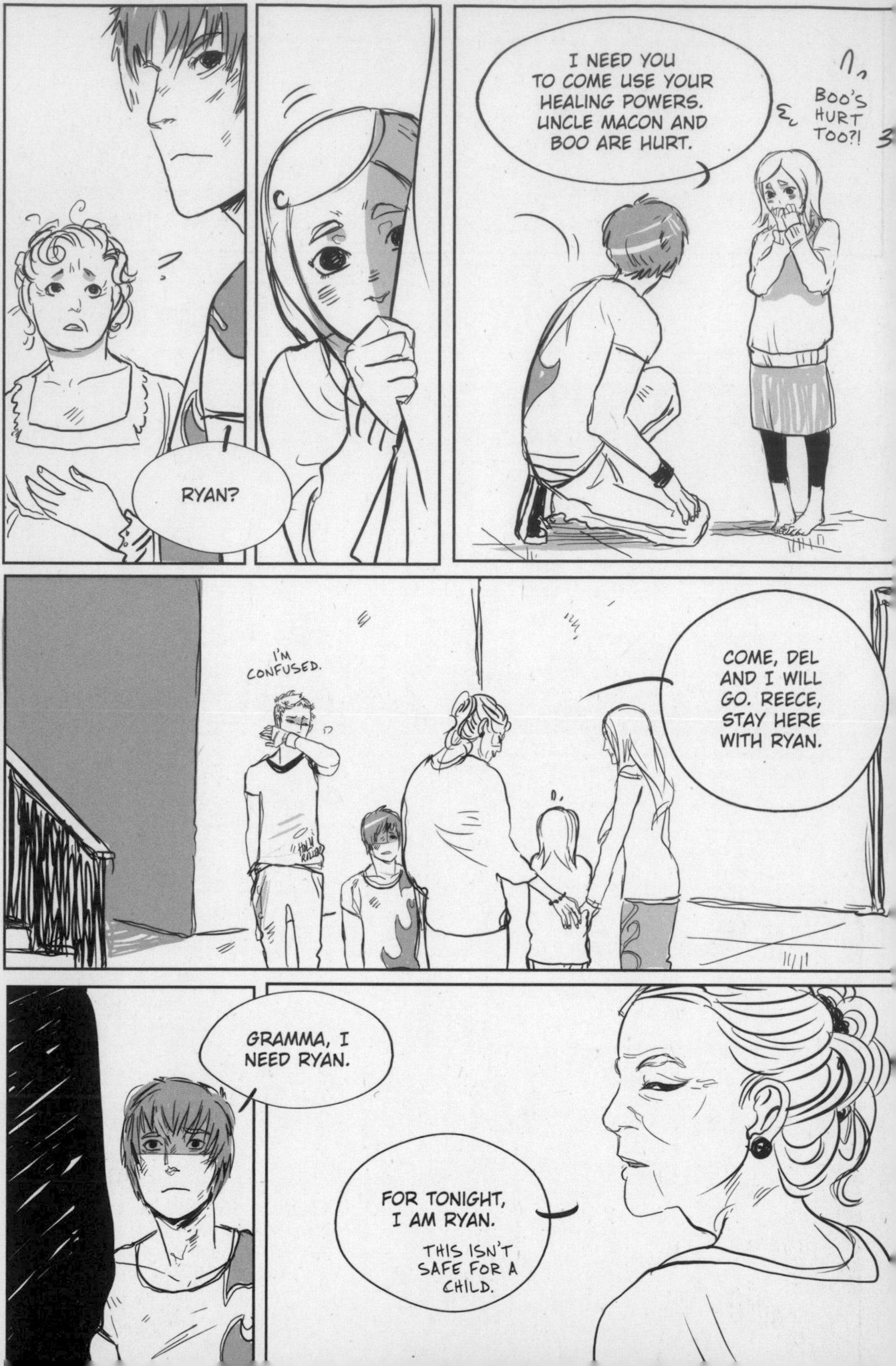
RYAN?
I NEED YOU TO COME USE YOUR HEALING POWERS. UNCLE MACON AND BOO ARE HURT.
BOO'S HURT TOO?!
I'M CONFUSED.
COME, DEL AND I WILL GO. REECE, STAY HERE WITH RYAN.
GRAMMA, I NEED RYAN.
FOR TONIGHT, I AM RYAN.
THIS ISN'T SAFE FOR A CHILD.

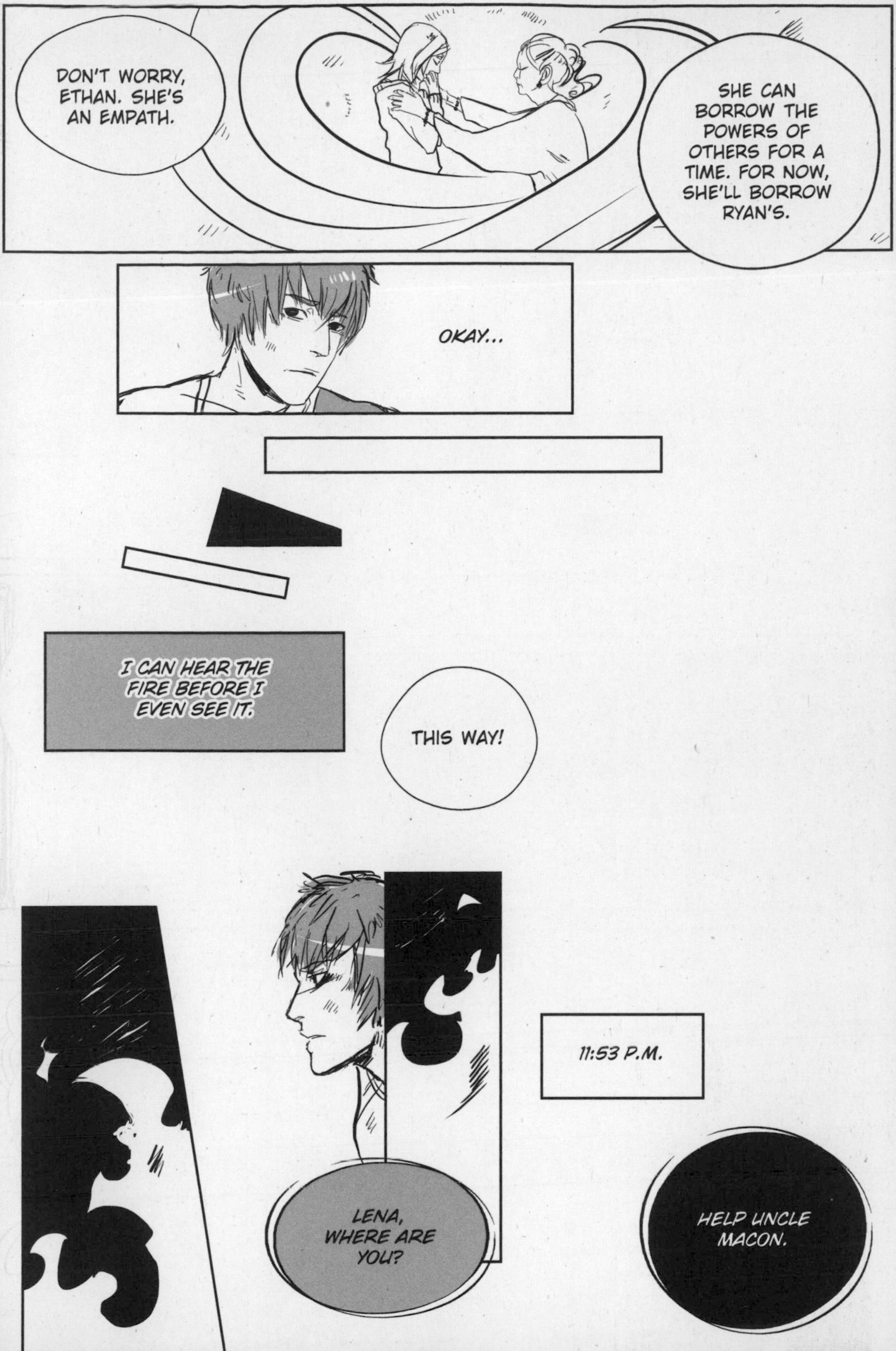
DON'T WORRY, ETHAN. SHE'S AN EMPATH.
SHE CAN BORROW THE POWERS OF OTHERS FOR A TIME. FOR NOW, SHE'LL BORROW RYAN'S.
OKAY...
I CAN HEAR THE FIRE BEFORE I EVEN SEE IT.
THIS WAY!
11:53 P.M.
LENA, WHERE ARE YOU?
HELP UNCLE MACON.

COUGH

THERE HE IS!

HE'S WEAK, BUT HE'LL BE ALL RIGHT.

UNNH...

WHERE'S LENA?

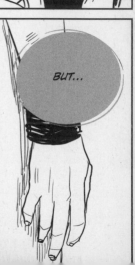

BUT...

ETHAN'S GOING TO FIND HER.

I'LL CHECK ON MRS. LINCOLN.

YOU REST!

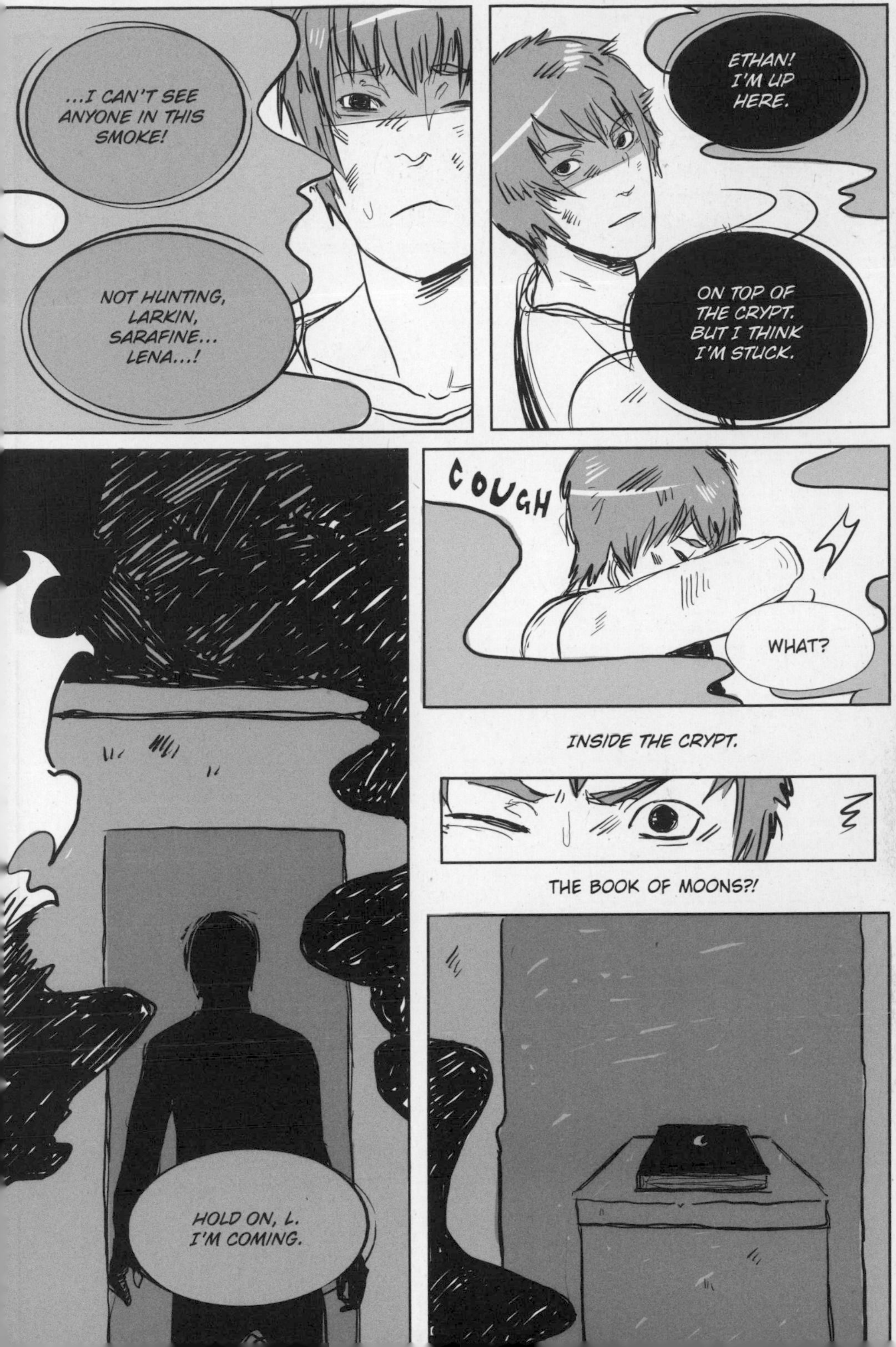
...I CAN'T SEE ANYONE IN THIS SMOKE!
NOT HUNTING, LARKIN, SARAFINE... LENA...!
ETHAN! I'M UP HERE.
ON TOP OF THE CRYPT. BUT I THINK I'M STUCK.
HOLD ON, L. I'M COMING.
COUGH
WHAT?
INSIDE THE CRYPT.
THE BOOK OF MOONS?!

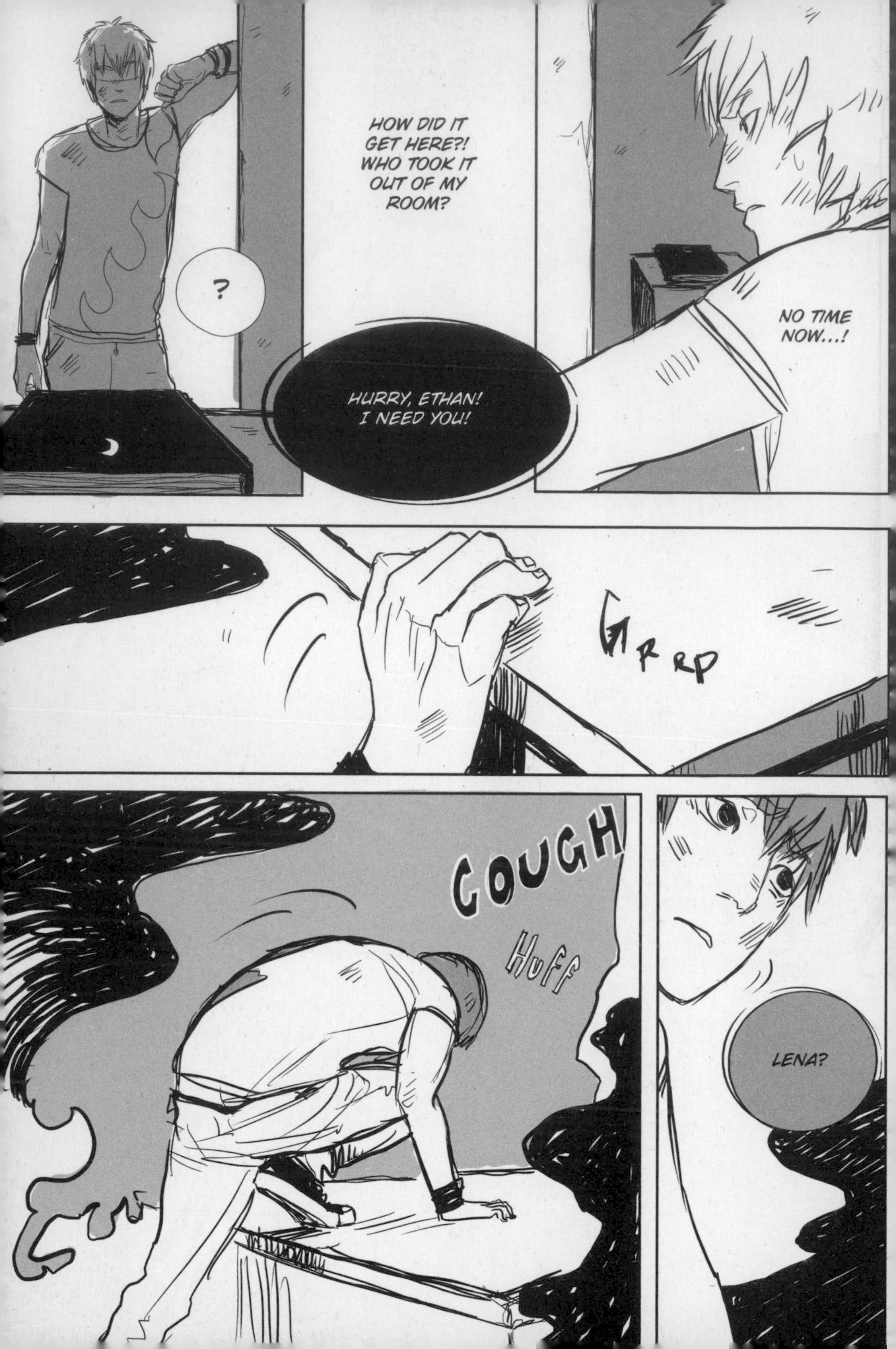
?
HOW DID IT GET HERE?! WHO TOOK IT OUT OF MY ROOM?
HURRY, ETHAN! I NEED YOU!
NO TIME NOW...!
GRRP
COUGH
HUFF
LENA?

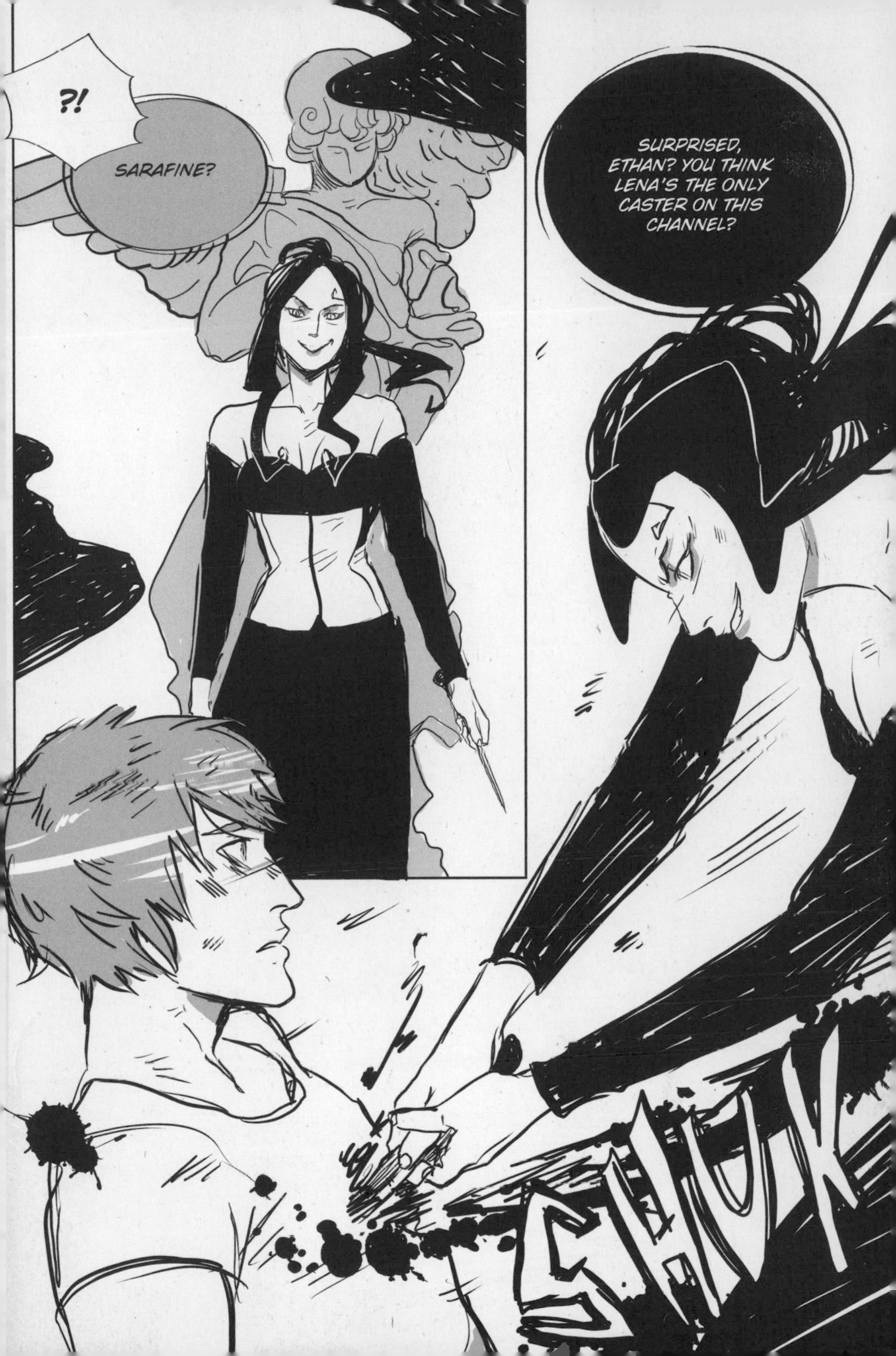
?!
SARAFINE?
SURPRISED, ETHAN? YOU THINK LENA'S THE ONLY CASTER ON THIS CHANNEL?
CHUK

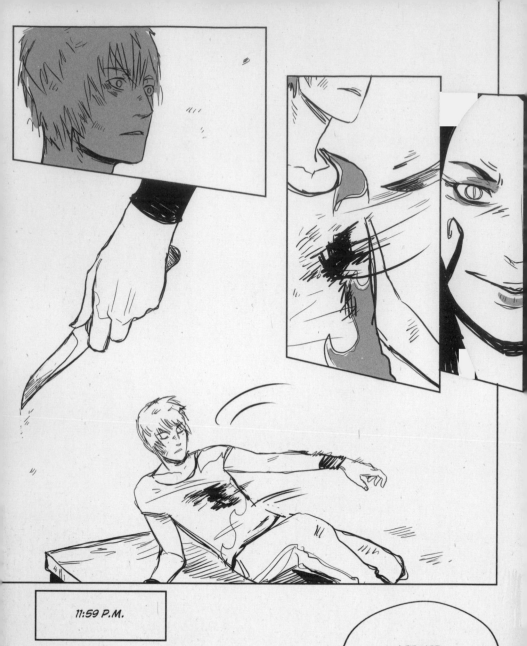

11:59 P.M.

LET HER
TRY TO STAY
LIGHT NOW.

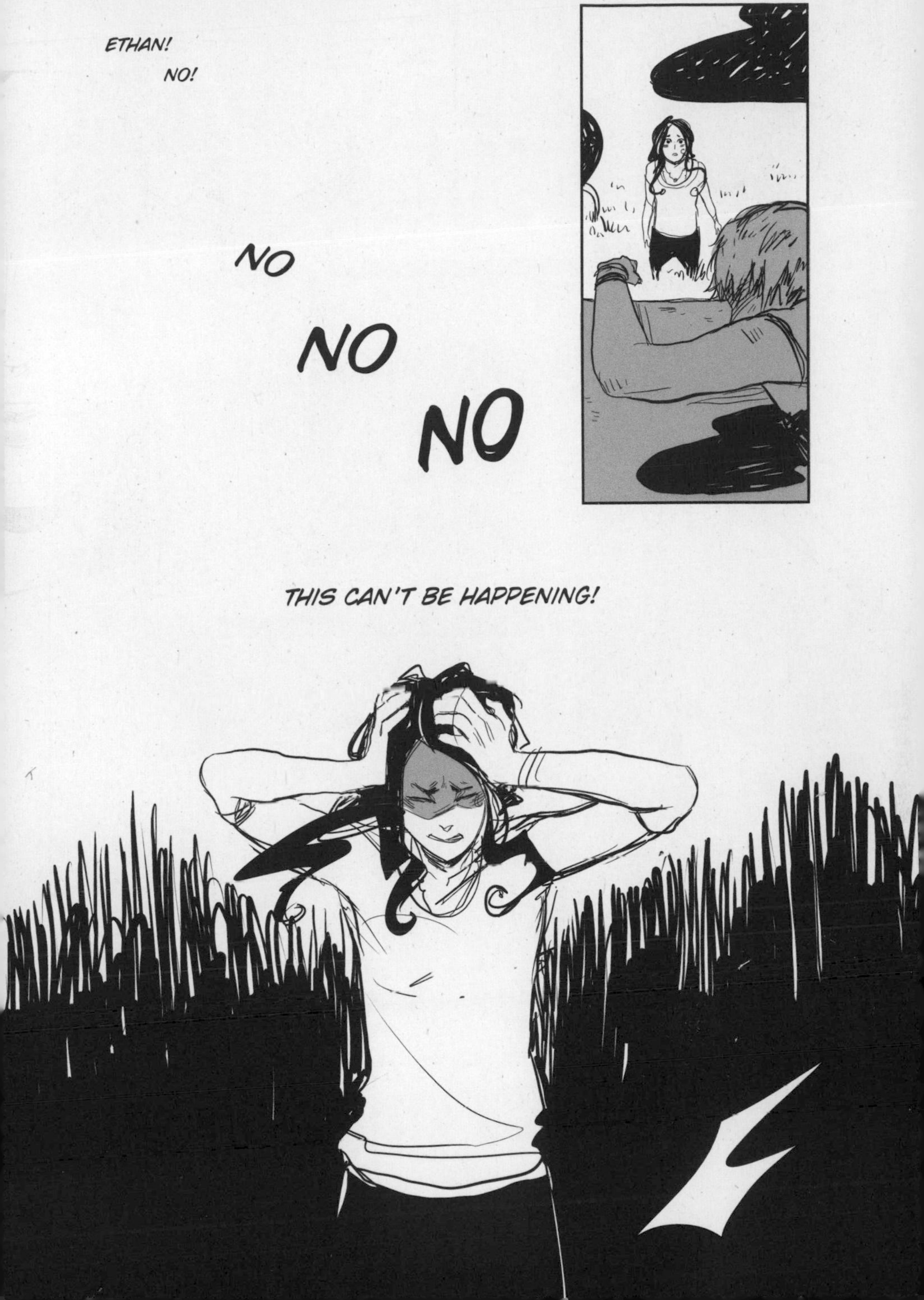
ETHAN!
NO!
NO
NO
NO
THIS CAN'T BE HAPPENING!

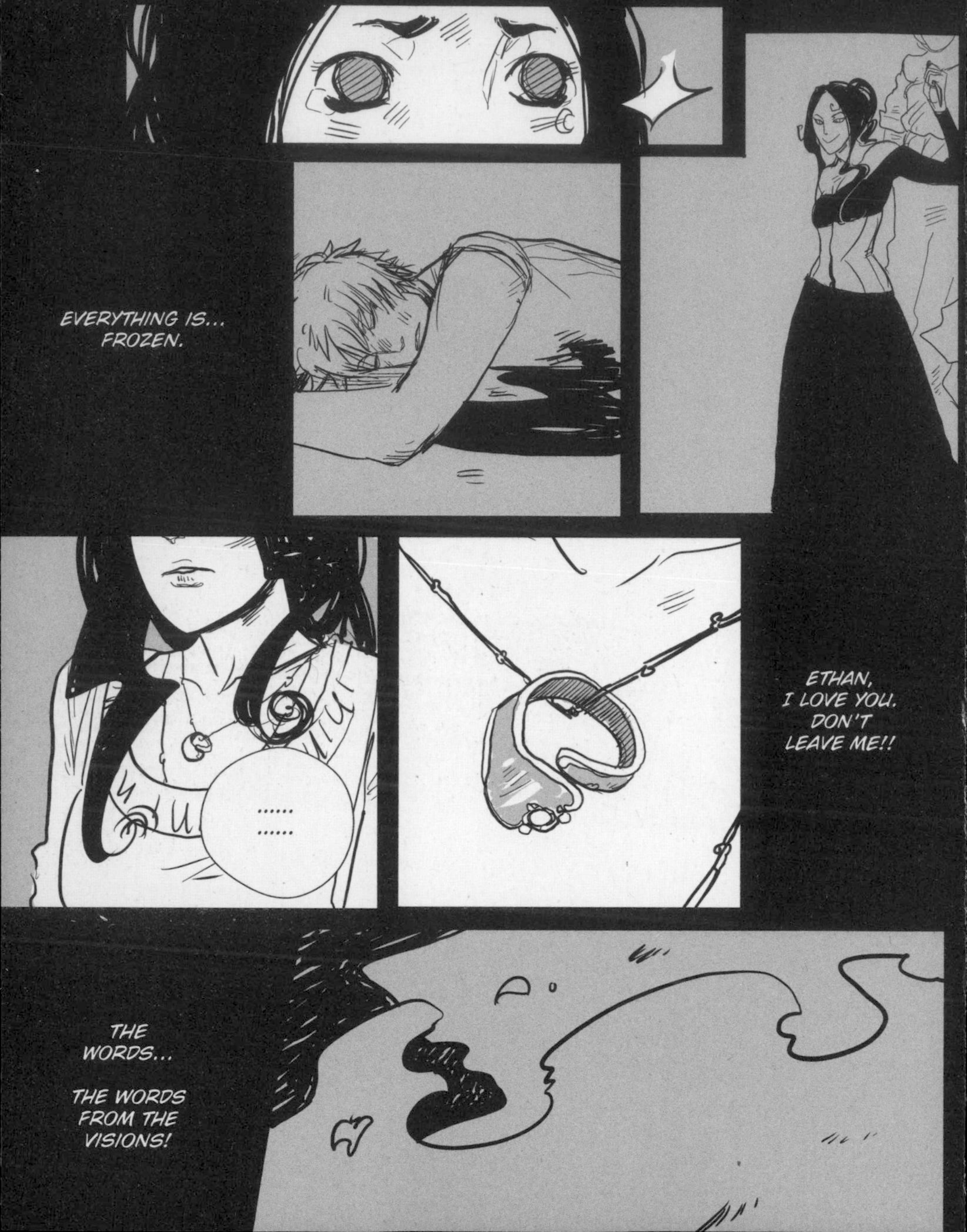
EVERYTHING IS... FROZEN.
ETHAN, I LOVE YOU. DON'T LEAVE ME!!
....
THE WORDS...
THE WORDS FROM THE VISIONS!

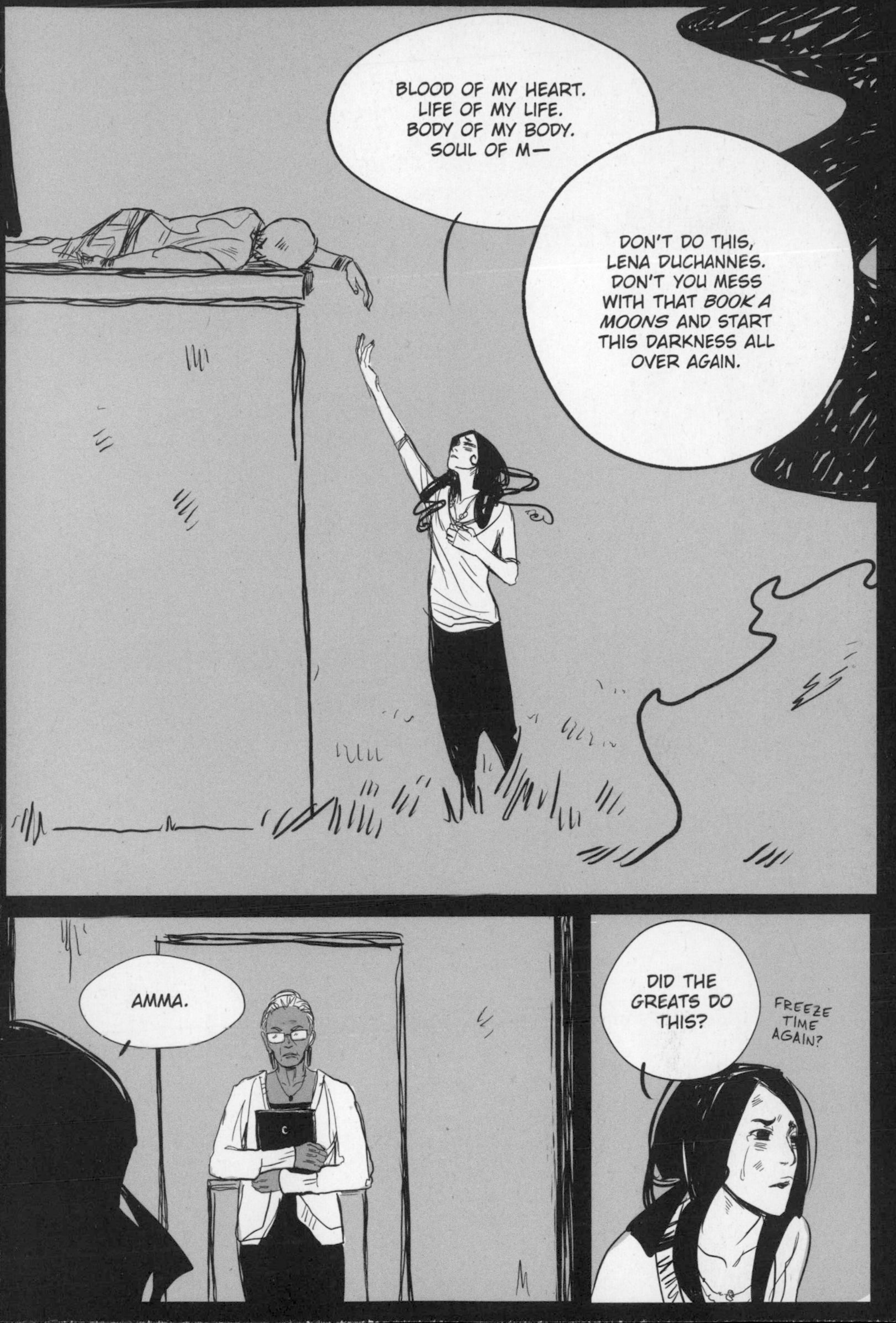
BLOOD OF MY HEART. LIFE OF MY LIFE. BODY OF MY BODY. SOUL OF M—
DON'T DO THIS, LENA DUCHANNES. DON'T YOU MESS WITH THAT *BOOK A MOONS* AND START THIS DARKNESS ALL OVER AGAIN.
AMMA.
DID THE GREATS DO THIS?
FREEZE TIME AGAIN?

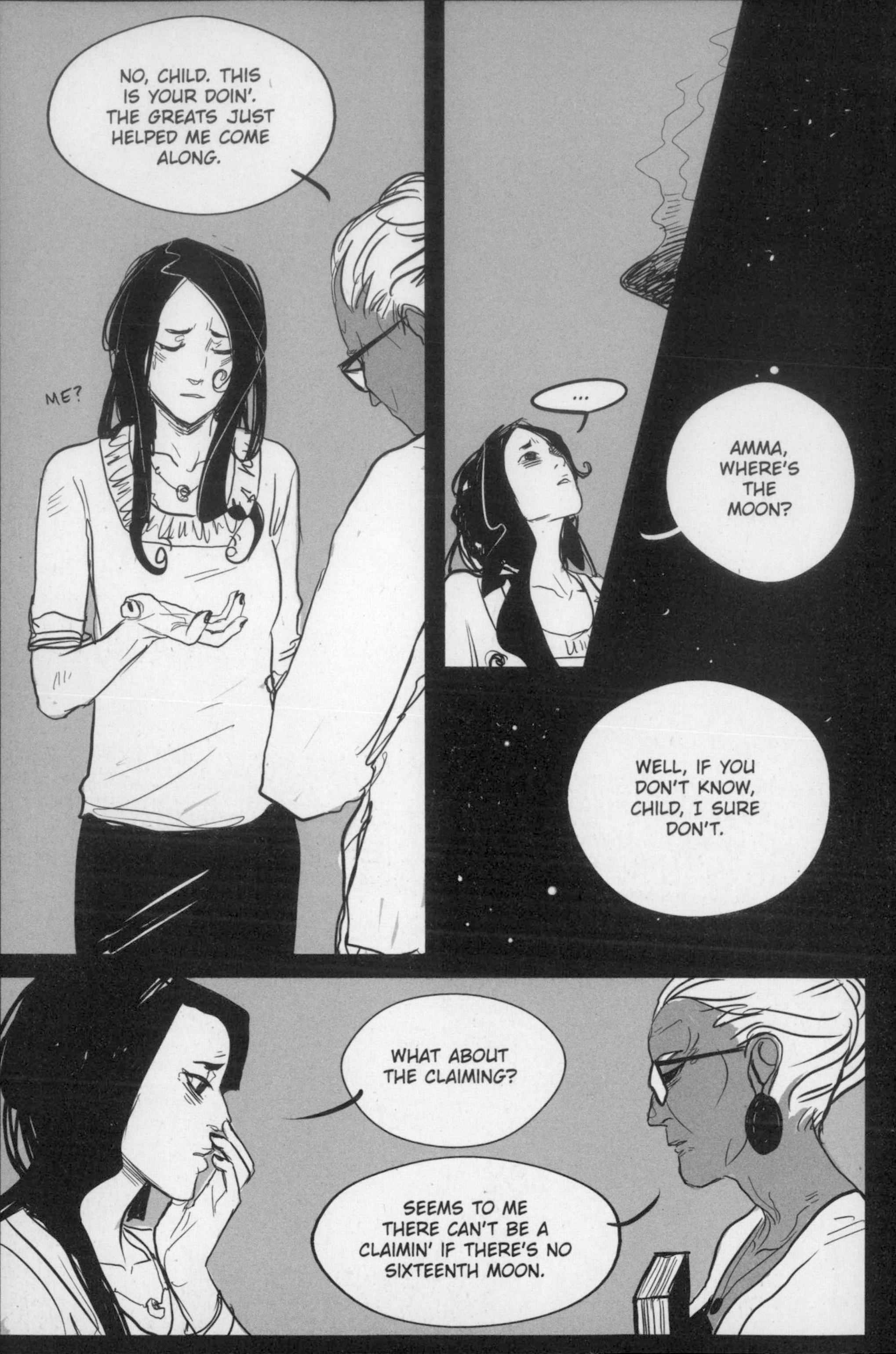

NO, CHILD. THIS IS YOUR DOIN'. THE GREATS JUST HELPED ME COME ALONG.
ME?
...
AMMA, WHERE'S THE MOON?
WELL, IF YOU DON'T KNOW, CHILD, I SURE DON'T.
WHAT ABOUT THE CLAIMING?
SEEMS TO ME THERE CAN'T BE A CLAIMIN' IF THERE'S NO SIXTEENTH MOON.

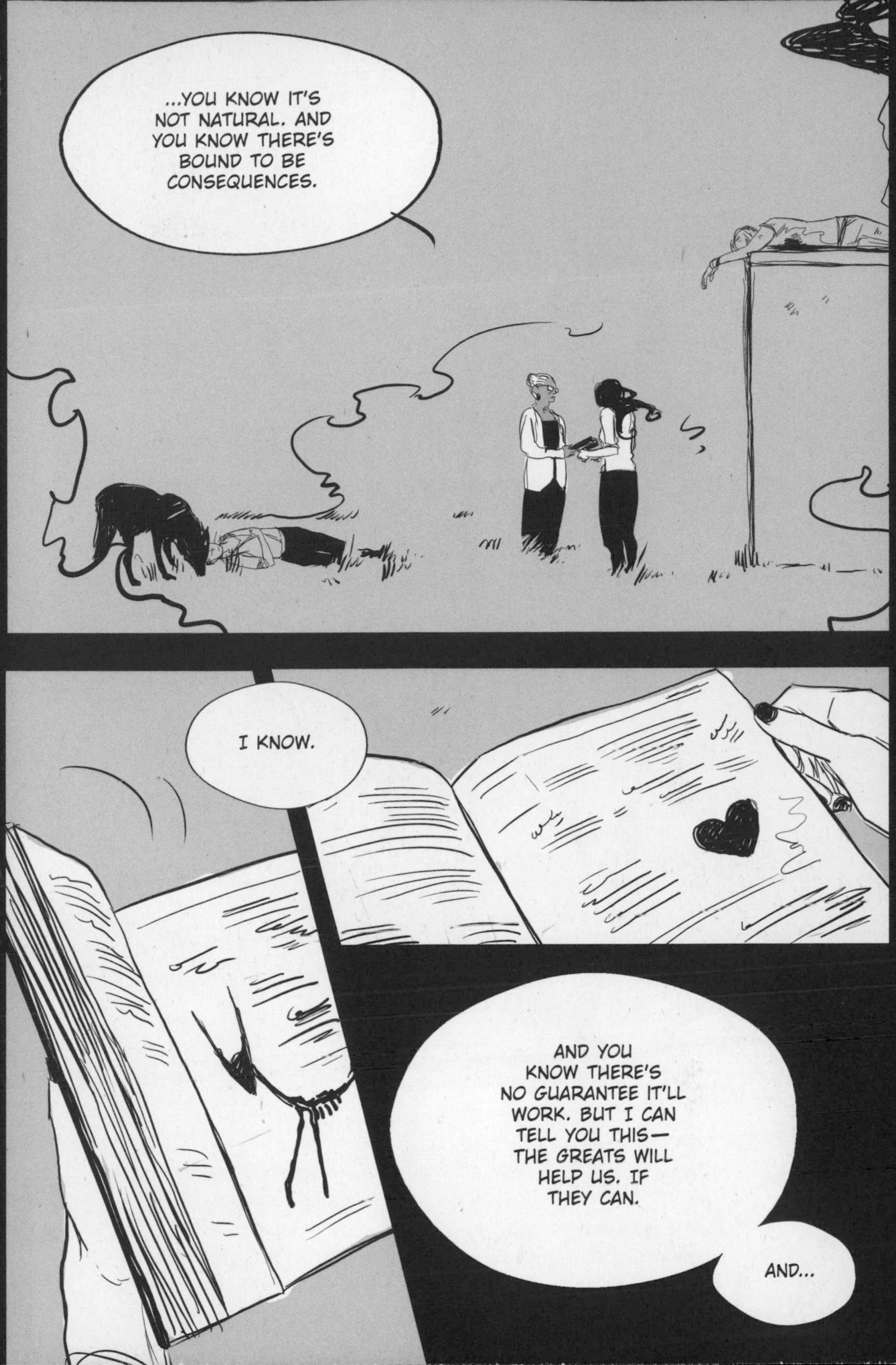
...YOU KNOW IT'S NOT NATURAL. AND YOU KNOW THERE'S BOUND TO BE CONSEQUENCES.
I KNOW.
AND YOU KNOW THERE'S NO GUARANTEE IT'LL WORK. BUT I CAN TELL YOU THIS— THE GREATS WILL HELP US. IF THEY CAN.
AND...

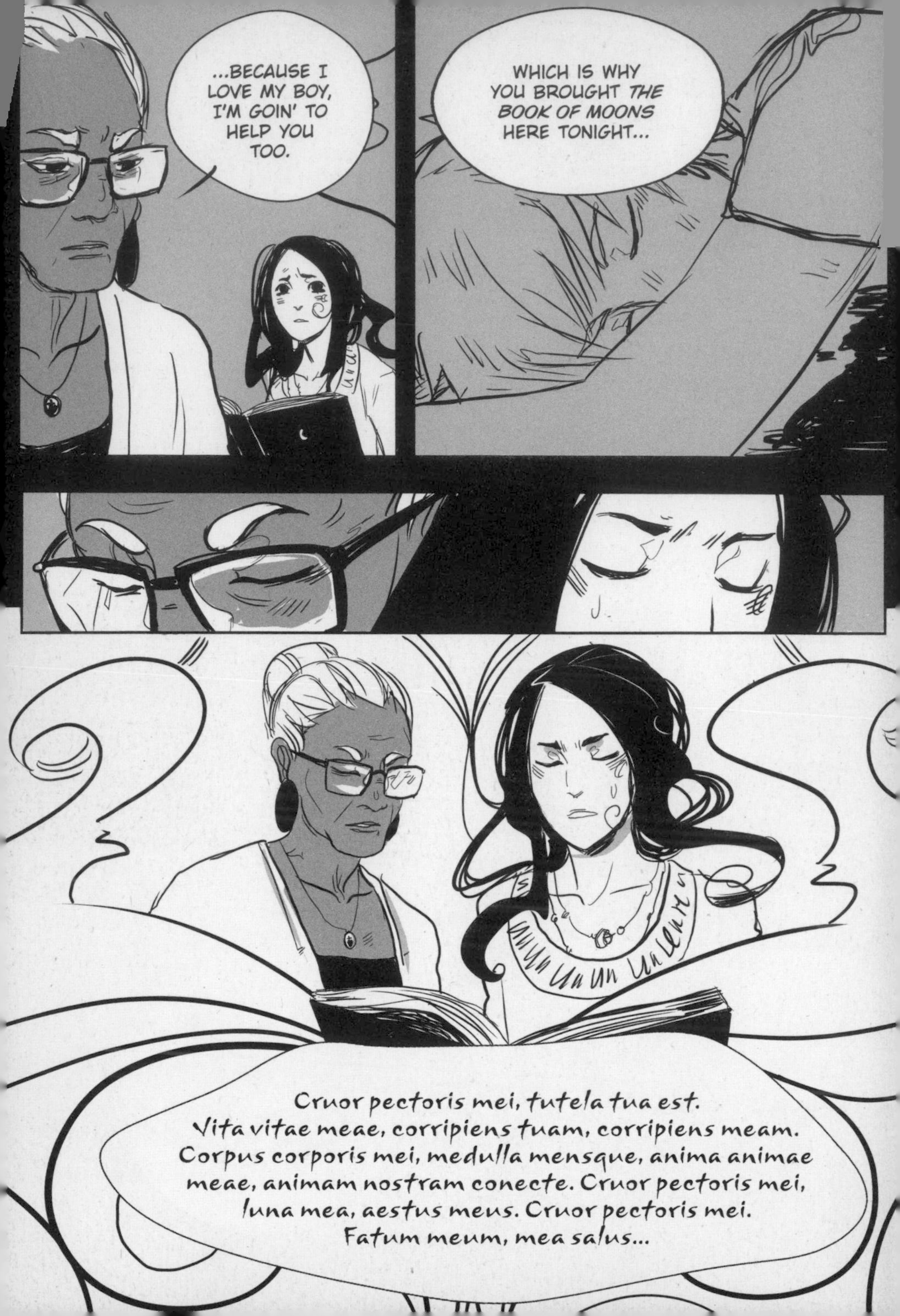
...BECAUSE I LOVE MY BOY, I'M GOIN' TO HELP YOU TOO.
WHICH IS WHY YOU BROUGHT *THE BOOK OF MOONS* HERE TONIGHT...
Cruor pectoris mei, tutela tua est. Vita vitae meae, corripiens tuam, corripiens meam. Corpus corporis mei, medulla mensque, anima animae meae, animam nostram conecte. Cruor pectoris mei, luna mea, aestus meus. Cruor pectoris mei. Fatum meum, mea salus...

BEAUTIFUL CREATURES

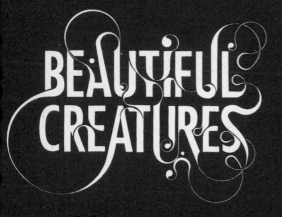

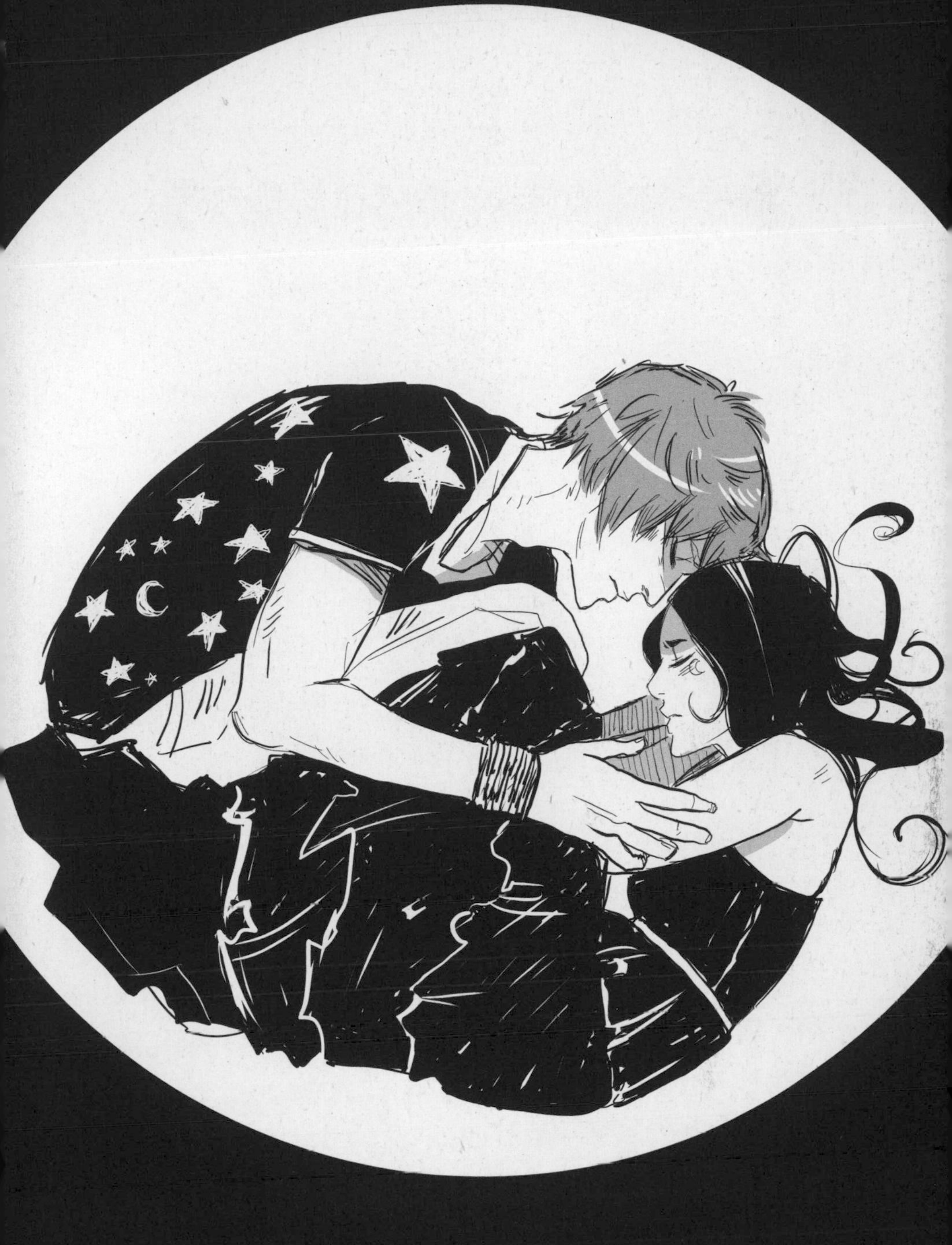

CHAPTER 8

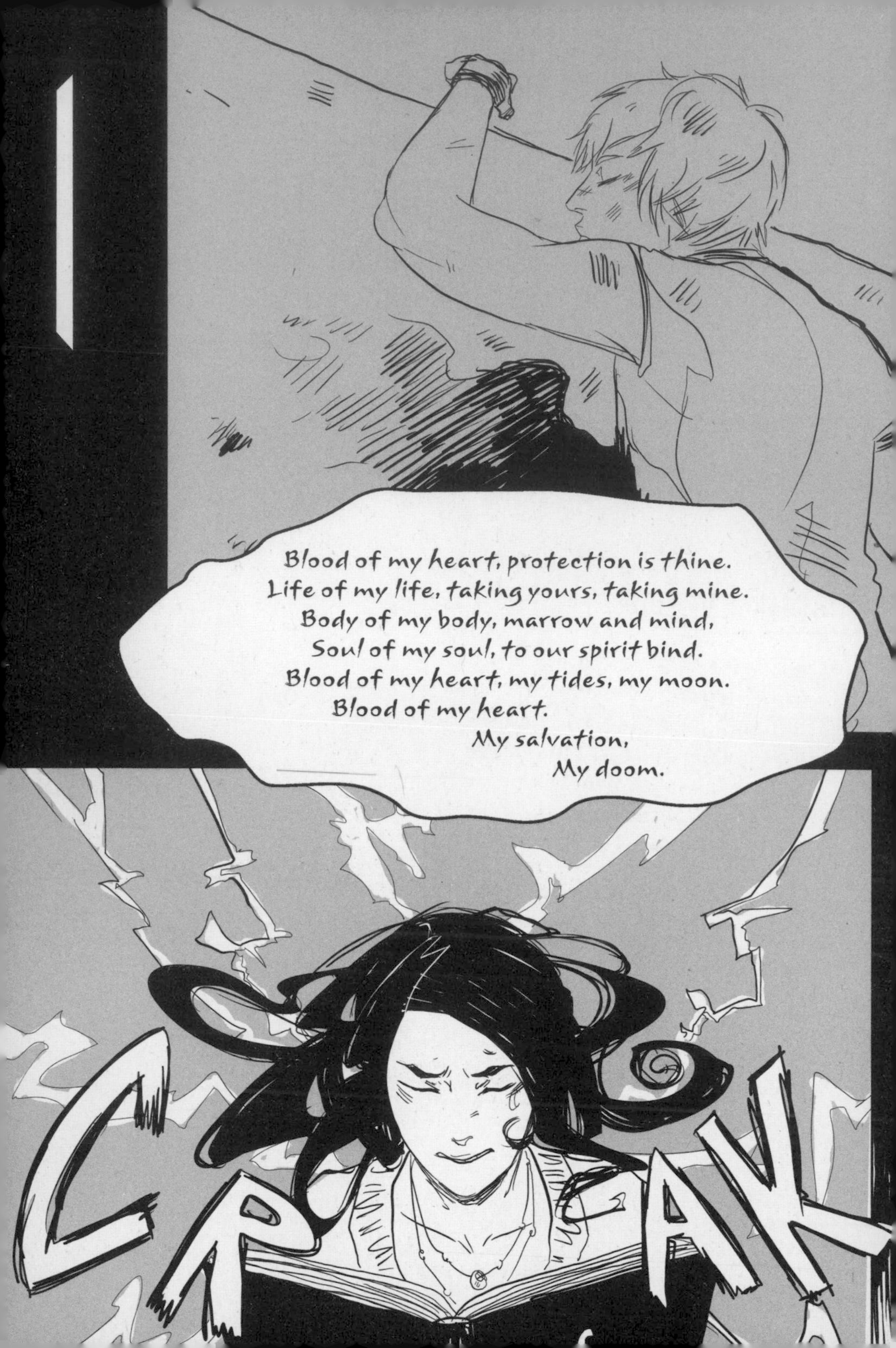
Blood of my heart, protection is thine.
Life of my life, taking yours, taking mine.
Body of my body, marrow and mind,
Soul of my soul, to our spirit bind.
Blood of my heart, my tides, my moon.
Blood of my heart.
My salvation,
My doom.

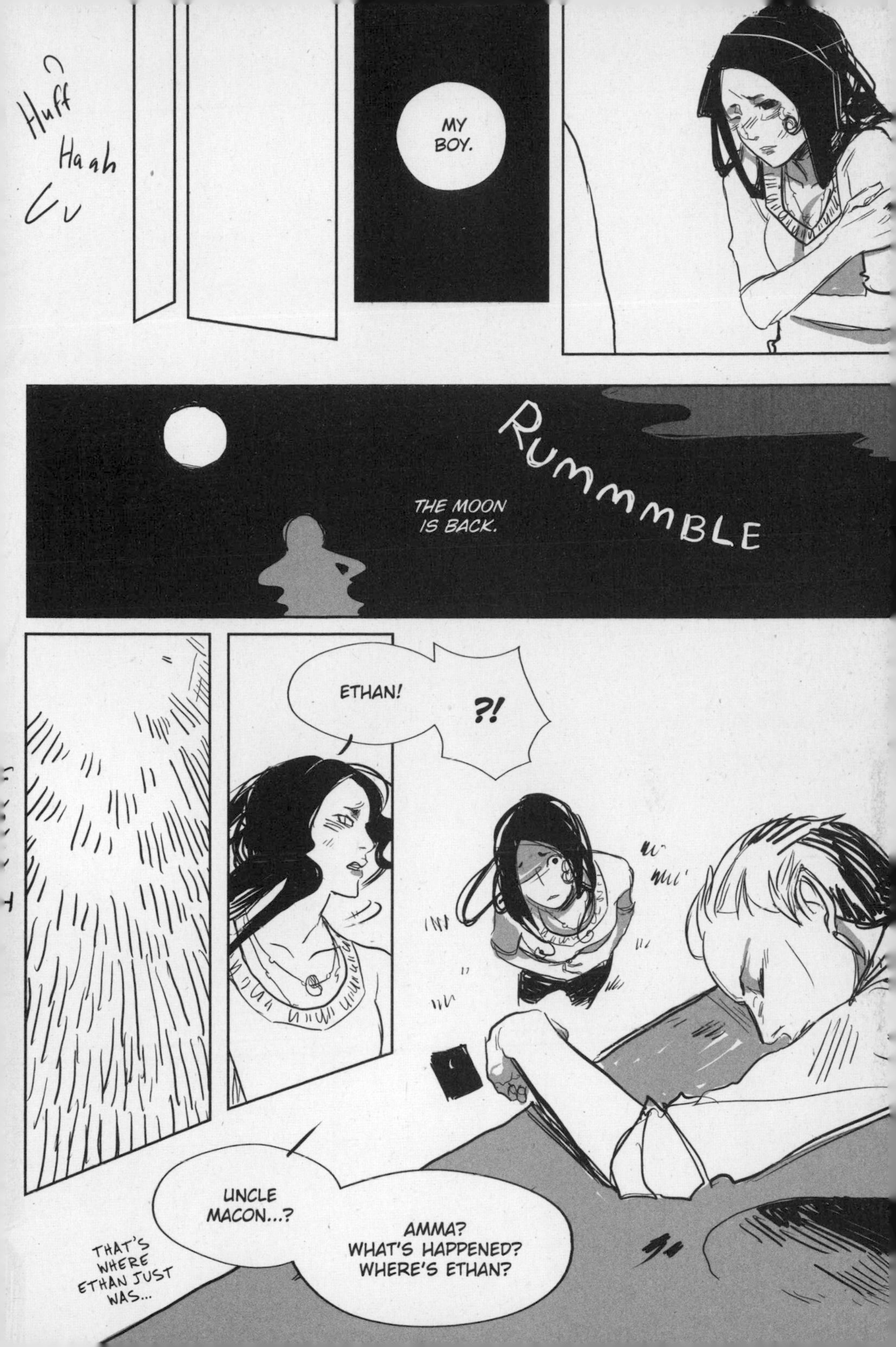
Huff
Haah
Uu
MY BOY.
RUMMMMBLE
THE MOON IS BACK.
ETHAN!
?!
UNCLE MACON...?
AMMA? WHAT'S HAPPENED? WHERE'S ETHAN?
THAT'S WHERE ETHAN JUST WAS...

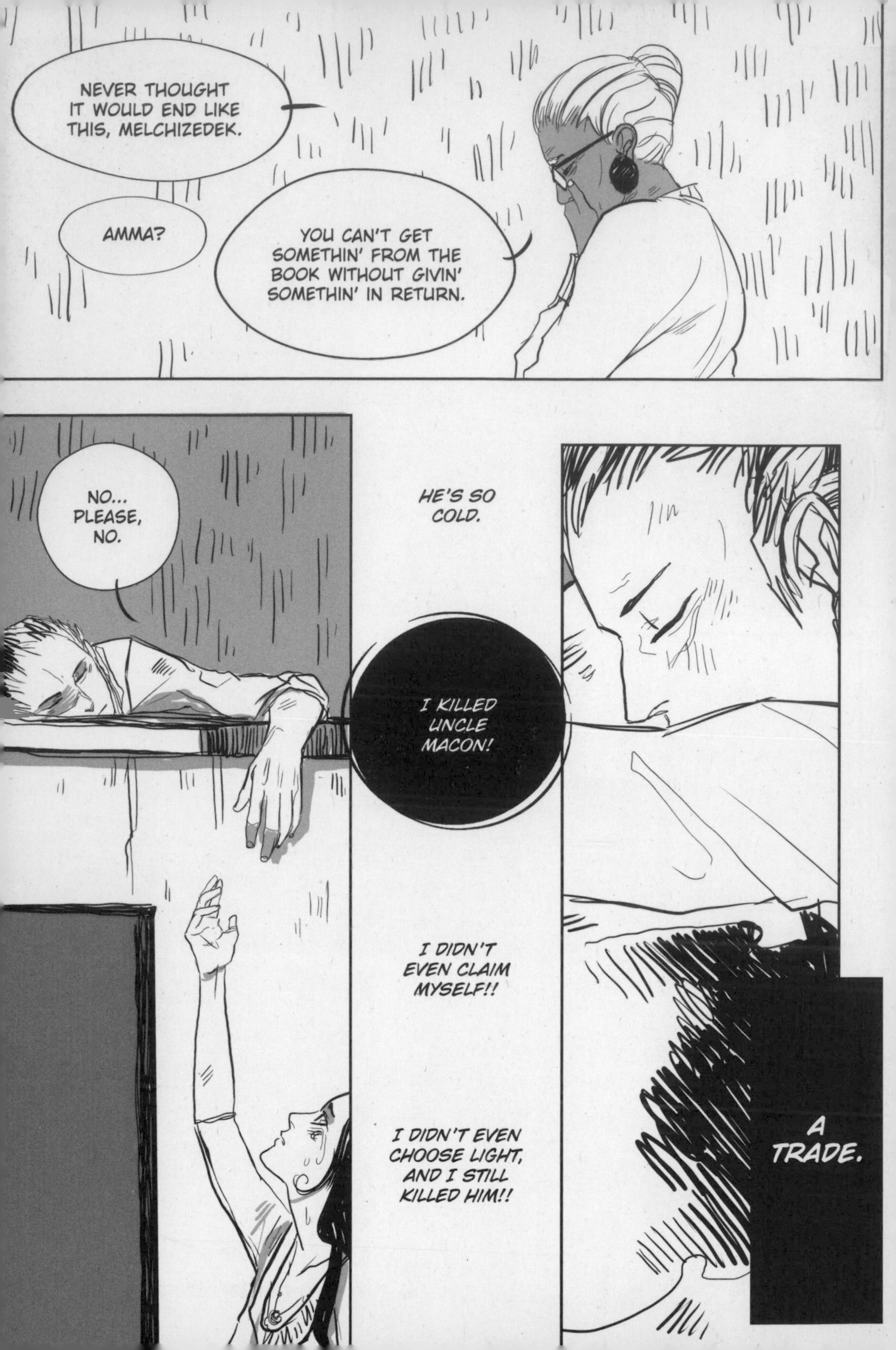
NEVER THOUGHT IT WOULD END LIKE THIS, MELCHIZEDEK.
AMMA?
YOU CAN'T GET SOMETHIN' FROM THE BOOK WITHOUT GIVIN' SOMETHIN' IN RETURN.
NO... PLEASE, NO.
HE'S SO COLD.
I KILLED UNCLE MACON!
I DIDN'T EVEN CLAIM MYSELF!!
I DIDN'T EVEN CHOOSE LIGHT, AND I STILL KILLED HIM!!
A TRADE.

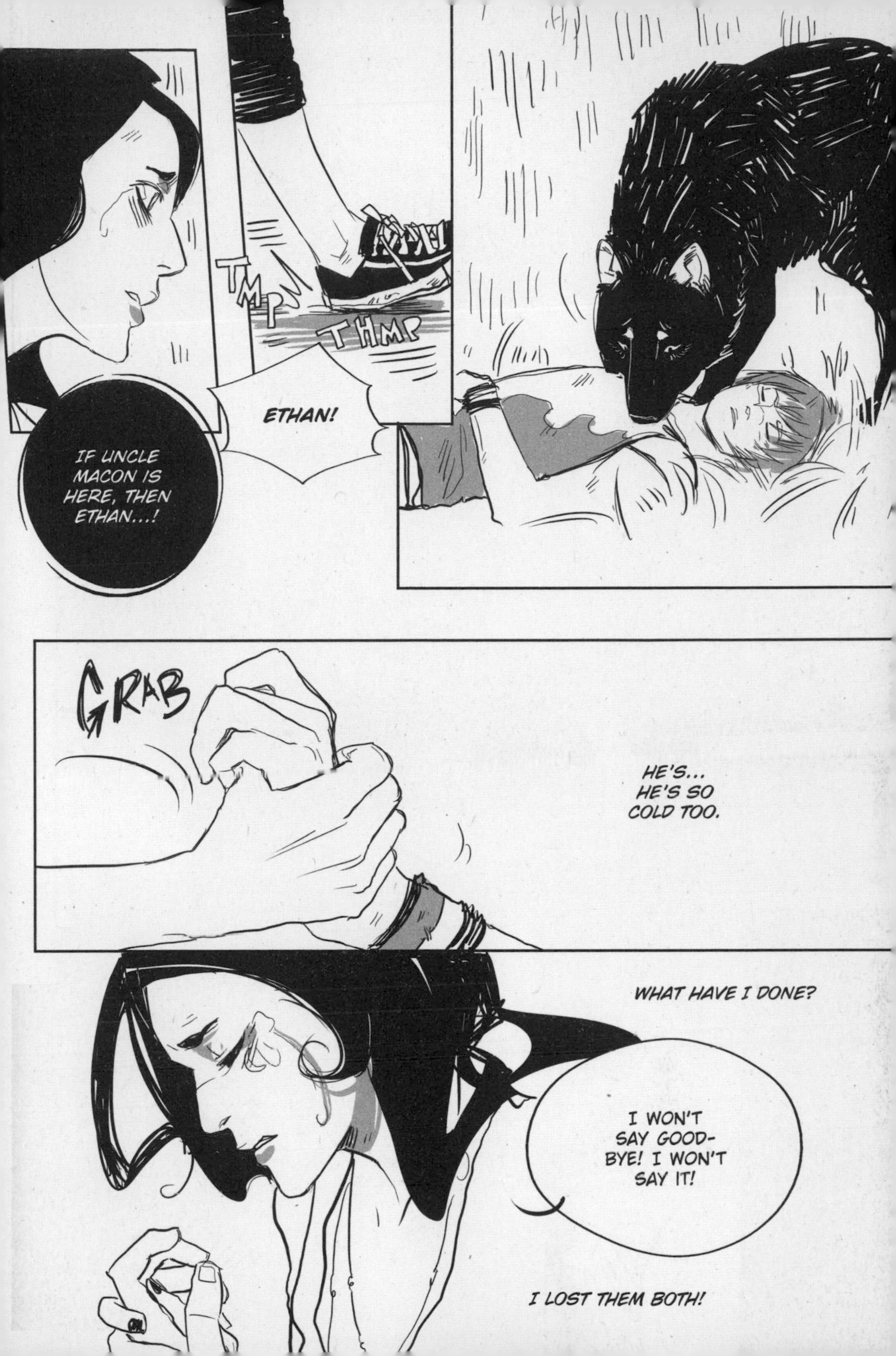
IF UNCLE MACON IS HERE, THEN ETHAN...!
TMP
THMP
ETHAN!
GRAB
HE'S... HE'S SO COLD TOO.
WHAT HAVE I DONE?
I WON'T SAY GOOD-BYE! I WON'T SAY IT!
I LOST THEM BOTH!

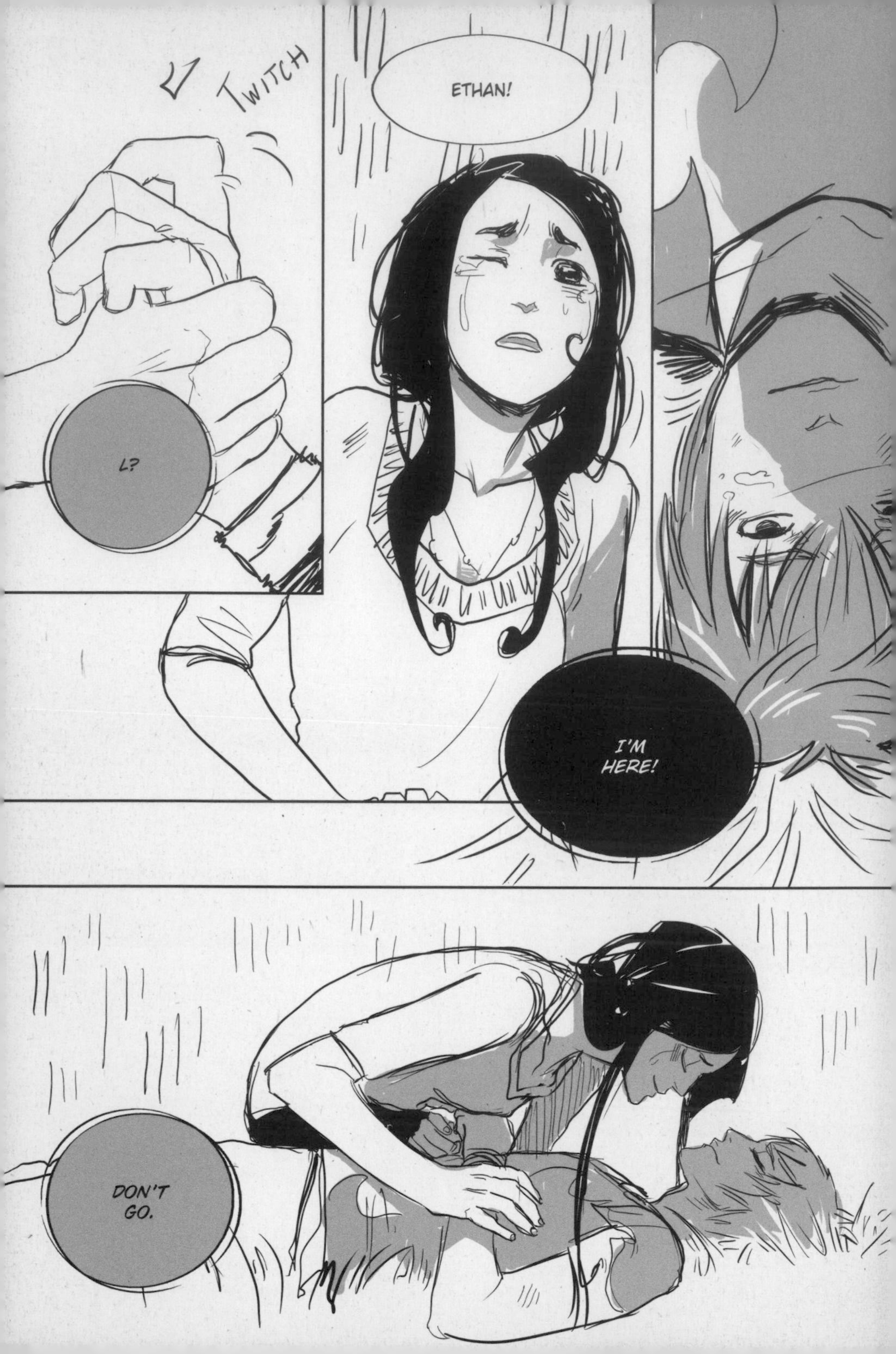
TWITCH
L?
ETHAN!
I'M HERE!
DON'T GO.

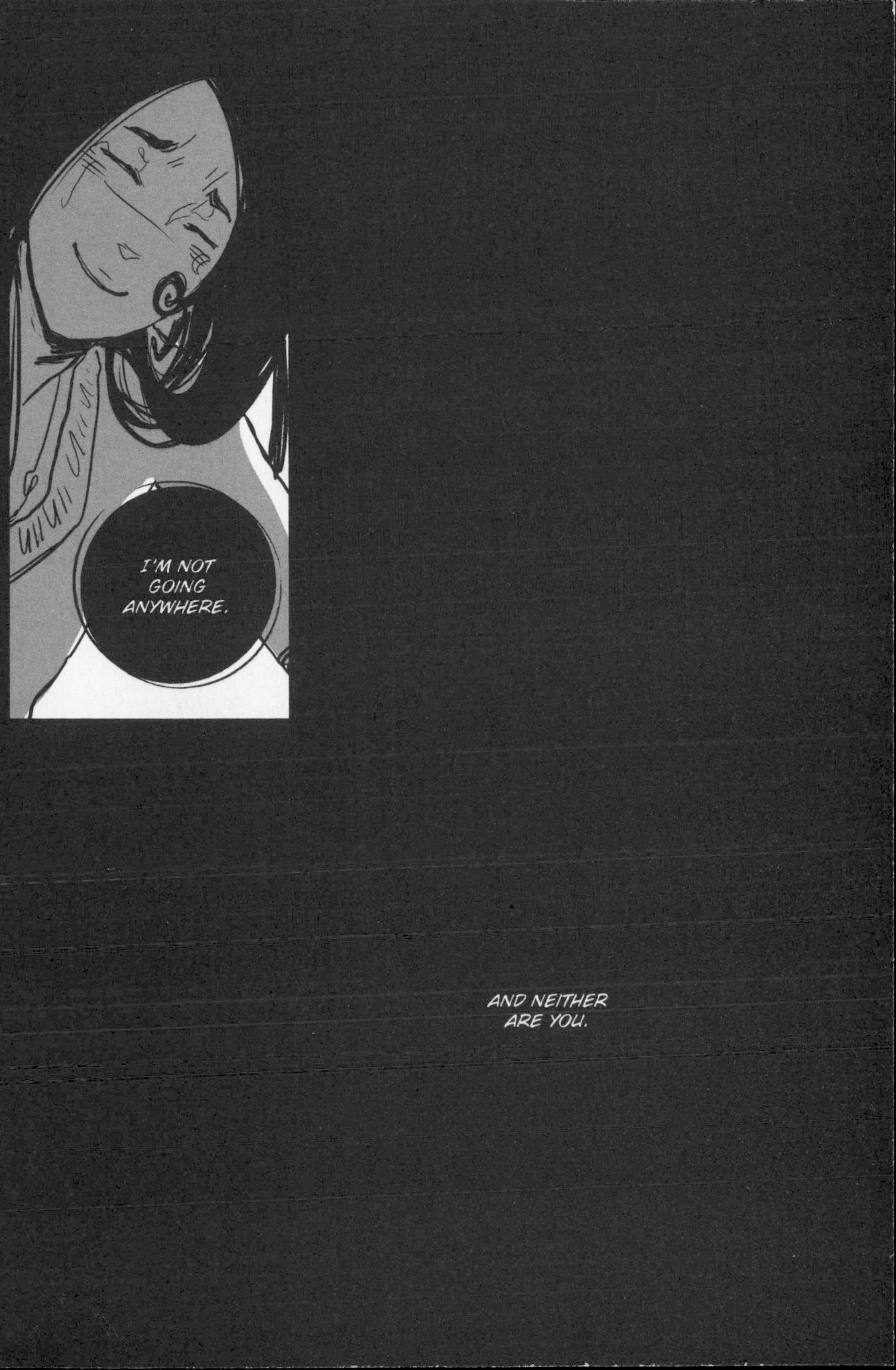
I'M NOT GOING ANYWHERE.
AND NEITHER ARE YOU.

LENA TOLD ME WHAT
HAD HAPPENED WHILE I
WAS PASSED OUT...

MACON WAS THE ONLY
CASUALTY. APPARENTLY,
HUNTING OVERPOWERED
HIM AFTER I LOST
CONSCIOUSNESS.

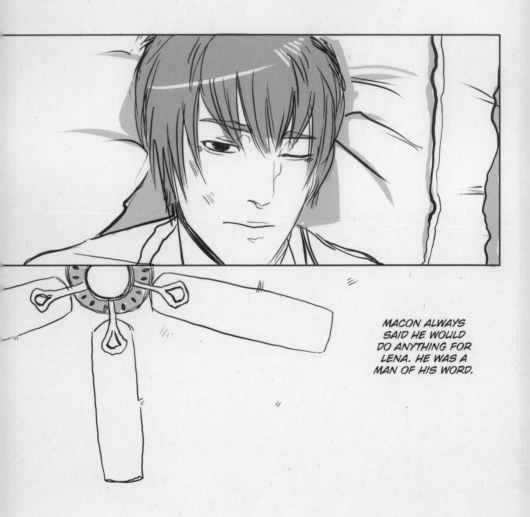

MACON ALWAYS
SAID HE WOULD
DO ANYTHING FOR
LENA. HE WAS A
MAN OF HIS WORD.

AND SARAFINE...

I'M FUZZY ON THE
DETAILS, BUT LENA SOMEHOW
MANAGED TO BLOCK OUT THE
MOON AND SAVE HERSELF
FROM BEING CLAIMED.

WITHOUT THE CLAIMING,
IT LOOKS LIKE SARAFINE,
HUNTING, AND LARKIN FLED,
AT LEAST FOR NOW.

AND THEN THERE'S ME.
I GUESS I FELL WHILE
CLIMBING THAT CRYPT AND
KNOCKED MYSELF OUT.

LIKE AN IDIOT.

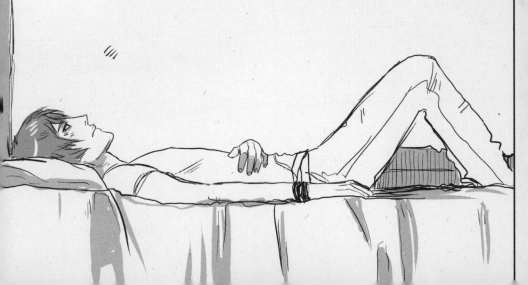

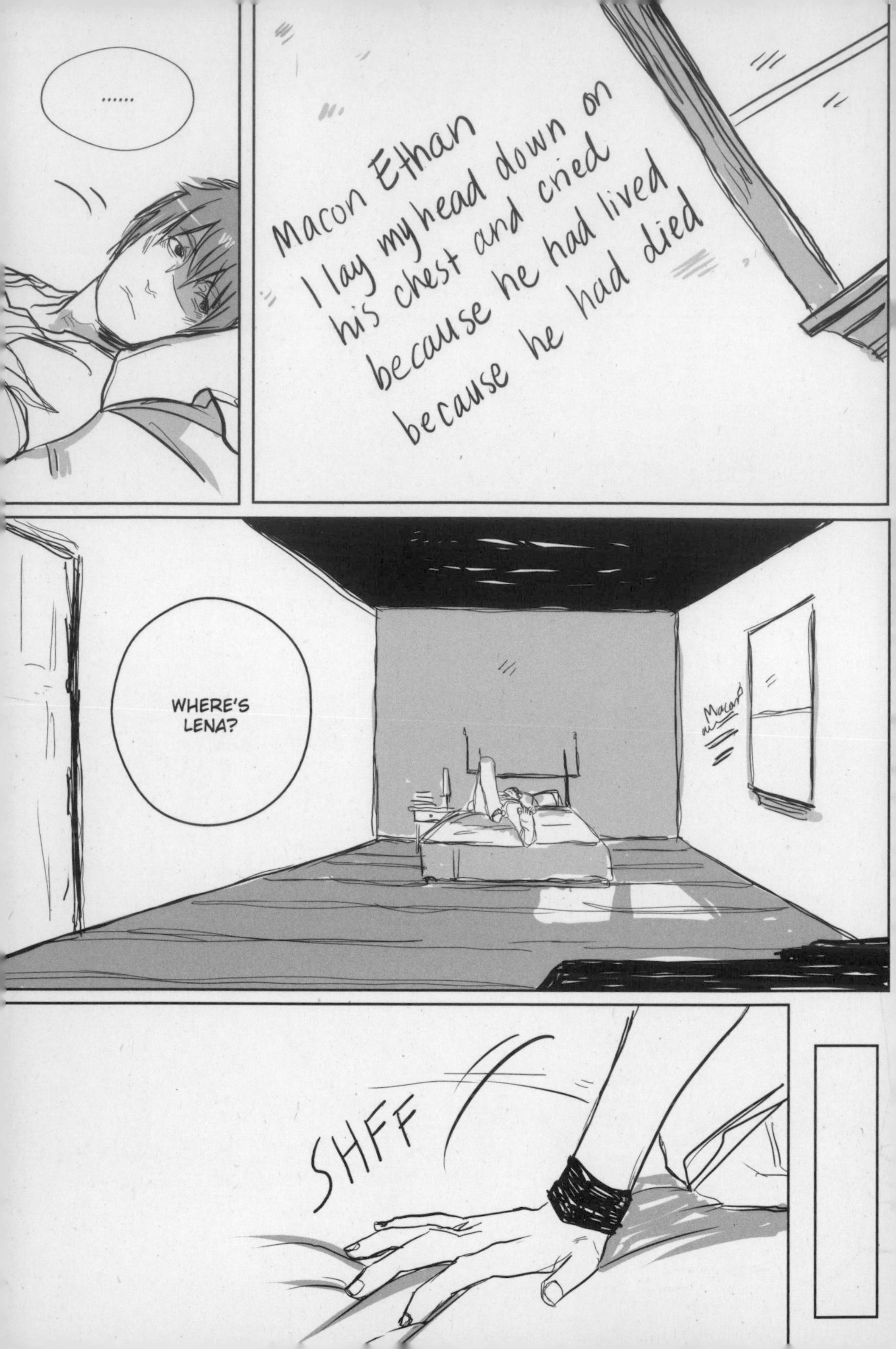
......
Macon Ethan
I lay my head down on his chest and cried
because he had lived
because he had died
WHERE'S LENA?
Macon?
SHFF

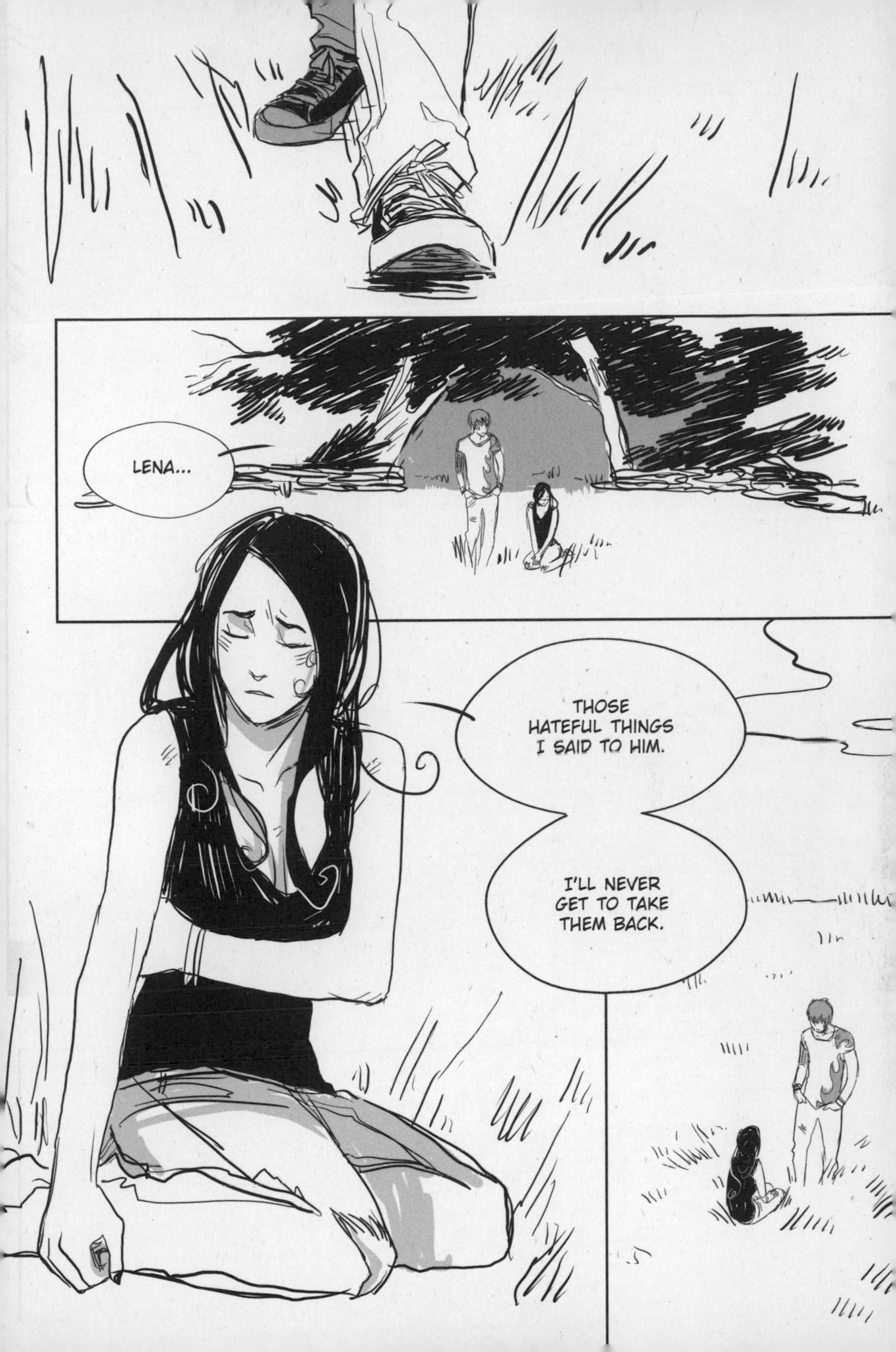
LENA...
THOSE HATEFUL THINGS I SAID TO HIM.
I'LL NEVER GET TO TAKE THEM BACK.

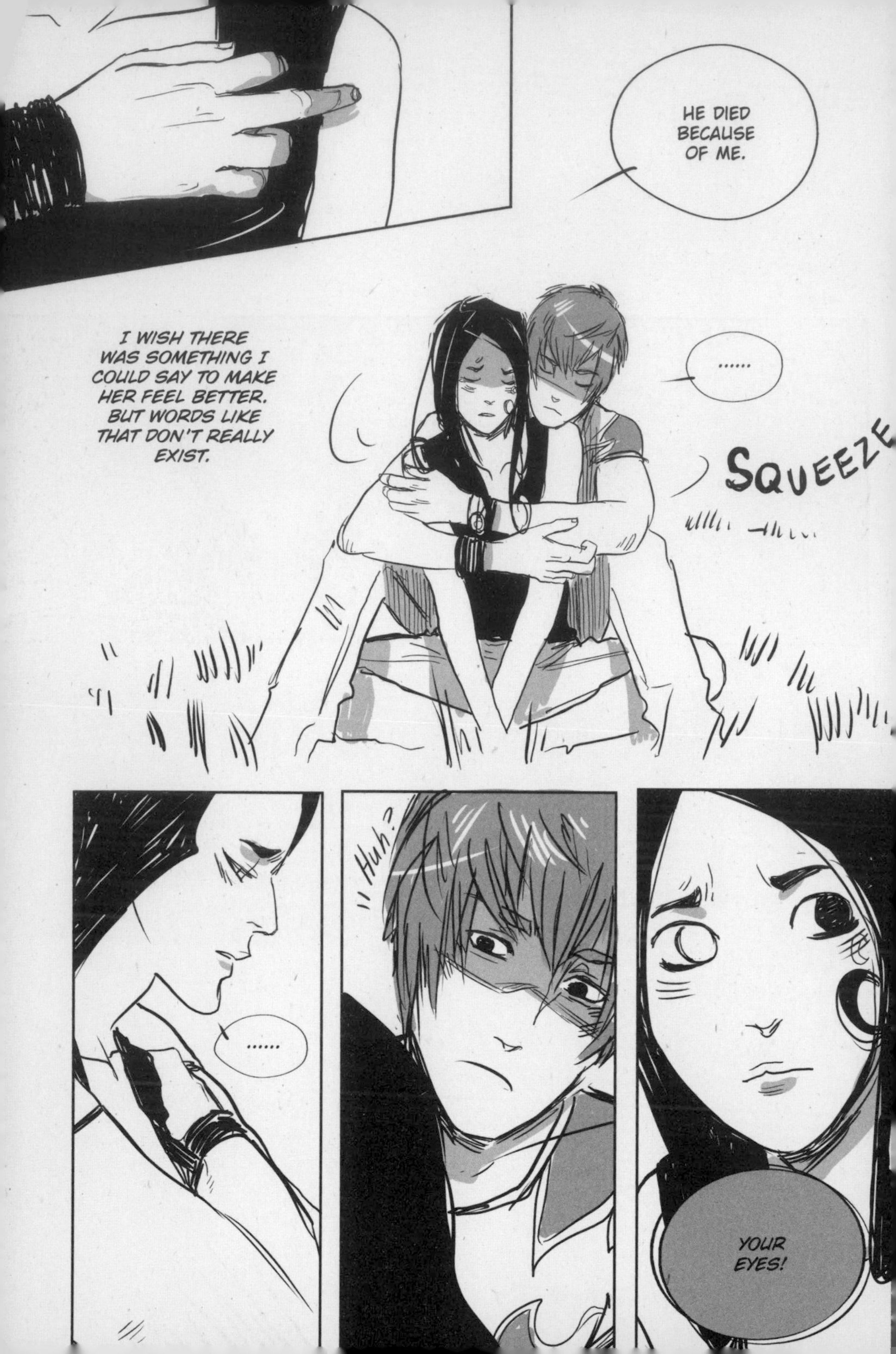
HE DIED BECAUSE OF ME.
I WISH THERE WAS SOMETHING I COULD SAY TO MAKE HER FEEL BETTER. BUT WORDS LIKE THAT DON'T REALLY EXIST.
......
SQUEEZE
......
Huh?
YOUR EYES!

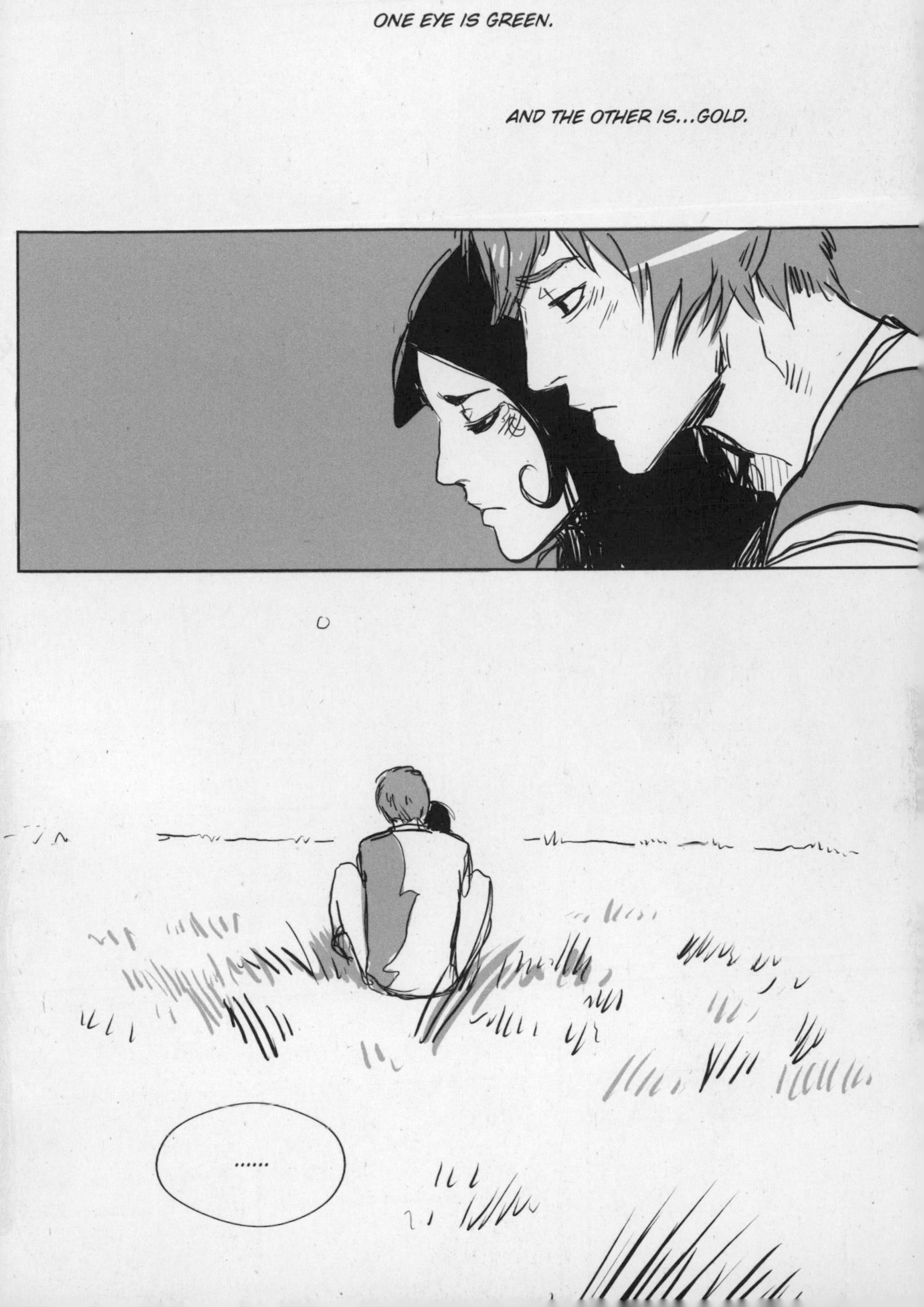
ONE EYE IS GREEN.
AND THE OTHER IS...GOLD.
......

DON'T
LET GO.

NEVER.

CRNCH

AUNT DEL OFFERED
TO DRIVE ME HOME, BUT
I WANTED TO WALK.

I NEED TO
CLEAR MY HEAD...

I STILL CAN'T
BELIEVE WE LOST
MACON.

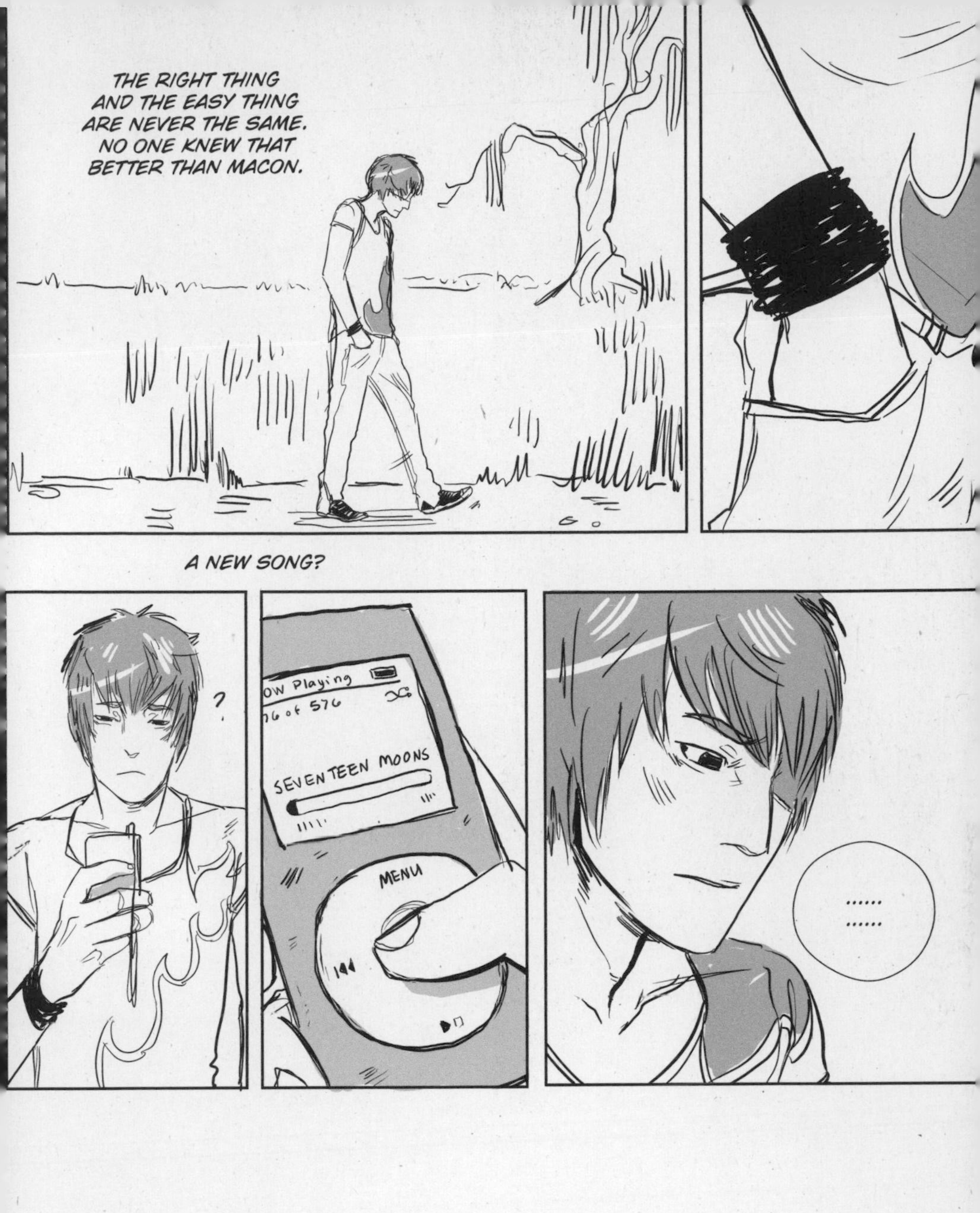
THE RIGHT THING AND THE EASY THING ARE NEVER THE SAME. NO ONE KNEW THAT BETTER THAN MACON.
A NEW SONG?
?
SEVENTEEN MOONS
MENU
......
......

☾

Seventeen moons, seventeen years.
Eyes where Dark or Light appears.
Gold for yes and Green for no.
Seventeen the last to know.

BEAUTIFUL CREATURES

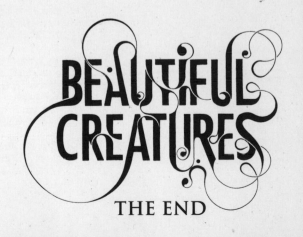

THE END

BEAUTIFUL CREATURES:
THE MANGA

KAMI GARCIA & MARGARET STOHL
CASSANDRA JEAN

Adaptation and Illustration:
Cassandra Jean

Lettering: Abigail Blackman

BEAUTIFUL CREATURES: THE MANGA
Text copyright © 2009 by Kami Garcia and Margaret Stoh
Illustrations © 2013 Hachette Book Group, Inc.

Yen Press
Hachette Book Group
237 Park Avenue, New York, NY 10017

www.HachetteBookGroup.com
www.YenPress.com

Yen Press is an imprint of Hachette Book Group, Inc.
The Yen Press name and logo are trademarks of Hachett
Book Group, Inc.

First Yen Press Edition: February 2013

ISBN: 978-0-316-18271-3

10 9 8 7 6 5 4 3 2 1

BVG

Printed in the United States of America